# FLYING FOR FREEDOM

*A man worth listening to: Wing Commander Cosme Gomm, DSO, DFC. Photo: Vincent Holyoak.*

# FLYING FOR FREEDOM

*Life and Death in Bomber Command*

*To David*

*With best wishes*

*Tony Redding*

## TONY REDDING

### CERBERUS

This edition published 2005 by Cerberus Publishing ltd.

Cerberus Publishing Limited
22A Osprey Court
Hawkfield Business Park
Bristol BS14 0BB
UK
Tel: +44 (0) 1275 54 54 70
Fax: +44 (0) 1275 54 54 72
e-mail:cerberusbooks@aol.com
www.cerberus-publishing.com

British Library Cataloguing in Publication Data.
A catalogue record for this book is available from the British Library.


ISBN 1 84145 011 1


PRINTED AND BOUND IN ENGLAND.

# Contents

*To Sidney Knott and his Brothers*

*in Arms in Bomber Command*

*Author's Note*

MY first memories are of the early 1950s. The first half of that decade was little changed in the general style of life from that of the 1940s, other than the fact that there was no longer a war on. Yet war had touched almost every street in South London. The brick-strewn bombsite next to our war-damaged home was once a school. Mercifully the bombs fell on a Saturday.

In the mid-1950s virtually all cars were black, dense smogs remained commonplace and young boys, arms outstretched, still imagined they were Spitfire pilots as they whirled around the playground.

The war had ended in Germany's unconditional surrender 10 years before. In 1940 Britain had come perilously close to utter defeat. Hitler's Germany was a nightmare, a distillation of all that is evil in this world. Millions of ordinary people, including Lancaster rear gunner Sidney Knott, stepped forward. They participated in the crusade against a new barbarism. Sidney Knott had the good fortune to survive 64 bombing operations over Germany, Italy and occupied Europe. Now in his eighties, he provided much of the narrative for this book. Many thousands of his comrades of 60 years ago – then young men in their late teens and early twenties and with everything to live for – were not so lucky.

In recent times, authors and TV producers have made much of the 'immorality' of area bombing – the mass destruction of German cities. In doing so, they ignore the fundamental immorality of war in all its forms. Sadly, the fact that thousands of young volunteers serving with Bomber Command died for our many freedoms (including the freedom to criticise) is too easily cast aside and forgotten.

Area bombing, of course, remains a controversial subject. Did the circumstances justify the adoption of area bombing? Were the results worthwhile, in both the military and political sense?

Taking the second question first, it is true that German war production continued to expand despite the bombing campaign. Yet what production levels would the Germans have reached but for Bomber Command's attentions? In the absence of the area campaign against German cities and industry, D-Day and the conquest of Germany might, perhaps, have taken place in 1946 and 1947, rather than in 1944 and 1945. There is also the uncomfortable thought that without the erosion of the enemy's frontline fighting capacity, arising from the German need to defend Reich airspace, the Allies might well have been tempted - at the highest political levels - to use nuclear weapons in Europe during late 1945, as they did against Japan.

As for the first question, concerning circumstances, it is a fact that Bomber Command represented Britain's only direct offensive capability against Germany for most of the war. Yet I prefer to consider justification in terms of the commonsense views of Sidney Knott and millions of his contemporaries.

The vast majority of ordinary men and women never had doubts at the time (or, indeed, later) about the area bombing of German cities. Many people had bitter, direct experience of German air attacks. They also harboured no illusions about the nature of the enemy and what was at stake, for them and for future generations. Attitudes hardened when the full extent of Nazi Germany's industrialised mass murder (and its boundless appetite for gratuitous cruelty) finally became known immediately after the war. It may not be fashionable to voice such views, or to point to Hitler's well-developed plans for the total subjugation and ruin of Britain, but it must be said that millions more would have died had the war in Europe lingered on.

Victory in Europe was due, in large measure, to the quiet courage and fortitude of men such as Sidney Knott. Bomber Command's young volunteers risked everything in a righteous cause.


Tony Redding
Ash, Canterbury, 2004

# Acknowledgements

I<small>T</small> has long been my intention to write a book about the human aspects of Bomber Command's war but business and family commitments, together with other interests, had first call on my time. I then had the good fortune to meet Sidney and Joan Knott. I owe a debt of gratitude to my wife, Philippa, and my late father-in-law, Stan Boylett, for arranging the introduction. I am also grateful for my wife's forbearance and active assistance by way of typing and proof-reading the various drafts.

Having been intrigued by our first discussion, I asked Sidney Knott if he would be interested in collaborating on a book describing his wartime experiences, set within a wider commentary concerning the bomber war. It took him three months to reply. As always, in the meticulous way I have come to know so well, he wanted to be sure that his memories were clear and sufficiently detailed to support the proposed project. He spent that three months making copious notes of his first tour of operations and then replied in the affirmative. It has been a pleasure to work with him. I am also grateful to his wife, Joan, for her support and active assistance – especially her help in tracking down the families of crew members.

The enthusiastic help of the crews' families was indispensable. I am grateful for their patience in reading drafts, researching material and offering encouragement throughout.

One of the greatest pleasures in undertaking this project was the opportunity to bring people together. One happy outcome was the first meeting in 58 years between Sidney Knott and Bill Harrall, his 582 Squadron mid-upper gunner. In addition, on Saturday August 9 2003, Sidney, Bill and members of the crews' families gathered at the Petwood Hotel, Woodhall Spa, for a reception and lunch to mark the completion of the manuscript. The party of 36 then drove the short distance to the wartime bomber station of East Kirkby, now Lincolnshire Aviation Heritage Centre. Sidney and Bill enjoyed a short taxi-run in 'Just Jane' (NX611), the Museum's Lancaster. The rest of the party took the opportunity to admire, at first-hand, the aircraft that, time and again, brought their fathers and grandfathers safely home from enemy territory.

This book was made possible by the generosity of many. In particular, I am grateful to the Foster family for allowing unrestricted use of Ted Foster's unpublished manuscript. The valuable advice and photographic material provided by Vince Holyoak made a major contribution, as did the research undertaken so enthusiastically by Bomber Command historian Barry Hope and the guidance offered by 467/463 Squadrons Association UK Secretary Jill Skeet and researcher Jim George.

I am also grateful to Kim Twyman, Mandy Taylor, Meriel Bailes and Fiona Cummings for their help and support during the preparation of this book.

Every effort has been made to check the facts and opinions presented in this text. That said, the responsibility for any remaining errors is mine alone.


Tony Redding

# CHAPTER ONE

# *The Choice*

ON a mid-March day in 1943 Wing Commander Cosme Gomm, DSO, DFC, looked up as the good-looking young Lancaster Captain entered the room. Gomm had established 467 Squadron, Royal Australian Air Force, four months previously. The Squadron Commander motioned Frank Heavery to a seat.

Measured by the grim realities of life and death in Bomber Command during early 1943, Heavery and his crew were experienced. They had survived 12 operations, including two trips each to Essen and Nuremberg. Heavery respected Gomm. He was a man worth listening to, having completed a first tour on Whitley bombers before flying Beaufighters in the night interception role. Gomm formed 467 at Scampton on November 7 1942 and had taken it to another bomber station, Bottesford, later that month.

Gomm came straight to the point. Air Vice-Marshal Cochrane, 5 Group's Commander, was charged with forming a 'Special Duties' squadron. Cochrane wanted talented crews for this new unit. Gomm looked hard at Heavery: 'I don't want to lose you, but I have made my choice and I have picked you. How do you feel about it?'

Heavery felt unsure. He countered with an obvious question: 'What does 'Special Duties' mean?'

Gomm smiled: 'I can't tell you more but I am prepared to give you 24 hours to think it over. If you want to go, fair enough. If you don't want to go I may be able to do something about it. This is an Empire squadron and more Aussies are about to join us. I could argue that I need my more experienced crews to help the new boys. Talk it over with your crew.'

Heavery closed the door, stepped outside and stared across the broad expanse of airfield. He decided to call a crew meeting and put the matter to a vote. The seven men got together and weighed up Gomm's proposition. Sidney Knott, Heavery's rear gunner, recalls that the choice was far from straightforward:

> *At that time casualties were high and many 467 crews had failed to survive beyond 10 trips. We had lived through our dangerous probationary period. We had developed into a strong team. We had confidence in each other and in the job we were doing. The halfway point in the tour was not far away. On the other hand, moving to a new squadron would mean more training and that implied*

*a break from operations. Each of our last six trips had involved heavily defended German targets. Would our luck hold? I felt it was unrealistic to hope to live through another 18 trips like that. 'Special Duties' could hardly be more dangerous! Perhaps the move would give us a life-saving break?*

*I decided to support the idea. Two of the others also said yes, but this left the crew split – three in favour of Special Duties and three preferring to stay with 467 Squadron. Frank held the casting vote. He paused and said quietly: 'I don't think so. We'll stay as we are.' That was it. Subject closed!*

Heavery and his crew had met Cochrane. The Air Vice-Marshal had visited Bottesford in recent weeks. He had sat waiting to talk to the crews as they filed into the debriefing room after a raid. Knott's brief encounter with the 5 Group commander left him with the impression of a man accustomed to getting what he wanted. Nevertheless, the outcome of the Special Duties vote was accepted and Gomm sent another crew.

Recently commissioned Vernon Byers, Royal Canadian Air Force, took Heavery's place. He and his crew found themselves at Scampton on March 28, mixing with others posted in to form 'Squadron X'. The Commanding Officer was Guy Gibson and Squadron X became 617 Squadron. They began a hectic work-up for the attack on the Ruhr dams in mid-May.

Pilot Officer Byers, at 32, was older than most Lancaster Captains. His home town was Star City, Saskatchewan[1]. After the war the story developed that all 'Dambuster' crews were hand-picked veterans. This was far from the truth; some had completed fewer than 10 operations[2]. Byers' crew had completed just three operations when they joined 617 Squadron's A Flight. He had been with his previous squadron for just seven weeks, having arrived at Bottesford on February 5 1943[1]. The story eventually hardened into the myth that all 617 Squadron aircrew were highly experienced and the very best in Bomber Command. Even some recent published work repeats this myth. Yet, Byers was an unknown and a new boy in every sense.

Heavery's casting vote led, indirectly, to a chain of events ensuring that Byers captained one of the 19 Lancasters dispatched on the night of May 16-17 1943 to attack the dams. Eight failed to return and there were only three survivors among the 56 crew on board these aircraft[3]. Two of the three suffered severe injuries. Byers died that night. Indeed, his aircraft, AJ-K (ED934), was the first casualty. This Lancaster was part of the second wave (but first away from Scampton). Byers was one of 13 Canadians who failed to return from the Dams Raid. His rear gunner, Flight Sergeant James McDowell, was also Canadian. The records (AM Form 700) show that the aircraft had just 13 hours on the airframe when it failed to return.

Byers' aircraft took off at 21.30, the third of five aircraft in the second wave briefed to attack the Sorpe Dam. After 87 minutes in the air AJ-K was hit by flak batteries on the island of Texel. Byers was slightly off track. His aircraft caught fire and crashed at 22.57 into the Waddenzee, just off Texel and around 18 miles west of Harlingen. There were no survivors. It appears that the end was witnessed by the skipper of another second wave aircraft, Pilot Officer Geoff Rice in AJ-H[4]. Byers' aircraft was seen at 300-450 ft (reports vary) when it was hit by flak. Byers may have been climbing to check a pinpoint when disaster struck.

On June 22, just over five weeks after the raid, McDowell's body was found off Harlingen by the crew of a fishing boat. The rear gunner is buried at Harlingen. Byers and the rest of his crew are remembered on the RAF's Runnymede Memorial to those with no known grave (Byers: Panel 175). The week before McDowell's body was recovered, AJ-K provided a fitting salute to its gallant crew. The mine exploded with great violence, to the consternation of locals[5].

These dramatic events remained some weeks distant when Frank Heavery took the decision that probably saved his life and the lives of his crew, including Sidney Knott:

> *Byers and his crew were not really established when they were posted to 617 Squadron. They had done just the three trips, although I believe Byers had done another two as 'second dicky' - second pilot - to gain experience of operational*

*Tea before take-off: Wing Commander Gomm (third, left) pictured before a March 1943 sortie. The sergeant next to Gomm is James Lee. This 20-year-old was the sole survivor of Gomm's crew when they were shot down on a sortie to Milan in mid-August. Photo: Vincent Holyoak.*

*flying. In any event, they were beginners. As for Squadron X, Scampton is not far from Bottesford. The first we knew of 617's existence was the appearance of some strange-looking Lancs flying low over our airfield, minus their bomb doors. Very low level flying at night was the main training task and it was rumoured that 617 Squadron pilots wore special dark glasses when flying in daylight.*

Following the raid, the Dambusters' success was celebrated throughout the country and far beyond. Human nature ensured, however, that 617 Squadron attracted jealous comments:

*It became known in 5 Group as the 'One Op Squadron'. The raid was big news on the wireless and in the newspapers. We knew Byers had been posted to the squadron and we soon discovered that he and his crew were missing. This was no secret: Frank visited the Intelligence Office and read the raid reports. The skipper had more time on his hands than the rest of us when not flying. He was a frequent visitor to Intelligence and the reports of 617's exploits were available about a week after the raid. We thought they had done well. Gibson, of course, was a big name. We were relaxed about it. We had made our choice and were completely wrapped up in 467 Squadron. Our future – or lack of it – belonged to Gomm and his squadron. There was no reason to assume we would be luckier than Byers in the coming weeks.*

When Cosme Gomm selected Byers for 617 Squadron he could not have known that the Canadian pilot had barely two months to live as a result of the posting. Gomm was a very popular Commanding Officer – highly professional but with some endearing eccentricities. They included his love affair with a large Oldsmobile and a favourite toast at the Mess bar: 'Never a dull!'[6]. Gomm was fated not to complete his tour with 467 Squadron. He was killed in action, probably as a result of a nightfighter attack, following a sortie to Milan on August 16 1943. It was his twenty-fourth operation with the squadron he had formed and worked so hard to turn into an effective fighting unit.

CHAPTER TWO

# *The Air Gunner's Brevet*

YOUNG Sidney Knott's two closest friends were already in uniform when war began. Johnny Martin had been called up and was in the army, while Bobby Hopkins had joined the Royal Navy as a Boy Entrant. Knott was discontented with life. He was in a rut, serving customers in the family's greengrocers in the Essex town of Leigh-on-Sea:

> *Twelve months earlier, in the Autumn of 1938, a new Territorial Army drill hall opened in town. The War Minister was due to speak and Johnny and I went along. We had much in common. We had left school at 14 and, three years on, we had been drawn into the family businesses. My mother had the greengrocers and Johnny's father ran a garage. While we had no particular thoughts about war at that time Johnny was impressed with the TA. He spent two weeks away at camp and promptly signed up on his return. I was more cautious. I felt obliged to continue to help my mother in the shop.*

Knott's father, a carpenter and joiner, had managed to steer clear of the shop. Wounded three times in the Great War, Sidney James Knott Snr. had something of a reputation as a drinker. This was not unusual. Most Western Front veterans had been brutalised, to some extent, by their wartime experiences. Some had spent many years trying to forget the horrors of the trenches in the company of their pals and a pint glass.

Sidney James Knott Jnr., while an unassuming boy, had a strong, independent character. He was no fan of school and occasional bouts of truancy did not go unnoticed. He went into hiding whenever the School Board Inspector made exploratory visits to the family home. The young boy preferred to roam Leigh Marshes. He and his mates developed an entrepreneurial past-time, using wheelbarrows to lift heaps of unwanted shells from the back of the harbour cocklesheds. They found a ready market, as cockleshell paths were all the rage in 1930s seaside towns. Sea Lavender was also plentiful on the marshes and could be sold in penny bunches.

These early adventures came to an abrupt end when 10-year-old Sidney developed osteomyelitis – an infection leading to inflammation of the bone marrow:

> *This was a big shock. Until then I had been full of life. I had two major*

*operations on my leg and spent 19 weeks in hospital. It took me a full year to walk without crutches. Eventually I grew fit again and managed to put this alarming episode behind me, but the year out of school did nothing for my education. I began working in the shop at a very early age; mother paid no wages and the small change in my pocket came from paper-rounds.*

*While not much of a scholar I loved sport – especially football. I was a good all-rounder and a sympathetic teacher introduced me to the Southend and District Amateur League. I was fond of cricket too but needed money to buy the whites, whereas football cost next to nothing. I had an easy-going attitude towards money. Few ordinary people cared about money before the war; they had none to worry about!*

There was overwhelming relief across the country when the 1938 Munich Crisis ebbed away and left Britain shaken but still at peace. Yet,

*Teenagers at the time of the Munich Crisis: Sidney Knott is sharply dressed, on the far right. Photo: Sidney Knott.*

deep down, most people realised that war was inevitable. On Sunday September 3 1939 Prime Minister Chamberlain's wireless address to the nation announced the outbreak of war. This news failed to move Sidney Knott, who remained locked within the parochial world of a small town greengrocers:

> *The possibility of war with Germany increased week by week during that last Summer of peace, but I remained preoccupied with my own future and the problem of those lost opportunities at school. I enrolled at nightschool soon after my sixteenth birthday and began to study book-keeping.*

The wider world's problems seemed remote and irrelevant, but this changed when the war suddenly took a direct interest in Knott's family:

> *My cousin Olive lost her husband during the first weeks of hostilities. Jack was in the Merchant Navy; he was reported 'missing, presumed drowned'. Suddenly, the war became a personal affair. In 1938 I had shied away from the Territorials. When Chamberlain broadcast in 1939 I listened politely, then left the house to continue a game of cricket. In May 1940, when Anthony Eden made a national appeal for men to join the Local Defence Volunteers, I had a different attitude. The war news was grim and I wanted to do something.*

> *The doors of the police station were wide open when I arrived. I went in and registered without hesitation. My LDV unit consisted of familiar faces – local boys of my age and old soldiers of Great War vintage. We received LDV armbands – there were no uniforms. There were also no weapons, so we concentrated on drill. We could march like soldiers even if we didn't entirely look the part.*

The LDV became the Home Guard as the Summer of 1940 unfolded and kit and weapons began to trickle through:

> *We made our headquarters in the garage of a large house. Leigh-on-Sea took on a warlike appearance – pillboxes were built and signposts and place names disappeared. My platoon's job was to guard Southend's railway and tram depots. As we stood guard the war news went from bad to worse: the Blitzkrieg ended in the collapse of France and Britain stood alone. The Home Guard was preoccupied with 'Fifth Columnists' and the more serious threat of a surprise attack by parachutists, should fears of invasion become reality.*

> *We visited Shoeburyness Garrison on several occasions, meeting the Regulars and experiencing life in a real army camp. We took along our elderly rifles and the single five-round clip carried by each platoon member as our contribution to the defence of the realm. While at Shoeburyness we fired our few rounds at the butts. This was my first opportunity to fire the .303, although I had used a shotgun successfully as a boy, providing occasional rabbits for the table.*

> *I wore my Home Guard uniform with overblown teenage pride. I can still recall the childish pleasure when a policeman stepped out of the Blackout shadows one evening, inspected me with veiled torch beam and said: 'Ok, Tommy, off you go.' When on parade with my platoon I enjoyed the company of the older men and their stories of life in the trenches.*

> *Only a few weeks before, Leigh-on-Sea's entire fleet of cockle boats had gone*

*to war, sailing to Dunkirk to help rescue the British Expeditionary Force. One boat struck a mine and the explosion killed everyone on board. I knew all the 'Cockle Boys', including the three who died.*

It was a sign of the times. The mountains of shells behind Leigh-on-Sea's cocklesheds – once a valuable source of pocket money for Sidney Knott and his friends – began to disappear. Nothing went to waste in a British economy mobilising for total war. The shells were shovelled into lorries and taken away, to provide grit for chicken feed.

*High Summer arrived and the Battle of Britain approached its climax. On a hot August Sunday my father suggested a walk along the cliffs. I knew exactly where he had in mind, a vantage point providing a wonderful view across the Thames estuary to the Kent shore. We sat together, sprawled on the grass, as a droning noise began to develop out to sea. As it grew louder three great formations of enemy aircraft crawled into view. The Thames anti-aircraft batteries added to the noise; puffs of black smoke suddenly appeared among the twin-engined bombers. We watched in silence as the formation of around 150 enemy aircraft continued its stately progress along the Thames, brushing aside the best efforts of the guns. They began a sweeping flat turn and smoke suddenly poured from one of the aircraft. It lost height and eventually came down on the Thorpe Bay mudflats. I had seen the first of many bombers shot down. Very few were to be German!*

*The Luftwaffe's systematic night bombing of London soon commenced. I developed a habit of watching the fireworks from the top of Southend's Pier Hill. The display was fantastic. The night sky was split by brilliant shellbursts and flares, searchlight cones and the glow of fires. An oil refinery was hit during one raid and burned round the clock for days. It was an incredible sight.*

*The anti-aircraft guns went into action every night, including the offshore batteries mounted on the Nore and other sea forts. Sited on sandbanks in the estuary, these steel-framed structures look rather like modern offshore oil platforms.*

Sixty years on, abandoned and rusty, the sea forts now stand in silent tribute to Britain's 'Finest Hour' (although they were far from silent in the 1960s, when some were occupied by 'pirate' radio stations). The forts were designed by G. M. Maunsell, built at Gravesend, floated downriver and positioned in the shallows, directly under the track of aircraft crossing the Kent and Essex shores, or turning in to follow the Thames to London. During the war years the forts' guns accounted for 22 enemy aircraft and 25 Flying Bombs.

In this increasingly insecure world Knott's daily life alternated between shop and Home Guard platoon. This routine came dangerously close to collapse one Sunday morning, when his father walked through the front door with alarming news:

*A notice had appeared in the window of the shop across the road. The citizens of Leigh-on-Sea were informed that their town had become a 'Restricted Area'. They were told to be prepared to leave this frontline zone within 24 hours (and with only one suitcase each). Our family was exempt because of the shop.*

*People didn't wait for their marching orders. Around half the town's population disappeared within 24 hours. Invasion was expected at any moment and the army wanted space to do battle on the Essex beaches, with the approach roads free of refugees.*

*These events were traumatic for those remaining in the town and there were painful consequences for my family. Our greengrocers, established in 1923, had been a busy shop from the day of opening. The shop and living quarters had been built by my father and grandfather. Now trade fell away and the staff had to go. I would have been more than happy to join them but still felt unable to turn my back on mother. Then I bumped into an old schoolfriend wearing pilot's wings. The urge to cut and run grew stronger by the day and father made it worse. He gave me a stern warning: 'You had better do something. They will catch up with you eventually and send you straight into the army.' I took his point, remembering that he had been wounded three times in Flanders.*

In no time at all the family business was a shadow of its former self. Ten staff had gone and the shop barely ticked over:

*There was nothing left for me at home and I began to map out my future. I decided to join the Royal Air Force. I had reached the age of 18 and had freedom of choice for the first time in my life. There was no recruiting office locally, so I took the bus to Romford – not the most exciting way to go to war! The choice was between the Navy and Air Force. At that time there was a relatively modest intake into the Navy, unlike the Air Force. My father favoured the RAF. While he came from a rough and ready family he was never without a collar and tie. He regarded the Air Force as the more gentlemanly option; all ranks wore a collar and tie.*

Sidney Knott's RAF medical had an element of farce. The doctor asked him for a water sample but he had listened to his mother's parting comment. He had peed just before going into the waiting room:

*A look of disgust came over the doctor's face when nothing came of his simple request. Several volunteers failed the first test! We were told to wait in a corner. Later, we were ordered to remove our shoes and socks and walk around on the cold stone floor. A psychological trick was employed: assistants ran the taps in a series of deep sinks. This did the trick and all outstanding samples were produced with ease.*

Beyond the supreme challenge of surviving the Battle of Britain, the RAF's many problems in August 1940 included a shortage of wireless operators. A cheerful Recruiting Officer at Romford dismissed Knott with an encouraging aside: 'I'll put you down for wireless op. It won't be long before you are called.' He was right. Within days Knott received instructions to report to RAF Uxbridge for attestation. He was still worried about his inadequate schooling. Knott's standard of English – especially spelling – was poor and he was not surprised to learn he had failed the test. There was one option left: the RAF 'General Duties' category was open to him and he seized the opportunity.

*In no time at all I had a service number and the rank of AC2 (Aircraftsman, Second Class). As a volunteer I had to take the oath. I took the Bible in hand*

*and read the official text. It included a striking phrase: '...to defend at all times our King and Royal Family' – or words to that effect. I remember thinking it odd that there was no mention of defending the country, but I had taken the King's Shilling. Despite my immediate availability I kicked my heels on 'deferred service' for another three months.*

Sidney Knott's call-up papers eventually arrived, together with a rail warrant. He was instructed to report to Blackpool for basic training on Monday January 6 1941:

*I was too keen. I set out a day earlier than necessary and caught the train to London. My walk through the capital, in the gloom of the early evening Blackout, made a deep impression. The Blitz-scarred streets were full of shelterers scurrying to the Tube stations. Going down myself, I was staggered to see hundreds of women and children filling the platforms, noisily chattering as they prepared their rough beds for the night. I realised, for the first time, just how much London had suffered night after night. My morbid interest in that 'fireworks display', viewed from the relative safety of Southend, now made me feel uneasy and rather guilty.*

Blackpool, while quite different, was another shock to Knott's system. The Corporal eyeing up the new recruits was a man of few words: 'You lot! Come with me. We'll find you billets.'

*We were soon housed in tired examples of the cheap Bed and Breakfast accommodation so popular before the war. Our billet provided a place to eat and sleep, but little else. The next step was the kitting-out parade, fixed for that first afternoon. This took place in the garish surroundings of Blackpool's famous Empress Ballroom. Well-known to radio audiences, this was a leading venue for popular cinema organists. The ballroom itself was unbelievable, with its huge chandeliers and plush décor. Yet war with Hitler had succeeded in reducing even this interior to drab reality. Trestle tables filled the vast room, each piled high with kit. I got into line and received a kit bag. I moved on and accepted each item in turn, without comment. There was no question of trying it on. Too bad if an item didn't fit. It came as a surprise, however, to discover our hosts' talent for spotting correct sizes with the most cursory of glances. Occasional mistakes were sorted out later by swapping over-long trousers or ill-fitting shirts with others in the billet.*

The six weeks' initial training yielded more revelations. Each day was filled with drill, PT on Blackpool Sands and endless lectures. The medical talks included a lurid briefing on VD:

*While in my late teens I had no idea such diseases existed! Perhaps this requires a word of explanation. The essential facts are simple: teenagers during the early 1940s were extremely slow to grow up. There were exceptions, of course, but most of us were more interested in sport than girls. Most of us became even less interested in the 'fair sex' after the VD lesson.*

Those with a more determined appetite for female company had rivals for the attention of the Blackpool belles. The Free Poles had a reception centre in Blackpool. Many of these natural charmers were hardened characters – their youthful innocence lost in the struggle to survive the catastrophe that had overwhelmed their country.

Knott's adult education continued as the weeks passed:

*I enjoyed the course, regarding it as designed by the RAF purely for my benefit. Our evenings were free but there wasn't much to do beyond cementing new friendships. We visited the local swimming baths once a week but that was no luxury. We were rationed to just 20 minutes: five minutes to undress, 10 minutes in the pool and five minutes to get dry and dress. It was almost impossible to get a decent bath at our B&B billets, so we jumped into the pool clutching bars of soap. We had no swimming kit and ran around starkers. This was a bit of a shock and I began to appreciate that men came in all shapes and sizes.*

*We made the most of Blackpool. It was a great place for entertainment, even with a war on, although our meagre pay didn't stretch very far. Blackpool had its Tower Ballroom and the entertainers. They included Reginald Dixon, 'Master of the Mighty Wurlitzer', the greatest of the organists and resident at the Tower from 1930 to 1970 – with a break for war service in the RAF. There were also several top dance orchestras, together with the aquarium, the zoo and, of course, the beach – although Blackpool Sands provided few delights during that bitter Winter of 1941.*

*Much of the training took place at Blackpool football ground, where stands were divided off into classrooms. Towards the end of the six weeks we drew rifles from the armoury and boarded a tram to Fleetwood. We spent the day on the range. Once again I fired a few rounds. I had the edge on some of the others when it came to rifle drill, thanks to my Home Guard days. In fact it didn't seem to take me long to pick up most things.*

*We were posted in mid-February and the Corporal who greeted us so warmly on our first day was unlucky enough to be put in charge of the move. We boarded an early morning train and headed south, eventually arriving at Bletchley. Our group of 25 then changed trains, having been informed that our destination was Horsham, Sussex. Some hours later, our train arrived at Norwich. We then discovered our true destination to be Horsham St. Faith, an RAF station close to Norwich (and now the local airport). The long-suffering Corporal was pleased to see the back of us.*

The new arrivals were fed and watered. There was cocoa from the WVS (Women's Voluntary Service) van and, shortly afterwards, Sidney Knott allowed himself to be impressed by his first meal on an RAF station:

*It was wonderful. The dish, described as 'cheese pie', was delicious. Thinking ahead about my future life in the service I was much encouraged. What's for tea?*

Accommodation proved more difficult. Beds were found but for the first night only. In the morning all new boys were packed off to nearby Blickling Hall. This large country house provided accommodation for personnel manning Horsham's satellite, a grass airfield at Oulton, around 12 miles to the north. Their arrival at Blickling Hall was less than auspicious. The Warrant Officer in charge explained that their quarters were unfinished. He gave them the good news: the walls and floors of the wooden huts were in position. The bad news followed: in most cases the roofs and windows were missing. Twenty men were allocated to each incomplete hut. Knott looked around, surveying the faces in his group. They were all 'General Duties' and from every part of the country:

> *We got as much sleep as we could under the circumstances, then paraded the following morning. Various jobs were allocated. I was told to report to the Fire Section, equipped with a solitary crash tender.*

> *Blenheim bombers operated from the airfield at Oulton, two or three miles from Blickling Hall. The Blenheim squadrons had been savaged by the Luftwaffe during the previous year's Blitzkrieg. Now they operated within 2 Group, part of Bomber Command at that time. My appointment to the Fire Section sounded more exciting than most General Duties but reality failed to live up to the promise. To make matters worse, conditions at Blickling Hall were abysmal. There was no Mess. We were expected to make do with a filthy-looking field kitchen. We grabbed meals when we could, taking our food into the draughty, leaking huts and eating while perched on our beds. There was no hot water and we took to 'boiling up' on the hut stove for a decent shave. Discipline was lax and there were no civilising influences. The NAAFI ladies did what they could by providing tea and snacks on the airfield during the day, but Blickling Hall and its surrounding buildings were depressing. This stately home was owned by the Marquis of Lothian, Britain's Ambassador in Washington. He left the pile to the National Trust on his death in 1940 and the RAF took it over for the duration.*

An Orderly Room was established in the large yard adjoining the main building. The new boys continued to arrive and were allocated rough quarters on the estate and in the surrounding area. The lax attitude prevailed. A few individuals were needed to man the Orderly Room. Others were required to peel potatoes and tackle other mundane jobs for the Officers' and Sergeants' Messes and for the field kitchen. More were needed to man anti-gas, sanitary, defence and other sections, including the bomb dump. Eight AC2s, led by a Corporal, made up the Fire Section at Blickling Hall/Oulton. Their duties included fire protection at the stately pile and custody of the satellite airfield's precious crash tender.

New arrivals soon discovered that there wasn't much to Oulton. The airfield opened in July 1940. It had a dangerous-looking hump in the middle, uncomfortably tall trees around most of the perimeter and no buildings other than a few Nissen huts serving as ground staff workshops. The Duty Pilot lived in relative luxury. He had a shack-like office facing into the airfield. Flying was restricted to daylight hours and local defence consisted of a few gun emplacements along the boundary, manned by General Duties airmen.

During Sidney Knott's stay the Blenheims were operated by 114 Squadron and, subsequently, 18 Squadron (the latter eventually succeeded by 139 Squadron)[1]. The twin-engined bombers made regular daylight sorties and the Duty Pilot's task was to log all aircraft movements. His shabby little office abutted the short concrete track providing access for the crash tender. This was crewed by a driver and three firefighters. The emergency facilities were completed by the 'blood wagon' (ambulance), with its driver and orderly. Most days passed peacefully enough for the emergency team, with excitement in very short supply. Crash duty was particularly tiresome for the unlucky one wearing the asbestos suit. The ungainly trousers had to be worn at all times by one of the crash team on watch. The top and visor could be put on in a hurry, however, when responding to an incident. The driver was expected to keep the crash tender's engine warm and ready for action at all times:

*I attended three crashes during my six months with Oulton's Fire Section. The first was a typical result of youthful exuberance. A Blenheim tore across the field low and fast, doing a 'shoot-up' after an air test. The pilot pulled up one second too late at the end of the airfield and clipped the trees. His machine lost flying speed and flopped heavily into an adjoining field. The Blenheim's numerous shortcomings included the reluctance of its engines to respond quickly in an emergency.*

*We set off in the crash tender, with the ambulance rattling along close behind. While the Blenheim had not caught fire, the impact had reduced much of it to matchwood. We approached from what remained of the tail. As we moved forward we could see the pilot, a young officer who had been alone in the aircraft. His flying clothes were visible but his head had slumped down into the cockpit. It took only a moment to appreciate our mistake – he'd been decapitated.*

*I remember my surprise at the lack of blood as we struggled to get him out of the wreck and into the ambulance. This wasn't easy as his legs were jammed beneath him. Our Corporal became impatient. With the sharp comment 'stop buggering about', he ordered us to chop off the trapped foot. The field amputation was performed with the crash tender's fire axe, leaving us with a body and head in the ambulance and a foot, still in its flying boot, lodged firmly in the wreckage.*

*A team from Bristol, manufacturers of the Blenheim, eventually arrived at the crash scene and they were not amused to find the pilot's foot still in-situ. We were ordered back, with strict instructions not to return without the missing body part.*

The second crash was also the result of pilot error – an attempted landing along the airfield's shorter axis. There was no choice due to the wind direction:

*We stood outside the Duty Pilot's office, open-mouthed and willing the Blenheim to go round again. It didn't! It came in too fast, ploughed through the far perimeter hedge, crossed the road and scythed through the hedge on the other side. We were on our way before it stopped moving. I happened to be wearing the asbestos suit that day but, once again, there was no fire. Two crew members scrambled out but the third was in difficulties. I helped him out and took him over to the ambulance. All three had escaped serious injury. I stood there, clumsy in my fire-suit trousers, surveying the wreckage and clutching the axe recently used in less fortunate circumstances.*

Such events were rare. Bored duty crews passed the time as best they could. There was no hot food for airfield ground personnel. Instead, a convoy system operated, taking airmen back to Blickling Hall for what passed for a meal. When not on standby at the airfield, Fire Section crews had their responsibilities at Blickling Hall. Fire pumps and sandbags had to be checked and a special key was used to enter the mansion's main rooms, to inspect the fire buckets. One NCO with too much time on his hands experimented with a chute for rapid evacuation from the Hall's top floor.

Knott's crew were off duty when the call came to respond to another crash:

> It wasn't one of our Blenheims. An Anson had crashed in a nearby field. It was the camera plane filming for the new picture 'A Yank in the RAF', starring Tyrone Power. The film star was lucky he wasn't on board. We found the pilot and two cameramen lying dead in the wreckage and I heard the full story a few hours later. A Spitfire and Hurricane were being filmed "attacking" the Anson. One pass came a shade too close and the fighter clipped the Anson, sending it spinning out of control and into the field. The fighter pilot baled out and survived. As for the unfortunates in the Anson, it took some time to recover their bodies. We were becoming hardened to gruesome sights, however, and took such things in our stride.

> The Anson's fuselage had burst apart and the two cameramen could be seen sprawled inside. They were civilians and looked foreign to my eye. Their large film canisters had broken up and there was tangled cine film everywhere, adding to the bloody chaos inside the wreck.

By this time there were serious concerns about the dismal living conditions at Blickling Hall. Some 400 men occupied the Hall and the many buildings scattered throughout the grounds:

> The limited mains water was reserved for drinking and cooking. Water for washing and laundry was drawn from the lake. Things continued to deteriorate and everyone suffered bouts of a dysentery-like illness. This threat to health prompted a much needed shake-up and improvements were made. A barn was converted into a large dining hall and a kitchen was built. There was even the novelty of a few hours off, thanks to the introduction of a liberty bus to Norwich. This journey passed quickly, in a barrage of filthy RAF songs.

More formal entertainments eventually arrived. A small stage was built at the end of the new dining hall and ENSA began to visit.

> Lady tap dancers, for reasons which conveniently escape me, were always popular. The entertainer who made the biggest impression, however, was Basil Radford. He was a talented man, a straight actor and also part of a popular comedy duo. He partnered Naunton Wayne in the 1938 Alfred Hitchcock classic The Lady Vanishes. They played two eccentric Englishmen (Charters and Caldicott, respectively) on a train in 'foreign parts' and more interested in cricket scores than bodies in the corridor and missing ladies. Basil would present a one-man show and then join us for drinks. He did much to improve morale at Blickling Hall.

Other 'entertainments' held an element of surprise:

> We were sitting by the crash tender when an aircraft flew over. It didn't sound like one of ours. We caught sight of it, bobbing in and out of cloud. I stood on the crash tender, looking up, when I noticed that the suspect's bomb doors had opened. Bombs then began to fall, each explosion marked by a tall

*plume of smoke. We set off to investigate.*

A railway line ran along one side of the airfield. One bomb had hit the track and a train had stopped in the cutting, the locomotive releasing angry clouds of steam:

*Other bombs had fallen close to the aircraft at their dispersals but had done little damage. They had penetrated deep into the soft earth before exploding. Real excitement at last! Our first taste of enemy action. There were some old Vickers gas-operated machine guns positioned around the airfield. We could have had a go but not without the blessing of an officer. This was an anticlimax – we felt we had missed our chance. Now squadron personnel were saddled with the job of washing the aircraft free of mud from near misses.*

During mid-August 1941 a paragraph in Daily Orders caught Knott's eye. The RAF needed more air gunners:

*Given the disturbing way the war was going, I felt I should do more. During my time with the Fire Section the day revolved around the aircraft and the urge to fly soon took hold. That said, I was one of only two volunteers. Our names were taken and, eventually, I found myself before the Group Captain at Horsham. The interview was very straightforward. There was no Selection Board – this officer made his own decisions. I was dismissed with a promising remark: 'Well, you look suitable enough! I'll recommend you.'*

*Volunteering for aircrew was a peculiar business. It was a once-only decision and a one-way ticket. Free choice disappeared the second I volunteered and there was no turning back. While waiting for a posting I had a change of scenery. I left the Fire Section for Oulton's bomb dump. Perhaps word had spread that I had volunteered for aircrew. I can imagine the logic: anyone silly enough to volunteer for operational flying surely belongs at the station bomb dump! The AC2s acted as labourers for the armourers and manhandled the 250 lb bombs carried by the Blenheims. We took the bombs from the store and loaded them onto trolleys. It took two or three men to lift each bomb.*

*I had busy days but, overall, most of my time at Oulton was spent doing very little. General Duties life in the RAF did not make the adrenalin flow. I passed the time by mucking in, even helping to wash up or peel potatoes in the Mess – anything to avoid boredom! The monotony was broken occasionally by guest lecturers, including MPs who addressed us on the progress of the war and other weighty topics.*

Two months passed before the call came.

Sidney Knott's Air Force career continued in London, at No. 1 Aircrew Reception Centre, St John's Wood. The volunteers were housed in blocks of flats around the perimeter of Regents Park, overlooking the zoo. The intake consisted largely of RAF ground personnel who had re-mustered, although a few were completely new to the service, having joined up just six weeks previously.

There were few medical checks to ensure the men were fit for flying duties. The Group Captain's recommendation worked its magic in Knott's case. He was, nevertheless, required to submit to the RAF's much-feared mercury test. This involved blowing into a U-tube and holding the column of mercury above the mark for 90 seconds. This was extremely difficult and a certain amount of practice was essential if the victim was to pass. Knott 'held the mercury'. He received his white flash, worn on the forage cap to identify him as 'Aircrew, Under Training.' He was posted immediately to an Initial Training Wing on the South Coast:

*I felt elated. While still a kid, that white flash showed my intent to contribute to the war effort. I was impressed with my new quarters: a hotel on the seafront opposite St. Leonards Pier. The entire ITW ate and slept there. Naturally, it was too good to be true. I had been posted in from an operational station where discipline was lax. ITW was very different. I was forced into an orgy of button-cleaning, boot polishing and marching at light infantry pace all over Hastings. What a pain!*

*With all this exercise we needed to take a bath regularly, but we had to respect the wartime rule specifying five inches of water only. The depth was checked meticulously by a bored Pilot Officer armed with a ruler. We soon accepted the bull. No matter how bright and sparkling we left the bath, we were always told: 'Not good enough. Do it again.'*

*We had evenings out but the Canadian Army's arrival in Hastings took the gloss off our excursions. Somehow or other we didn't mix well. Within a day or two Brits and Canadians were restricted to alternate evenings out. Money is said to be the root of all evil. Well, that was certainly true in this case. The Canadians were much better paid, they were not afraid to spend it and we resented our status as poor relations.*

The days passed quickly in that strangely subdued seaside environment. Lectures were held in the large properties along the seafront, all requisitioned by the RAF. When not marching at double time, Knott and the other volunteers were introduced to the obsolete Vickers gas-operated machine gun – still in widespread use – and the more modern, belt-fed Browning. They were taught how to strip and reassemble the guns. Some elements of the course were technical, but Knott enjoyed them all the more for their complexity.

The volunteers began the painful process of learning Morse on the 'buzzer'. This was soon cast aside and they switched to the Aldis signalling lamp. Their introduction to the Aldis took place in a car park built beneath the promenade. The signallers had to find a convenient corner, as this underground car park was full of building materials, stored for the construction of tank traps and other seafront fortifications.

*We were required to meet a basic standard – using the lamp to send six words a minute. Each word was calculated at four letters long, a point not without its element of humour. We paired off for practice, one working the lamp and the other taking down the messages. As we grew more proficient signals were sent from the roof to the top steps of the Lido sun terrace, over a mile away.*

*I did well in the practicals but soon got into trouble in the classroom. I couldn't keep up with the torrent of dictation at the end of each lecture. My Elementary School was not known for the academic brilliance of its pupils. My marks, overall, left much to be desired. I did my best to keep up and spent most evenings copying out what I had missed, consulting a room-mate's notebook.*

*This was frustrating as I remained very enthusiastic about the course. We had lectures on the basics of navigation, aerodynamics and the theory of bombing. There were frequent aircraft recognition sessions. I continued to please in the practicals, but the paperwork went from bad to worse.*

As the six-week course continued the volunteers were introduced to R/T (radio-telephony) procedures and the phonetic alphabet. This was subject to fashion and a growing American influence. 'A – Apple', for example, was scrapped in favour of 'A – Able' and 'B – Beer' became 'B – Baker' halfway through the course.

An introduction to the theory of parachuting caused great unease among students. The news that a body accelerates as it falls – until it reaches 'terminal velocity' – did nothing to increase Knott's desire to give it a try. There was genuine relief when it became clear that the syllabus did not include a jump:

*Now fully familiar with the guns we were introduced to the turrets. There were two basic types: the Boulton Paul, with joystick controls, and the Frazer-Nash, with handlebar-type controls. The largely unsuccessful Defiant fighter had a four-gun Boulton Paul turret. The Frazer-Nash, however, was the more significant as it equipped the RAF's heavy bombers.*

*Some of the finer points of gunnery were introduced. They included deflection shooting, relative speeds (from zero, when flying in formation, to double when closing head on), harmonisation of the guns and gun sights. I lapped it up but found the maths confusing. I was aware of my weaknesses but it came as a blow to learn that I had failed the course due to 'lack of mathematical ability'. I now faced a 'Return to Unit', a prospect more embarrassing than being drummed out of the Brownies. There can be nothing worse! In the services, the last place anyone wants to go is back to the unit they have just left.*

*Happily, I won a reprieve – along with half the others, who had also failed. Fortunately, the RAF could not afford to be too fussy in 1941. The Air Force was desperate for more air gunners as the new four-engined bombers began to roll off the production lines in increasing numbers. A pragmatic solution was found: the introduction of the extended course. This solved two problems. It avoided a catastrophic 50 per cent wastage rate on the course by making it much more difficult to fail. It also bought time. The Gunnery Schools, representing the next stage in our education, were full to capacity. There were simply not enough places to go round.*

*Our extended course began with the arrival of the RAF's secret weapon, a team of experienced Education Officers. They split us into small groups and provided concentrated coaching in our weakest subjects. I spent the next few weeks doing nothing but drill, PT and maths – lots of maths. I took the exams again and passed.*

The ITW moved during the extended course. In early December 1941 Knott's group boarded a train at 7 am. They had no knowledge of their destination. Could it be to the far north, to the Orkneys? Or the isolation of Wick? Some hours later they were shunted into a siding:

*We had no idea where we were until a railway worker ambled past the carriage. Responding cheerfully to our question, he replied: 'Wembley, mate!' My enthusiasm for football got the better of my imagination. A posting to paradise! Sadly, however, we stayed on the train. Some hours later another engine hitched up and we were off again, still none the wiser. We passed the time eating our rations, dozing or playing cards until the mystery tour arrived at a Midlands town around teatime. The WVS had turned out in force and were ready with steaming mugs of cocoa. It wasn't long before we were ordered back into the carriages and the journey continued until the train finally stopped at around midnight. We had been travelling for the best part of 17 hours and felt thoroughly fed up and disorientated. We formed up with full kit and marched out of yet another anonymous station. The cold night air caught in our throats and we smelt the sea. We had swapped one coast for another. The stiff-legged march to our billets served as a sombre introduction to the delights of Bridlington, Yorkshire.*

The waiting billets were empty houses. The rooms were cold and there were no beds. The men were told to sleep on the floor, using 'biscuits' – three small, square mattresses – to form makeshift beds:

*Our only defence against that freezing night was a single blanket each. One enterprising room-mate slipped away and returned a few minutes later with a bundle of wood to burn in the grate. We admired his enterprise but felt differently the next morning when asked to pay for a missing garden fence, now a pile of ashes. On a happier note, real beds soon arrived.*

Inshore fishing was still permitted off Bridlington at this time:

*During the first few days we were amazed to see fishermen walking around town carrying enormous cod by the gills, with tails brushing the pavement. This was an appetising sight given the strict food rationing. Virtually every street in Bridlington had its fish and chip shop and we intended to visit as many as possible.*

A greasy meal of fish and chips would have been the worst possible prelude to Bridlington's challenging air sickness test:

*I found the whole thing preposterous. We had spent many weeks training and no-one had bothered, at least until now, to find out whether we suffered from airsickness. It was hard to make sense of this but even harder to beat back a laugh when we saw what had been rigged up for the test. There we were, lined up on Bridlington's windy seafront and confronted with two large fairground swing-boats. The ropes had been removed from each boat and wide boards had been fixed from end to end. Divided off into pairs, we were strapped to the boards, lying on our backs.*

The men were told to keep the swings moving, virtually through 180 degrees, for around 20 minutes. Medical Officers were on hand, armed with notebooks, stop-watches and buckets. The victims were expected to hold a lucid conversation until they turned green and could no longer endure the torture. Some lasted a few minutes. Others did much better but only three or four held out for the full 20 minutes.

*After this ordeal we were required to sit down and recover for 15 minutes. My turn came just before lunch. I held out for 20 minutes but then realised I would be late for lunch if I rested. As I hated to miss my food I tottered to the Mess on rubber legs.*

*I never heard any more of this experiment. I assume it was a complete failure. In any event we were all posted to Gunnery School, to the great relief of those who managed only a few minutes on the swings. Perhaps a record of this nonsense still exists in the Air Ministry's dusty archives. What a way to train for war! What did Bridlington's residents make of it? Grown men enjoying the war on a fairground ride! Perhaps they concluded that the men strapped to the planks had committed some dreadful deed and were now paying the price?*

Sidney Knott's six weeks at St Leonards and at Bridlington stretched to five months due to the lack of places at Gunnery School:

*We were all fed up – 'browned off', as the saying of the time went – but some bright spark decided to liven things up by putting us through a three-day evasion exercise. This would come in handy if we were shot down. We were issued with field rations and moved out in small groups. The idea was to avoid capture and return to camp unseen. My group succeeded. We took to hiding in haystacks and the search teams failed to find us. The course then came to an end, at long last, and we were given leave. I was pleased to see the back of ITW. It turned out to be more of a trial than any three-day evasion exercise. My next stop was No.1 Air Armaments School at Manby, Lincolnshire.*

Knott arrived at Manby in May 1942. Events had conspired against him, resulting in an unusually lengthy stay at ITW. Even so, he still had some way to go to complete his training and emerge as an operational air gunner. Manby was the venue for yet another six-week course. In this instance, however, the system's bottlenecks worked in Knott's favour. The insatiable demand for places encouraged those in charge to condense the Gunnery School syllabus into four weeks.

Manby was a pre-war station. Its facilities included a large parade ground, an unwelcome indicator of plenty of bull. The course opened with two weeks in the classroom. Knott and the other student gunners were then ready to begin flying:

*My big moment arrived some seven months after I began training. On June 6 1942 I took off from Manby on board Wellington 9295, with Pilot Officer Carruthers as skipper. I had never flown before. My first impression was one of overwhelming space – the sheer expanse of the countryside below took my breath away. What a wonderful view! We were in the air for just 45 minutes but that was enough. The main purpose of the flight was 'air experience' and it was certainly an enjoyable experience. Even better, I repeated it later that day. My second short hop in the Wellington was with Warrant Officer Tilbury at the controls. I had practised manipulating the turret on the ground, but found things very different in the air. Turning the turret onto the beam was bloody frightening! As I rotated out to 90 degrees I had to fight off the terrible feeling that my turret was about to fall off. The perspex bubble rattled and roared in the slipstream as it moved out to the beam. I had to dare myself to go out to 90*

degrees at first, but I soon got used to things. I was proud to be on Wellingtons. I regarded the Wimpy as a fine, modern aircraft – so effective that it remained in service on some fronts until the war's end.

Three days later I was aloft in another Wellington, 9220, piloted by Flight Lieutenant Marawski. During this 65-minute trip I fired 200 rounds. I was overwhelmed. I felt a tremendous sense of power when I fired the guns for the first time. Some accounts describe our .303s as pea-shooters. All I can say is that it felt very different behind four Brownings. Surely it was impossible for any attacking fighter to escape such a hail of fire?

I flew twice the following day, firing 400 rounds in all. The air-to-air targets were drogues towed by Martinets. The target tug let out the drogue to around 400 yards (better safe than sorry), then took up station on the Wimpy's beam. Several gunners were aloft in my aircraft. The ammunition was colour-coded and each gunner had 200 rounds of a particular colour. Strikes on the drogue left tell-tale traces of paint.

Other exercises included firing astern (done over the sea) and air-to-ground firing over the Mablethorpe Sands range. We flew at low level over the sands, following the water's edge and firing at targets mounted on pontoons. After each exercise a range attendant would mount up and ride out to pick up the sea targets – all done without getting his feet wet. There was just one hiccup, the occasion when I let fly at what I thought was the target, only to be stopped by an hysterical shout over the intercom. Whatever I had fired at, it was not the target! I never found out what that large object was but no deaths were reported and no harm done.

Ground instruction and practical exercises also filled the days. The

*Sprog air gunners: No. 42 Air Gunners' Course, No. 1 Air Armaments School, Manby, Lincolnshire. Sidney Knott is standing in the middle row (third from right). The white flashes on the caps indicate Aircrew/Under Training. Most of these men had ground jobs in the Air Force and re-mustered for flying duties. They went their separate ways on completion of the course. Many were to die on operations. Photo: Sidney Knott.*

*Air gunner: The initial training is over and Sidney Knott wears the 'AG' half-wing. Later, while on operations, he was described as 'fearless, or just bloody barmy'.*
*Photo: Sidney Knott*

subjects included harmonisation of the guns and the use of the cine camera gun. A Martinet or Lysander would roll in for a slow attack. Each gunner practiced turret manipulation skills, following the target with the cine camera gun as it approached the Wellington:

> *The cine camera gun was temperamental and often jammed. Nevertheless, we always managed to return with some useful footage. Typically, we used one magazine during each attack sequence, with the 'enemy' aircraft usually approaching on the beam.*

> *I used the cine camera gun for the first time on Thursday June 11 1942. By the time Manby had finished with me I had logged flights totalling 23 hours 40 minutes and had fired 2,400 rounds, together with cine film. I had trained for many months. I had no nerves when flying and suffered no airsickness. I had scrambled over the academic barrier and continued to enjoy my flying. As for air-to-air firing, my hits averaged 12 per cent – a score regarded as quite respectable. Best of all there was now an Instructor's endorsement scrawled in my logbook: 'Should do fairly well'.*

Air gunner, as a distinct crew category, did not become established until early 1939. The air gunner's cloth badge was introduced that December and it was decided that all gunners should hold the rank of Sergeant (as a minimum). Some gunners were commissioned, but only in a proportion of around one-to-three to pilots and navigators[2].

Knott received his air gunner's half-wing during a parade on July 3 1942. He had finished with a course mark of 78 per cent.

> *I was content with this result. I happened to be a marker on the parade*

*ground and the Group Captain taking the parade slowly made his way towards me as he inspected the men. When he reached me he paused, looked me straight in the eye and said: 'You could have done better than that!' What flannel! I didn't believe a word of it – he didn't know me from Adam!*

Knott went on leave. Whilst at home he didn't talk much about his experiences and achievements:

*I now wore the air gunner's brevet. Father didn't ask questions. Much later, however, I heard that he had told his drinking pals all about it. As for the potential dangers of life as an air gunner, I didn't have much to say as I had no real understanding of the risks. That would come later. As for mother, she remained totally pre-occupied with the shop. Greengrocery was her life. Her two brothers had a shop in town before the First World War. When they were called up she ran the shop in their absence.*

*My mother expected me to spend my leave serving customers. I didn't want to know. I needed to relax and felt surprised at my lack of guilt over this unprecedented refusal to cooperate. I took comfort from the fact that father was now more involved in the shop. Let them take care of it! My head was full of Brownings, deflection angles and German aircraft profiles. A few days of peace and quiet, walking Leigh Marshes, would do no harm.*

# CHAPTER THREE

# *Crewing Up*

RAF Finningley, a station opened in the pre-war years, was occupied by 25 OTU (Operational Training Unit). Sidney Knott's leave came to an end. He arrived at Finningley in early August 1942 with a healthy appetite for more flying in Wellingtons:

> *We were to spend a few weeks at this Yorkshire airfield, then move to Bircotes – its southerly satellite in Nottinghamshire – for extensive crew flying. First find a crew! That was tomorrow's problem. My first job was to find the OTU Gunnery Leader and make myself known.*

The Gunnery Leader took charge of the fresh intake of novice gunners:

> *Under the Gunnery Leader's supervision we spent the next two weeks in the workshops, alongside the armourers. I had three short night flights in a Wellington (each with a different pilot). I had to wait until the end of the month to add to my air-firing experience. By Saturday September 12 I had fired 2,200 rounds (bringing my total to 4,600 rounds) and my flying hours had almost doubled, from 23 hours 40 minutes to 44 hours 25 minutes. The gunnery exercises had included air-to-air and air-to-ground firing. There were also 'fighter affiliations', with friendly aircraft making mock attacks on us.*

> *Crewing-up was the highlight of my stay at Finningley. This took place during the second week. Many pilots, observers, wireless operators, navigators and air gunners were posted in as individuals, but there were also a number of ex-Blenheim crews.*

> *The RAF had a simple yet surprisingly effective system for crewing-up. We were assembled and told to get on with it! Crewing-up had the atmosphere of an old-fashioned teenage dance. There was a vague fear of being left on the shelf, with everyone looking on and savouring your embarrassment. We stood outside in groups, hands shading our eyes against the Summer sunshine. Some chatted nervously while others were silent, busily scanning faces. We had been arranged in groups according to 'trade' and the embarrassment eased as the bolder souls among the pilots began recruiting. I caught our Gunnery Leader smiling, viewing the proceedings with wry amusement. I shuffled over to two gunners I knew. A bit of company felt most welcome at that point.*

Some embryonic crews already stood together. There were 12 sets of pilots, observers and wireless ops from the Blenheims. They had completed an OTU course in readiness for action in the Middle East but the

Air Ministry then had a change of heart. They were sent to join Bomber Command's Main Force. These three-man crews needed a navigator and gunner to fly Wellingtons, but they had a head start on the rest:

*Naturally, I turned out to be a wallflower. Most gunners had been picked but I had yet to be approached. Someone standing close by whispered: 'You'd better hurry up or you'll be stuck with that young bloke over there.' Then a wireless op came over and invited me to meet his pilot – who happened to be the 'young bloke'. I walked over and looked him up and down. He was Frank Heavery, a country chap from the Cotswolds. Heavery had good looks and a quiet, pleasing manner. We hit it off immediately.*

*Frank was just 19. He was nicknamed 'hollow legs', for his legendary ability to put away the beer. He was shy and reluctant to assert himself. He was also a slow learner. Once he had the hang of something, however, it stayed inside his young head for good. Frank was of medium height, slim and fit. He always claimed to be six months younger than me but the real gap was 20 months. Frank had a habit of embellishing the truth about his age. He had joined the RAF at 17 but, in reality, was nearly a year younger. Frank became more talkative with a few beers inside him, but he was always in control and never lost his temper.*

*Frank entered the Air Force straight from school and on the strength of a good education. He had no girlfriends. His life was flying and beer, in that order. Gradually, he built a reputation as an excellent pilot. He wasn't a big man. A heavy bomber demanded plenty of physical strength from the pilot and, for that reason, I often thought that Frank might have made a great fighter*

*Freshmen: Pilot Frank Heavery (right) with his navigator, Ted Foster. Photo: Sidney Knott*

*pilot. As our skipper he didn't say much. He was in charge but didn't throw his weight around. Frank was not a commanding figure but, when it came to flying, he knew how to look after a Lanc and its engines. He was the tops in that department.*

Heavery had trained as a Blenheim pilot. Knott had been approached by BPH 'Johnny' Lloyd, Heavery's wireless op on Blenheims. The former Blenheim crew was completed by observer RM 'Nick' Murray, who had been the navigator until that point. It was Murray who invited Ted Foster to join Heavery's crew as navigator. Nick then moved over, to become the five-man Wellington crew's bomb aimer and front gunner. Murray's knowledge of navigation would be a useful back-up, particularly when map-reading and identifying pinpoints.

Nick Murray and Ted Foster were old friends, having been in the same intake at Aberystwyth ITW. Nick wangled Ted into the crew. He introduced him to Frank and Johnny, to prepare the ground. Later, over a beer, he promised to continue to work on Heavery. He kept his word and lobbied hard for Ted when the big day arrived. Eventually, Frank took the bait, walked over and extended the invitation.

Ted Foster was a Yorkshireman but always claimed to be special as he 'really came from Bradford'. He started work in the textile mills and became a sorter – a good job in relative terms. Foster had things in common with Sidney Knott, including a strong desire to better himself. Ted had also attended nightschool before war came and his decision to volunteer for aircrew.

Foster had left school at 14. Worried about his lack of formal education, he thought his best chance was to apply for air gunner. In true Yorkshire style, however, he became an observer on discovering that the job paid more. He was also fortunate enough to train in the United States. On his return to Britain he was surprised to be given a choice of

*End-of-course photograph: this ITW Observers' Course was completed at Aberystwyth in mid-1941. Nick Murray and Ted Foster first met on this course. Nick is in the front row (fifth from right), while Ted is in the third row from the front (eighth from right). After ITW, Nick and Ted went their separate ways for further training but were destined to meet up again at Finningley and, subsequently, to fly 29 operations together. Photo: Wendy Bird.*

three venues for OTU training. He selected Finningley as it was the nearest to Bradford[1]. Foster made a tremendous effort to make the grade as a navigator. Knott felt drawn to him by their similar backgrounds and a common interest in navigation:

> *I knew I would never make it as a navigator but I picked up a lot of basic knowledge about navigation from Ted. Physically we were much alike – both slim and fit. Ted had trouble with my accent early on. He tried and failed to locate 'Sarfend' on a map of Essex. Ted was known for his shock of naturally wavy blond hair and this unruly mop often got on his nerves. On returning from leave while at Finningley he surprised everyone by coolly announcing that he had just married his childhood sweetheart. Ted delivered this thunderbolt in a rich Yorkshire brogue, emphasised by a slight stammer. We took in the news and wondered, silently, whether the responsibilities of marriage would take the edge off Ted's work in the air. We kept a close eye on him for a while.*
>
> *Ted was my closest friend at OTU. He occupied the next bed in the billet. We were the odd ones out, as we had joined an established Blenheim crew. One quiet evening, when we were on our own, I asked Ted the obvious question point-blank: 'Don't you think it would have been better to have waited?' He dismissed the idea: 'I've known her since school. And, don't forget, if anything happens to me she'll get a pension.' Ted's Yorkshire roots showed on occasion!*

An even-tempered man, Ted Foster had his emotions well in hand. He grew up fast in the Air Force and the responsibilities of married life never influenced the high standards he set himself.

> *Ted's early working life in the mill left a mark. In an odd way it prepared him for his wartime role. In a pre-war mill every job was timed to the last second. In the RAF, pilots, navigators and wireless ops were issued with excellent Omega watches. Ted delighted in his and became our timekeeper. He woke early every morning and set a brisk pace with his favourite catch-phrase: 'C'mon, C'mon, C'mon!' – these repetitions increasing in urgency. He became known as 'Hurry-up Man'.*
>
> *Ted's greatest quality was total loyalty to his crew. Some months later, when we were operational, we had a break and took the train into town. We walked three miles to the station and caught the train. We went to the pictures, had a drink or two and headed back to catch the last train. There was a fish and chip van parked outside the station, with a huge queue already formed behind it. We were hungry and got into line but Ted said it was a waste of time. We would never get served before the last train came in. We were willing to chance it. Ted became frustrated and gave vent to a rare outburst: 'This is stupid! If we miss the bloody train we'll have to walk back and that's nine miles! You're all mad!'*
>
> *Ted was furious. He turned to walk away several times but his legs brought him back, almost against his will. In any event the train pulled in just as we were about to be served. It then pulled out without us. We faced a nine-mile footslog and, worse still, the fish and chips were disgusting. Ted was purple with*

*rage as we began our long hike. He may have moaned every step of the way, but he had been unable to catch that last train without his crew!*

Heavery's crew meetings were enriched with a variety of accents. Nick Murray contributed to this mix:

*Nick was from Belfast. Small in stature but with a giant personality, he was a little older than most of us. His few extra years had been spent working as a trainee estate agent.*

*Nick and Ted trained together as observers but were now air bomber and navigator respectively. In common with most former observers they refused to take down the half-wing with the 'O' (known as the flying arsehole badge). As sprog crews advanced towards operations most senior officers became tolerant of such idiosyncratic behaviour. As bomb aimer/front gunner, Nick was also our second navigator. This recognised his experience while training on Blenheims.*

*Belfast Boy: Nick Murray pictured during training. The white flash on Nick's forage cap denotes 'Aircrew/Under Training'. Photo: Flo Murray.*

*Nick was well educated and his comments were spiced with a distinct Belfast patter. While a quiet man he walked with a spring in his step and his Irish spirit surfaced occasionally, especially when he'd had a drink or two. We saw this side of him during an evening in the local pub. Licensing hours were strict during the war, with no drinking up allowance when 'Time' was called. We squeezed in a last round, but our drinks had only just arrived when the landlord came over and said 'I must have your glasses'. That was it. Our Belfast boy hit the roof! He hated to rush his beer and explained his position, in very graphic detail, to the dumbstruck publican.*

*Nick began to lose his hair in his early twenties. This was a sensitive point and he always took care to wear his forage cap at a rakish angle, covering the bald patch. He spent a lot of time combing the surviving thatch.*

*Our five-man Wellington crew was completed by wireless op Johnny Lloyd, a Londoner. Johnny was reserved yet somehow took on the role of crew spokesman. We never got much out of Johnny. While not exactly secretive he had his own little ways. He wasn't far short of Nick's age and, after the war, Ted persisted in his belief that the wireless op was the senior of the two. Johnny was always around to keep us in order – rather like an elder brother.*

Sixty years on, Knott has little to say about how the crew reacted to him as a personality:

*I regarded myself as an ignorant fellow. I suppose I was over-conscious of my poor education. Under-confident and with no real conversation, it took me a while to get to know people. Yet things changed completely when we lived together as a crew at Bircotes. I emerged from my shell and became less self-conscious. I do know they thought I was keen – perhaps too keen. After the war Ted told me that Nick had once said to him: 'I never know what to make of Sidney. Either he is fearless or just bloody barmy.'*

The crew settled into their training. Heavery flew regularly in the OTU Wellingtons and familiarised himself with the type. Most Finningley Instructors were veterans with operational experience. Young Heavery was quiet and asked few questions. One Instructor got impatient with him and this contretemps said much about the challenge of instructing. The personal chemistry between Instructor and pupil had to be right and, on occasion, the relationship developed in ways which were far from ideal. Frank's early experiences may have influenced his attitude and contributed to his excellence as an Instructor later in his flying career.

When flying from Bircotes Knott enjoyed following the R/T exchanges between Heavery and his Instructors. The new skipper practised 'circuits and bumps' (repeated take-offs and landings), overshoots and flying on one engine. Then it was Murray's turn. He dropped small practice bombs as the Wimpy droned high above Wainfleet Bombing Range, in a remote area of the Wash. Within a few weeks the five began to fuse together as a crew. They soon reached a milestone when Heavery became a solo Wellington pilot:

*Having completed our initial training we made the move to E Flight at*

*Bircotes. This airfield was in Nottinghamshire, next to the Great North Road. We began crew flying from Bircotes on Sunday September 20 and Frank made his first flight as a Wellington captain within 48 hours. Frank's debut, however, was a bit of an anticlimax as the aircraft went u/s in flight and we spent only 15 minutes in the air. During the Wednesday Frank was joined by an Instructor for the first in a long series of simulated raids. This was also aborted, after just 30 minutes, due to a duff aircraft. We were disenchanted by this time and with good reason. Four of our first five flights from Bircotes were aborted (three due to technical faults with the aircraft, rather than the weather). I became wary of Bircotes' Wellingtons. They were thoroughly clapped out and undeserving of love.*

Saturday September 26 was a better day. Unaccompanied by an Instructor Heavery and his crew flew 'Raid II' without a hitch, logging two hours 25 minutes in the air. At 13.20 the following day they took off in a Wellington to fly a mock raid lasting five hours. This exercise gave the gunners their chance and Knott fired 200 rounds air-to-ground.

*Training at Bircotes continued at a gruelling pace. We flew mock raids on most days. The seventh and eighth – night flights of three to four hours' duration – were complex enough to put the entire crew to the test. On Sunday October 11 we took off at 15.45 for an 'oxygen climb'. This flight of 90 minutes was a preparation for high altitude flying, with the pilot controlling the oxygen. This exercise was largely for Frank's benefit. We landed, rested for an hour or two and then began preparing for our first 'Bullseye' later that day. This was a carefully planned mock raid, designed to give the sprog crew a greater insight into operational conditions.*

*We took off in Wellington 963 at 19.40 that Sunday evening, while British searchlight crews and gun teams prepared to do battle with us. We flew west, reached the Welsh coast and headed down the Irish Sea, penetrating as far as Cornwall. There was bright moonlight. Bullseyes were flown in such conditions for safety reasons. We flew several dog-legs and searchlights attempted to cone our Wimpy as we finally turned onto the correct heading and began the run-in to the target. We were about to 'bomb' Weston-super-Mare! Then came a rush of adrenalin as a Spitfire appeared out of the night, curving in to attack 963. Frank reacted quickly to my instructions and took violent evasive action, shaking up the army officer who flew with us that night as an observer. We landed back at Bircotes at 0110 and the skipper taxied the Wellington to E Flight dispersal, our longest flight to date successfully completed.*

The crew flew a second Bullseye four nights later and came under repeated mock fighter attack. For some reason Heavery had been ordered not to take evasive action. The crew shook with laughter when informed that the Spitfire pilot claimed to have shot them down four times in four passes. The simulated night raid had lasted six hours 40 minutes. Flown on Thursday October 15 it marked the end of the crew's work-up at Finningley's satellite. Knott's flying hours, once again, had more than doubled (from 44 hours 25 minutes to 100 hours 55 minutes). During their time with E Flight at Bircotes Heavery's crew had flown 56 hours 30 minutes (25 hours 55 minutes at night). Knott's total flying time at 25 OTU amounted to 77 hours 15 minutes. So far he had fired 5,250 rounds and used 150 ft of cine camera gun film.

*Pre-war Finningley's facilities were grouped together. Bircotes, in contrast, was a typical wartime station and its designers had in mind the possibility of enemy action rather than convenience. Bikes were essential on this dispersed station. It was at this point that we discovered something surprising about Frank. Our pilot could fly a Wellington bomber at night as well as the next man, but he couldn't ride a bike! His shaky efforts on two wheels produced hoots of laughter from bystanders. This problem could not be overcome. Our skipper was born without a sense of balance – at least on the ground!*

*Friday October 16 was our last day at Bircotes. We planned to celebrate at the Granby, in nearby Bawtry, a popular aircrew watering hole. The pub was around two miles from the airfield and we discussed the problem of getting Frank there and back in one piece. The outward leg was straightforward. It was downhill and the skipper could be accommodated on a crossbar. One of us would run his battered bike down to the pub. The return would be uphill and made at a far slower pace. If Frank fell off he'd have plenty of beer inside him and wouldn't feel a thing!*

*We had a great night. Later, outside the pub, Frank was launched in the general direction of Bircotes. Having been told to think of nothing but the need to pedal, he was given a single, violent shove towards the airfield. He wobbled out of sight but was later found entangled in a hedge near the camp perimeter. Dazed and sorry for himself he said he had 'sideslipped' into the ditch.*

The crew went on leave before reporting back to Finningley. Knott had a nasty shock on his return. He had been made Orderly Sergeant, responsible for a mass of unfamiliar work riddled with the petty

*Bill Blundell: Knott's cousin appears to have shot down the first of two attacking nightfighters before his own aircraft crashed near Brussels. Photo: Raoul Lloyd.*

bureaucracies of service life. By now the entire crew eagerly awaited their next posting, marking the final stage of the long journey to an operational squadron. Their last hurdle was the Heavy Conversion Unit (HCU). The crew was about to increase in size, from five to seven, in order to fly four-engined bombers. They would then commence operations.

Heavery's crew were fortunate during their training. Flying accidents were commonplace under wartime conditions. They had also escaped a dangerously premature introduction to operational flying. Many OTU crews found themselves 'roped in' to make up the numbers for Bomber Command's great set-piece raids.

The first of the 1,000 bomber raids was launched against Cologne on the night of May 30/31 1942. Everything was thrown into this attack. Cologne was followed by less successful mass raids on Essen (June 1/2) and Bremen (towards the end of the month). Instructors and pupils were stripped from OTUs without hesitation in order to boost the numbers. The obvious risks were outweighed by a political need to do damage on a vast scale and so save Bomber Command from its many critics.

*I had been sitting in Finningley's Mess when I suddenly spotted a familiar face across the room. It was my cousin, William Blundell. Surely not! He was three years younger than me and this individual certainly looked older than 18. Yet people look so different in uniform! The boy gazed hard at me and then we greeted each other.*

*My cousin played an important part in my young life, as I had the habit of staying at my Aunt Gert's house in Woolwich every Summer. My parents had also lived with Aunt Gert when they were first married. I spoke first: 'What are you doing here? I didn't even know you were in the Air Force!' Unfortunately we managed only a few words as he was rushing off. He laughed at the coincidence of our meeting, suddenly became serious and said he had to go. He promised to talk later. I never saw him again and he was killed the following year.*

Air gunner Sergeant W J 'Bill' Blundell died on May 30 1943. He was a member of the five-man crew of Wellington HE212. This aircraft, captained by Pilot Officer Henry Lloyd, participated in a raid on Wuppertal, taking off at 22.23 that fateful evening. Another Captain had taken Lloyd's aircraft on an attack several nights before and they had failed to return. Lloyd took another aircraft, Yvonne Proudbag, the usual Wimpy of an all-New Zealand crew. The Wellington crashed at Vollezele, Brabant, 26 km west south-west of Brussels. The entire crew were buried together on June 1 at Vollezele Cemetery. Lloyd's crew had completed over 20 ops with 466 Squadron, Royal Australian Air Force, based at Leconfield, Yorkshire. William Blundell was born on May 9 1924. He had just turned 19 when he was killed in action. The average age of the crew was 21. It was a bad night for 466 Squadron. They lost three aircraft. Knott's cousin was shot down by Oblt. Rudolf Altendorf. During 1994 a memorial at Vollezele was dedicated to Lloyd and his crew.

Lloyd's Wellington was attacked by two nightfighters. During the first encounter, Blundell damaged the attacking Bf110, which lost an engine. The nightfighter crew successfully baled out. It is possible that Altendorf attacked an already crippled Wimpy. The bomber crashed onto a house, killing one of the occupants.

Large-scale raids began to employ a new concept – the bomber stream. The aircraft were concentrated, flying along a set route and at a set speed. Aircraft were allocated height bands and times in the stream, to reduce collision risks[2]. Bomber Command's tactics were evolving rapidly as Heavery's crew moved ever closer to operational status. A three-week wait ended when their postings arrived. The next stop was RAF Scampton and 1661 Conversion Unit. It was time to say farewell to the Wellington:

*The Wimpy was still very much a front-line aircraft. It had a distinctive character. It looked the part in flight and sat with a purposeful squat on the ground. Crews liked it as its 'geodetic' construction gave it immense strength. It could survive an amazing level of battle damage. The Lancaster succeeded the*

*Wellington as the elite bomber but the Wimpy retained some advantages, including a spacious interior. It had more room than the Lancaster (perhaps because there was less equipment in the fuselage). The Wimpy was also less noisy than the Lanc, although those four Merlins did make a sweet sound. All in all the Wellington was a great aircraft and it was easy to forgive the way its light yet immensely strong wings appeared to flap as it flew.*

1661 Heavy Conversion Unit flew Manchesters and Lancasters drawn from 44 (Rhodesia) Squadron's Conversion Flight. There were three Flights: A and B at Waddington and C at Scampton[3]. This HCU had a distinguished pedigree, having been formed by Squadron Leader J D Nettleton, VC. His squadron had been the first to receive the Lancaster.

A South African from Natal, John Nettleton led the dashing yet costly raid on the MAN diesel engine works at Augsburg on April 17 1942. This was an experimental low level daylight raid employing the new Lancaster. Seven of the 12 aircraft from 44 and 97 squadrons failed to return. Nettleton received the Victoria Cross[4]. He was to be killed in action just over a year later, during his return from a raid against Turin on July 13 1943[5].

Heavery and crew arrived at Scampton during the first week of November 1942. They felt relieved. Hanging around at Finningley got on everyone's nerves:

*We had been at a loose end for a few weeks. Nearly a month separated our last flight at Bircotes and our first at Scampton. Ted used the wait to drop yet another of his famous bombshells (he should have been a bomb aimer!). He had married his childhood sweetheart from Bradford (then a WAAF driver at Finningley). Now the couple had started a family. Mary was pregnant by the time Ted arrived at Scampton. This meant she had to leave the service, but we were to meet again when I took up Ted's generous invitation to accompany him*

*Edging closer to operations: pictured (left to right) are: Sidney Knott, Nick Murray, Frank Heavery and Ken Butterworth. Frank and Ken shared a love of beer, even the weak wartime brew. Note that Nick's forage cap is worn at a rakish angle, to cover his thinning hair. Photo: Sidney Knott.*

*on leave. I stayed at their modest yet comfortable house in Bradford – purchased at a bargain price, of course!*

Two additional crew members were required before Heavery could convert to four-engined aircraft:

*Two sergeants were detailed to us. Our mid-upper gunner was Ken Butterworth, a Lancashire lad. Ken was a former butcher's boy from Bolton. He made an instant impression as a noisy yet likeable individual, with a sharp sense of humour. Having been introduced to Ken, Ted Foster walked away, muttering darkly: 'If they parachuted him into a village full of cannibals, he'd be on first name terms with them within the hour'. Later, Ted was generous enough to acknowledge his error of judgement as Ken blended in very well. He was bigger built than the rest of us and had an expressive Lancashire voice. Looking back, we were a bit too reserved as a crew. Ken injected some life into the mix.*

*Ken and I had a chat about a very serious matter. It was agreed that, given my experience on Wellingtons, I should stay in the rear turret.*

*The second of the two sergeants, our flight engineer, was a former RAF Apprentice who had been in the service for some time. Unfortunately he was an Apprentice who had failed to grow up! Apprentices were the very backbone of the pre-war RAF Technical Branch and all wartime flyers were in their debt. That said, we had serious doubts about our flight engineer from the first. On one occasion, while at Scampton, he failed to turn up for a cross-country flight. We searched high and low but he could not be found. We had no choice but to fly without him and we covered up the whole business. Luckily Frank had command of the aircraft that night. Our missing man would have been for the high jump had an Instructor joined us for the exercise.*

*Back on the ground and with our engineer still absent, we called a crew conference. We were unimpressed and some argued strongly that he should go. Our engineer was unpopular and lazy and yet, incredibly, we gave him another chance. Sadly, the engineer showed no gratitude and his persistent bad attitude did nothing to ease the ill-feeling towards him. He even failed to turn up for another exercise. While outraged, once again we rather stupidly covered for him. Nick and Ted split his work between them. Our engineer knew King's Regulations from cover to cover. He had an answer for everything and, unfortunately, not every response was truthful. In short he was a menace – an unwelcome destabilising factor. We wanted to begin our operational tour in perfect harmony (or at least as close as possible to that happy state). The engineer stood in the way of this goal.*

The crew walked around the Avro Manchester. The aircraft certainly looked purposeful despite its reputation for engine problems. There was a view that its Vulture engines had entered service prematurely[6]. Fortunately a development of the Manchester, fitted with four reliable Merlins, had been envisaged as early as the first quarter of 1939. In fact, Avro had been ready to commence building the Lancaster prototype before the twin-engined Manchester reached RAF bomber squadrons[7]. Contrary to the popular claim that the Lancaster resulted from the failure of the Manchester, the reality had more to do with the fact that the day of the twin-engined heavy bomber was over. The Lancaster's crowning advantage was a huge bomb-bay free of obstructions and capable of housing stores of great size. This aircraft emerged as a war-winner.

A total of 7,377 Lancasters were produced. Each cost an average of nearly £59,000, excluding equipment such as the bomb sight, radar and radio. Some 1,150,000 men and women helped build the Lancasters (although many were also engaged in producing components for other aircraft)[8]. A total of 156,192 Lancaster sorties were flown during the war and 3,431 of the bombers were lost on operations[9].

Heavery had to wait three weeks for his introduction to the Lancaster. Meanwhile, there was work to be done flying the Manchesters. On November 13 an Instructor, Pilot Officer Hartley, watched over Heavery as he released the brakes on Manchester 7493 at 11.20. The big bomber roared across Scampton's grass. The crew politely ignored the fact that it was Friday the Thirteenth and their faith was rewarded: Heavery went solo on type that very day, after just two hours' dual. Five more Manchester flights followed, the last on the morning of Sunday December 6. One trip gave Knott his opportunity and he fired 500 rounds at ground targets. Most of the exercises, however, concentrated on local flying and circuits and bumps.

Another landmark was reached during the afternoon of December 6 when 1661 Instructor Pilot Officer Rodley took the crew for a Lancaster familiarisation flight lasting just under an hour. Heavery received instruction on Lancaster 4258 as his crew absorbed the sounds, smells and atmosphere of the aircraft type in which they would fight their war in the night sky.

The Lancaster had made its operational debut on March 3 1942. With a wingspan of 102 ft and a fully laden weight of 65,000 lbs, it carried 14,000 lbs of bombs with ease. The maximum range was 2,530 miles with a 7,000 lb bomb-load (1,730 miles with 12,000 lbs). Later in the war specially modified Lancasters carried Barnes Wallis' 22,000 lb Grand Slam earthquake bomb.

The Lancaster B.I had four Merlin XX, 22 or 24 engines, rated from 1,280 hp to 1,620 hp. The B.III had American Packard-built 28 (1,300 hp), 38 (1,390 hp) or 224 (1,640 hp) Merlins[10]. The B.II was an insurance policy, with its Hercules radial engines anticipating a shortage of Merlins that never materialised.

The Lancaster was much loved by the crews. One description will suffice: '...a pilot's aeroplane without a single vice, the Lanc inspired confidence...'[11] The aircraft was also known to Sir Arthur Harris as Bomber Command's 'Shining Sword'. In terms of bombs dropped on night operations, per aircraft that failed to return, it stood head and shoulders above the other 'heavies' (Stirling, 41 tonnes; Halifax, 51 tonnes; and Lancaster, 132 tonnes)[12].

*Frank continued to build his reputation as a skilled pilot. On Tuesday December 8 he went solo in Lanc 4185, after two dual flights on type. During these early excursions we visited Syerston in Nottinghamshire.*

*Syerston was home to two operational squadrons, 61 and 106, flying Lancasters. More instruction followed and we practised feathering, three-engined overshoots, circuits and bumps and air-firing. We had a short night flight in a Lanc on December 9. Two days later I participated in a two hours 20 minutes night exercise with Sergeant Vine's crew. It was common practice to join other crews for training flights, to gain an insight into how others reacted in the air.*

*Vine was to die on operations within a few months. He and his crew did not live to see the end of February. Two other crews on the conversion course also lost their lives within a short period while flying with our squadron. Sergeant (later, Pilot Officer) Mant, who shared an exercise with Frank on our third flight in a Manchester, was killed in action in March. In addition, I flew twice with Flight Lieutenant Desmond, who was to die in late May during the last operation of our tour. He often took up sprog gunners for air-firing exercises.*

*War-winner: the Avro Lancaster. Sidney Knott was to fly 64 operations in this superlative heavy bomber. Photo: Trustees of the Imperial War Museum.*

Scampton was very crowded in late 1942. Beyond 1661 Conversion Flight, it accommodated two operational squadrons: 49, an elite 5 Group unit, and 57, another good outfit with a growing reputation.

On one occasion Heavery was invited to join the back of the queue, as aircraft of both squadrons lined up to depart on a raid. While they were merely on a short hop to Woodhall Spa, this clever psychological move did much to convey the atmosphere of the 'real thing':

*This gave us a buzz. It was impressive to see the Lancs lined up in front of us, ready to depart. We got a 'wave-off' for the first time although we hardly deserved it, given our brief trip to Woodhall Spa for circuits and bumps.*

*As for our rogue flight engineer, matters came to a head. One night we were down for circuits and bumps at Woodhall Spa. On the way, some members of the crew saw a horrifying mid-air collision between two bomb-laden aircraft. It was a truly gigantic explosion. Twelve months later I was to learn that this collision had also been witnessed that night by my second tour mid-upper gunner, Bill Harrall.*

*We attempted to close our minds to this disaster on arriving at Woodhall Spa for the night exercise. An account of that evening, written by our navigator some years after the war, noted that Frank had trouble gaining flying speed on our first take-off run from Woodhall Spa that night. The airfield perimeter was dangerously close by the time we finally clawed our way into the air. Frank's urgent request for 'wheels up' was lost on our engineer, who had frozen solid. By the time he reacted we had already clipped the hedge. Frank had yet another shock some minutes later, back on the ground, as he taxied round for another take-off. He was startled to see his crew preparing to leave the aircraft. We were in a state of near mutiny. The sight of the collision and the instant destruction of 14 young lives was disturbing enough. This was followed closely by the Reaper's attempt to terminate our own careers – bungled despite the assistance of our dozy engineer. It was just too much! Flying that night was over unless another engineer could be found. Strong words were exchanged, reducing the engineer to tears, but Frank finally persuaded us to see sense. Flying resumed, although the mood was sombre.*

Scampton was so crowded that conversion crews frequently flew to other airfields to carry out their exercises. Heavery's crew settled in, although the Scampton 'pecking order' was all too obvious:

*The Mess was as crowded as the station and there were always two sittings for lunch. The operational squadrons, of course, had priority and we were on the second sitting. Scampton's facilities were comfortable and the Mess served wonderful food, with the added benefit of waitress service. We made ourselves comfortable in the anteroom, awaiting our turn. There were plenty of opportunities to listen in on the operational crews' conversations. We were always eager to pick up tips.*

The Americans were flooding into Britain at this time and they began to revolutionise popular music.

*They set up their own radio station – AFN (American Forces Network). This played all the latest jazz and big band hits. AFN had 'DJs'. We'd never heard of DJs before! Many of the best records played had yet to be released in Britain.*

*Even AFN, however, failed to shake our habit of always listening to the BBC at one o'clock. If there had been any operational flying the night before, the news announcer would give brief details and casualties would be mentioned. The news created a tension between first and second Mess sittings. The first sitting wanted to finish lunch and get out quickly enough to hear the news, while the second sitting held back and occupied the best chairs, ready for one o'clock. After the news, we would amble into the Mess, picking up two or three vitamin pills from a bowl at the door. Our Medical Officer was a firm believer in vitamins and their power to preserve aircrew.*

The RAF Doctors experimented with vitamin tablets, in the optimistic expectation that night vision could be improved. Vitamin A deficiency can result in night blindness[13]. Halibut oil capsules, a concentrated source of Vitamin A, were put out for the aircrew. Pathfinder Force Commander Don Bennett later admitted that he had tried vitamins himself 'in vast quantities without any noticeable improvement'[14].

> *Beyond the possibility of a flying accident, our biggest hazard at Scampton was the danger of tripping over the boozy dog occupying the Mess bar. He loved beer and never knew when to stop. He drank until his back legs refused to work, then sank to the floor in a contented, highly alcoholic daze.*

By now, all newly-arrived crews knew the purpose of the build-up at Scampton. A new unit, 467 Squadron (Royal Australian Air Force), was to be formed:

> *We were to join this new squadron. I first became aware of the new unit's identity when it was announced that the King was to visit Scampton. The alcoholic dog was hidden away. A hangar was cleaned until spotless. A Lancaster was towed inside and it was polished like a diamond. The crews of 49 Squadron were ranged along one side of the hangar. They stood in neat groups of seven – pilot, navigator, flight engineer, air bomber, wireless op and the two gunners. The crews of the new squadron, 467, lined up opposite 49, while 57's crews stood in front of the aircraft. We happened to be the last crew in the 467 line-up, standing in the front corner of the hangar. The King's car drew up outside. Flashbulbs popped amongst the Press contingent and we enjoyed our grandstand view of the proceedings.*

> *King George VI stepped out briskly, to be greeted warmly by Scampton's Station Commander. His Majesty moved forward to shake hands with his glove on and our 'ambassador' had an anxious second or two trying to remove his glove in time. The King then toured the hangar, speaking to each Lancaster captain in turn. He had something to say to every pilot. We were the very last in line. Finally, His Majesty stood eye to eye with Frank and asked him how the conversion was going. He asked what type we were converting from and questioned Frank about the qualities of the Lancaster. They talked together for some time. Later, back in the Mess, we suddenly realised that the King's conversation had been entirely free of stutter. Perhaps his well-known public speaking difficulties disappeared when he was at ease?*

> *During the parade the King presented an award to a Squadron Leader and then moved off to dine in the Officers' Mess. There remained just one item on the agenda: an inspection of Scampton's pigeon loft. Even at this stage in the war the Air Ministry regarded a bomber crew as incomplete without a brace of homing pigeons. We carried pigeons on every operation. It is little appreciated that Bomber Command's war, so tragically expensive in human terms, also cost the lives of thousands of pigeons, shot down over Germany and elsewhere. These unpleasant realities were not brought to His Majesty's attention as he inspected Scampton's pigeon loft, said to be the best in the RAF.*

On the subject of pigeons, while at Scampton Heavery's crew were briefed for an unusual mission:

*Pigeons on ops: two 467 Squadron aircrew, Johnny Lloyd (right) and Flying Officer Cazaly, check the birds while awaiting transport to their aircraft. Photo: Vincent Holyoak.*

His Majesty was unaware that the Scampton loft held at least two birds worthy of the Dicken Medal, the avian VC. One evening, while still flying Manchesters, we were briefed for a very exotic exercise. We were told to fly out across the North Sea, climb to 10,000 ft and air-launch two pigeons! As an aside, I often wondered how our pigeons managed to survive long flights at up to 20,000 ft or more without the benefit of oxygen. Anyway, they seemed to tolerate these conditions without problems. No birds died on us!

We set out on our mission and, frankly, I didn't give much for the chances of our pigeons. We had worked out a launch method. I would rotate the rear turret fully to the beam. This left a convenient gap between fuselage and turret, with just enough room to extend an arm. When we reached the correct position and height Johnny Lloyd made his way back to the rear turret, clutching the unsuspecting birds in their boxes. There is a definite knack to holding a pigeon. Johnny had been taught to insert the two legs between his fingers and draw the bird close to the chest, where it soon got comfortable. Our wireless op worked his magic on one bird and then successfully jettisoned it through the gap. Within a minute the second pigeon was also released and, mission accomplished, we turned for home – certain in the conviction that our feathered friends would be *logged as 'Failed to Return'.*

> *On landing back we followed the usual routine and went to the Mess for a pint. After a while we could no longer resist calling up the pigeon loft. We asked to be informed the moment our birds returned. Pigeons have a good turn of speed but our birds had the wind against them. We called up on the hour and, as expected, our pigeons were in danger of being posted missing. Johnny said he had tried to throw them down, to miss the worst of the slipstream. Even so, the violent launch must have been an unwelcome surprise for the birds. Suddenly there was a phone call for Johnny and he came back beaming. Two very tough RAF pigeons had just made a perfect landing at Scampton's loft. I regarded their survival and return as a minor miracle. Later we were told the flight had been organised to test the idea that pigeons carrying messages giving an aircraft's position could be released in flight, before ditching. We gave them the answer but I felt sure that only exceptional pigeons were up to the job.*

The Air Ministry rejected an early design for 467 Squadron's badge – a Kookaburra perched on the branch of a gum tree[15]. The problem concerned the fact that the snake in its beak featured Hitler's head. This was superceded by a more conventional snake's head. Curiously, 467's badge is not displayed at the RAF Museum, Hendon, but it is to be found among the floor plaques in the RAF church of St Clement Danes, in the Strand, London. It never became 'official'. At one stage in the war, squadrons in 467's position were asked to defer applications for approval. Later, when asked if the squadron wanted to submit a new application, the offer was not followed up.

While the new squadron's early artwork caused some controversy, the Heavery crew's conversion syllabus at Scampton continued on schedule and was completed on December 21. They had logged 26 flights in Lancasters in just over two weeks, including a number of night flights. They had often used Woodhall Spa's hard runways to practice circuits and bumps. At that time Woodhall Spa housed 97 Squadron, flying Lancasters. Heavery and the other captains converting to heavies had to tolerate some good-natured sarcasm from the operational crews, due to their lack of aircraft. Slowly, however, 467's Lancasters began to appear, in ones and twos. The first Lancaster taken on charge was W4384, arriving on November 9 1942[16]. The ground crews also arrived. They were posted in from all corners of the RAF, not just Bomber Command. Some had never worked on four-engined aircraft before. They trained on the ground as the crews trained in the air.

Knott had taken to the Lancaster. He had fired 1,250 rounds while at Scampton, bringing his total rounds fired to 6,500 – including 4,250 to drogue and 1,850 air-to-ground. The crew had logged 36 hours 40 minutes in the air with 1661's C Flight. They had 12 hours 35 minutes in Manchesters and 24 hours five minutes in Lancasters (nine hours 20 minutes at night). Knott's flying now totalled 137 hours 20 minutes, including 39 hours five minutes at night. Crew and squadron were ready to go to war.

# CHAPTER FOUR

# Operational at Last!

T HE spire of the 13th Century church of St Mary the Virgin soars 210 ft above the stunning countryside of the Vale of Belvoir. Said to be the tallest village spire in Leicestershire, it was both a landmark and a hazard for the pilots of 467 Squadron, Royal Australian Air Force, based at nearby Bottesford[1].

The station was built by George Wimpey & Co on 700 acres near the hamlet of Normanton, just north of Bottesford village. A satellite airfield was built at Langar, Nottinghamshire. Bottesford's location was less straightforward, as the airfield straddled the corners of three counties: Nottinghamshire, Lincolnshire and Leicestershire[2]. The station opened in September 1941. The main gate and station sick quarters were in Nottinghamshire and the guardroom, technical facilities and billets in Lincolnshire, while the main runway and bomb dump were in Leicestershire[3].

Built to a typical wartime pattern with three concrete runways, Bottesford was a 5 Group station. This all-Lancaster Group was headquartered at Grantham, six miles away. The Group reached its full strength of 10 squadrons on the formation of 467 Squadron at Scampton on November 7 1942. These squadrons (9, 44, 49, 50, 57, 61, 97, 106, 207 and 467) represented around two-thirds of Bomber Command's Lancaster strength[4].

The squadron moved to Bottesford later in November and stayed for almost exactly a year. In November 1943 the station transferred to the USAAF (50th Troop Carrier Wing, US Ninth AAF)[5]. It returned to RAF control in July 1944 and accommodated 1668 HCU[6].

Sidney Knott was posted in from Scampton on Tuesday December 22 1942. At that point the new squadron had 19 Lancasters and a total strength of 611 personnel[7]. Heavery's crew began flying the next day. The pressure was on. The entire squadron was working up to commence operations as early as possible in the New Year. The major enemy during these formative weeks was the weather. Frosty days were interspersed with periods of mist and drizzle[8].

*As new arrivals on B Flight we took a Lanc, 4283, into the air at 15.25 on the Wednesday. We were up for 75 minutes and I made a contribution by firing 600 rounds at a drogue. We were now in the final few weeks of training before our first operation. We logged three more flights before the end of the month, the last being a Bullseye simulated night raid of four hours 50 minutes. In those last few days of 1942 we logged exactly nine hours in the air – just over seven at night.*

Ted Foster wanted to celebrate his twenty-second birthday but didn't see much prospect of a party at Bottesford. He was wrong. On the very day of their arrival the new boys were invited to a 'Christmas do' in the Sergeants' Mess.

*Naturally, our flight engineer got a skinful and stayed the course until the beer ran out in the early hours of the morning. Our navigator saw him develop undercarriage trouble. According to Ted, on leaving the Mess the engineer fell down the steps and injured his ankle. What a Christmas treat for us! During the following day our 'present' arrived – a new engineer. In fact we flew with various engineers until Sergeant F 'Jock' Rodgers arrived in March.*

*Jock was a Lowland Scot and a very different type from our renegade engineer. We had difficulty understanding him over the R/T at first, but there was no questioning his ability. Jock had completed five ops as a member of Pilot Officer J. H. Smith's crew. They were experienced and had been posted in to complete their tour. The last trip was to Turin on the night of February 4/5. Jock then flew with Squadron Leader Thiele on the March 1/2 Berlin raid.*

On January 1 1943 Bomber Command had some 206 Lancasters with the operational squadrons. They represented 31.7 per cent of the heavy bomber strength. In the space of 12 months these figures increased to 586 and 53.8 per cent respectively.

The new 5 Group Australian squadron operated for the first time on Saturday January 2 1943[9]. Five aircraft were dispatched on minelaying sorties to the French Biscay ports[10]. Flight Sergeant M.P. Stewart made 467 Squadron's first operational take-off that night, in Lancaster W4795. Stewart and his crew had only a few weeks to live. They were dead before the end of February.

Heavery's crew still had five non-operational flights before them – two night flying tests and three Bullseyes. The first Bullseye was flown on Sunday January 3 and involved a flight of four hours 20 minutes. The Winter weather, however, offered few opportunities for flying and the third Bullseye was not flown until Tuesday January 26.

The Vale of Belvoir is susceptible to fog[11]. Bottesford, in particular, is notorious in this respect. In January, however, fog was so widespread and persistent that all 1 Group and 5 Group airfields were closed on occasion[12]. The lack of flying weather had one virtue: it allowed the crews more time to settle into squadron life. While an Australian unit, the majority of 467's personnel in those early months were RAF and most of the more experienced officers were New Zealanders.

Bottesford was well dispersed, to protect its bombers and facilities from enemy intruders. Its layout looked rather like a lopsided 'A' from the air. The main runway had a length of 1,933 yards and ran parallel to the Bennington – Normanton road. The two shorter runways had a length of 1,400 yards. The station's buildings were of the prefabricated type and sited a long way from each other:

> *Our billets were Nissen huts, with the windows in each end wall. Internally, a partition ran across the middle and each half of the hut accommodated six men. On entering the hut there were doors to left and right, each room having three beds. Frank, Nick and Johnny – the original Blenheim crew – took the right-hand room, while we gunners and Ted moved into the other. Our various engineers did not billet with us.*

The station's population of around 2,000 lived in primitive buildings that lacked adequate heating and other basic facilities. Human waste was collected and spread on the fields (but this was not unusual in a deeply rural area at that time). Bottesford was not connected to mains water until 1951 and sewerage arrived a decade later[13].

> *The Squadron's two Flights were engaged in a punishing flying training schedule. This gave us opportunities to familiarise ourselves with the local area. Our final Bullseyes were handled in a new way – a reminder that we were about to make our operational debut. We were briefed exactly as if they were real raids. The only difference, in terms of preparation, was the absence of an escape kit. We also flew in the 'right direction', being required to make for specific points on the Dutch and Danish coasts. In one sense we were already operational, as we were acting as decoys.*

Group Captain FRD 'Ferdie' Swain had been Bottesford's Station Commander since 207 Squadron's arrival in November 1941. The third Lancaster unit to form, 207 Squadron converted from Manchesters at Bottesford in March 1942[14]. Swain made his reputation in the pre-war Air Force by capturing the world altitude record, reaching 49,967 ft in a Bristol 138A. He was awarded the Air Force Cross[15].

> *We were proud to be part of the new squadron. The royal visit to Scampton helped to build this sense of pride. The King's visit meant a lot and I was reminded of my oath on joining up. As for company, we shared Bottesford with plenty of other sprog crews. In contrast, our leaders were very experienced. A few senior crews, some with only a few trips to do, were also posted in to give 467 Squadron a boost.*

> *Scampton introduced us to the feel of an operational station. Our stay at Scampton had been a form of extended briefing. Now the wait was over. I had fired thousands of rounds during training. The crew had flown a series of Bullseyes and four had been spoofs to draw attention away from real raids. I had been training for over 17 months, since August 1941. One of my gunner friends, Len Whitehead (from Deal, in Kent), went to the other extreme. He was in a 'reserved occupation' at Shorts, building Sunderland flying boats on the Medway. They released him when he volunteered for aircrew and he began training in 1943. Len did his squarebashing and a gunnery course, then went straight to an operational squadron. At that point he had never flown at night! His second night trip was to Berlin (the first being a 45-minute night flying*

*test). This initial sortie added significantly to the modest total of 24 flying hours in his logbook.*

Everyone joining 467 Squadron during those early weeks soon formed a favourable impression of the senior officers. The Squadron Commander was especially popular:

> *Cosme Gomm was a tall chap, softly spoken and very affable. In fact, we liked all our commanders. A group of outstanding individuals led us into battle.*

> *We had picked up much of value from the operational crews at Scampton. I now had the ability to spot people worth listening to. More often than not, those 'shooting lines' – boasting – were the inexperienced.*

At that point the air campaign against Germany entered a new phase. Casualties were increasing but Bomber Command was gaining strength. We also had the wonderful GEE box, developed at the Telecommunications Research Establishment and a solution to so many navigational problems. We felt ready!

# CHAPTER FIVE

# Under Fire for the First Time

THE crew's tour began at a time when Bomber Command's capacity to destroy German cities was expanding rapidly. British determination to use strategic air power to bring ruin to Hitler's Germany was set out in a paper prepared under the auspices of Sir Charles Portal, Chief of the Air Staff, in November 1942 – the very month 467 Squadron formed at Scampton. The paper outlined Portal's aims for 1943 and 1944. The objective was to drop 1.25 million tonnes of bombs on Germany (killing an estimated 900,000 people and seriously injuring another one million), destroy the enemy's industrial and transportation infrastructures and make 25 million people homeless[1]. At least one-third of German industry would be laid waste[2]. Portal painted a chilling picture of the 'whirlwind' promised by Harris when he stood on the Air Ministry roof in 1940 and watched London burn.

Bomber Command dropped 35,000 tonnes of bombs on German targets in 1942. The bomb tonnage trebled in 1943. In just one month in the Spring of 1945 Bomber Command dropped the equivalent of 1942's total tonnage[3].

The great area bombing offensive entered a new phase in March 1943 when the 'Battle of the Ruhr' began. The main instruments required for the catastrophic ruin of German cities were assembled at last. They now rested in the hands of Arthur Harris. The Pathfinder Force (PFF) had won its independence and had become 8 Group. There had been dramatic advances in target location. Technological milestones included the first use of H2S airborne radar by Pathfinder aircraft (an attack on Hamburg, Germany's second city, on January 30/31). The new Target Indicators were dropped for the first time on January 16/17 to mark Berlin.

The highly effective Oboe blind-bombing aid was also introduced at this time. The first operational trials of Oboe took place on December 20 1942, in an attack on a coking plant at Lutterade in the Netherlands[4]. The primary role of the Oboe-equipped Mosquitos was highly accurate target marking for the heavy bombers, regardless of cloud conditions[5]. Oboe marking held the promise of concentrated bombing of targets even when they were totally obscured. As Pathfinder Force Commander Donald Bennett pointed out, during the bad weather month of January 1943 Bomber Command would have been 'practically paralysed' without

blind marking[6]. Instead, the bombers attacked Essen six times and Duisburg twice. He saw Oboe as 'probably the most effective single instrument of warfare in our entire armoury[7].'

The strategy for highly accurate, concentrated bombing had crystallised: PFF target location by visual or flare-dropping means, using Oboe-equipped 'Finders' when possible, followed by extensive flare-dropping by 'Illuminators', primary marking, continued marking by 'Backers up' and bombing by the 'Main Force' – arriving in a dense concentration over the target and swamping the defences. Later, the 'Master Bomber' concept was employed. This allowed for direct control of the attack by VHF, while over the target.

Bennett (*Pathfinder*) said the Finders were drawn from the best crews, to drop flares in the area of the aiming point a few minutes before Zero Hour. A Finder or Finders would then drop flares on the exact aiming point. The Illuminators dropped more flares, to help the Primary Markers – crews with a reputation for bombing accuracy. Their job was to drop TIs on the aiming point. Backers-Up added more TIs, as required[8].

Oboe's full operational debut coincided with Sidney Knott's first operation. On the night of January 27/28 1943 Mosquitos used Oboe for ground-marking. The target was Düsseldorf. Oboe's range was limited by the Earth's curvature but it was an effective solution to the persistent industrial haze hiding the Ruhr. Oboe-equipped PFF Mosquitos operated at around 30,000 ft. Their height and speed made for relatively low casualty rates, despite the fact that they had to fly an approach run of some 50 miles for Oboe-controlled marker release[9].

The Casablanca Directive was agreed by Churchill and Roosevelt at this time. The two leaders had fresh instructions for Harris: 'Your primary object will be the progressive destruction and dislocation of the German military, industrial and economic system and the undermining of the morale of the German people to the point where their capacity for

*Mosquito: A 105 Squadron aircraft. Oboe-equipped Mosquitos offered the prospect of concentrated bombing of targets, even when totally obscured. Photo: Trustees of the imperial war museum.*

armed resistance is fatally weakened[10].' There was nothing new in this reference to German morale.

On August 18 1941 the Butt Report (an objective assessment of the effectiveness of British bombing) had told the harsh truth about Bomber Command's ineffectual early war years. The report was based on an analysis of some 600 sets of aiming point photographs[11]. It found, inter alia, that only around one in four crews claiming to bomb a German target put their bombs within five miles of the target. Bombers could not survive daylight operations but when operating at night many crews had trouble finding a large city, let alone a specific target within a city.

Area bombing, clearly, was the only option if the bombing war was to be prosecuted. In February 1942 an Air Ministry communication to Bomber Command stated: '...it has been decided that the primary objective of your operations should now be focused on the morale of the enemy population and, in particular, of the industrial workers.' In that month Harris became AOC Bomber Command[12].

In response to the growing ferocity of the British night attacks and the prospect of heavy American bombing by day, major improvements to German air defences were in place or in the process of implementation by early 1943. The Luftwaffe had some 600 radar-equipped nightfighters in service. Furthermore, radar had much increased the effectiveness of the flak batteries[13].

On Wednesday January 27 1943 Frank Heavery's Lancaster, W4823, climbed away from Bottesford's main runway at 17.40. This was the real thing but the crew were not going to Düsseldorf. As an introduction to operations they had been briefed to drop five mines in the shipping lanes off the island of Juist:

> *Crews frequently started a tour with an 'easy' minelaying trip. Earlier, we had been briefed to lay mines off the French Biscay coast. Bad weather led to a decision to scrub the operation at the last minute, just as we were about to board the aircraft. After this let-down we were ready again on the Wednesday. These operations were known as 'gardening'. The mines, referred to as 'vegetables', had a length of 10 ft and entered the water by parachute.*

During the Second World War Lancaster crews flew 2,929 minelaying sorties[14]. On the night of January 27/28 the minelaying involved 54 aircraft and 'vegetables' were dropped into the waters off Texel and along the Frisians. One bomber, a Stirling, failed to return[15].

> *The Frisians run from the top of the Zuider Zee – now known as the Waddenzee – to North Germany. Our target area, Juist, was located off the Ems estuary. The Flight Plan involved crossing Juist, to a point just beyond the island, followed by a sharp turn onto the reciprocal course. This would offer a brief opportunity to gain a pinpoint on the island. We would then fly a timed run from that pinpoint. If all went well our mines would drop neatly into the deepwater channel. In order to lay the mines successfully, our Lanc's altitude at release must not exceed 1,500 ft, putting us within easy reach of light flak and searchlight defences.*

*During the briefing we were told there were no defences on Juist, although a neighbouring island to the west, Borkum, had a reputation for enthusiastic flak crews. This claim of a flak-free Juist appeared to be substantiated on crossing the island, but all hell broke loose as we returned and searched for our pinpoint. Lesson No.1: take what you hear at briefing with a pinch of salt.*

*We were sitting ducks at 1,500 ft. This is the worst possible height to fly over ground defences, as the light flak gunners are offered a generous arc of fire. Within seconds we were held by two searchlights and tracer came up from all angles. It was extremely frightening to be robbed of night vision in an instant. I was in no mood to sit there and take it. I began to fire down the searchlight beams and at the sources of the tracer.*

*This was my first experience under fire. I found the tracer almost hypnotic as it rose slowly and then accelerated past the turret at a fantastic speed. It was all over very quickly – a matter of a few seconds – and the searchlights disappeared. I had fired 500 rounds and, hopefully, the short bursts had disturbed Juist's flak gunners. Meanwhile, Frank and Nick were busy. The bomb doors opened and we began our timed run along the shipping lane. Frank held the Lanc steady as we flew over the dark waters and laid the large mines.*

While over Juist, members of Heavery's crew spotted another Lancaster getting the full treatment from Borkum's gunners. A few hours later, after the debriefing, Ted Foster suggested that Sergeant Vine's crew may have over-estimated their ground speed and turned in too early, placing them squarely over the flak guns.

During the return flight Heavery's crew were in a subdued mood:

*We were very shaken. As novices we had swallowed the line that there were no defences on Juist. As a result we were surprised and ill-prepared for our hot reception. We were hosed with light flak yet, somehow, emerged unscathed. I felt sure we had escaped with our lives because those gunners were probably Home Guard ('Heimatflak'). It might have been a different story had those guns been manned by the Ruhr's seasoned flak troops.*

*Ted had remained at his navigator's station. He was behind his curtain and had no view of what went on outside during our brief and violent introduction to light flak. He had just one terse comment to offer: 'Blimey! We were lucky!'*

*Our BI Lanc had been in the air for four hours 55 minutes. Nick had performed well. He had been responsible for obtaining that all-important pinpoint and had carefully positioned our aircraft for the timed run to the target area. After the debrief and back in our billets, we sat up and talked things over, re-living our experiences. Ted pencilled the word 'Juist' on the wall by his bed. The fact that we stayed up, swapping stories, showed our raw state. We had yet to appreciate the importance of getting to bed and conserving our strength. Chit-chat can always wait for the morning.*

*Our fellow gardening enthusiast, Sergeant Vine, was a special character. After the war Ted recalled that Vine's history included some unauthorised low flying. The offender's vigorous denials were brushed aside in favour of the physical evidence: twigs and other debris found embedded in the underparts of his aircraft. His punishment was 'loss of seniority' (being required to wait an extra six months to reach Flight Sergeant). This made no difference to Vine as he went missing within the space of a few weeks.*

This trip to Juist was the only sortie made by the crew in a B.I Lancaster. The first of 467's B.III Lancasters arrived in January. Over 3,000 B.III Lancasters were built. During this first month of operations, 467 Squadron dispatched 66 aircraft against 12 enemy targets and two crews failed to return (Pilot Officer Wark and Sergeant Aicken)[16]. Al Wark was an American, from Seattle[17].

*Blast and fire: this bomb-load consists of a 4,000 lb Cookie, cans of incendiaries and general purpose bombs. Photo: Vincent Holyoak.*

Heavery's first trip had been successful despite the unpleasant surprise over Juist. Yet this was something of a false dawn for the crew as the weather then deteriorated. They were to wait nearly three weeks for their second operation. January 1943 ended with Heavery taking E-Easy (ED363) on a half-hour night flying test. At that point Knott had 166 hours 45 minutes in his logbook, including 64 hours 25 minutes at night. He had fired 7,600 rounds, the last 500 in anger.

The crew next flew on February 4. They took off in T-Tommy (ED524) at 14.05, having been briefed for an eight-hour cross-country. Wireless op Johnny Lloyd received a recall signal well into the flight and they were back at Bottesford for a night landing after six hours 10 minutes in the air. During the following day they took the same Lancaster on a combined night flying test and low level bombing practice. Murray dropped practice bombs from a height of 1,000 ft.

The crew appeared on 467's Battle Order for the second time on February 16. During the day ED523 was bombed up with a dark green, dustbin-like 4,000 lb 'Cookie' high capacity blast bomb and 12 containers, each packed with eight 30 lb (J-Type) incendiaries. The latter contained a vicious mixture of phosphorus and other combustibles.

This sortie to Lorient introduced the crew to a typical Lancaster war load: a 4,000 lb Cookie (or 'Blockbuster') and incendiaries. Bomber Command dropped 68,000 Cookies during its long bombing campaign.

*Getting ready: aircrew prepare for the night's raid. Photo: Vincent Holyoak.*

High capacity blast bombs opened up buildings and made it easier for incendiaries to take hold.

The 4lb incendiary emerged as Bomber Command's most destructive weapon. The bomblets had an hexagonal section (for easy packing) and were carried in cans known as Small Bomb Containers, or SBCs. Some of these unpleasant little fire-raisers held an explosive charge, to make life more dangerous for the Germans on the ground.

Bomber Command adopted codewords for the various warloads. An area bombing all-incendiary load was codenamed 'Arson'. In the case of a Lancaster it consisted of SBCs, each carrying 90 4 lb No. 15 incendiaries (including No. 15 X explosive incendiaries). The two types were often loaded in a 10:1 mix.

A warload offering both blast and fire, codenamed 'Cookie/Plumduff', was used against heavily industrialised urban areas. This consisted of a 4,000 lb impact-fused high capacity bomb (the Cookie), 1,000 lb short-finned, short-delay high explosive bombs and SBCs with 4 lb or 30 lb incendiaries.

The most common warload, however, was the blast/maximum incendiary mix dryly codenamed 'Usual'. This consisted of a 4,000 lb Cookie and SBCs of incendiaries[18]. Heavery's crew were briefed to drop the 'Usual' on the French port of Lorient.

> *In the late afternoon we attended the Lorient briefing. We were told that the port had been developed into one of the principal U-Boat bases along the French Atlantic coast.*

A total of 377 aircraft were readied for the Lorient attack: 131 Lancasters, 103 Halifaxes, 99 Wellingtons and 44 Stirlings[19]. Four weeks before, on January 14, a new Air Ministry Directive had been issued. A desperate struggle was under way against the U-Boats in the Atlantic. The French ports used by the submarines were to be destroyed in heavy area bombing attacks. Lorient, the first priority, was raided that very night and the following night. During January and February Bomber Command flew some 2,000 sorties against Lorient but achieved little. The U-Boats were moored safely under the thick concrete roofs of their pens.

When preparing to attack targets in occupied France Bomber Command planners went to great lengths to minimise French casualties. Such concerns were set aside in the case of the U-Boat ports, due to the disastrous losses suffered by the Atlantic convoys. The area raids on Lorient reflected the harsh terms of the new Directive. The raid of February 16/17 was the last large attack in the series flown against Lorient since the Directive was issued. The town itself was the target and much of what had survived the earlier attacks was flattened:

> *We took off at 19.00, having been briefed in detail on the significance of this target for the Allied war effort. Our Lanc made good progress through the night sky. We headed for Start Point, on the Devon coast east of Salcombe and our pinpoint for the Channel crossing turn. When over Start Point Ted told Frank to fly 090. The skipper quietly rejected his navigator's offer and asked him to reconsider. The next proposal was 270. It was obvious that Ted had a serious*

*problem as our target was on a southerly heading. Frank told Nick to go back and sort him out. The reason for Ted's uncharacteristic behaviour was readily apparent. His oxygen tube had become twisted, virtually cutting off the supply. A man starved of oxygen acts like a drunk. Happily, recovery is swift when the oxygen supply is restored (unless the victim is too far gone).*

*We crossed the enemy coast without further incident and turned onto track, having been briefed to attack Lorient from the land side. Frank and Nick began their double act as we flew over the town's lively defences. There was plenty of flak. I felt our Lanc lift as the bombs fell. Suddenly everything went red, white, then black. The huge flash seemed to smother our aircraft and we were all blinded for a few seconds. I could see, imprinted on my retina, a ghostly image of our tail engulfed in flame. Gradually my eyes focused. Night vision had gone but I could see and feel enough to know we were heading in the wrong direction – straight down! The night sky filled the entire view from the rear turret. We were diving at great speed, out of control and at an angle so acute that my shoulders were thrust firmly against the turret doors.*

*I could hear faint voices on the intercom. The crew seemed to be whispering. Perhaps the intercom had been damaged by the flak shell? Then there was complete silence from the crew as ED523 became increasingly nose-heavy and steepened in the dive. The Lancaster's maximum speed in a dive is 360 mph. The vibration and noise suggested we were close to 'never exceed' speed. Looking straight up at the heavens I felt curious at my lack of fear and the ease with which I had already accepted oblivion. I wondered if Frank had been killed by the flak burst. I then felt the Lanc begin to pull out. We recovered from the dive and levelled out at an extremely low height over the sea. I felt a cold surge of fear pass from head to toe.*

*Ghostly voices returned to the intercom. I heard Frank say: 'We're OK'. He then gave instructions and the crew began to check for damage. Nick made his way down the fuselage to inspect the bomb-bay. He came on the intercom with bad news. Our Cookie had failed to drop. The large, ominous-looking cylinder was still firmly in place, despite our steep dive and last-minute recovery. We could not land back at Bottesford with a Cookie in the bomb-bay. There were standard instructions for such situations. The big bomb would have to be dropped manually over a designated area free of Allied shipping. Our skipper had more pressing problems, however, as ED523 was extremely reluctant to climb to a safe dropping height, despite the fact that all four engines were running well. It was not our night!*

*We were in a bit of a fix. The Cookie could not be dropped in a safe condition and more height was needed if we were to avoid the risk of being blown out of the sky by our own bomb. The safe height for a Cookie was 4,000 ft – the usual rule was 1,000 ft per 1,000 lb of explosive charge, but it was wise to allow more when over the sea. Frank struggled to make the aircraft climb while Nick grabbed some handtools and returned to the bomb-bay. The Lanc grudgingly made 5,000 ft and we arrived over the drop zone as Nick did his best above the bomb-bay. Finally, the bomb doors opened and we parted company with the unwanted Cookie. It plunged towards the sea and I saw the brilliant flash as it*

*High capacity blast bomb: a 4,000 lb Cookie on the trolley at Bottesford. This photograph was taken after Sidney Knott's first tour was completed, as this crew (led by Pilot Officer Doug Harvey) were posted to 467 Squadron on August 11 1943. Photo: Vincent Holyoak.*

detonated on impact. *The blast wave reached up and shook our Lanc from end to end. Ted needed no second bidding and gave Frank a course for Bottesford.*

Heavery landed at 01.10. It should have been a relatively short trip, but the unwelcome visit to the designated drop zone stretched an eventful second operation to six hours 10 minutes. The crew sat round the table with an Intelligence Officer and told their story:

*I thought it was flak but the Intelligence Officer had other ideas, using the word 'scarecrow' for the first time. He claimed the Germans were firing shells that simulated exploding aircraft. This was news to us. I thought 'scarecrow' was a good name – it certainly scared the hell out of me! I had hardly any experience of flak at that time, but the explosion seemed impressive enough to mark the end of an aircraft laden with bombs and petrol. Much later, after the war, I considered this possibility. The Germans maintained that scarecrow shells were a myth. Only one aircraft failed to return from this raid. Perhaps it had been flying alongside us when it received a direct hit and vanished in a fireball?*

The night's adventures were over. The crew made their way to the billet and attempted to settle down. Sleep refused to come. Sidney Knott closed his eyes and recalled the moment when the Lancaster had been thrown sideways and then plunged earthwards with great violence:

*I turned it over in my mind. Why had I felt fear only when there seemed a possibility of survival? It didn't make sense. During training I had often wondered how I would cope in the final seconds of a 'sticky end'. I found the answer in that dive over Lorient. I felt relaxed, not the least bit worried. Perhaps real fear requires the chance of survival? When we entered that dive I felt sure we were finished.*

Many other aircrew in extreme situations had similar experiences, with the apparent certainty of death accompanied by calm acceptance. One such account is given by Rolfe (*Flying into Hell*)[20].

*After a few hours rest we decided to give ED523 the once over. We were told that a hole had been found in the port inner oil tank. Incredibly, this small hole was the only visible evidence of damage.*

A total of 363 aircraft bombed Lorient that night. In all, 1,675 aircraft claimed to have bombed this port during the month since the Air Ministry Directive was issued. Close to 4,000 tonnes of bombs had fallen on Lorient; 24 aircraft had failed to return[19]. Having flown on the last of the Lorient raids, Heavery's crew participated in the first attack against another U-boat port, St Nazaire. Two weeks after Lorient they took T-Tommy (ED524) to this target, together with a 4,000 lb Cookie and incendiaries. On this occasion the big blast bomb dropped without hesitation.

The Germans, meanwhile, moved more nightfighters to French airfields, to defend the U-boat bases[21].

Three days after Lorient, Heavery and his team entered Bottesford's briefing room and joined four other 467 crews (led by Squadron Leader Paape, the Flight Commander, together with Flight Lieutenant Michie, Flight Sergeant Howie and Sergeant Vine). It was the afternoon of Friday February 19. The wall map revealed the target – another port but this time in Germany. A force of 338 aircraft, including 52 Lancasters, was being prepared to attack the docks and naval base at Wilhelmshaven[22].

Disenchanted with ED523, Heavery was happy to hear he had been

*Taking a chance with Lady Luck: Sergeant Brian Howie in the cockpit of his usual Lancaster, A-Able (ED541). Other crews sought to avoid this aircraft, with its skeleton throwing dice. Nevertheless, it was lucky for Howie on 50 Squadron and continued to be so on 467 Squadron. He and his crew finished their tour on March 9 1943. Photo: Vincent Holyoak.*

allocated O-Orange (ED530). As the crews were briefed the armourers completed their work. Heavery's Lancaster now held a Cookie and 12 cans of incendiaries. Bomber Command had raided Wilhelmshaven with 195 aircraft the previous night but the results were disappointing. It was hoped that the follow-up would prove much more destructive:

> *While the target required a long crossing of the North Sea this was straightforward for Ted. It involved a clear run over the ocean followed by a quick penetration into Reich airspace. We got the green at 17.55 and O-Orange gathered speed, the four Merlins producing a healthy roar.*
>
> *This trip began well. Everything went according to plan on the outward leg but the flak was very heavy over the port. We had never seen anything like it. Was this 'normal' for a German target? Nick disregarded the fireworks and dropped accurately on the Pathfinder markers, despite some cloud and ground haze. It felt a bit dicey but the built-up area was compact and we were quickly away and out of the worst. We turned for home and left the hostile coast behind.*
>
> *Once over the North Sea Frank began to let down through a cloud layer. We had a terrible shock when we broke through. We were over a very large city! Our minds worked overtime as we searched for an explanation. The obvious and most alarming possibility was that we were flying a 'reciprocal' – eastwards, rather than westwards towards England. Frank was careful to maintain an even tone of voice as he raised this possibility with Ted but our navigator was emphatic. He remained fully confident that we were flying in the right direction and it soon became obvious that he was correct. We had fallen victim to a very convincing optical illusion. The regular patterns on the 'ground' were, in reality, the white caps of waves highlighted across the dark surface of a rough sea. It served as yet another painful reminder of our inexperience.*

O-Orange was down safely by 22.40 after four hours 45 minutes in the air. On landing, the flaps were raised, the radiator shutters opened and the Lancaster began to taxi to the dispersal. The crew soon discovered that two of the five aircraft dispatched by 467 were overdue. The aircraft and crews disappeared without trace:

> *Vine's crew had gone and so had Michie's. On the crew status board the letters FTR (failed to return) appeared. It was at this point that we began to appreciate the reality of life on operations. Here today, gone tomorrow! We took Vine's loss very hard. This crew had included a former three-man Blenheim team. They had occupied the other half of our hut.*
>
> *It was time to take stock. We didn't need anyone to tell us we were green. We had made plenty of mistakes during our first three ops and, at that point, no-one in our crew expected to be around for the 'last all-clear'.*

Fourteen telegrams were dispatched that morning. They would be read and re-read by families distraught with grief. They would have drawn no comfort from the disturbing findings of an intelligence assessment of the second raid on Wilhelmshaven within 24 hours. The first attack had put most of the bombs to the west of the target. The second raid's bombing concentration was to the north and, once again,

little damage had been done. Four Lancasters failed to return on the first night and 12 on the second (including the two 467 aircraft).

There was an investigation into the PFF marking. This yielded a startling revelation: the Pathfinders had been issued with obsolete maps that failed to show recent, large-scale urban development[22].

Heavery's crew would have been dismayed if they had known that at least one in five high explosive bombs dropped by Bomber Command aircraft failed to explode. In addition, the explosive power of British bombs, weight for weight, remained far less than that of German bombs (containing aluminium powder) until relatively late in the war[23]. Aluminised explosive was introduced eventually and this greatly increased the destructive power of British bombs[24].

Bad weather restricted flying for a few days after Wilhelmshaven and provided a welcome respite. The crew continued to chew over their experiences:

> *The rotten weather was a godsend. We held numerous crew meetings and carefully picked over the many errors made on our probationary trips. We knew we had to keep intercom chatter to a minimum. We also recognised the crucial importance of accurate navigation. Some solutions were simple. We decided, for example, that every crew member should be capable of checking the correct position*

*Up you come: a helping hand for Ted Foster, Frank Heavery's navigator. The Skipper is standing to the left and Nick Murray is to the right, waiting to board. Photo: Vincent Holyoak.*

*of the North Star on the outward and return legs. On the Wilhelmshaven raid Ted was sure of himself as the North Star was in the right place.*

The pace of operational flying began to intensify. On Thursday February 25 the crew attempted to push aside their vivid memories of Lorient and climbed into ED523 at just before eight o'clock in the evening. Having run through the 'vital actions', the checks made immediately before take-off, they were soon bound for Nuremberg with a Cookie and 10 cans. ED523 was part of a force of 337 aircraft dispatched for this attack on the city. The weather was poor and the bombing scattered, yet over 300 buildings were damaged. Nine aircraft failed to return, 2.7 per cent of the force dispatched[22]. Heavery's crew spent seven hours 25 minutes in the air.

> *We lost Flight Sergeant Stewart on this operation. Ted took the loss to heart as Flight Lieutenant Rowcroft, our Australian Navigation Leader, had decided to fly with Stewart that night. Ted's consolation was personal survival; he quietly pencilled the word 'Nuremberg' on the wall by his bed.*

*Bombs on target: the certificate received by each member of the Heavery crew on bringing back a good aiming point photograph from an attack on Nuremberg on February 25/26 1943. Sidney Knott.*

After the debrief and a few snatched hours in bed the crew woke to find themselves on the new day's Battle Order. For the first time they were to experience the grossly excessive physical and mental demands of sorties on consecutive nights. The target for February 26 was Cologne and ED523's bomb load combined a Cookie with 12 cans of 4 lb incendiaries.

The crew rested on February 27 but joined the St Nazaire attack the following day. A safe return just after midnight brought February to a

NURNBERG

25/26·II·43·

SGT· HEAVERY         SGT· FOSTER         SGT· MURRAY

SGT· HODSON         SGT· LLOYD         SGT· KNOTT

SGT· BUTTERWORTH

close, with six sorties completed and 33 hours 50 minutes of operational flying in Sidney Knott's logbook.

By February 1943 Bomber Command had 53 squadrons in six Groups. They operated nearly 1,000 front-line aircraft, including 650 four-engined Stirlings, Halifaxes and Lancasters. The Command held stocks of five million 4 lb incendiaries, with production running at around 60,000 per week[25]. During February 467 Squadron had dispatched 75 aircraft to 13 targets, losing three crews (Sergeant Vine, Flight Sergeant Stewart and Flight Lieutenant Michie). There were no survivors among the 21 aircrew[16]. The Reaper had also visited German nightfighter units. Three of the most successful pilots – Knacke, Gildner and Becker – had been killed in February. By a strange coincidence each had 44 night victories at the time of their deaths[26].

# CHAPTER SIX

## *'It All Looked Very Unfriendly'*

OPERATIONS during the first half of March put Heavery's crew to the test. They made five trips in the first nine days. Each involved a tough target: Berlin, Hamburg, Essen, Nuremberg and Munich.

Over 50 years on, Bottesford Section Officer Marie Cooper reflected: 'Everything was intensified, both on the ground and in the air: the numbers of aircraft sent out, staggered heights at which to fly, routes to saturate enemy defences, the critical relationship of bombload to petrol, new marker techniques by PFF (and) the production of large mosaics of principal targets, against which aiming point photographs could be plotted. Briefings became longer and the number of information charts proliferated, as did the Intelligence staff[1].

On Monday March 1 the port inner Merlin engine of Heavery's Lancaster stuttered into life, followed by the three others. He manoeuvred the bomber off one of Bottesford's 36 dispersal pans. He got the green at 18.45 and took T–Tommy (ED524) into the air. The crew were bound for Berlin with a 4,000 lb blast bomb and 10 cans of incendiaries. The Lancaster was one of a force of 302 bombers flying to the 'Big City' that night. T-Tommy soon ran into problems:

> *After just 20 minutes in the air we were dismayed to hear Ted tell Frank that the GEE box had failed. This was a serious matter. Our navigator's electronic 'right hand' packed up just seconds after we had set course over the base. Ted tried changing fuses but the box failed to come to life. He applied all the first aid he knew but still couldn't persuade it to work. GEE fixes were crucial as they were used to verify wind strength and direction. Ted and the skipper reviewed the options. Ted later confessed that he had become desperate enough to ram his finger into the socket, to check whether the GEE set still had power. He received a vicious shock for his trouble but the GEE screen remained blank.*

GEE utilised signals from three ground stations: a 'master' and two 'slaves'. The time difference between the reception of these signals was used to determine the aircraft's position. GEE allowed navigators to find their position to within six miles, even at extreme range. It was said to have been named after the first letter of 'Grid', as the aircraft's position was found by reference to a map-grid[2]. Its range was limited by the Earth's curvature to around 350 – 400 miles.

*'Everything was
intensified': Section
Officer Marie Cooper, an
Intelligence Officer at
Bottesford. Photo:
Vincent Holyoak.*

GEE lacked the accuracy required of a blind-bombing aid and it was
susceptible to jamming. Yet GEE remained in service throughout the war
as it gave crews reliable fixes for at least part of the outward leg (allowing
the bomber stream to concentrate) and, most importantly, assisted
during the tiring last leg home[3].

*We faced a long sea crossing (336 miles precisely, according to the
navigator's log), yet Frank and Ted decided to continue. We were going to do it
the hard way! Better to press on than turn back and abort the sortie. When we
crossed the coast Ted called up the wireless op and asked Johnny to drop a flame-
float. This gave me the chance to take drift readings from the rear turret. We
were doing things the old-fashioned way in the absence of Ted's electronic box
of tricks. The long hours spent practising turret manipulation and taking drift
readings paid off on this trip. I could achieve an accuracy to one degree by
snatching quick readings from the turret drift dial. I took three readings from
the glowing float and gave Ted the average.*

*When Johnny dropped the first flame-float down the flare chute I was ready
– crouched over the guns, with the barrels depressed, and waiting for it to
appear under the tail. It became visible in a second or two, directly underneath,*

*and showed up well in the darkness below. The readings averaged five degrees to starboard.*

*Ted called for another flame-float as we continued to climb. He knew our necks depended on getting this right. A mistake could result in Frank unwittingly taking us over a coastal flak hot-spot. Sightings on the second float produced an average reading of seven degrees to starboard. Ted then asked for a third float but we entered a layer of thinnish cloud just before I could get the final drift angle. The second, however, was 11 degrees and this suggested the wind had continued to strengthen during the climb. Ted acted on these readings as he had nothing better to go on. His next hope was a recognisable landfall on the Danish coast somewhere near the island of Mando, south of Esbjerg. Nick was told to obtain a pinpoint as we crossed the coast and he moved forward into the bomb aimer's position.*

Murray struggled to make the most of occasional breaks in the cloud:

*Nick suddenly reported an island which appeared to be Mando. Ted worked swiftly at his curtained-off station and produced a new course for the skipper. This brought us back on track for the next leg across Denmark and to our turning point on the Baltic coast. Meanwhile, Nick prepared for his non-lethal duties that night – dropping morale-boosting leaflets to the Danes. Leaflet dropping was known as 'nickelling'. With this accomplished we settled down for the final leg to Berlin, with T-Tommy following a south-easterly track.*

*The Big City eventually came into view. It was an unbelievable sight! While this was our first visit to Berlin we could hardly miss it! The German capital was ringed by a thick band of searchlights. Their beams played above the vast urban area and its environs. A string of brilliant fighter flares drifted across the sky ahead of our track. It all looked very unfriendly.*

A dense barrage of flak rippled and flickered in the sky over the city. Most were exploding 88mm shells, each designed to burst into 1,500 pieces of shrapnel[4]. Brightly coloured pyrotechnics dropped by the Pathfinders were already suspended over the target. Many were 'hooded', to protect the night vision of aircrew above. One 467 Squadron Lancaster Captain, Bill Manifold, has described how the Target Indicators looked from bombing height: 'A red TI, cascading down to form its characteristic shimmering pool, looked just like a cigarette carelessly knocked against somebody's trouser leg in the dark...[5].' The Germans called the TIs Christbäume – Christmas trees[6].

*Flak burst all around us as Frank and Nick took T-Tommy across Berlin at 19,000 ft. We were slightly earlier than our allotted Time on Target but got on with it anyway. The bomb-bay doors were opened. It took around two minutes for the doors to fully open at this height. We dropped on a vivid concentration of markers. The aircraft shook with the release of the load and we held our track, waiting for the 3ft long, 20 lb photo-flash to detonate. The camera then took a series of photos. Ted counted off seconds as long as minutes. The 5 Group reward of an Aiming Point Certificate seemed most inadequate at such moments. Nick reported that our bomb doors were closed as we banked away*

DANSK PROPAGANDA I U.S.A.: Danske i Amerika har ladet fremstille denne Plakat, som henleder Amerikanernes Opmærksomhed paa, at 5000 danske Sømænd sejler for De forenede Nationer.

*Nickelling: Front cover of the leaflet dropped over Denmark on March 1/2 1943, to boost the morale of an oppressed population. Sidney Knott.*

*from the maelstrom below. At that stage the briefed coastal crossing point near Texel, on the Zuider Zee, seemed an extremely long way away. T-Tommy levelled out on a westerly heading.*

*We were coned for the first time that night, as we returned across Germany. Frank didn't mess about. He threw our Lanc all over the sky. One searchlight beam had found us, followed by another three and then too many to count. We were blinded by the harsh, white glare. The skipper's aerobatics were successful, however, and we suddenly escaped the beams. There was no flak in the area – the searchlights must have been for the benefit of fighters. The cloud was increasing rapidly and we were grateful for the swift build-up to full cover.*

*The Berlin flak was bad enough but the searchlight trap robbed us of night vision and it took 20 minutes for our eyes to recover. We needed cloud cover as we were now very vulnerable to fighter attack. During the minute or two it took to enter the cloud the hairs on the back of my neck stood up. I scanned the sky for hostile aircraft, eyes straining into the darkness. Was there a fighter out there, creeping up on us? Then T-Tommy slipped into the cloud layer.*

Foster gave Heavery a new course. T-Tommy continued to fly towards the coast, with the GEE box still resisting the navigator's persistent attentions. During the long flight back across Germany Knott informed Heavery that he could see the glow of Berlin on fire at a distance of 160 miles. When the ETA near Texel was reached cloud cover was solid once again and it was impossible to gain a pinpoint:

*We assumed all was well. Ted gave Frank a course for the homeward leg across the North Sea. We hoped to cross the coast at Skegness. At the halfway point, Ted asked Johnny for a loop bearing. We didn't use this on the way out due to its general lack of reliability and to avoid assisting the German wireless monitoring service. The bearing put us around 20 miles north of track and Ted gave the skipper a course correction. Frank then began to let down through the cloud. We broke cover at 4,000 feet and I shared in the relief greeting our almost immediate glimpse of the coastline. Even in the Blackout, the outline of Skegness Pier was unmistakable. Our Lanc soon entered the Bottesford circuit and Frank must have been glad to see the two green lights that confirmed our undercarriage was locked down. We would be on the ground in a couple of minutes, bringing to a close that rather harrowing night.*

*Safely back at Bottesford and off the runway, we opened the bomb doors, as it took 15 minutes of high energy pumping to open them with the engines stopped. We headed towards the dispersal and T-Tommy eventually came to a standstill. We climbed out into the cold night air, the engine noise still throbbing in our ears. We felt different as we stretched our legs beside the aircraft. We had left our sprog status behind, somewhere over Berlin. We had completed seven trips – four to German targets, the last being the Big City. I recalled the moment at OTU when someone asked an Instructor: 'What's it like flying on operations?' He replied: 'You'll know when you have Essen in your logbook.' Well, I had Berlin in my logbook and that was good enough for me! We were fully operational, in every sense of the word.*

Seventeen of the 302 bombers dispatched to Berlin on March 1/2 failed to return. The casualties, 5.6 per cent of the force, included seven Lancasters. The bombing results were good despite the Pathfinders' difficulties in achieving concentrated marking. The problems were due, in the main, to the challenge of identifying specific city districts on the H2S radar screens. While bombing was far from concentrated the extent of the damage was unprecedented[7].

During the first half of March Flight Sergeant Brian Howie's team became the first 467 Squadron crew to complete a tour (they had been posted in – from 50 Squadron – with operational experience). Howie had a close call over Berlin in January. The sortie began badly when, shortly after take-off, they discovered they were flying towards Ireland

*Bill Manifold's crew at
Bottesford: they completed
their tour with 467
Squadron and a second
tour with 156 Squadron.
Photo: Vincent Holyoak.*

rather than in an easterly direction. With this problem identified they
sought to make up time, only to be coned over Berlin. They had
attempted to re-enter the bomber stream by increasing speed and
adjusting their track on the approach to the target, but they over-
compensated and found themselves one of the first, rather than the last,
over Berlin[8]. As such, they received the full and devoted attentions of the
Big City's fearsome defences.

CHAPTER SEVEN

# The Turret and the Guns

ASIDESTRAND bomber fitted with a Boulton Paul gun turret underwent service trials with 101 Squadron during early 1934. It was armed with a single Lewis gun. This was the RAF's first totally enclosed, power-operated rotating turret[1]. The trials soon confirmed that it made for much improved gunnery. Turrets evolved rapidly in subsequent years. The Lancaster's rear turret was the FN20, manufactured by Captain Archie Frazer-Nash's company. This turret had hydraulic power and could be rotated with the guns moving simultaneously[2].

Sidney Knott was slim. He had the agility required to get in and out of a Lancaster's rear turret without too much difficulty:

> The crew used a small ladder to enter the aircraft by the rear side door. I had the shortest walk. On entering the fuselage I turned left and walked past the Elsan chemical toilet and wall-mounted ammunition pans, pausing to stow my parachute pack. It was then a question of wriggling over the rear spar. This required technique. I could swing my legs over this barrier by grasping two straps attached to the roof. With the turret doors free to open I pushed my feet through. Once my flying boots were inside the turret it was easy to persuade the rest to follow – but there wasn't much room! You had to be a bit of a contortionist to do it in reverse and get out. Getting in was bad enough and a few rear gunners never quite mastered it. Some rear and mid-upper gunners reached an understanding. The mid-upper gunner would help his rear gunner in and then shut the doors behind him. I got it down to a fine art and never needed help, but I always worked up a sweat inside my bulky flying kit.
>
> Abandoning a Lancaster in an emergency was far from easy, as evidenced by the poor survival rates. The rear gunner had to get out of his turret, wriggle over the rear spar, clip on his chute, reach the door, open it and bale out without getting his head knocked off by the tail. This struggle often took place with the aircraft in a steep dive or rotating in a vicious spin. There was no room in the turret to sit on a seat-type parachute or wear a chest-type, as my body filled virtually the entire space. The FN20 was very cramped; in the normal sitting position my back rested against the doors.

Once inside, the rear gunner sat on a crude seat – a metal plate covered with a thin cushion. When the early Lancasters reached the squadrons their rear turrets were equipped with armour. The steel plates concertinaed as the guns were depressed.

*Sting in the tail: Flying Officer Roy 'Juggo' Hare, from Stourbridge. Hare became 467 Squadron's Gunnery Leader and operated a policy requiring gunners to work closely with armourers on the ground. Hare was killed when flying with Wing Commander Balmer in May 1944. At that time, Balmer was 467 Squadron's Commanding Officer. Photo: Vincent Holyoak.*

*The armour plate gave a degree of protection but it was soon removed (together with a good deal else) to increase the Lanc's bomb-carrying capacity.*

The seated rear gunner's eyes were level with the reflector sight. This followed the guns as they moved. A dimmer switch controlled the brilliance of the illuminated sight. It would be turned to its lowest setting on dark nights and to maximum in daylight:

*The gunner had to recognise an enemy aircraft in an instant. By knowing the incoming aircraft's wingspan, its distance could be estimated using the sight. The reflector sight was extremely reliable; it was fault-free throughout my two operational tours.*

Oxygen entered the turret to the rear gunner's right. The drift indicator, or dial, was also located to the right. Dead astern read as zero on the drift dial, which was marked by a coloured scale in degrees, red for port and green for starboard. As on the March 1/2 Berlin raid, a flame-float could be dropped to allow the rear gunner to measure the aircraft's drift. Knott would sight on the float when it ignited. He would then snatch a quick look at the dial and report the angle of drift – remembering, as always, that port and starboard are reversed when facing rearwards.

The intercom plug was situated close to the oxygen inlet. There was also a handle, to wind the turret dead astern and lock it in the event of hydraulic failure. The turret's main controls were similar to a motorbike's handlebars. The grips were twisted to depress or elevate the guns. Rotation was produced by turning the control column. The turret's speed of rotation depended on the force exerted.

*Gunners always talked about 'turret manipulation', the ability to control the turret and the guns. Total command of turret movement required excellent coordination between the gunner's hands, eyes and brain. I practised turret manipulation whenever I flew in daylight and, given enough light, on the way out at night. I would sight on a field boundary and attempt to follow the hedgeline as the countryside rolled away beneath me. This was difficult at first but, after a while, I found I could manage it even in turbulent conditions. I put in some extra practice after each leave, as it didn't take long to get rusty.*

Every air gunner did what he could to improve visibility. Battle experience had changed attitudes towards the turret. It had been designed as a totally enclosed perspex bubble with a small window facing aft. This opened with a sliding action:

*The window guides attracted dirt, especially when flying through cloud. A tiny speck of dirt could be mistaken for an approaching fighter. The window was removed but this didn't help as the guides remained in place. Then the entire rear-facing perspex panel was removed. Scientific trials later established that the resulting temperature difference was negligible – just a few degrees. Who cared, when turret temperatures of -30 deg. and lower were the norm, perspex or not? Improved vision was well worth that insignificant temperature difference.*

*Our squadron eventually decided to leave the perspex turret top in place, but removed the rearward-facing panel in its entirety, up to eye level. I got into the habit of giving what remained of the perspex a final polish in the late afternoon, before every operational flight. The best cloth for this purpose was the muslin used in the meat trade to cover carcasses.*

The Lancaster's sting in the tail consisted of four .303 Brownings, each with a rate of fire of 1,150 rounds per minute. This machine gun was evaluated by the RAF as early as 1918 and Armstrong Whitworth acquired manufacturing rights. The gun's calibre was modified from .300 to .303 inch and improvements were introduced over the years. Around 2,000 Brownings were being manufactured weekly by 1941. It was an ideal weapon for the RAF's new generation of heavy bombers as it was belt-fed[3].

The rear turret's Brownings were 'harmonised' to produce a tight grouping of rounds at a given range. The guns were adjusted on the ground to achieve this grouping, typically at 400 yards. Some Gunnery Leaders, however, had different ideas and preferred 250 yards.

The RAF evaluated the heavier American .50 calibre machine gun during the early 1920s but used it sparingly during World War II[3]. A few squadrons did have .50 calibre guns. They had a slower rate of fire and only two were accommodated in the 'Rose' rear turret. Bomber Command might have made more use of the .50 machine gun but for the Japanese attack on Pearl Harbour in late 1941. One of the more minor consequences of the United States' entry into the war was the decision to requisition four factories, established by the Ministry of Aircraft Production to manufacture these weapons for Britain[4]:

> *We would have liked heavier guns but this subject didn't play on our minds. I knew my four .303s threw out an awful lot of rounds and most night combats took place at very close range.*

This point about range was confirmed during the interrogation of leading German nightfighter pilots conducted immediately following the end of the war in Europe. Nachtjagdgeschwader 4's Major Heinz-Wolfgang Schnaufer, for example, stated his preference for opening fire at 100m, closing to a range of as little as 30m on a dark night (Appendix 3; 6).

For most of the war RAF and Luftwaffe gunnery experts alike were firm believers in tracer. British attitudes changed, however, when operational research revealed that many gunners preferred to watch (or 'follow') tracer rather than rely on deflection shooting.

> *Tracer was very frightening when it came your way. At the same time it was hopeless to aim by following tracer, due to the 'hosepipe' effect of a stream of bullets. Tracer deceived the eye and Bomber Command eventually concluded that its use should be curtailed. The Germans took the same decision. Tracer gave the game away in night combat.*

Schnaufer held a different view on that final point. He told his interrogators that, in his experience, tracer did not give away a bomber's position. He added that a greater readiness to open fire and the use of brighter burning tracer would have done much to discourage the more inexperienced nightfighter pilots (Appendix 3; 21).

The maximum ammunition load for the Lancaster's rear turret was 10,000 rounds. The belts were folded into aluminium canisters feeding into ducts running along the rear fuselage wall. Early on in the tour Knott's four Brownings had a full ammunition load, with the canisters full. Later much less ammunition was carried, to save weight and increase bomb-carrying capacity. Short bursts – just a second or two – were favoured by the gunners.

> *We did everything possible to reduce the risk of a stoppage. It was important to ensure there were no kinks in the belts. I always carried out these checks myself; it was a job too important to delegate. Nevertheless, a stoppage could occur at any time. For this reason every gunner carried a toggle. This was a small hand grip and wire loop – used to pull back the breech block and clear a jammed round. I always cocked the Brownings immediately we became airborne and tested them over the sea. This was good for morale. The noise of the guns always gave the boys a bit of a boost when outward bound.*

The practice of test-firing the guns on the outward leg was suspended during Knott's tour with 467 Squadron:

Clear vision the priority: a 467 Squadron aircraft with the rear turret sliding window removed. The crew is that of Flight Lieutenant Leo Patkin, RAAF. On the extreme left is mid-upper gunner Cliff Cooper, who went to 582 Squadron in 1944 for a second tour (as did Frank Heavery's rear gunner, Sidney Knott). Sergeant Ralph Chambers, second from left, was Patkin's flight engineer and the uncle of Jim George, now a researcher specialising in 467/463 Squadrons. This aircraft is believed to be M-Mother (ED547) and the photograph was taken in October 1943. This aircraft failed to return from Berlin in late December 1943. Sidney Knott flew four ops in this turret during March 1943 (to Hamburg, Essen, Nuremberg and Munich). Photo: Vincent Holyoak.

*I think this decision was taken due to the ever-increasing size of the raids. With so many aircraft flying in close proximity, in the dark, it was thought that test bursts could have tragic consequences.*

Loss of the rear turret's hydraulic power was a constant worry. The port outer engine provided hydraulics for the rear turret[5]. The master cylinder was located in the rear fuselage at a position close to the turret doors:

*If the spindle on top of this cylinder could be pushed down there was air in the system. This meant some loss of control over turret movement. One particular aircraft on the squadron had a reputation for such problems. Try as they might the ground crew failed to find the leak. If enough air got in the complete loss of hydraulic power – and turret failure – would follow. Nothing could be done in flight as the entire system had to be bled. I ran into a similar problem, with a vengeance, during my second tour.*

*The squadron ground crews and armourers set high standards. I had daily contact with them and got to know some very well. A Flight Sergeant had charge of a group of three aircraft. An important part of the ritual, on the ground, was the moment when the Flight Sergeant presented our skipper with Form 700. A signature on this document marked Frank's formal acceptance of the aircraft.*

*On 467 Squadron the ground crews were distributed between A Flight and B Flight (and, later, C Flight on its formation in March 1943). Squadrons had different ideas about the responsibilities of gunners and armourers. In 467's case, we gunners assisted the armourers whenever possible, stripping down the guns and cleaning them in the armoury. In contrast, gunners on some squadrons never touched their guns on the ground. The armourers did everything.*

The air gunner had a panoramic view of bursting flak shells, fighter flares, searchlights, air combats and aircraft going down in flames. Each operation imposed great strain and tested the resilience of the toughest individual. Terraine (*The right of the line*) observed: 'The air gunner's role was intimately linked to the turret; his task, especially at the rear, was essentially solitary, calling for both deep moral reserves and great physical fitness[6].'

Knott's behaviour in the turret was governed by self-discipline:

> *Everything was subject to a drill. There was a drill for searching the sky for fighters and another for ditching in the sea. All crews interested in survival knew these procedures by heart. Those not prepared to trust everything to luck did what they could to improve performance by practicing these drills. We were that type of crew. I used the gunner's search drill but added my own refinements. The full search pattern began as soon as we left the coast.*

Search reporting, by the book, was orientated from nose to tail, port or starboard, up/down: ahead, fine bow, bow, thick bow, beam (at 90 degrees to the aircraft fuselage), thick quarter, quarter, fine quarter and stern:

> *I had the habit of crouching over the guns rather than sitting. I rested on my elbows, taking the weight off my feet. This 'turret crouch' gave me the best view of the danger area below, where a fighter, lost against the dark ground, would be especially difficult to see.*

The Lanc's blind spot was directly below and this cost the lives of many unsuspecting crews[7]. Pilots of Schnaufer's nightfighter unit regarded 'banking search' defensive flying as an effective counter, as an attacker could never be sure whether or not he had been seen (Appendix 3; 20).

*Experten: Major Heinz–Wolfgang Schnaufer (centre) with his crew: gunner Wilhelm Gänster (left) and radar operator Fritz Rumpelhardt. Schnaufer wears the Knight's Cross with Oak Leaves, Swords and Diamonds. His companions wear the Knight's Cross. Schnaufer preferred to open fire at 100m. He was the most successful German nightfighter pilot of the Second World War. Photo: Trustees of the Imperial War Museum.*

*My turret was always on the move. The search pattern covered a full 180 degrees: the rear, below and both quarters to the beams. There was a rhythm to this task – searching to one side and below, then switching to the other side and down again. This pattern offered the best chance of a timely warning of fighter attack. Keeping busy also gave me confidence.*

Ken Butterworth was in the mid-upper turret. He had a different search pattern: to each side and down, together with the area to the rear, directly above Knott's head. The critical areas were on the beam, where he could see much more than the rear gunner.

In a dangerous sky, particularly during times of intense fighter activity, the Lancaster's lookout was reinforced. The wireless op kept watch from the astrodome, a perspex bubble, while the bomb aimer manned the front turret guns. Everyone understood that survival depended on keen eyes:

*It was a question of spotting the fighter before the fighter spotted us. If I could see a fighter attacking another bomber, it was almost certainly out of range of my guns. To put it bluntly, it was someone else's problem. We wanted to live and that meant staying in the dark zone and avoiding trouble. There was an element of 'I'm alright, Jack!' in this strategy. It was a matter of being realistic: a gunner spoiling for a fight would not live long. In fact he would almost certainly take the rest of the crew with him, in a pointless and literal blaze of glory. Our job was to drop bombs and survive, so allowing us to continue to drop bombs.*

Major Schnaufer's debriefing by an interrogation team in late June 1945 offers an interesting perspective from the German side. He said that, once in the stream, a nightfighter pilot could expect to spot one to three bombers, but perhaps 20 or more under conditions of bright moonlight. An experienced pilot would attack an average of three bombers on a dark night. Schnaufer claimed nine kills during February 21 1945 – two in the early hours of the morning and seven more in the evening. This German nightfighter ace had attacked many bombers with upward-firing Schräge Musik cannon (used for the first time during the August 1943 Peenemünde raid). His preferred range was around 80 m and only one bomber in 10 saw him at a range of 150-200 m and corkscrewed before he could fire (Appendix 3; 5,8).

*Crews were not briefed on the existence of Schräge Musik upward-firing cannons, at least in my experience. It was a revelation to me. I first heard the term many years after the war.*

Bomber crews, of course, saw the survival value in a methodical lookout for fighters and instant reaction to a warning. The degree of effort put into practicing these skills, however, varied greatly from crew to crew:

*The gunner spotting a fighter took command of the aircraft. A crisp, precise call for evasive action – such as 'Corkscrew port, go!' – required an instant, unquestioning response from the pilot. The best tactic was to turn into the attacking fighter. If the bomber turned away, it presented an easier and larger target for a longer period.*

*Gunners prepare for Berlin: this photograph was taken at Bottesford on March 29 1943, as the crews dress for an attack on the 'Big City', Berlin. Pictured centre is Ken Butterworth, Frank Heavery's mid-upper gunner. Also patting 'Jock' the Scottie is Pilot Officer George Currie, of Bill Manifold's crew. The gunners here are wearing the electrically heated Taylor Suit. Photo: Sidney Knott.*

The corkscrew consisted of a diving turn of some 30 degrees and 500 ft, going into a climbing turn of 30 degrees and 500 ft in the opposite direction[8]. Schnaufer's pilots regarded the corkscrew as an effective response to fighter attack. A violent corkscrew, beginning with a very steep dive and turn, stood a good chance of success due to the fighter's inability to pick up speed quickly enough to follow. Schnaufer was amazed at the violence of some manoeuvres performed by Lancasters. He also said, however, that a fighter could follow the first phase of a less violent corkscrew and open fire 'at the top', as the bomber changed direction. The danger in this tactic was exposure to fire from the mid-upper turret in the opening phase of the corkscrew. Experienced nightfighter pilots often broke off the engagement if the target began to corkscrew or fire back, preferring to re-join the hunt and seek easier meat (Appendix 3; 8, 9, 10, 11, 16, 17, 18).

> *People eager to avoid the chop put extra effort into practicing evasive action. We certainly did! We took it very seriously and refined our technique. It helped to look at things from the perspective of the German pilot, who regarded the entire night sky as his hunting ground. Some parts of the sky are darker than others. No matter how black the night, the view towards the ground is always darker, while the north is nearly always lighter. German pilots understood the significance of these differences and were just as keen to stay alive. An attack was more likely to come in from the dark side.*

This is confirmed by German nightfighter pilot Paul Zorner, who flew the Ju88. He recalled his operational training and the advice given to him by leading experten: 'From them, two things always remained in my mind. Firstly, that at night you could creep up on an enemy aircraft like a Red Indian: in other words, there were heights and directions, depending on the weather conditions, from which to approach with minimum risk of being seen. The second point was to keep your nerve and aim carefully between the fuselage and engine, in the case of a twin-engined bomber, and between the two engines on one wing with a four-engined machine, and then the enemy would catch fire after the first burst[9].'

The Lancaster was a big target. If a fighter was seen but showed no interest in his aircraft Heavery took immediate but *gentle* evasive action. A steep turn might attract attention, with what light there was reflecting on the four-engined aircraft's large wing surfaces.

> *Any hint of fighter activity – such as the sudden appearance of a group of flares or a suspicious absence of flak in a 'hot' area – encouraged Frank to move slightly off track and into the dark zone. His random height changes then became more frequent. People out there were trying to kill us and Frank was determined to make it difficult for them.*
>
> *As we became more experienced we began to appreciate the extent of our ignorance at the start of the tour. We were developing animal-like instincts impossible to teach in an OTU classroom. As the tour progressed we became self-taught specialists in survival.*

Many factors influenced the chances of staying alive. A late aircraft might attempt to catch up, as the bomber stream offered safety in numbers. This required more speed. When engines are pushed they get hotter, producing a brighter exhaust glow. This, in turn, increased the risk of being spotted by fighters. Where did the balance of advantage lie?

According to Major Schnaufer the exhausts of a Halifax could be seen from below at a range of up to 400m-500m. In contrast, a Lancaster's exhausts could be seen by a nightfighter pilot only when flying directly astern and in line with it. On a dark night the Lancaster's exhausts could be visible at up to 800 m (Appendix 3; 26).

Contrails were another headache:

> *Contrails were deadly. They could form at any time and without warning. They suddenly flicked out from the rear of the aircraft. There was no choice in this situation – the aircraft had to lose height. It was better to accept this than leave a gigantic signpost for patrolling nightfighters. We ran into this problem many times. One puff of white was enough for me to issue a sharp warning: 'Contrails'. Frank would put the nose down without comment.*

Some nightfighter experts such as Schnaufer were experienced enough to be able to estimate the range of a bomber flying ahead purely from the density of its contrails (Appendix 3; 28).

If Heavery's crew had a survival 'secret' it was total commitment to teamwork. Early on in the tour their experiences left them in no doubt that teamwork was a life-saver:

> *We were a team in every sense of the word. Later, when looking back on the first three trips – our probationary period – a queasy feeling grew in my stomach. We were so green! It took some time for this unease to recede but it was displaced eventually by a growing confidence in our abilities. The problem of our first flight engineer had been dealt with. We went to great pains to ensure nothing else disturbed the equilibrium and we now worked to make a good team even better. Constant training and growing operational experience bound us*

*together. We developed the habit of holding regular crew conferences. These discussions were always open and often quite blunt.*

*We introduced new routines to improve efficiency. One early lesson concerned the use of the intercom. There had been too much chatter in flight – a reflection of nervous tension. The chit-chat contributed nothing and increased the risk of being surprised if it got in the way of a sudden warning of fighter attack. We gunners found a solution.*

In part the problem had its roots in the dangers of anoxia. The gunners were isolated from the rest of the crew and especially vulnerable. Some gunners suffered a lonely death from oxygen starvation due to icing, a kink in the tube (as experienced on the February Lorient raid by Ted Foster) or a technical fault in the system. During a long flight, moisture and saliva (even vomit, in the case of secret sufferers of airsickness) trickled into the thin, corrugated rubber tube feeding the mask. This froze in the extreme temperature, forming a deposit that eventually blocked the tube. Typical symptoms of anoxia are feelings of well-being, followed by euphoria, coma and death.

On the night of January 16/17, during the first of two raids on Berlin, the rear gunner of future 467 Squadron C Flight Commander Keith Thiele died of oxygen starvation. This resulted from a tragic chain of events recounted in On the wings of the morning, Vincent Holyoak's excellent history of RAF Bottesford. The rear gunner who lost his life was 21-year-old Canadian Sergeant Alvin Broemeling.

Temperatures at operating height were abnormally low that night, at around -50 deg. C. Broemeling told Thiele that his oxygen system was freezing up. His flying helmet had been stolen a few days before. Early on during the Berlin flight the gunner had complained that the replacement was a poor fit. Thiele told him to use the spare carried on board but this was an obsolescent type prone to freezing. The skipper then told his rear gunner to use the emergency oxygen bottles. This helped for a while but Broemeling was in trouble again by the time Lancaster ED360 began its bombing run. The wireless op went to his aid while Thiele ignored the defences and put the aircraft into a steep dive from 19,000 ft immediately the bombs were dropped. When at 8,000 ft he left the flight engineer at the controls and went back himself, only to find, sadly, that it was too late. All attempts at resuscitation failed[10].

There may be no connection but it is interesting to note that a contemporary photograph shows Squadron Leader Keith Sinclair and flight engineer Sergeant Paddy Traynor wearing flying helmets clearly displaying their names, in very large letters[11].

*It was standard drill to flex the oxygen tube at regular intervals to prevent the potentially lethal accumulation of ice. We were also expected to check in on the intercom every now and then. These routines saved many a gunner's life. Unfortunately, however, this did tend to encourage unnecessary conversation. Ken and I put a stop to this. We reduced communication to the simple confirmation that we were both alive and well. I gave an occasional blow into the mike and Ken would respond with two shorter blows. This left the intercom free for a fighter warning.*

*Ken kept his eye on me from the mid-upper turret. He could see my turret moving around. Even so there would be two blows in the mike if he hadn't heard from me for a while. These brief signals were heard by the rest of the crew and assured them that their gunners were alive and alert. While the intercom was silent most of the time, our noisy, vibrating Lanc was filled with the tension of human concentration.*

The rear turret was a harsh environment. It was cramped, cold and remote from the rest of the crew. There was no room to move around and ease discomfort in the limbs. There is a myth that all gunners (especially rear gunners) were short and of slight build but this was not the case. Sidney Knott is no giant, at 5 ft 7 inches, but he knew other gunners who were taller, including one who was around 6 ft:

*Gunners came in all shapes and sizes but a slight build was an advantage as the Lanc's rear turret was a tight fit. Anyway, tall or short, many rear gunners were affected by the profound loneliness of their station. Since the war much has been written about this sense of isolation, but it never bothered me. The intercom kept us together in the air, even if used sparingly. I always felt close to the crew and in touch with what was going on. I found it helped to have a clear picture of the Flight Plan in my mind.*

*It is true, however, that some rear gunners developed unusual attitudes that reflected their physical situation. After all, we always looked back rather than in the direction we were heading! To add to the confusion my port was starboard for the rest of the crew and it took a while to get accustomed to this when using the intercom. Later, after the war, I was amused to learn that some people cannot tell left from right. They would have been in big trouble in a Lanc's rear turret!*

Knott became familiar with the turret's noise and vibration during training. The fear he knew at Gunnery School, during those first few flights, had long since disappeared. Nevertheless, he was appalled, long after the war, when shown the modest bolts that held the rear turret in place.

Of all hardships faced by rear gunners, cold was the most severe. Frostbite was commonplace:

*The turret thermometer's scale went down to −40 deg. C. I remember staring at the mercury, stuck at -40, and wondering just how cold it really was. I could cope with dry cold as the heated suit made it bearable. Temperatures in the icing range were the real menace and frozen eyelashes were one of the more bizarre effects. A well-fitted oxygen mask sat tight around the nose but some moist air always escaped from the top, near the eyes. Gradually my eyelashes froze solid. This was irritating and affected my vision. Every now and then I had to remove an outer glove and gently use a finger to clear my eyes.*

*Scientists occasionally visited bomber stations to interview operational crews and seek views on the equipment in use. It was difficult to offer sensible comments about clothing, due to the bewildering range of attire adopted by operational aircrew. I looked conventional enough, dressed in a gunner's yellow 'Taylor' suit (I found this much superior to the earlier, brown suit). An electrically-heated garment was worn underneath. This looked like a boiler suit and was fastened with press-studs. It provided heat from neck to toe but offered no protection for the head. I pointed this out to one group of 'boffins', adding that the silk and chamois-lined leather flying helmet was no help. No superstitious air gunner, of course, would trade in his old helmet for a new issue. That would be asking for trouble on the next raid! Gunners solved the problem in their own way. I took to wearing a Balaclava over my flying helmet. Others experimented with scarves of various types.*

The electrically-heated suit was essential but it took a while to get used to its foibles. If the gunner got too hot it could be switched off, but he would then cool off very quickly. It was all too easy to go from one extreme to the other and end up with frostbite. Too much heat could make the gunner sweat – although fear was the more likely cause! Either way, a perspiring gunner would soon find himself in trouble as the sweat froze on his skin.

Fatigue was just as dangerous:

*The station Medical Officer distributed 'wakey-wakey' pills at the briefing – one for a four to five hour trip and two for a longer flight to eastern or southern Germany. It was important not to take this pill until airborne. The inexperienced often swallowed them before take-off. They would then stay awake all night if the operation was scrubbed! The wakey-wakey pill has been described as Benzedrine or caffeine. I seem to recall that we were issued with caffeine tablets. In any event they certainly worked in a curious way. The pill had little or no effect for a while. In fact I often found it made me more drowsy at first. On a long flight I never took the second pill when the defences were active. I waited for everything to calm down. Anyway, after 20 minutes or so the pill would work its magic. I was wide awake and stayed that way.*

As Heavery's crew gained experience they emerged as a fine team,

*Two Flight Commanders: Squadron Leader Keith Sinclair (left) and Squadron Leader Keith Thiele. The aircraft is believed to be N – Nuts (ED764). Both men survived the war. Thiele's rear gunner died as a result of an oxygen supply problem during a sortie to Berlin in January 1943. Note that the rear turret's guns are pointing towards the ground. This indicates that the armour plate remains in place. Without the armour, the guns rested in the elevated position. Sinclair, a journalist, once interviewed Hitler. Photo: Vincent Holyoak.*

*Ready to go: Squadron Leader Keith Sinclair and flight engineer Paddy Traynor in the cockpit of 'Pregnant Winnie'. Note that their names are clearly lettered on their flying helmets – possibly a response to the theft of a flying helmet that contributed to the death of Keith Thiele's rear gunner over Berlin. Photo: Vincent Holyoak.*

totally committed to survival in the night skies over Germany. They knew the odds were against them but this was never discussed. They were well aware, of course, that Lancaster crew survival rates were poor.

This is a complex issue. Middlebrook analysed statistics concerning 607 aircraft written off during the 'Battle of Berlin' 1943-44 Winter raids. An average of 1.3 aircrew survived from the seven-man crews of the downed Lancasters, as against 1.8 in Stirlings and 2.45 in Halifaxes[12]. Yet aircrew flying in Halifaxes and Stirlings had a greater chance of dying, due to the higher casualty rates associated with those types. It seems clear, however, that the Lancaster was the most difficult of the three bomber types to leave in an emergency (almost certainly due to the position and height of the main spar across the fuselage)[13].

All too often there was simply no time to get out. An entire crew would perish in a catastrophic explosion or ride their aircraft down to oblivion, pinned inside by the centrifugal force. Many aircrew survived only because their aircraft broke up. Heavery's response was to organise frequent practice of the emergency drills, especially procedures for abandoning the aircraft:

*The rear gunner and mid-upper gunner would make for the rear door, having clipped on their chest-type parachute packs. The idea was to kneel on the step, curl into a tight ball and roll out head first. Hopefully, your head would go under the tail rather than smash into it. Given enough time, however, everyone would leave by the forward emergency hatch as this was safer. It was a Bomber Command tradition, of course, that the skipper was the last to leave the aircraft.*

German flak had a well-deserved reputation for deadly accuracy but fighters were the main threat. By this time a relatively small group of German nightfighter aces had emerged. The Luftwaffe adopted policies designed to reinforce success. A nightfighter pilot required extraordinary courage and skill. Early victories were recognised by greater personal freedom of action. The talented were permitted to pick the best nights to fly, so maximising their chances of gaining more victories[14]. A small, elite group of experten destroyed the flower of Bomber Command in 1943-44.

One expert, Peter Spoden, recalled that the nightfighter war was regarded by the elite as a 'crazy kind of sport'. The nightfighter pilot achieving his first kill would receive the Iron Cross First Class, followed by the Ehrenpokal (Cup of Honour) at four victories. The German Cross of Gold would be awarded at 10 kills and the Knight's Cross at 20 victories[15]. Evidence of the remarkable success of a top-scoring expert was exhibited in Hyde Park after the end of the war. One of Schnaufer's Bf110s attracted much attention, its tail fins covered with a display of 121 victories. One of the nightfighter's twin fins is now exhibited in the Imperial War Museum, London. Ironically, Schnaufer, the great survivor, was fated to die in a road crash in France during 1950. After escaping death in air combat he was killed by a French truck with faulty brakes[16].

*I feared the fighters more than the flak but both were highly efficient killers. I also hated the searchlights as they helped the flak and fighters. The guns, of*

*'That's Henderson, our rear gunner.' This cartoon was found amongst the late Ted Foster's papers. It was attributed to the Toronto Star but subsequent enquiries suggest this is incorrect.*

*course, were concentrated around the cities and in the coastal strip, but a fighter could appear at any time. We were very fortunate. We never had a fighter combat – a combination of sheer luck and our determination to stay out of trouble.*

*Fighters had many advantages, including a small profile, heavy armament and time enough to select the best approach for an attack. On one occasion, during the March 26 raid on Duisburg, Ken saw a Ju88 begin to approach us. There was some doubt about whether we were the fighter's intended target but Frank reacted immediately to Ken's warning. He put the Lanc into a flat turn, to avoid reflection from our wing surfaces. It soon became clear that the Ju88 was stalking another target. We moved into the dark zone and lost him.*

Heavery was right to be wary. The Ju88 C-6, for example, had a fearsome nose armament of three 20 mm cannon and three 7.9 mm machine guns. A three second burst delivered 81 cannon shells and 177machine gun rounds[17].

*After the Duisburg trip Ken and I reviewed our responses on sighting the Ju88. Did we act correctly? We brought Frank into the conversation and eventually concluded that we had done the right thing. There had been no shouting or panic. Frank's flat turn made it more difficult for the nightfighter to obtain a visual. Ted then came over. It was all news to him. He hadn't appreciated exactly what had happened, being fully occupied at the time. I smiled and told him: 'Don't worry mate. You're better off behind your curtain!'*

Later, 5 Group became increasingly worried about losses from fighters exploiting the blind spot below and experimented with a ventral machine gun. This required the removal of the H2S radar blister. The under-gun was given a trial by 61 Squadron. The arrangement required an eighth crew member and met with little success. Len Whitehead – who got to know Sidney Knott many years after the war, when they were both members of the Kent Branch of the Air Gunners' Association – made four trips as an under-gunner in late April-early May 1944.

Whitehead's tour began in December 1943. He completed 35 operations, amounting to an impressive 240 hours. Many of his sorties were trips to Berlin. When the tour finished, he became a Gunnery Leader at Swinderby. Len Whitehead told Sidney Knott that the under-gun was ineffective. The .5 machine gun, free-mounted on a swivel, protruded through a 2 ft 6 in diameter hole in the aircraft floor. It was intended that the under-gunner should sit on a seat only a few inches above the floor, with his back resting on the bomb-bay step, but this gave him no view directly underneath. It was then decided that the gunner should stand up, braced in a harness, to fire the weapon. In this position, his field of view was still very limited. This point was rammed home when Whitehead's 61 Squadron aircraft left a German target with one bomb hung-up in the bomb-bay. The bomb-aimer made his way back, determined to release it over Germany. The bomb doors were opened. He arrived at the inspection door panel, looked down and shouted 'Weave!'. This was his last word. Cannon shells ripped through the floor

and killed him. Yet he had saved the crew. He had seen a Schräge Musik nightfighter immediately below and about to open fire. Yet the gunners – including Len, with his limited view through the hole in the floor – had failed to spot the fighter.

Bomber Command, however, may have under-estimated the deterrent value of the ventral gun position. Major Schnaufer said he and his pilots had been warned about the under-gun in 1942. This had been a significant concern until it was found that aircraft with such gun mountings were few and far between (Appendix 3; 22).

> *It seemed to us that survival rested largely in our own hands. I don't know if it is possible to 'manufacture' luck but we certainly tried. Confidence was the key. Our confidence was built on the certain knowledge that every crew member knew exactly how to respond in an emergency.*
>
> *We knew how to cope if some of us were killed or wounded. One of our great strengths was the ability to cover for each other. We had four trained gunners: the two 'regulars' and two others, our wireless op and bomb aimer. I had an understanding with Ken. If I became a casualty he would leave the mid-upper position and replace me in the four-gun rear turret, assuming it was still operational. In turn, I had picked up the basics of navigation, while the bomb aimer knew how to control the fuel, the critical function of the flight engineer. Most importantly, the navigator could fly the Lanc if Frank became incapacitated. Ted couldn't land the aircraft but he could fly it to a point where we could bale out over friendly territory.*

By the time Heavery's crew had completed seven operations they had begun to acquire a casual air of experience that is difficult to define:

> *A few weeks later, when we had reached the half-way point in our tour, we were regarded as a very senior crew. Attitudes changed. We commanded respect and people picked our brains, recognising that we had survived, to some extent at least, through our professionalism. We had dealt with the intercom chit-chat. We also made it more difficult for flak and fighters by constantly changing height and weaving. At the personal level I had developed a keen instinct for knowing when trouble was brewing.*

# CHAPTER EIGHT

# *'This Stuff is All Around Us!'*

DURING March 1943 Heavery's crew switched from B to C Flight. The squadron had started life with two Flights, each of eight aircraft. Flight Commanders were expected to maintain six Lancasters serviceable and ready for operations at all times. Since the squadron's formation additional aircraft had arrived and the third Flight was formed.

Heavery's crew got into their stride as the Battle of the Ruhr opened. This was the first of three major campaigns fought by Bomber Command (the others being Hamburg and Berlin). Aircrew, with a fine sense of irony, called the Ruhr 'Happy Valley'. The only 'happy' factor associated with a Ruhr target was the relatively short trip. For too many crews it was extremely short – being one way only. The Ruhr gun and searchlight belts were around 20 miles thick and the defences had a well-deserved reputation for excellence.

There were 43 major raids on German targets during the Battle of the Ruhr period (with just over half the targets actually in the Ruhr). These attacks amounted to 18,506 sorties. Happy Valley became a Bomber Command graveyard. The campaign cost 872 aircraft and a further 2,126 bombers damaged. The loss rate over the near five-month Battle of the Ruhr averaged 4.7 per cent[1].

*March 1943 was very busy. We made nine trips in all, including three to the Ruhr – two to Essen and one to Duisburg. We also bombed Berlin three times, visited Hamburg and made two deep penetrations, to Nuremberg and Munich. The pace was punishing but we managed to squeeze in some leave during the month. Operational aircrew received six days' leave around every six weeks.*

The March 1 flight to Berlin in T-Tommy (ED524) set the tempo for the rest of the month. The crew dropped a Cookie and 10 cans, returning to Bottesford after a flight of seven hours 10 minutes. Hamburg followed on March 3, this time in M-Mother (ED547). The Lancaster carried a Cookie and 12 cans – the closer target permitting a slight increase in bomb-load.

On Friday March 5 Heavery's crew once again filed into the briefing room, already filling with the blue mist of cigarette smoke. They listened quietly as the Intelligence Officer gave his appraisal of Essen, the 'target for tonight'. A total of 442 Bomber Command aircraft opened the Battle of the Ruhr that night. The Ruhr campaign was to continue until July 24.

Heavery's crew – flying M-Mother once again – contributed a Cookie and 12 SBCs (containing a total of 1,080 4lb incendiaries). They were back at Bottesford just before midnight, their ninth operation safely completed. Others were less fortunate. Sixteen aircraft were written off (3.6 per cent of the attacking force). The results of this raid were encouraging, however, with heavy damage across 160 acres of the city. Some 53 buildings within the Krupps complex were hit and more than 3,000 homes were destroyed. Over 450 people died[2]. Photo reconnaissance indicated that around half of all bombs fell within one mile of the aiming point and that about 30 per cent of Krupps had suffered significant damage. Eight 109 Squadron Oboe-equipped Mosquitos laid a 15-mile long approach path of yellow markers leading to the target, the very centre of Krupps[3]. The first red target indicators were dropped over the target at 20.58. The flak was heavy and many aircraft suffered damage over the target[4].

The crew's fatigue level soared after the next two raids, long hauls to Nuremberg and Munich. Each trip exceeded seven hours and they were flown on consecutive nights (March 8/9 and 9/10). The crew took M-Mother to both targets. Nine aircraft failed to return from Nuremberg and eight from Munich. During the Munich attack the flak batteries fired over 14,000 rounds[5].

Heavery kept quiet when the March 5 target was revealed. He had no wish to disturb his crew by talking about his first operational trip flown as second dicky with another crew and with Essen as the destination. His

*Fatal rendezvous with Düsseldorf: the crew of C Flight's Jack Parsons (seated, left). Parsons and two of his crew died on the night of May 25/26 1943. Photo: Vincent Holyoak.*

skipper on that sortie had been Squadron Leader Thiele, the highly-decorated New Zealander who would shortly form and command C Flight, 467 Squadron. Keith Thiele, 22, was on his second tour. He had avoided posting as an instructor, in a successful bid to continue operational flying[6]. Another 467 Lancaster Captain, Bill Manifold, said the squadron regarded him as 'indestructible'[7]. Thiele was to be awarded the DSO in May.

> *Frank might have been to Essen before, but this target was new to us and it turned out to be just as unpleasant as anticipated. The city appeared to have grown a roof of exploding flak. Mosquitos dropped red TIs, followed by PFF heavies dropping greens. Somehow, once again, we came through safely, although a shell fragment cracked our Lanc's windscreen. While glad to get back we found that the first aircraft to return to Bottesford had crashed on landing, blocking the main runway. We diverted to nearby Swinderby, just to the north, where a long queue for landing had developed. After a miserable few hours at this base, including a poor breakfast of Spam and fried potato, we flew back to Bottesford – only to be briefed for an immediate return to Essen. This idea gave everyone dyspepsia! Fortunately the attack was scrubbed at the last moment, just as our Lancasters were lining up for take-off. 'Scrub nights' triggered hard drinking and boisterous behaviour, if we could summon up the energy. We sent Ken on ahead to the Mess bar, with instructions to set up the drinks. His job was to line up the beers before the rush, while we looked after his kit.*

*Berlin, March 1/2 1943: the chaotic scene over the city during Bomber Command's attack. This oblique shows smoke drifting from fires in the Steglitz area (A) and a concentration of fires around the Tempelhof marshalling yards (B). Photo: Trustees of the Imperial War Museum.*

*On its formation the squadron had been stiffened by one or two experienced crews posted in towards the end of their tours, but the rest were novices. Only a few weeks later we now ranked as experienced, with nine trips. It was after the March 5 sortie to Essen that attitudes towards us began to change. People talked to us – and about us – and we were approached for advice. Most ground crews knew Heavery. I was never known by my own name, but as 'Heavery's rear gunner'. It was the same for the others. The skipper gave us new identities.*

In March Group Captain William McKechnie, GC, succeeded Ferdie Swain as Bottesford's Station Commander. McKechnie won the Albert Medal while a Cranwell cadet. He had rescued a fellow cadet from a

*'Indestructible': Squadron Leader Keith Thiele took command of C Flight, 467 Squadron.*
*Photo: Vincent Holyoak.*

crashed and burning aircraft.

McKechnie had an informal style. He was happy to tolerate the energetic V-signs from aircrew as he waved them off[8]. On the debit side McKechnie suffered severely from air sickness and, therefore, was unpopular as a flying companion[9].

On one occasion, in February the following year, Bottesford Intelligence Officer Marie Cooper joined McKechnie for a flight to Edinburgh in a Tiger Moth. The aircraft circled repeatedly. Marie assumed the Group Captain was searching for pinpoints on his map. In fact, he was busy vomiting over the side of the biplane's open cockpit. His face had turned pale green by the time the Tiger Moth had landed. On boarding the bus for the city, he then confessed to having no money on him. Marie ended up paying both fares[10].

Other events during March included Air Vice-Marshal Cochrane's unannounced visit to Bottesford. The 5 Group AOC was sitting in the debriefing room as the first of 467's tired crews filed in from a raid:

> We were taken aback to see Cochrane in the room and shocked when he rose from his chair and shook hands all round. He'd had a good look at Frank as he ambled in, in his typically casual way. Our skipper always had a tendency to walk with a bit of a sway, even without the beer. Cochrane looked Frank in the eye and said: 'You look as though you've just taken the dog for a walk'. Some dog! A wolf, perhaps? Anyway, a Lanc with a Cookie and over 1,000 incendiaries was certainly a very dangerous animal.

On Friday March 12, exactly a week after their first visit to Essen and with Nuremberg and Munich also behind them, Heavery's crew took their chairs in the briefing room in Bottesford's shabby headquarters block. As usual, strict security measures prevailed. The station was sealed off from the outside world. No-one was allowed to leave the base and all telephone boxes were padlocked. No calls were permitted.

As the air war grew in intensity and complexity the briefings became more sophisticated. Bottesford's Intelligence Section was headed by a Welshman, Squadron Leader Hewitt. The Intelligence staff had a rich mix of characters: a former West End actor, a 'country gentleman' Flight Lieutenant, a friend of Gomm's known as 'Latin American Joe' and two Section Officers – Marie Cooper (an archaeologist before the war) and Anglo-Irish Paula Fisher. 'Paul', relatively new to Intelligence work, was very attractive and became the Squadron Commander's girlfriend[10].

> The navigators' briefing usually took place an hour or more before the main briefing. Consequently, Ted was already seated at our usual place. Frank led the way as we joined Foster. The skipper sat next to Ted, stared hard at the big wall map and then glanced over his navigator's charts. Many other eyes followed the tapes leading to the night's target and this prompted subdued yet clearly audible groans. We were less than thrilled at the prospect of returning to Essen, the most heavily defended target in the central Ruhr valley. This was western Germany's industrial heart. The briefing followed the usual pattern – an appraisal of the target and information on weather, timings, route markers and the target-marking plan.

*Our Lanc for the night, Q-Queenie (ED500), had been bombed up and now awaited us on the dispersal pan. We took off on our twelfth operation at 19.25 with a Cookie and 12 cans in the bomb-bay.*

A total of 457 aircraft were readied for this raid. The attack was delivered by 156 Lancasters, 91 Halifaxes, 42 Stirlings, 158 Wellingtons and 10 Mosquitos. Twenty-three aircraft failed to return – five per cent of the force[11]. Twenty-five aircraft were written off that night (*Chorley, Bomber Command Losses, 1943*).

*As we neared the end of the outward leg Frank's steady voice came over the intercom. He asked Ted for our ETA at the target. Before Ted could reply, however, Essen's defences woke up with a vengeance. Searchlight beams instantly illuminated a huge area of sky around us. It was as though someone had flicked on a light switch. Initially, there was very little flak. Perhaps the fighters were around? We always favoured staying well within the bomber stream, believing in safety in numbers. Flak and fighters loved stragglers.*

*The aim was to pass some 450 bombers over the target in the shortest possible time, with the raid commencing at the specified zero time for the dropping of the first markers. Each aircraft had a 'zero time plus' to bomb. Every bomber had a designated height, with the Lancasters concentrated in the 18,000-20,000 ft band, the Halifaxes some 2,000 ft lower and the Wellingtons at around 14,000 ft. The Wellingtons were timed to go through after the higher flying aircraft, but I often saw them directly below as the Lancasters and Halifaxes began dropping their loads.*

This developed into another successful attack against Essen, largely thanks to Oboe. The bombing was concentrated on Krupps. It received 30 per cent more damage than in the raid a week earlier[11].

*Here we go again! Q-Queenie continued over the Ruhr valley at around 18,000 ft – our specified bombing height. Frank finally got a reply to his earlier*

*Cheers: four of the six 467 Squadron stalwarts would not survive operations at Bottesford. Pictured (left to right) are: Mess landlord Jock Murray, Cosme Gomm, Keith Thiele, Group Captain McKechnie, Don MacKenzie and 'Ray' Raphael. Photo: Vincent Holyoak.*

question. I heard Ted say: 'Ten minutes to target. The early markers should show in eight minutes.' The view from the rear turret was impressive, with flak and searchlights everywhere. Someone – I can't remember who – muttered quietly into the intercom: 'This stuff is all around us!'

Our track on the run-in was north-south. We almost always attacked Essen from this direction in the hope of seeing the Rhine, but I couldn't see much through the thick Ruhr haze. I heard the bomb-aimer report: 'Markers – well ahead.' Nick then took control of the Lanc, guiding Frank onto the target and aiming point. This raid was going like clockwork. The Oboe PFF aircraft had marked accurately and Essen was about to be clobbered.

Things happened quickly. Nick gave his final instructions and I felt the aircraft jump as our bombs fell at 21.36. The release system dropped them at half second intervals. Then we stayed on track for long seconds, waiting for the photoflash. There was a sudden dull thud and the aircraft shook itself. I smelt cordite as we flew through the shell burst. The gunners below had our height! As the bomb doors closed my turret flooded with white light as a searchlight crossed our track. Once out of the beam the turret interior glowed a dim orange from the fires below. Then a newly-laid belt of fighter flares became visible.

I looked down and saw the photoflash detonate, followed instantly by the blast wave from our Cookie – or someone else's. It mushroomed across the ground in a second. There was enough light below to see many other bombers overflying the target at various heights. It was a picture of pure chaos. Some aircraft in

*After the show: relaxing in Bottesford's Officers' Mess after an ENSA concert. Pictured (left to right) are: Pilot Officer Ciano, Flight Lieutenant Davis, Squadron Leader Hewitt, Section Officer Betty Davies, Squadron Leader MacKenzie (and his dog, Prinny), Section Officer Paula Fisher and (far right) Bill Manifold. Photo: Vincent Holyoak.*

*close view were on their bombing runs, with bomb doors open. I then spotted an aircraft with flames streaming back. Inside, seven men were fighting for their lives. I could picture their struggle to bale out. I wouldn't fancy jumping over this target and dropping into an inferno. Desperate civilians needed no further excuse to turn into a lynch mob.*

*I continued to search for fighters as Frank reacted to Nick's confirmation that we now had our photo. The Lanc's nose went down and the throttles were opened. We didn't hang around! It was a long way into Essen and it took even longer to get out. The skipper eased Q-Queenie out of the dive and Ted gave him a new course. We were making for the dark zone beyond Essen but it seemed very far away. The sky over the target was almost as bright as day. I saw another aircraft going down, trailing fire. A huge ball of flame then erupted to one side of our aircraft. Was that a direct hit on a bomber flying alongside? Only a few seconds later Nick reported that we had left the flak behind. This probably meant we had entered a fighter patrol area. The contrast between the fireworks and nothing made me very uneasy. It was far too quiet. Ken and I continued to work our turrets in search of nightfighters. It was tempting to relax at this point, with the bombs gone and the target behind us. That could be fatal. We had to negotiate several busy fighter beacons before reaching the coast.*

Heavery followed the instructions given at the briefing, delivered just a few hours before in a quiet room, in another world:

*As soon as we were clear of the German hills the skipper put the nose down once again and dived to an unusually low level – around 500 feet – in an effort to outsmart the defences. We then went lower still, right down on the deck. Our Lanc flashed across the dark landscape and crossed into Holland. Nick*

*Devastation on the ground: Krupp's factories burnt out and flattened by raids on Essen. This photograph was taken in April 1945. Krupps occupied an area of 2.5 miles by 1,500 yards. Photo: Trustees of the Imperial War Museum.*

*went into the front turret to watch for masts, pylons and barrage balloons. The aircraft roared along, the flat countryside rolling away at great speed.*

*I heard Nick report a town coming up to port. He was still speaking when our Lanc was hosed with tracer. We were surrounded by streamers of light flak and illuminated by searchlights. I gave the defences 600 rounds from my Brownings, in the hope of spoiling their aim. It was over in seconds and Nick warned Frank that the coast was fast approaching. The skipper responded by diving lower still, to just above tree height. The beach zipped past and we were soon out to sea and able to climb to a safer height. Frank asked everyone to report in. We had no damage and Queenie was going strong.*

*Later, when discussing our adventures at debriefing, we concluded that Queenie had clipped The Hague defences instead of crossing the coast a little further north at Noordwijk.*

The rest of the homeward flight was uneventful and the crew were relieved to pick up Bottesford's beacon. Heavery put the Lanc into position above the bottom of the circuit. The usual height was 4,000 ft but if the cloud base was lower the aircraft were positioned just underneath. It was time to break radio silence – always strictly observed from take-off to arrival over base after an operation. Heavery used the base call-sign: 'Babette. Q-Queenie.' This was the first indication that we had survived the night. Flying Control knew Heavery was back. The crew waited for the WAAF's sweet response: 'Q-Queenie, circuit 25.' The skipper had been instructed to hold at 2,500 ft. He then received the QFE (barometric pressure at Bottesford), allowing him to adjust the altimeter to take account of changes since take-off.

There were three Lancasters ahead of Q-Queenie and waiting to land:

*Normally, the circuit was flown anti-clockwise, with aircraft descending progressively as others landed. The exception applied when circuits overlapped, due to the close proximity of two airfields. By flying one circuit clockwise and the other anti-clockwise, all aircraft flew in the same direction within the area of overlap.*

*Our procedures produced a landing every two minutes. As one aircraft reported 'Runway clear', the next would declare 'Funnels' (final approach). At that point the following aircraft would be approaching downwind, with the one after that on the upwind leg. Adjustments were made by widening or shortening the circuit. Following a large raid, hundreds of aircraft wanted to get down as quickly as possible. With so many aircraft in the air, heading for their bases, the skies were very congested and the danger of collision was ever-present for homecoming crews.*

*I heard Frank report our progress: 'Q-Queenie – downwind' (as the undercarriage was lowered, together with a little flap), followed by the crosswind leg and the crisp words 'Q-Queenie – funnels'. Until the aircraft in front could be seen all R/T instructions were followed to the letter. Q-Queenie settled into the approach and Frank checked the threshold lights. Two greens indicated correct height; ambers meant too high and reds, too low. Frank lined up the Lanc and waited for confirmation that the aircraft in front had cleared the runway. He was ready to go round again should the runway be obstructed.*

*These final minutes demanded immense concentration. It was important to get it right as battle damage could make it dangerous to go round again. Any ungentlemanly attempt to jump the queue caused great offence. One well-known dodge was to call up for a slot while still some distance from the airfield – in effect, taking a theoretical place in the queue for landing. Those who broke radio silence while still too far out would be invited to visit the Squadron Commander and explain themselves.*

*Safely back: B Flight Commander 'Pappy' Paape does the paperwork as Section Officer Paula Fisher debriefs the crew. Photo: Vincent Holyoak.*

Communications priorities included SOS, a general broadcast (not to a specific station) from an aircraft that would be forced to land within 15 minutes (with the following letter codes: F, due to fighter attack; A, due to anti-aircraft fire; and M, due to mechanical trouble). A 'P' signal could be sent by an aircraft with a 45-minute endurance or a dud engine. Throughout the landing procedure pilots had to be ready to give way to aircraft in distress or with casualties. This convention is said to have led to the development of a very slick trick. Ted Foster told Knott about such a case, during a discussion long after the end of the war[12].

*Ted said it happened during his second tour, with 227 Squadron. They were returning from a raid on a synthetic oil target when fog closed many English airfields and aircraft were diverted to Scottish bases. It had been a long haul, fuel reserves were low and everyone was anxious to get down. While circling the diversion airfield, attempting to establish his place in the queue, Ted's skipper was browned off to hear that an aircraft coming in on two engines had received priority. The pilots flying the other Lancasters, also low on fuel, cursed their luck. Later, they were ready to lynch the skipper of that aircraft 'coming in on*

'Spare bod': Flight Sergeant 'Mac' McGalloway took Nick Murray's place as bomb-aimer on the Heavery crew's flight to Duisburg on March 26. McGalloway was a member of Pilot Officer Alan Fisher's crew. Photo: Vincent Holyoak.

two engines', when they discovered it was a twin-engined Wellington. As Ted well knew, of course, this is just one of a large number of popular jokes and 'Mess stories' told and re-told at Bomber Command stations during the war years and not to be taken too seriously.

One WAAF at Flying Control had the most wonderful voice. She became the spirit of Bottesford. Whenever I heard her voice, at the end of an operation, I felt elated. After the war I came close to naming our first child 'Babette'. My wife, however, objected strongly to the idea of naming a baby girl after a bomber station call-sign. Today, Jean (with a grown-up family of her own) is grateful I saw sense and relented.

Safely down, Q-Queenie taxied to dispersal and the engines fell silent. Moving slowly with stiff limbs, the crew climbed out of the aircraft and found their lift to the Locker Room. They knew it was important to take good care of their flying kit:

*The electrically heated suit was vulnerable. It had to be kept bone dry. Any moisture could cause an electrical short and leave a limb to freeze. Frostbite was inevitable if the suit developed a problem. We did things properly on the ground as well as in the air. Any slack behaviour on the ground could turn into a killer in the aircraft. Parachutes were an obvious focus of attention. The Parachute Section informed the Flight Office whenever a particular chute was due for re-packing. Occasionally, a D-ring (ripcord handle) was pulled in error. This meant an embarrassing visit to the Parachute Section and the traditional payment of a ten shilling fine. It happened to me once – bloody fool! I was tired, became clumsy and allowed the ring to catch an obstruction. Out came the silk.*

With their kit stowed the crew made their way to the debriefing:

*There were two entrances to station headquarters. Officers used the front door. NCOs used the side door. This custom was set aside at Bottesford (and many other stations) when aircrew returned from ops. Sergeants walked through the front door for the debrief, enjoying this implicit recognition of their worth.*

No matter how tired the crew, their attendance at debrief was mandatory. Beyond helping in the general assessment of the raid's effectiveness, a well-conducted debrief revealed many specific details while the crews' experiences were still fresh in their minds. The information sought ranged from new developments in German defences and tactics to the accuracy of the weather forecast given immediately prior to the raid.

*We tried to get through the debrief as quickly as possible. It stood in the way of our flying meal in the Mess and, finally, bed. We were really organised by this stage. There was no question of hanging about, talking to other crews, and we didn't bother trying to unwind. Nothing worked! The best plan was to tuck into the meal and get some sleep, if possible.*

*Essen was a relatively short trip of four hours 15 minutes. We landed at 23.40. After the meal we walked back to the billets. Everything seemed at peace and it was a clear, starry night. When inside the room I glanced at my watch. It was 02.00. It had been a 'short day' but had started at 09.30 yesterday. No wonder our days seemed to merge together!*

*Sprawled on the bed, I studied the ceiling and mulled over the past two weeks. Since February 25, when we first flew to Nuremberg, we had completed a further eight trips. Another three operations had been scrubbed following considerable preparation and much expenditure of nervous energy. We had completed six trips so far in March and we were only on the thirteenth of the month! One of my worst moments occurred when a trip was scrubbed at the very last moment, with the Lancasters on the peritrack as the red Very light soared above Flying Control. The anti-climax was appalling.*

*Later, after a few hours' sleep, Ted woke me with his usual: 'C'mon, C'mon, C'mon!' He wanted lunch. After the meal I made my way to the Flight Office and was pleasantly surprised to find we were not required that night. We could have a real rest. Before long Ted urged us to head for the*

*Mess again. He wanted tea. We sat around afterwards in the anteroom, waiting for the bar to open. The room began to fill and small groups formed as crews swapped stories. One distinctive aspect of life on an operational squadron was the isolation of each crew. They took off on the same raid and returned with very different experiences. Everyone had his story to tell and every story was different.*

*Ted and I had a couple of drinks and returned to the billet, while Frank and Ken had a few more. We stepped outside into the dark, clear night. As Ted and I strolled back to the Nissen hut he continued my education. Ted had been teaching me about cloud formations and stars. I was keen enough and it certainly passed the time on those long, cold Winter walks to our hut. The evocative star names – such as Regulus and Canopus – remain fresh in my mind to this day.*

The pressure eased during the second half of March. Heavery's name appeared on the squadron Battle Order on just three occasions. They should have made four trips. On Sunday March 14 they were airborne in Q-Queenie for a half-hour night flying test but the intended operation was scrubbed – producing the usual mix of relief and stress. In his honest and sober account of life on an operational bomber squadron, Don Charlwood (*No moon tonight*) reflected: 'To live until his next leave became the greatest hope of each man[13].' Heavery's crew went on leave the following morning:

*Nick was at a disadvantage. Our bomb aimer's tortuous journey to Belfast and back swallowed some 36 hours of his precious few days away. He made his way north by slow wartime trains to Stranraer, then boarded the ferry. Inevitably, he was back late on one occasion (through no fault of his own) and we flew with a 'spare bod' bomb aimer, Flight Sergeant J 'Mac' McGalloway.*

It may have been during this leave that a curious incident entered Bottesford's folklore. The Lancasters were formed up on the peritrack, waiting to go, when a fox darted across the line of aircraft, followed closely by the Belvoir Hunt. The scarlet-clad riders charged across the runway, oblivious to the needs of war and ignorant of the obscenities over the intercom from Lancaster captains concerned about overheated engines[8].

The crew – minus Murray – re-assembled at Bottesford. During their absence, on March 22, the squadron had operated against St. Nazaire. There was bright moonlight and good visibility over the target, but thick cloud covered the bomber bases on the return and some crews were diverted north, to Lossiemouth. Pilot Officer Hooper had a close call. He was told to land downwind and ran off the end of the runway[8].

Heavery's crew flew again on Friday March 26, when they took O-Orange (ED530) on a visit to the important Ruhr target of Duisburg. With the help of McGalloway, Nick Murray's stand-in, they dropped a Cookie and 12 cans of incendiaries. O-Orange was one of 455 bombers raiding the city that night. Six failed to return. The bombing results were disappointing due to technical problems among the small force of Mosquito markers[14]:

*March concluded with a sortie to Berlin the next night, followed by a day's rest then a return to the Big City on the 29th – our last trip of the month being*

*flown in J-Jig (ED695).*

The first of the Berlin attacks was a failure due to inaccurate marking. Nevertheless, many bombs fortuitously hit an important Luftwaffe stores complex hidden in a wood. Nine aircraft failed to return. The second raid fell foul of weather difficulties and, once again, the results were poor[14]. In all, 26 aircraft were struck off charge that night.

The first of the late March Berlin trips produced an unpleasant surprise for Heavery's crew:

*Running up: a 467 Squadron Lancaster shortly before departure. An operation could be scrubbed at the very last moment. Photo: Vincent Holyoak.*

> *We were about to begin our bombing run, with the markers in sight, when all four Merlins spluttered and died. It is hard to imagine a more frightening scenario – over the Big City with no engines! Frank diagnosed the problem as petrol starvation and invited Jock to check the fuel gauges and tank selector cocks. The Lancaster had six fuel tanks. We took off using the two No. 2 tanks between the inner and outer engines, then switched to the No. 1 tanks between the fuselage and the inner engines. Fuel was then pumped from the No. 3 tanks (each holding 114 gallons) to top up the No.2 tanks. While over enemy territory, the flight engineer was supposed to keep the contents of the Nos. 1 and 2 tanks roughly equal by running on each for*

around half an hour at a time. In all the excitement, the flight engineer had failed to switch back to the inboard tanks. He moved fast at the controls and the welcome sound of four Merlins returned. This problem took long seconds to fix. In order to reach his panel, which was located behind him, the engineer had to stand up, fold his seat away, unplug the intercom, do the necessary and then reverse these actions. I recall this example of bad timing as our worst attack by 'Gremlins', the mischievous creatures who haunt all RAF aircraft with the express purpose of terrifying innocent aircrew. If all four engines are to cut, why not ensure it happens over the centre of Berlin?

In March 1943 467 Squadron dispatched 112 aircraft against 12 targets and one crew failed to return (Pilot Officer Mant)[15]. Within a few months the squadron had become firmly established. In The Avro Lancaster, Francis Mason wrote of 467 Squadron in March 1943: 'With three months of Lancaster operations behind it, the squadron was steadily building a very good reputation for reliability and efficiency, with a lot of 'press on' spirit among the crews[16].'

During Monday March 29 the Press descended on Bottesford as preparations for the return to Berlin were under way:

> The Press party included a Daily Sketch photographer. He took photos of 467 Squadron crews preparing for the night's attack. Many of the photos were taken outside the Flight Offices, with people standing around enjoying a cigarette, clutching their flight rations or adjusting their flying clothing. The Daily Sketch must have regarded our skipper as especially photogenic. They took group photos but Frank's face was singled out and printed very large in the newspaper, opposite a photo of First World War hero Albert Ball, VC. Fortunately for Frank, he was not named but described in the caption as 'an unknown hero of this war'. This is a rare example of entirely accurate newspaper reporting.

From the earliest days of the war Bomber Command had engaged

*Outside the Flight Office: crews ready for transport to their aircraft for the March 29 Berlin attack. Three members of the Heavery crew are pictured. Third from the right is the skipper, Frank Heavery. Immediately left, with a cigarette on, is mid-upper gunner Ken Butterworth. On the far right is wireless op Johnny Lloyd. Between Lloyd and Heavery is Flying Officer Cazaly, Flight Lieutenant Desmond's mid-upper gunner. Cazaly had only eight weeks to live when this photograph was taken. Photo: Sidney Knott*

in 'Nickelling' – dropping propaganda leaflets (initially leaflets only, but now usually accompanied by a full bomb-load). Some leaflets were designed to boost morale in the occupied countries. Those dropped over Germany were rather gruesome – featuring dead German soldiers and prisoners of war. This was supposed to undermine morale. On the occasion of the March 29 Berlin attack, a different approach was tried.

It was well known that crews often kept examples of leaflets as souvenirs:

*At the briefing, we were warned that these leaflets were top secret and that the bundles were not to be tampered with. The packages were handed to the bomb-aimers by Intelligence Officers. They were then told that, on landing back, they were to check that no copies were left before the aircraft taxied to dispersal. Nick was curious and kept a few examples. We then discovered that we had been carrying thousands of sheets of counterfeit German emergency ration coupons. They looked extremely authentic, covered with the Berlin stamp. This novel form of economic warfare subsequently led to German claims that we had breached the Geneva Convention. The British Government stoutly denied all knowledge of the affair.*

CHAPTER NINE

# The Hardest Month

A PRIL 1943 was the hardest month for Heavery's crew. The physical
and mental strain increased day by day. They had made one trip in
January and five in February, followed by nine in March – three to Berlin
and six to other heavily defended German targets. Another nine
operations were to follow in April. During March the crew logged 56
hours of operational flying. This was exceeded in April, with a punishing
total of 62 hours 45 minutes.

The psychological stress was offset, to some extent, by the anaesthesia
of sheer exhaustion. The month included three consecutive trips of nine
hours or more. These marathons left the Heavery crew's rear gunner
with a physical problem. Prostrate on his bed, Sidney Knott found his
eyes refused to shut. His body was in the Nissen hut but his eyes were still
in the turret, quartering the night sky for fighters.

*We started the new month with an attack on Essen on Saturday April 3. We
took off at 19.35 in J-Jig (ED695) – our second op in this aircraft. This was
to be our third visit to a target widely regarded as the most heavily defended in
Europe. I consoled myself with the thought that J-Jig had brought us back safely
from Berlin only a few days before. In my view, the Big City was just as bad as
Essen. Our bomb-bay held a 4,000 lb blast bomb and 12 cans (each holding 90
4 lb incendiaries) for Essen's war industries.*

Heavery touched down at Bottesford at 00.50 after five hours 15
minutes in the air. Essen, as always, had been a sobering experience.
Knott and Butterworth had seen four bombers go down over the target.

A total of 348 aircraft were dispatched and 317 attacked the home of
Krupps. The Main Force included 225 Lancasters; nine failed to return,
together with 12 Halifaxes. The bombing was accurate and over 600
buildings were destroyed[1]. Sadly, the British losses included the aircraft
of Squadron Leader AM Paape, DFC and Bar, 467's outstanding B Flight
Commander. This was a loss the squadron could ill-afford. Paape, an
experienced New Zealander, died in T-Tommy (ED524) on the
eighteenth trip of his second tour.

The mood was recalled by Intelligence Officer Marie Cooper: 'I don't
think any of us doubted that we would eventually win the war, but when
and at what cost? The unknown future became a blank. Here and now
took over[2].'

Paape and A Flight Commander Dave Green were former 207 Squadron Manchester pilots. This squadron had occupied Bottesford prior to 467's arrival[3]. Paape, however, had flown his first tour with 207 at Waddington, while Green was on his second tour from Bottesford[4]. Paape always claimed that his technique on approaching the target was simplicity itself: he switched to 'George' (the autopilot) and closed his eyes[5].

On the Sunday morning, after a few hours' rest, Heavery called in at C Flight's Office. He studied the board and found he was on the Battle Order once again. Kiel was the target. At the dispersal F-Freddie (ED737) awaited them. It had a full bomb-bay – a Cookie and 12 cans. Bomber Command sent 577 aircraft to this major port and naval base but the results were disappointing. Marking was difficult, due to cloud cover and strong winds, and little damage was done. Twenty-six people died on the ground; many more were killed in the attacking aircraft – 12 bombers failed to return that night[1]. A total of 14 aircraft were struck off charge.

Heavery's aircraft arrived back at 02.45 after five hours 50 minutes in the air. Knott craved a rest:

*After two nights on ops we expected the day off. Our squadron, together with many others, tried to follow this practice unless a 'maximum effort' was ordered. Then everyone had to fly, tired or not. In the event we were lucky and rested until Thursday due to bad weather.*

The three Lancaster pilots looked at each other in surprise when told to ready their aircraft for a formation flying practice on Thursday

*Swapping stories: the scene at one of Bottesford's dispersal pans. This is Squadron Leader MacKenzie's crew. Photo: Vincent Holyoak.*

morning. The flight included air-to-sea firing. Rumours spread, with the crews suspecting that a special, low level daylight raid was planned. They were accustomed to the mantle of darkness and found this prospect unwelcome:

*Training never stopped but daylight formation flying was very unusual. We set off in ED772 at 11.15, accompanied by two other experienced crews. Flying in close formation – a novel experience for all concerned – we headed for the coast and found our sea target. I logged 300 rounds fired. We were a little apprehensive about what might come next but we didn't let it ruin our appetite. We landed back just in time for a late lunch. I never discovered the reason for the formation practice and that night (and the rest of the month) continued with the usual night flying.*

*Promoting 'Wings for Victory': Bill Manifold's crew at Bottesford in February 1943. Pictured (left to right) are: mid-upper gunner Eric Rosie, bomb aimer Austin Brown, wireless op Harold Hernaman, pilot Bill Manifold, navigator Tom Moppett, rear gunner George Currie and flight engineer Fred Jarvis. Photo: Vincent Holyoak.*

Bill Manifold, a 467 Squadron Lancaster Captain at that time, offered a more pedestrian explanation for the formation flying. It appears that he and Stu Hooper captained the two Lancasters accompanying Heavery's aircraft. Manifold and Knott have the same flight time logged (one hour 35 minutes). According to Manifold the main purpose of the daylight formation flight was nothing more sinister than a promotion for the 'Wings for Victory' savings campaign[6]. Manifold later referred to a contemporary report recording that Wings for Victory weeks in the March-June 1943 period raised an impressive £615 million[7].

*On our return from formation flying Frank announced that the day's main briefing was fixed for 17.00. We were allocated V-Victor (ED621) for the raid. This Lanc was brand new, having arrived on the Squadron just over two weeks*

*before, and it proved to be something of a racehorse. Frank galloped it up to 23,000 ft over the target that night. He did even better without the bombs and attained a remarkable 25,000 ft plus on the return.*

*We kept busy during the day. Ken and I went out to the dispersal pan, to inspect V-Victor's turrets and guns. We made ourselves known to the Flight Sergeant and climbed into the aircraft. Slipping over the rear spar, I had a close look around the turret. Moving back into the fuselage I checked the ammunition belts and confirmed that everything was clean. The belts were laid correctly, to run freely in the ducts. Our armourers worked to a high standard but any dirt in the ducts could cause a stoppage at the very moment deciding life or death. I preferred to satisfy myself that all was well.*

*I made sure the turret floor was clean and dry. When it rained water collected on the floor if the ground crew failed to cover the turret in good time. This froze during the climb to operating height. I also gave the surviving perspex a last polish and wiped away any dampness on the ammunition. The next job was to check the hydraulics to ensure the system was free of air. Ken continued working at his position in the mid-upper turret. When satisfied with his two guns he repeated the routine in the front turret.*

*The navigators' briefing was already under way. Ted was accompanied by our bomb aimer. Nick Murray, a Blenheim navigator prior to joining the heavy brigade, was now our 'second navigator'. He was available to give Ted a hand when required or to take over should he be hit. This briefing took place earlier than the main briefing, in order to give the navigators enough time to study the routes in and out and prepare their charts.*

*Later, on entering the briefing room, we discovered our destination was heavily defended Duisburg, yet another Ruhr target. With the main briefing over we met up for our pre-flight meal at 18.15. We were down at the Flight an hour after the meal, having collected our kit. Our pockets were emptied of all personal items. Nothing of a personal nature could be taken on an op. Letters, even a cinema ticket, might be of use to German Intelligence. The idea was to arrive by around 20.15, no later than half an hour or so before take-off. Frank walked slowly around the aircraft, checking the tyres for creep and ensuring all locking tabs were removed from the control surfaces.*

*This op took just over six hours. We dropped the usual load: a Cookie and 12 cans, scattering more than 1,000 incendiaries over Duisburg. As each Small Bomb Container fired electronically, the incendiaries were freed and fluttered briefly before settling on the nose, where the weight was concentrated.*

The crew arrived back from Duisburg at 02.55 on Friday April 9. It had been a long day – around 20 hours by the time they finally got to bed at 05.30. At that point they had completed 18 trips and flown nine different aircraft on operations. Many crews found themselves expected to fly whatever aircraft were available:

*We never thought of a particular Lancaster as 'ours' and there was always an element of the unknown when taking an unfamiliar Lanc on ops. Aircraft may be mass-produced but there are tremendous differences in their flying qualities. One aircraft on 467's strength, for example, had a twisted airframe. It preferred to fly in an alarming, crab-like fashion. Great care was needed when taking off and landing in this unhappy machine.*

*Another Lanc with a problem had a violent tail wheel shimmy. This shook the aircraft from nose to tail. On take-off, the idea was to lift the tail wheel as quickly as possible and, when landing, to do the opposite and hold it off. It wasn't very pleasant. It felt as though the tail could break away at any moment. We were told there was nothing to be done about it, but I noticed that later aircraft had larger tail wheels (Modification 696). Perhaps this was the answer.*

Bill Manifold had a different recollection of 467's practice concerning the allocation of aircraft: 'The squadron had some excellent policies and one of these was that a crew should stick, as far as possible, to its own machine. It seemed such an eminently sensible idea that it came as quite a surprise later to find squadrons which did not subscribe to it[8].'

Manifold's memory is correct. Records show that 23 of his 30 ops with 467 Squadron were flown in ED539. In contrast, other contemporary Lancaster Captains, such as Heavery and Sinclair, had a different experience. Squadron Leader Sinclair's crew, for example, made 27 trips in 10 different aircraft. Several factors may have been at work here, including the rank of the pilot and his degree of assertiveness, the seniority of the crew, the availability of aircraft – and the importance the Captain attached to the issue.

Leonard Cheshire, VC, had no doubts about the importance of 'ownership'. He wrote: 'We each owned our own aircraft and, almost more important still, our own ground crew, both of whom we looked

*Time for a smoke: Keith Sinclair (third from left) and crew members on a muddy Bottesford dispersal. Photo: Vincent Holyoak*

upon as part of ourselves and which only under dire necessity would we lend to anyone else. Proportionately, as these ties of mutual understanding and confidence developed, one flew to greater effect, was the more likely to survive damage or injury and served out one's time in the squadron with more peace of mind[9].'

Guy Gibson, VC, when with 106 Squadron, held the opposite view. He saw an advantage in flying 'pool' aircraft, as Captains and crews flew more carefully, being aware that every aircraft had its individual characteristics[10].

Heavery's crew were exhausted on returning from Duisburg on April 9:

*We were desperate to get to bed but still found just enough energy to demolish our flying breakfast. Aircrew on operations always had a fried meal. Eggs, scarce in wartime, were a dead cert for a flying breakfast, although bacon was more hit and miss. We turned in. Later that Friday morning we woke to unpleasant news. We were on again. Even worse, we discovered later that we were to return to the same target that very night – again in V-Victor and with the same bomb load. Duisburg's status as a hub of the German war economy was receiving full recognition.*

*The time passed quickly. We got to lunch at 13.30. Our aircraft was serviceable and take-off was set for around 20.30, a little earlier than the previous night. Our time in the air was only four hours 35 minutes – a full 90 minutes shorter than the night before. We took a much more direct route (presumably chosen in deliberate contrast to the complex Flight Plan of the previous night). Unfortunately, the weather information we received at the briefing proved to be inaccurate.*

Thick cloud led to poor bombing results on both Duisburg raids. Damage was modest and 63 people died on the ground. Once again, the casualties in the air were more severe; 27 aircraft failed to return from these raids[11]. Thirty-one aircraft were struck off charge.

Section Officer Marie Cooper flew with some 467 Squadron crews during night flying tests and exercises, amassing over 60 hours. She found the rear turret by far the most uncomfortable station. 'I flew with Keith Sinclair, who was older than most of the others. He had a crazy but effective navigator from the Outback, Jack Gordon, who frequently designed his own route out and back[2].'

Navigators were expected to follow specified routes but the unconventional Gordon was effective as his crew always returned safely. Marie recalled this navigator's fruity Australian English: 'about as original as his routeing plans...[2].'

Marie had a frightening flight with Flight Lieutenant Forbes later in the year. It was a bombing practice and the range was crowded. At one point Forbes commented tersely: 'Let's get the hell out of here.' The Lancaster turned for Bottesford, only to find the sky above the airfield almost as crowded and the visibility poor. The congestion over the range drew some sharp protests, with many reports of 'close encounters'[2]. Forbes did not survive the war. He was killed in action on the night of

*Ready to fly: Section
Officer Marie Cooper
with 'Fish' Whiting.
Photo: Vincent Holyoak.*

*Ready to fly: Section Officer Marie Cooper with 'Fish' Whiting. Photo: Vincent Holyoak.*

February 21/22 1945, during an attack on the Mittelland Canal near Gravenhorst. Four of his crew survived.

Marie also flew with 'Fish' Whiting. His navigator, Bill Close, was a former maths teacher. He was known for his attachment to bright red braces. Fish and Bill conspired together to win the pilot's wager with 5 Group AOC Cochrane. Whiting bet Cochrane 'Ten Bob' that, no matter how long his take-off was delayed under the threat of a cancelled operation, he would still get to the target on time and be first back to Bottesford. Thanks to Close's creative routeing he did just that, claimed his winnings and, to everyone's amusement, eventually received ten shillings from 5 Group HQ[2].

Marie recalled: 'I flew with this crew occasionally over a period of six months, when Fish went from Flight Sergeant to Flying Officer, until they finished their tour. As an honourary crew member I received a portion of the red braces. They were cut up and handed out[2].'

The brittle, precious quality of infrequent free days remained fresh in Marie Cooper's mind in the early 1990's. They were lived with great intensity as they ended back in the unreal world of an operational station: 'This intensity probably also explains the quality of human relationships against the background of the unspoken thought that tomorrow might just not be another day. If one knew someone, then one knew them for life. When Fish visited us recently, in spite of a full complement of careers on both our parts, it was as if the 40 years in between had never existed! Was it this intensity that was missing in the post-war world?[2].

The contrast between the intensity and fragility of life is underlined by the story of one WAAF officer said to be confined to bed with shingles. In fact, she had become pregnant and eventually left the service to have her baby. The father went missing soon after she learned she was pregnant and her fortitude in facing things alone won the respect of Marie and others 'in the know'[2].

Having operated on consecutive nights the crew rested on Saturday April 10. They took ED772 for a 90-minute fighter affiliation and night flying test on the Sunday morning. At that time Bomber Command often used general duties aircraft on its own strength, rather than Fighter Command's Hurricanes and Spitfires, for fighter affiliation work:

> We were up against slow, clumsy aircraft like the Lysander and Martinet. Their awkward mock attacks gave Ken and I plenty of time to call for evasive action and get the attackers in our sights.

There were no ops on the Monday but there was intense activity at the dispersals during the following day, April 13. Another trip was in prospect and the heavy fuel load suggested a long haul. Typical fuel loadings were 2,100, 1,800 or 1,400 gallons. On this occasion full tanks (2,154 gallons) were required, indicating a very long flight.

The crews were about to be surprised. They were briefed to bomb their first Italian target, the port and naval base of La Spezia. Heavery's name appeared on the Battle Order and preparations began for the marathon ahead.

> We were allocated ED772 for our twentieth op that Tuesday. We first became

*Winner of the 'Ten Bob bet': Flying Officer J.H. 'Fish' Whiting's crew. Pictured (left to right) are: mid-upper gunner Warrant Officer Blair, wireless op Sergeant Self, 'creative' navigator Pilot Officer Close, Fish Whiting, flight engineer Sergeant Pyke, rear gunner Sergeant Fowler and bomb aimer Pilot Officer Simpson. Photo: Vincent Holyoak.*

*aware we were on at around 09.30. Take-off was set for mid-evening and the whole day stretched before us. With a full petrol load there was less weight available in the bomb-bay. The armourers lifted four 1,000 lb bombs and five cans of incendiaries into our Lanc. The pace quickened at the dispersals as bomb trolleys circled the aircraft.*

Heavery's aircraft was one of 208 Lancasters and three Halifaxes briefed to bomb La Spezia that night. Four Lancasters failed to return. The raid caused severe damage[12]. Sidney Knott was confined to his cramped and icy turret for over 10 hours that night:

*It was a grand tour. We flew across France and, eventually, the lights of Switzerland came into view. This was a rare treat: Switzerland, together with Sweden, Spain and Portugal, remained neutral. As the long outward flight neared its end we approached La Spezia and flew across the Bay of Naples. We were briefed to attack from the landward side. The bomb aimer had a better view when looking out to sea.*

*There was flak over the target but not much to speak of. From where I sat, this raid looked very successful. We didn't think much of the briefed bombing height, a dangerously low 7,000 ft, but the defences fell quiet as soon as we started to bomb. We had no problems over the target other than the fact that Nick, unusually, requested three runs before 'pressing the tit'. Later, he said he had been looking for the battleship reported to be at the naval base.*

*The return flight was trouble-free but seemed to go on forever. This turned out to be my longest operational trip of the war and we were probably close to the limit for a Lanc carrying a useful load. The flight turned out to be even longer than expected due to navigational problems. Ted had noticed a southerly drift on the last leg to La Spezia but, for some reason, had failed to act on it. During the return he discovered – as GEE slowly came into range – that there had been a dramatic shift in wind direction. We were around 100 miles south of track. A course correction put us back but this took extra time and fuel. An error of 100 miles was significant and Frank asked Ted, on several occasions, whether it was time to return to our intended heading. Ted sounded a little shaken: 'No. No. Carry on!' Our navigator was embarrassed but he felt much better when he got back and found that every 467 navigator flying that night had been caught out by the unexpected wind change. In fact, we were one of the first crews to return.*

*On arriving back from a sortie we followed the usual practice and painted a small bomb symbol just below the main canopy, marking another successful trip for the aircraft. Our return from Italy, by way of contrast, saw the addition of a miniature ice cream cone rather than a bomb.*

Heavery and his crew badly needed rest but they rose early that day as Bottesford was in turmoil. Diphtheria had been discovered on the station. Doctors invaded the station and everyone was confined to camp until further notice.

Bottesford remained sealed for 10 days. The outbreak was serious, with many airmen and WAAFs going down with the disease. One WAAF died. Eighteen WAAF cooks were kept in quarantine, forcing others to

work virtually round the clock, cooking and serving the meals. Some benefited from this interruption to the routine. Bill Manifold's wireless op, for example, won £80 playing poker.

Heavery's crew were pronounced fit and were informed immediately that operations from Bottesford would continue, diphtheria or not. Within 48 hours, on the morning of Friday April 16, they were told they were flying that night. Their twenty-first operation was at hand.

The word spread rapidly among the crews. Bottesford's Lancasters were receiving a full petrol load from the Matador bowsers. Another long haul, perhaps nine hours or more, was in prospect. The Lancaster had six self-sealing tanks: two 580 gallon tanks between the fuselage and

inboard engines, two 383 gallon tanks between the inboard and outboard engines and two 114 gallon tanks between outboard engines and wing tips[13].

Diphtheria and another lengthy sortie were no inducement to eat a hearty lunch. Even Heavery's permanently hungry crew found their appetites subdued. Later in the day the target was revealed: Pilsen, in Czechoslovakia.

During that night the attackers were to run into strong nightfighter opposition and heavy casualties resulted. Two of 467 Squadron's aircraft were posted missing on the Saturday morning and the pilots' names, Sergeant Stuart (ED780) and Sergeant Wilson (ED651: Y-Yankee), were erased from the board in the Flight Office.

The pace was relentless. After Pilsen, Heavery's name appeared on the Battle Order again on the Sunday morning. The crew were allocated N-Nuts (ED764) – yet another stranger. This aircraft had some interesting nose art, with Popeye's Olive Oyl becoming very aggressive with Hitler. A full petrol load was required. Knott and the rest of the crew struggled to put aside their memories of the long and dangerous Pilsen op. Had that been yesterday? Or the day before? Where now? The strain was beginning to show and some faces hardened into masks:

*I went down to the Flight Office after breakfast but there was no squadron meeting that day. I returned to the Gunnery Section, still feeling restless. It was time to begin preparing for our twenty-second operation. We had reached another crisis point in the tour. At this stage crews ran the risk of getting sloppy. Unless we stayed sharp, fatigue would chip away at our hard-won fighting efficiency. During the afternoon N-Nuts' bomb-bay filled with 14 cans of incendiaries. This was unusual – our first all-incendiary bomb-load. All became clear at the main briefing. We were returning to La Spezia.*

Bomber Command sent 173 Lancasters and five Halifaxes to La Spezia that night. While the aiming point was over the docks, much of the bombing centred on an area to the north-west. One Lancaster failed to return[14].

N-Nuts touched down at Bottesford at just after 06.00, in the dim light of an early Monday morning. The Lancaster had been in the air for exactly nine hours. During the night, the incendiaries that had filled its huge bomb-bay had joined many thousands of others, tumbling down and starting fires across a wide area beyond the docks.

The main challenge for Heavery's crew arose just 10 minutes into the long flight, when Ken Butterworth reported problems with his mid-upper turret. Heavery was grateful that this was an 'ice cream raid', rather than a trip to Happy Valley.

When safely back on the ground the crew attended to the rituals of the debrief, then enjoyed their flying breakfast before settling down to bed. Later, Heavery felt relieved to hear they were not flying that evening. They were required, however, the following day, Tuesday April 20. Most 467 Squadron aircrew were so tired, at this point, that they simply failed to react to the news that they were flying again that night, with a full petrol load once more.

By 21.00 that Tuesday the crew had settled into their positions within J-Jig (ED695). This Lanc had taken them to Berlin and Essen over the past few weeks. Now they were prepared for yet another long trip. The target was Stettin, on Germany's Baltic coast. Heavery ran up the engines on full brake as the Lancaster got the green. Well-wishers waved as J-Jig began to roll, its bomb doors wrapped around a 4,000 lb Cookie and nine

*Recognition: the Heavery crew's certificate for a good aiming point photograph over La Spezia, April 18/19 1943. Sidney Knott.*

cans of incendiaries. The aircraft's four engines roared, held at maximum boost and rpm. A laden Lancaster, at around 65,000 lbs, would unstick at around 105 mph plus[15]. Undercarriage and flaps were retracted as Heavery's Lancaster joined a procession of 339 aircraft making for Stettin. Twenty-one failed to return, a loss rate of 6.2 per cent[16].

The crew switched to oxygen and began the climb to operating altitude:

> *We were routed across Denmark. The bomber stream then turned sharply out into the Baltic and turned again, to make the attack from the sea.*

Knott kept his turret moving over Stettin on that April night. By the time J-Jig turned for home the target was covered with a carpet of fire. Good visibility and accurate marking produced highly concentrated bombing. A city centre area of around 100 acres was destroyed and 586 people died in the tidal wave of high explosive and incendiaries[16].

Heavery brought his Lancaster into Bottesford at 05.40, eight hours and five minutes after take-off. He and his crew had now completed a series of four long trips: La Spezia, Pilsen, La Spezia again and, finally, Stettin. These sorties alone added another 36 hours to Sidney Knott's operational flying. There was still one third of the month to go. They were not to know that they would fly only one more sortie in April.

On returning from Stettin the crew wanted nothing more than a good day out. They felt the need to get away from airfields, Lancasters, runways, briefings and the paraphernalia of Bomber Command's war.

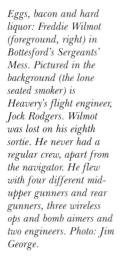

*Eggs, bacon and hard liquor: Freddie Wilmot (foreground, right) in Bottesford's Sergeants' Mess. Pictured in the background (the lone seated smoker) is Heavery's flight engineer, Jock Rodgers. Wilmot was lost on his eighth sortie. He never had a regular crew, apart from the navigator. He flew with four different mid-upper gunners and rear gunners, three wireless ops and bomb aimers and two engineers. Photo: Jim George.*

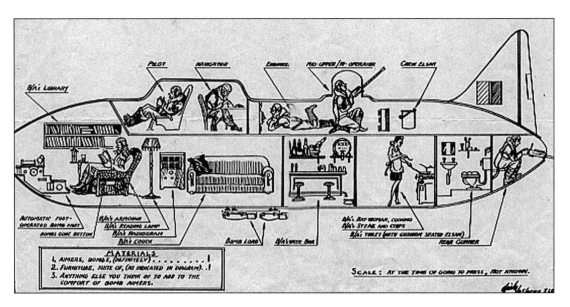

They managed to squeeze in a well-deserved break before the last trip of the month.

The crew climbed into J-Jig once again at just before midnight on Monday April 26. They had been briefed to bomb Duisburg for the third time that month. It was a 'same again' bomb-load – a Cookie and 12 cans. A total of 561 Bomber Command aircraft took off for the Ruhr; 499 attacked the target and the raid results were poor. Seventeen aircraft failed to return[17]. Twenty-one bombers were struck off charge.

Accurate marking was followed by inaccurate bombing, with extremely heavy flak and industrial haze contributing to the difficulties. Yet the effects were devastating for those under the torrent of bombs. Over 130 people died on the ground. Subsequently some aircrew expressed their feelings. One Lancaster rear gunner, 101 Squadron's Harry Quick, looked down on Duisburg that night: 'It was horrific what was happening down there. There were explosions, huge fires: a monstrous, bubbling stew of reds, oranges, blues and searchlights[18].'

During April 1943 no less than 11 major raids were unleashed by Bomber Command[19]. As for 467 Squadron, there were 147 sorties to 17 targets. Four aircraft failed to return (captained by Squadron Leader Paape, Sergeant Wilson, Sergeant Stuart and Flight Lieutenant Craigie)[20]. Despite these painful losses the squadron's morale remained solid. In total, the April 1943 raids cost Bomber Command 96 Lancasters.

*The bomb aimer's fantasy: this drawing was found in Nick Murray's papers. The 'design' is credited to Warrant Officer J.Leiper of 92 Group. Note the comforts of the in-flight bar, cooked meals and elaborate Elsan (with standard arrangements for the rest of the crew!). Flo Murray.*

# CHAPTER TEN

# It's a Long Way to Pilsen

PILSEN made a big impression on Sidney Knott and many other Bomber Command aircrew. The casualties during the night of April 16/17 were catastrophic. Yet, by the end of April Heavery's crew had completed 24 operations. Pilsen was followed in quick succession by a second trip to La Spezia, then Stettin and Duisburg. Could they stay alive and complete a first tour?

Pilsen was a long, tough trip. In the very early hours of Saturday April 17 Frank Heavery sat at the controls of ED772, high above the Czech countryside. Crouching over his guns in the rear turret, Knott's thoughts returned to the briefing. He had never heard of Pilsen until that afternoon. Now this town was somewhere below, in a landscape etched by moonlight. He felt naked and vulnerable as ED772's four Merlins took them closer to the target, the Skoda armaments complex:

*I had seen some fighter combats on the way out. I wasn't too worried about Pilsen's defences but I saw enough to know we could have problems getting there. The real trouble, however, started on the way back. The nightfighters were well positioned and the bombers were clearly visible thanks to the moon.*

*I saw many more combats after leaving the target. The fighters were waiting for us and one aircraft after another went down in flames. There was no subtlety to this raid. We were briefed to return along a reciprocal course. The idea of flying back the same way we came in unnerved us. Apparently, the planners decided that the Germans would conclude that we wouldn't be stupid enough to return on the same track used to fly to the target. The opposition, unfortunately, had a rather lower opinion of British creativity!*

*On the other hand, dog-legging back from Pilsen – whatever the route – was also very dangerous. On passing south of Nuremberg it was easy to go too far and run into Munich's strong defences. There were also the unpleasant possibilities of bumping into the defences at Stuttgart and, later, Strasbourg.*

As ED772 approached Pilsen Heavery's crew placed their trust in self-discipline and experience. Regardless of the trip's length Knott followed a strict rule. He never left his turret under any circumstances:

*The desire to urinate can be overwhelming during a flight of eight hours or more. The Elsan chemical toilet was in the rear fuselage, but I never used it. To my mind, leaving the turret during an operational flight was no different from deserting a post on the battlefield. Anything I wanted to do was done in the turret.*

*We were very young, of course, and free of the 'waterworks' problems so familiar in old age. My need to pee depended on how cold I got. If I had to, I stood up in the turret, removed a glove, pulled down the zip on the Taylor suit and went where I stood. Assuming a crouched position I'd pee over the ammunition belts, in the area where they entered the turret through the floor.*

*On landing back, after a few hours' sleep, I'd return to the aircraft and check the 'damage'. The urine turned the .303 rounds bright green. It took just a few minutes to break the belt, remove the offending strip, pull the belt back to the breech and wipe the floor.*

A total of 6,000 lbs of high explosive bombs were loaded into ED772's 33 ft long bomb-bay in readiness for Pilsen. The large Cookie and two 1,000 lb bombs represented a modest war load for the Lancaster. Full fuel tanks were required to reach Pilsen and return and this meant an unusually light load. Later in the day Knott settled down in his turret as Bottesford's runway fell away beneath him.

Take-off was planned for just after 21.00. As usual, the Germans knew a big raid was in preparation. The radio transmissions monitored by their intelligence services gave ample warning that Bomber Command would operate in strength that night.

*I walked into the main briefing and did exactly what everyone else did. I looked straight ahead at the big map on the wall. My eyes followed the line of coloured tape going east towards the target. On this occasion the tape seemed to go on forever!*

*As I took my seat I could hear people filing in behind me gasp with displeasure as they caught sight of the tape. The wall map looked like it had measles. It was covered in red blotches along the route to the target. The red hatched areas indicated concentrations of flak and searchlights, together with fighter bases and beacons.*

*We received a quick introduction to Skoda, a huge munitions producer. The briefing then developed in much the same way as all the others. Routes were outlined and timings given. The defences were described and the Met Officer gave his overview of weather conditions expected on the way out, over the target, during the return and, finally, over eastern England's bomber bases.*

*We had a surprise when the Medical Officer stepped forward. 'Doc' wanted to talk about Bottesford's diphtheria problem. Someone whispered pointedly: 'Pilsen – well they can't send the afflicted much further away!' Holding the full attention of an incredulous audience, he ordered us to report that we could be diphtheria carriers, should we be shot down and captured by the Germans! I'm sure many people in the room found it difficult to stifle their laughter.*

*Our crew got together immediately afterwards. Normally, we accepted all orders without question. They could tell us to stick our heads into a lion's mouth and we would do it, but this seemed ludicrous. We could just imagine the kindly Gestapo man's reaction to such frank disclosure. There could be no quicker way of attracting a bullet in the back of the neck! In the event of being shot down we would keep our mouths firmly shut on the subject of Bottesford's medical problems.*

The Intelligence Officers then distributed escape aids, contained in sealed packages with a clear perspex cover. The contents varied according to the countries along the route flown:

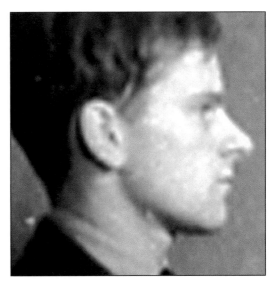

*Just in case: Sidney Knott's two 'evasion photos.' He flew with the photographs in his battledress pocket. They would be of use if false papers had to be produced for him by the Resistance. Photos: Sidney Knott.*

*We were under orders never to open this package unless shot down. The contents included money, emergency rations, a slab of chocolate, a map and other survival aids, including water-purifying tablets and Benzedrine. The small package fitted neatly into the battledress pocket. In addition, two buttons from my battledress top formed a crude compass when put together. My comb was a back-up. With the ends snapped off and suspended from a length of grass, the marked end of the comb would swing to the north.*

*We were issued with 'wakey wakey' pills. We were given our flying rations – a can of Californian orange juice and chocolate. I drank my orange juice as soon as we were airborne. All gunners did the same, as it froze solid during the climb to operating height. We worshipped this orange juice. We had never had anything like it and it couldn't be bought in the shops. It was delicious.*

There were some good-natured if caustic remarks during the Pilsen briefing when 467's crews were told, with magnificent understatement, that the route to the target was 'difficult'. The bomber stream would filter into Europe through France, much as usual, but problems were inevitable later, when negotiating the narrow gap between Stuttgart and Mannheim. These cities' vicious defences virtually merged into a single, dense belt of searchlights and guns.

A second group of bombers had been briefed to strike at Mannheim. The Pilsen attackers would continue eastwards, slipping past Nuremberg. There was a chance that the defenders might think they were going for that city, but the route would take them further east and into Czechoslovakia.

*Ken and I worked overtime in our turrets as ED772 closed with Pilsen. As always, there were few exchanges on the intercom, to reduce the risk of blocking a fighter warning. The bomb aimer suddenly said he could see flares going down dead ahead. We were on track. The navigator gave his estimate of the time left for the run-in. Then a clutch of markers burst a short distance away, on the Lancaster's port side. Ted had doubts about their accuracy but our Lanc moved over as the bomb aimer prepared to take control. Nick said he could see the target.*

*Getting ready to fly: Pilot Officer George Tillotsen's crew at Bottesford. They were to survive their tour, finishing in early October. They came through despite a close encounter with a nightfighter over Peenemünde in August. Photo: Vincent Holyoak.*

*I remember the surprise in his voice: 'It's small! Really small.' The bombing run was very short and there was no flak as our Lanc was freed of its bombs.*

*As Frank asked for a course for home Nick reported more markers ahead. Ted left his navigator's station, went forward for a look and he said: 'Well, I think they are the right ones!' We now had a grandstand view of a serious marking error by the Pathfinders. Some innocent location had already received most of the Main Force bombs as we turned for home. There was nothing to be done about it. I kept busy, looking out for fighters as a corner of my mind wondered whether we had bombed a German decoy – a spoof target.*

*Private thoughts are dangerous luxuries. I kept the turret moving, looking for a silhouette or the tiny points of light from the exhausts of a stalking nightfighter. It was time to take the second of my wakey wakey pills. I knew most of the fighters would congregate around the network of beacons covering the bottleneck between Stuttgart and Mannheim. I felt the pill take effect as the ache at the back of my eyes gradually eased.*

*During the return we methodically reported and logged the vivid splashes of flame appearing regularly in the skies around us. The inexperienced were dying, minute by minute, as they flew straight and level away from the target. Frank was no novice, however, and he kept ED772 weaving through the night. The random height changes made it much more difficult for a nightfighter to bring its cannons to bear.*

The crew had plenty to worry about during this trip. It was mid-April. The nights were getting shorter and long distance targets were becoming marginal:

*We knew it would be light before we reached the French coast. A low level crossing at 1,500 ft had been recommended, but light flak in the coastal belt was murderous at that height. We crossed the coast at an altitude much lower than 1,500 ft and travelling very fast. Even so, our Lanc was surrounded by webs of light flak and the shells reached up very slowly towards us. This was very unhealthy. I gave the German gunners something to think about, firing 300 rounds in very short bursts as we roared over the ground defences and headed out to sea.*

Ted left his navigator's station to find out what all the excitement was about. He told me later that, as he went forward, Frank turned round, his mask hanging free. The pilot stuck his tongue out at the navigator and gave him a vigorous V-sign. The flak hadn't dampened his spirits!

As ED772 left the French coast behind, on the final leg of its long return flight from Pilsen, wireless op Johnny Lloyd received instructions to divert due to weather problems. Their new destination was Boscombe Down, the experimental station. Boscombe Down was one of 14 Regional Control Stations designated for emergency use. Heavery put the Lancaster down carefully at 06.30, after nine hours 10 minutes in the air. As ED772 moved across the all-grass field Sidney Knott could see other 467 Squadron aircraft dispersed around the perimeter. The aircraft parked up and transport arrived to take them to a billet.

*It seemed odd not to go to a debriefing but there was no-one to debrief us at Boscombe Down. This suited us. We wanted breakfast and a bed although we didn't much care for the standard of local hospitality. The welcome was muted, to say the least.*

*We were driven to a hut at the far end of the airfield and left to our own devices, with only a vague promise that someone would try to rustle up some food and something to sleep on. Then came the parting shot: we were not to leave our hut under any circumstances and on no account were we to enter the Mess, as we were diphtheria carriers. Christ! Not again! This disease followed us around, wherever we went. Perhaps someone had opened his mouth on landing here? Perhaps Bottesford's Medical Officer had decided it was his duty to make a telephone call? Either way Boscombe Down was anxious to see the back of us.*

*After two or three hours' rest we were roused and told by one of our own squadron officers that weather conditions now permitted a return to Bottesford, given a serviceable aircraft. We had no great desire to hang around and wearily went to attend to ED772.*

*The skipper and flight engineer made a visual inspection, walking around the Lanc. They decided the minor flak holes should not prevent a return to Bottesford and climbed inside to continue their checks. We took on more fuel. The engines were started. The starboard inner was started first, as this drove the compressor for the brakes and radiator shutters. The engines sounded healthy and the Lanc appeared flyable.*

*We were the last of 467's aircraft to leave. As we completed our preparations, I became aware that Boscombe Down had an impressive collection of odd-looking aircraft. One caught my eye as we taxied out, a Lysander fitted with a rear turret. It was a real ugly duckling. As we finished our checks Flying Control instructed us to carry out a night flying test on the way home. Wonderful! In effect, we had been told we were 'on again' while still struggling to arrive back from Pilsen!*

Frank Heavery's take-off at 11.30 that Saturday morning was far from trouble-free. He was accustomed to a hard runway:

*Exhaustion probably contributed to what followed. The grass field was very rough and our Lanc hit an outsized bump during the take-off run. We had insufficient clearance under the tail, struck the bump and staggered into the air. Fortunately, Frank got us out of trouble by easing forward on the control column.*

*He had just enough speed to keep the Lanc off the deck until there was sufficient power to begin the climb-out.*

*With this boisterous farewell to Boscombe behind us, we got on with the night flying test. I practised turret manipulation by following hedgerows with the gunsight and I took drift readings by sighting on tractors and even the occasional horse. This Lanc had a perfect turret, supported by an excellent hydraulics system. We were back at Bottesford by 12.25.*

*Ken and I made our way to the Drying Section, to get rid of our outer flying kit before a much delayed debriefing. We had the usual cup of cocoa despite the unusual time of day. We then headed for the Mess and an extremely late flying breakfast. Ken had plenty of nerve. He was never slow to ask for someone's egg if he had failed to return. We knew the squadron had taken casualties and Ken pressed hard for extra eggs, but with no success on this occasion.*

*With the meal over we walked into the Mess anteroom and claimed the most comfortable chairs. We were asleep within minutes. An hour or so later we were roused and told that the planned op had been scrubbed. We were free to sleep until breakfast the next day. We needed the rest as our next trip was another long haul.*

Pilsen was a failure. Many Lancasters and Halifaxes bombed the wrong target that night. The arrangements adopted over the target were unusual, with the Pathfinder markers regarded as a general guide only. The Main Force crews were required to confirm the target visually[1]. Pilsen, of course, was far beyond Oboe range. When Heavery's crew made their late return to Bottesford they were told a large cigarette factory had been bombed by mistake. The truth was too embarrassing to be disclosed at the time. Many crews had bombed a large asylum at Dobrany. The Skoda Works, just a few miles away, was undamaged.

Almost a year later, in March 1944, Bomber Command suffered its greatest setback when 95 bombers failed to return from an attack on Nuremberg (a catastrophic 11.9 per cent loss rate). Yet losses in percentage terms during the April 16/17 Pilsen raid were almost as bad, at 11 per cent. Thirty-six of the 327 bombers dispatched failed to return[1]. Over 250 young men were in the missing aircraft. The vast majority were now dead – many still trapped inside smoking wreckage:

*They made the figures look better by combining the Pilsen casualties with the losses on the Mannheim raid also flown that night. The Mannheim loss rate was high, at 6.6 per cent, but still low enough in relative terms to bring down the combined loss rate to 8.8 per cent.*

*There were empty places in the Sergeants' Mess that morning. Wilson's crew were missing. Four died but Wilson and two others survived as prisoners of war. Pilsen was this crew's seventh operation, but Wilson's ninth trip. He had done two as second dicky, one to Duisburg and the other to Berlin. Wilson had been on the squadron for just five weeks, having arrived on March 10.*

*Sergeant Stuart's crew also failed to return. They were members of C Flight and had arrived at Bottesford in February. All members of this crew died on the Pilsen raid, their sixth operation. Perhaps they were tired – after all, they had made the long trip to La Spezia immediately before Pilsen.*

# CHAPTER ELEVEN

# Odds Against Survival

A ROUND 125,000 aircrew served with Bomber Command during the Second World War. Some 93,000 were British. Most of the rest were Canadians, Australians and New Zealanders, although many other Allied nations were represented. During the main area bombing offensive, the Command's frontline squadrons required a maximum of around 10,000 aircrew available for operations[1]. A total of 55,500 aircrew died; 47,268 were killed in action or died while prisoners of war. The ranks of the dead include thousands of air gunners[2]:

*I came to accept I wouldn't live to see the end of the tour but never said as much. I hoped to live but felt I wouldn't make it. We had been told to make a will. I never did as it tempted fate. Besides, what did I have to leave? I was just 21 and owned nothing worth giving away.*

Bomber Command's loss rate averaged five per cent for much of the war. The chance of an individual completing 30 operations might be as low as one in five. In Bomber Command's 'black periods' perhaps 20 out of every 100 aircrew starting a tour could be expected to survive 30 trips. At the end of a second tour of 20 operations just seven or eight might remain alive[3].

Bomber Command's Commander-in-Chief, Sir Arthur Harris, put the odds of surviving a first tour as 'scarcely one in three'[4]. The severity of the losses varied over time, in line with Bomber Command's changing fortunes in its long war with the German defences. Only committed optimists, however, expected to survive beyond 15 trips (the first tour half-way point).

The first 10 operations were regarded as the most dangerous. The second 10 were viewed as safer, in relative terms, while the final 10 were thought to be riskier, due to insidious over-confidence or what would now be described as combat fatigue[5].

*The odds against personal survival seemed overwhelming so the crews lived for the day. I didn't waste time looking ahead. I made it a rule not to be too bothered about 'ordinary things'.*

*Fear crept into my mind if I allowed myself to think about the chances of survival. People had different attitudes towards fear and its management. As a crew, we kept our thoughts (and prayers) to ourselves. I suspect, however, that even hardened atheists found themselves praying when they flew over the North Sea or Channel and crossed the enemy coast.*

People were expected to put on a brave face at all times. Bottesford Intelligence Officer Marie Cooper often stayed up to listen to the R/T exchanges as each aircraft called in on its return. She soon knew if an aircraft was missing: 'As someone who has a distinct tendency to have eyes filled with tears saying goodbye in the ordinary way, this had obvious advantages in potentially directing any such impermissible show of emotion onto my pillow. Pilots I had flown with were my special protégés, of course, and, of these, all came through[6].' Many

*Nightfighter victim: Flying Officer Cazaly, Pilot Officer Desmond's mid-upper gunner. The entire crew died on May 28 following a combat with a nightfighter. Cazaly and rear gunner John Ryalls shot down their attacker. The crew of the German aircraft also died. Photo: Vincent Holyoak.*

others didn't, including Desmond, MacKenzie, Mant, Raphael, Wilmot and Vine.

Knott was never much good at praying but noticed that it did become easier as the aircraft approached hostile territory:

*I knew the Lord's Prayer and I taught myself to say it with my eyes wide open and searching the sky for fighters. We never shared our innermost thoughts but I'm sure all members of our crew prayed at some point during every operational flight.*

Others were open about such intimate matters:

*After the war I met a navigator who had developed the habit of saying 'Let's hope we succeed' over the intercom as his aircraft approached the coast of occupied Europe. This, perhaps, is the most fundamental of prayers. He said it amounted to 'putting in a word' for his crew. Another crew favoured an open line to God. The former navigator of this crew told me his pilot always said a prayer over the intercom as they approached the coastal flak belt.*

Death was described in many euphemistic ways by bomber crews. One of the most common was 'gone for a Burton'. According to 467 Squadron Lancaster Captain Bill Manifold this alluded to the well-known beer. It was said to have come into use as an easy way of dealing with female callers asking awkward questions about the missing. Manifold always took care to ask for Whitbread's[7]. He needn't have bothered, as the saying's origins as a euphemism for death are much older and unconnected with beer.

*We never discussed the likelihood of dying but we did occasionally talk about why we accepted such outrageous risks. Our job was to cut back Nazi Germany and make a major contribution to its eventual defeat. Our enemies had introduced us to the destruction of entire cities. Our role was to ensure they suffered the consequences.*

*All the aircrew I have met, during the war and afterwards, regard 'Butch' Harris as a good leader. He had to be callous, if that is the right word, in order to win Bomber Command's war (and win it he did). Harris was a remote figure, unseen by the operational crews. He had a talented headquarters staff but the ultimate responsibility rested on his shoulders alone. Night after night he took calculated risks with our young lives. I feel sure he was always conscious of the frightful human cost.*

Harris knew area bombing had to go on, as the alternative – a longer war – was even more awful to contemplate:

*This was a just war, in so much as any war may be described as 'just'. Hitler's Germany revelled in an orgy of industrialised mass killing and its victims were, for the most part, the weak and defenceless. Beyond genocide, the ruthless exploitation and degradation of Europe's conquered peoples continued unabated, in many instances until the very last day of the war.*

*We had an unspoken appreciation of the fundamentals. This, perhaps, is the real key to the resilience of morale on the squadrons. We were not philosophers and the key issues were black and white for most. The appalling character of Nazi Germany gave the whole filthy business a stark clarity.*

*At the personal level our chances of staying alive were so small that life had a "here today" purity. In a strange way this gave a wonderful sense of freedom. We were volunteers, proud to belong to an elite and, in my experience, never in doubt about the essential justice of our war.*

*There were black periods, occasions when it seemed the war would continue forever and put us all in our graves. The Germans were extremely tough opponents and, at times, they really got the measure of Bomber Command. In the final analysis, however, 467's crews never faltered. They held solid.*

*The reality behind 'Gone for a burton': The twisted remains of ED531 on a Swiss mountainside, on the morning of July 13 1943. T-Tommy was one of three 467 Squadron aircraft that failed to return from a raid on Turin. Flying Officer Graham Douglas Mitchell, RAAF, and his crew were all killed when their aircraft hit high-tension wires. They were buried with full military honours at Vevy, on the shores of Lake Geneva. Photo: Vincent Holyoak.*

The human losses were horrific. The consequences of a flak hit, or a stream of fighter cannon shells striking fuel tanks or fuselage, were all too apparent to the bomber crews who happened to be flying close to the victims. A fully-laden heavy bomber was nothing more than an enormous bomb. It might hold some 2,000 gallons of petrol, 150 gallons of oil and 14,000 lbs of blast bombs, incendiaries and pyrotechnics, together with thousands of rounds of belted ammunition.

As German nightfighters penetrated the closely packed stream, the bomber navigators began to log the kills. Time and again, crews witnessed the sudden red, orange, yellow and white eruptions of flame signalling the violent conclusion of yet another nightfighter combat.

Gradually, the idea took root (or was planted) that some of the more spectacular explosions were 'scarecrows' – special shells developed by the Germans to simulate a heavy bomber's destruction:

> *Our Intelligence Officers claimed scarecrows were being used and that they had no lethal effect. After the war the Germans steadfastly denied their existence. Whatever the truth, the appearance was that of an aircraft blown out of the sky. Scarecrows were never mentioned at OTU or HCU but, perhaps naively, we were quite prepared to believe an Intelligence Officer attached to an operational squadron. We had to believe someone!*

> *Scarecrows may have been a complete fabrication, perhaps motivated by a perceived need to buttress morale on the squadrons. The scarecrow story masked the severity of our losses. If this is so, it offers a new perspective on our leaders' capacity for ruthlessness.*

Aircraft departing on ops were waved off by well-wishers. Bottesford Intelligence Officer Marie Cooper, when not on duty in the Ops Room, developed the habit of joining the group stationed at the point where each Lancaster paused before receiving the green. She

*Blind chance: Wing Commander Gomm (far left) pictured with other 467 Squadron officers at the front door of Bottesford's rather primitive station headquarters. Next to Gomm is Gunnery Leader Roy 'Juggo' Hare. Gomm had vast experience yet failed to return from an attack on Milan in August 1943. Photo: Vincent Holyoak.*

recalled: 'In response to complaints that they couldn't see if I was there or not I took to wearing a pair of Norwegian ski gloves for identification[6].'

This got her into trouble on one occasion. On returning to Flying Control she was confronted by the Station Commander and a visiting group of very senior officers. This provoked an immediate salute, greeted by raised eyebrows as the party took in her garish gloves, in the appropriate colours of red, white and blue. Marie was called in for reprimand the following day but was excused after her explanation – with a verbal caution to stay well clear of senior visitors in the future[6].

Ironically, there was a German parallel to the scarecrow story – at least in terms of a 'light-show'. During his interrogation in June 1945 German nightfighter ace Major Schnaufer commented that, during 1942-43, some British bombers fired off a brilliant white flash when attacked. He said this was an extremely effective form of defence, as it blinded the nightfighter crews and made them lose their targets. He and his fellow pilots had wondered why the idea was not pursued (Appendix 3; 37). Perhaps this 'secret weapon' was also non-existent? In all probability the white flash resulted from the detonation of pyrotechnics as the nightfighter's rounds struck home in the fuselage.

Some bombers struggled home with complete engines or turrets blown away by shell or cannon fire. Others were struck by bombs from friendly aircraft flying at higher altitudes. Many bombers stayed in the air despite severe damage caused by explosion and fire:

> *We were a lucky crew but we still collected our fair share of flak holes. On one occasion, Frank banked the aircraft as we left the target and this was the usual cue for Nick to move from the bomb aimer's prone position and man the front turret's twin Brownings. He was still settling behind the guns when a shell fragment ripped through the floor, exactly where his body had been just moments before. It left a hole the size of an orange. It also damaged a line and showered our Belfast boy with hydraulic oil.*

> *A tornado of frozen air penetrated the fuselage in an instant. Ted's charts took flight, adding to the chaos. The crew forward sorted things out as Ted rescued his papers. Frank eased the nose down as the crew members forward lacked the gunners' warm clothing. Frostbite was a certainty unless the Lanc descended rapidly into warmer air. The two inboard engines provided heating but that didn't reach the gunners. Now the others had a taste of cold as Ken and I knew it. From our turrets we offered one or two weak jokes, asking Frank to 'turn down the heat'. Later, however, I realised that Nick was severely shaken. Without doubt that shell splinter would have killed him, had he stayed put just a few seconds longer.*

> *We had other close calls. One night shrapnel smashed through the mid-upper turret's perspex. It penetrated the collar of Ken's Taylor suit but was 'spent' and came to rest without so much as breaking the skin. Nevertheless, it had enough force to give him an alarming smack on the back of the neck – an unpleasant reminder of his own mortality. Later, safely on the ground, he found the jagged metal fragment on the aircraft floor.*

*We collected plenty of holes in our aircraft but we never lost an engine during the first tour. We knew our luck could run out at any time and we did our best to conserve it by working hard to build teamwork and confidence. We did everything by the book. Some crews cut corners and they soon went missing. These losses were a great incentive to 'follow the drill'. Frank was a conservative pilot and we appreciated this quality. He was professional to the core and we developed a crew style in harmony with his careful approach.*

During early 1944 Bomber Command Headquarters staff considered the findings of an Operational Research statistical study. This appeared to demonstrate that experience and expertise had no detectable effect on crew losses[8]. Blind chance was the key.

*Sole survivor: 20 year-old Flight Sergeant James Lee jumped from Gomm's aircraft as it exploded. He suffered burns and was captured. This photograph was taken in Stalag Luft IVB. Photo: Vincent Holyoak.*

*We were realists and understood the importance of blind chance. We could die at any time, professional or not! Yet we also felt certain that a confident, efficient crew had more chance of getting through. Operational flying is a unique experience due to the fear factor. The odds were against us and we responded by trying harder and becoming more professional. What else could we do?*

Many photographs of Bomber Command's war show flak and fighter damaged aircraft on the ground, with surviving crews lined up and

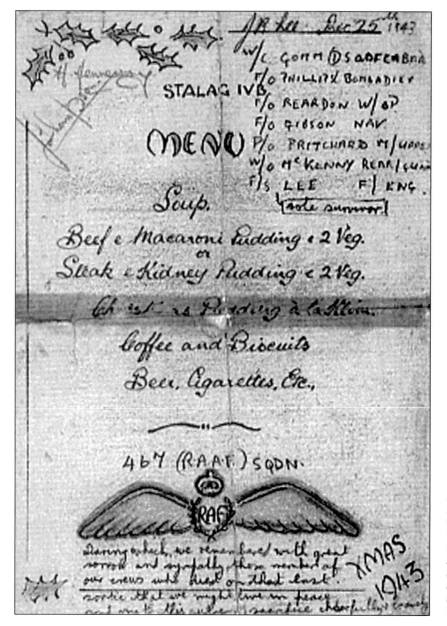

*Memorial lunch: James Lee's Christmas meal, in memory of his crew. 'During which we remembered with great sorrow and sympathy those members of our crews who died on that last sortie...' Photo: Vincent Holyoak*

grinning sheepishly for the camera:

> *The practice at Bottesford was to tow a damaged aircraft into a hangar corner, for patching and repairs. We never had much chance to inspect these casualties. Perhaps this was deliberate – part of a wider strategy to maintain morale.*

Some badly damaged aircraft were dismantled and taken to Langar, Bottesford's satellite and one of a group of major Avro repair bases.

At the human level, concern about morale influenced the way in which lockers were cleared and arrangements made for releasing the personal effects of the missing. The Adjutant was responsible for supervising this delicate task. The work was done by the 'Committee of Adjustment.' Some squadrons took a down-to-earth attitude towards these matters. Auctions of personal effects were organised, with the proceeds going to the next of kin. The prices paid were often inflated, reflecting the destination of the money raised. Very occasionally, a survivor would evade successfully, turn up and demand the return of his property.

The possessions of those who had failed to return from the night's raid were removed by the Committee of Adjustment during the early morning. This was done quietly, efficiently and with discretion. Each item was examined with care before being released for return to the families. There was always the possibility that a locker, kitbag or wallet might contain a letter from 'another woman'. In one case at Bottesford two fiancés turned up, asking after the same missing man. Fortunately, they arrived on different days, but missing letters proved difficult to explain[9].

The Adjutant or Squadron Commander wrote to the next of kin. In many cases the letters included a cautious expression of hope that the missing man might have survived:

> *It was usually possible, at a later date, to discover whether a man had been killed or taken prisoner. If we wanted information about someone, Frank would visit the Intelligence Office for news. At the same time we had no opportunity to indulge in morbid reflection. Life on an operational squadron unravelled at a furious pace and feelings of sadness and loss soon wore off. When someone failed to return we drank to him in the Mess. The chat sounded callous to outsiders. Someone returning from leave might ask: 'Where's so-and-so?' The response would be facetious: 'He's gone for a shit.'*

Some everyday items took on a special value in wartime Britain. The billets at Bottesford were a long way from the ablutions and 467 Squadron crews got into the habit of leaving their holdalls in the washrooms. Whenever a man went missing his bag was always searched for soap – notoriously hard to come by in 1943.

Such harmless, petty larceny was exceeded by 467 Squadron's crooked Adjutant. He was exposed when Pilot Officer Mant failed to return from a sortie to Stuttgart during the night of March 11/12. One of 'Dinny' Mant's crew (named by Bill Manifold as bomb aimer Will Campbell) had been lucky. He had been on commissioning leave when his crew went missing. This was overlooked and his belongings were also removed from the billet. He went to recover the items but his wireless had disappeared. An investigation led to the discovery of the wireless – and much more besides – at the Adjutant's rented house in Bottesford village. He was court-martialled, publicly stripped of his rank and sentenced to a six-month prison term[9]. Sidney Knott has no recollection of the parade, but there are accounts describing the ritual humiliation of this officer.

> *Stealing from dead aircrew left no room for excuses, yet some of us felt sorry for the Adjutant and argued that his treatment was too severe. Our thoughts soon returned, however, to our own plight. Many of us were going to die. It is natural, however, to assume that death is a matter for others. Some refused to be shaken in this belief, regardless of the close calls and horrors they experienced in the air. I felt sure that, sooner or later, I would be killed in action. As I sat in the turret, waiting for take-off and with everything vibrating around me, I would say to myself: 'It's going to happen but not this time. Not tonight.'*

Others felt differently. Jack Currie, in the evocative book *Lancaster Target*, described his view of the odds on reaching his fifteenth operation with 12 Squadron in late September 1943: 'When we joined the squadron the odds against our finishing the tour were about seven to one, now they had shortened to better than four to one. These statistics never meant much to me, however, except when I was cold and tired and frightened. I always thought we would survive the tour...'

Many accounts of Bomber Command's war describe circumstances in which individuals experienced an overwhelming premonition. One example was recorded by a 61 Squadron Lancaster Captain: 'On April 22 1944 our target was Brunswick... For reasons I could not define, an intense feeling of foreboding refused to go away. I felt compelled to write letters to my parents and my girlfriend, telling them not to worry as I somehow felt that I would survive. I wrote a further letter to the Station Adjutant requesting that he made arrangements for my car to be taken care of. I also asked one of my groundcrew to look after my little dog, Boris. I had not felt the need to do any of these things prior to other operations[10].' This pilot's Lancaster failed to return. He became a prisoner of war.

Such feelings were often accompanied by a sense of resignation. Occasionally, however, there were outbursts of anger and rebellion. Later in the year, as 467 Squadron crews were briefed for the Peenemünde attack on August 17/18, 'Ray' Raphael – holding the fort as Squadron Commander after Gomm's loss only two nights before – had a premonition that he would not return. During the briefing he became extremely agitated about fighter concentrations along the chosen route and found it impossible to hide his discomfort. The Squadron Leader, a Londoner, was right. His Lancaster was hit and it crashed into a lake near Peenemünde[11]. Raphael was succeeded almost immediately by Wing Commander JR 'Sam' Balmer, 467 Squadron's first Australian Commanding Officer[12].

Intelligence Officer Marie Cooper also felt that Raphael would not return from Peenemünde. She remembers: 'He emerged from the briefing with his usual calm gone, muttering 'Too many fighters on that route!' When the rest came out they all looked a bit ruffled and one chap said: 'He got more than a bit worked up about the fighters[6].'

*I never had a premonition and I believe the same can be said of the rest of the Heavery crew. At least, if they did they never spoke about it. Keeping busy was the secret of staying sane. Some of us had deeper thoughts and wrote 'last letters,' usually hidden, self-consciously, in a kitbag. I received an occasional parcel from home – usually containing sweets and cakes, together with a short note. Yet my war was a remote affair. It seemed better that way. There was a telephone in the shop but I never called Mother. I never wrote a last letter to my family. What could I say? They had no idea of life on an operational squadron. Would my words have had any meaning for them?*

*It would be quite wrong, however, to conclude that the atmosphere in our billets and Mess was all doom and gloom. Quite the opposite! We lived for the moment and enjoyed our strange release from worries about the future. It was liberating. No-one cared about money. I seem to remember that air gunners received 14 shillings and sixpence a day, as did wireless ops and engineers. Navigators and pilots got an extra few shillings. The money built up as there were few opportunities to spend it. Gambling was rife. People showed no restraint and smiled as they lost everything. Card-playing for money was banned but bets were placed on the quiet during darts matches and games of Crown and Anchor, a popular dice game. Later in the war I watched Crown and Anchor schools play all night and five pound bets were commonplace. Huge sums, by the standards of the day, changed hands and no-one cared. A man with no future has no need of money!*

The crew's tour with 467 Squadron began at a time when the Germans were improving their air defences. The squadron's losses mounted but Knott noticed no deterioration in morale:

*Occasional bad weather periods grounded the squadron. This gave people time to think – always a dangerous habit. The solution was to keep busy. Our Station Commander made a point of keeping minds and bodies active. On one occasion we were briefed in groups, driven out by lorry into the night and told to find our way to another airfield. Our job was to evade security patrols and 'capture' Flying Control at one of the neighbouring stations. We had a lot of fun that night and the objective changed hands several times.*

*Some individuals drank too much but it was hard work getting drunk on weak wartime beer. Nevertheless, drinking and socialising were close companions and they played an important part in the life of an operational squadron. When I started to fly I was determined to avoid heavy drinking. My Father was a different man when sober and painful boyhood experiences had coloured my views. When the tour started, however, I found it impossible to avoid every boozy session in the Mess. I had a tendency to nurse a half-pint but there were many occasions worthy of a real binge. For most of us drinking was*

*the obvious way to relax and relieve the strain.*

Heavery's aircraft never turned back during the tour. An 'early return' could trigger ugly suspicions and close questioning. An individual might find himself accused of 'LMF' (lack of moral fibre). Fear of being branded LMF encouraged crews to put up with one or more significant technical failures on the outward leg. It was better to 'press on' and bomb the target rather than face an embarrassing inquest over a decision to turn back. There was also the strong desire to add one more sortie to the tally. An operation, once under way, had already consumed too much courage to be aborted without a struggle:

*We had our fair share of problems, with GEE box failures and other faults, but we carried on regardless. We had all heard stories of crews who had turned back having experienced problems in the air. Later, some were confronted with the news that their aircraft had been tested on the ground and found free of fault. This left an unpleasant taste in everyone's mouth.*

It has been suggested that LMF was commonplace but those making the claim have no direct experience of life on a bomber station during 1943 and 1944:

*I came across no case of LMF during my tour with 467 Squadron. It is only right, however, to add the qualification that these matters were dealt*

*Premonition: 'Ray' Raphael (far right) and crew are interviewed by a war correspondent on returning from Dortmund on May 4, 1943. Three months later, they all died during the Peenemünde attack. Raphael, who had become Squadron Commander only 48 hours earlier, following Gomm's loss, had a strong premonition that he would not return from Peenemünde. Photo: Vincent Holyoak.*

*with discreetly. There is always the possibility that some LMF cases occurred and were covered up. Nevertheless, my main point holds good: instances of LMF were extremely rare. Successful cover-ups would have been impossible had LMF been commonplace.*

Terraine (*The right of the line*) records the observations of Wing Commander J Lawson, of the Air Ministry Personnel Department. Lawson stated that in the 12 months to June 1944 (a period including the horrific losses of the Berlin campaign), suspected LMF cases represented less than 0.4 per cent of Bomber Command aircrew[13]. During the Battle of Berlin 2,938 aircrew died and 716 became prisoners of war[14]. The view that LMF cases were very few in number is backed by those who know best – the men who served with the squadrons. They include Searby (*The bomber battle for Berlin*), Hampton (*Selected for aircrew*) and, of course, Sidney Knott of 467 Squadron.

It is also true, however, that aircrew volunteered in a state of ignorance of the facts of life and death in Bomber Command and the powerful psychological stress imposed by ops. As Hampton observed: 'The realities of war came as a surprise, if not a profound shock, to everyone.' Yet the system offered no honourable way out for those who felt themselves crumbling under the pressure[15].

A man who refused to continue to fly might be offered the chance to think things over and change his mind. In general, however, there was no attempt to approach the problem as a potential medical condition. Certainly, there was no 'counselling' in the modern sense.

*Good reason for a binge: Squadron Leader Thiele's DSO party. In the second row are Paula Fisher and Cosme Gomm, standing together but later separated by the Squadron Commander's death over France. Photo: Jim George.*

The 1943 equivalent might be the brusque instruction to 'pull yourself together!'

Everyone recognised the importance of removing the LMF individual from the operational environment as quickly as possible. The manner of his going depended on the attitude of his station and squadron commanders. Some unfortunates disappeared quietly overnight, posted to unpleasant RAF receptacles for the unwanted or inadequate. Some were subjected to humiliation before their comrades. Harsh treatment, in any event, conflicted with the fact that LMF was not recognised as a disciplinary offence under the Air Force Act[16].

Fear of failure is a strong motivator. The threat of disgrace is an effective means of keeping people in line. This is beyond dispute, regardless of the many moral questions surrounding Bomber Command's insensitive, often brutal LMF system. Sixty years on, it is hard to escape the conclusion that LMF was a system deliberately and ruthlessly engineered to exploit fear of humiliation. This is quite different from suggesting that such fear was necessary in order to ensure aircrew continued to fly on operations. This would be an unforgivable insult to a body of men who showed the greatest courage in the face of terrible odds. Perhaps the LMF system is more a reflection of the inadequacies of those who devised it, rather than any failings, or potential failings, on the part of Bomber Command's volunteer aircrew.

*LMF was a crude, unjust system. 'LMF' was stamped across the individual's documents and that stigma stayed with him for the rest of his life. I'm sure most of them wanted to do their duty. All aircrew, time and again, had to swallow their fear when flying on ops. In some cases, inevitably, nerves snapped and minds and bodies could take no more.*

*It is interesting to contrast this with attitudes today. In recent conflicts, a few soldiers and pilots have refused to participate in combat BEFORE their first battle or mission. This is a very different situation – a sharp contrast to the position of a man who might have had 20 or more operations in his logbook at the point of failure! What of the poor devil who had squeezed out his last drops of courage and just couldn't climb that ladder, enter the fuselage and take off for his twenty-first trip?*

*There must be a cut-off point for courage, sealed deep inside everyone. Many aircrew had the tell-tale signs of the condition known as 'flak-happy'. The remorseless build-up of tension materialised in a facial twitch or a tendency to talk too much. Occasionally, it turned a man inwards and locked him in a box of detached silence.*

*I was surprised at my ability to cope. When my operational service ended I felt tremendous pride and, at the same time, profound gratitude that my reservoir of courage had been large enough to meet the demands of the bomber war. No doubt there are exceptions, but I'm sure most aircrew would feel for the man who had repeatedly dipped into his reservoir of courage and, on one dark night at the dispersal, found to his horror that the reservoir was dry.*

Bomber Command suffered the highest casualty rate of any arm of the services[17]. Due to the nature of the bomber war many stories of great courage in extreme circumstances will never be told – as there were no survivors. During his interrogation at the end of the war, NJG.4's Major Schnaufer paid tribute to the courage of British aircrew in doomed aircraft. He recalled that, in some instances, the gunners continued to fire accurately even though their aircraft was in flames and going down (Appendix 3; 25).

Perhaps this extreme form of courage has its counterpoint in the man who had the guts to 'go LMF', rather than jeopardise the lives of his crew through his own impaired performance. Surely a proportion of LMF cases would have soldiered on but for the added pressure of putting the lives of six close friends at risk? Courage is expressed in many ways.

*Today, when I look back, I can smile at my own fears. They were always strongest on the ground, when given some unwelcome administrative responsibility such as Orderly Sergeant. Things were different in the turret. I was my own boss and, to some extent at least, I had control of the situation.*

Superstitions and rituals helped many operational aircrew cope with the stress:

*We never changed our flying kit. No matter how filthy or decrepit a helmet or jersey became, it was treasured. This principle always applied and new equipment was spurned. One Londoner on 467, a sergeant gunner called Robson, refused to wear the superior Taylor suit. He stuck with his existing oily and battered kit.*

Sidney Knott wore the same sweater throughout the tour. It went unwashed for five months and his sole concession to personal hygiene was a decision to wear it inside out. His battledress took on the shabby appearance that marked out the veteran. No-one took much notice on an operational station. There was no 'dress code' other than the freedom to be different. Many a man flew over Germany with a girlfriend's stocking tucked inside his sweater:

*I contented myself with a Balaclava to keep my head warm. Others carried items of female underwear in their pockets. Some crews developed the habit of 'group peeing' on one of the wheels immediately before take-off. Lucky charms were commonplace. I had a wishbone and a rabbit's foot. My father made tiny wooden boxes to hold these talismans. My mother was superstitious. She was responsible for a wishbone wrapped in red, white and blue ribbons. It disintegrated with age but, in 2003, I still have the rabbit's foot. Back in 1943 I never took them on sorties – they stayed in my kitbag. Before flying I would stare at the kitbag and say to myself: 'I'm coming back for them!' And I did!*

Superstition made no concession to rank. The air gunner badge was designed in late 1939. Marshal of the Royal Air Force Sir Cyril Newall, Chief of the Air Staff, noticed that the wing had 13 feathers. He approved the design but with the caveat that aircrew would prefer a wing with 12 or

14 feathers. One feather was removed[18].

In the Summer of 1943 Flight Sergeant Bob Gates, an Australian pilot with 467 Squadron, put his faith in the Antipodean equivalent of Knott's rabbit foot. He draped a 'lucky kangaroo's foot' around his neck and developed the habit of kissing it before taking off on a raid. He also changed his socks before every sortie, favouring the brightly coloured rugby variety for ops[19].

*Lucky charms aside, we preferred to rely on skill and judgement. I wouldn't have thrown away my wishbone but I concentrated on avoiding mistakes which might cost lives! Early on, we decided we would never, under any circumstances, go round again over a target. With one exception, La Spezia, we followed this rule. We also adopted official advice never to fly over British convoys. The Royal Navy was famous for its trigger-happy tendencies and ignorance of aircraft recognition.*

*We practiced escape drill at the dispersal. I knew the difficulties involved in abandoning the aircraft. The safest exit was through the front escape hatch, in the floor of the nose. The hatch was released by a central handle and lifted inwards. If there was no time to reach this hatch my way out was through the rear door. The drill was to find my chute, clip it on, kneel down by the door, curl into a ball and roll out head first, legs tucked in tight. The main thing was to avoid being struck by the tail when jumping from the rear door. Aircrew were warned to use this only in extreme emergency. Many years after the war I met a former gunner (Ken Apps, from Ramsgate) who had escaped without injury from a Lanc's rear door, to become a prisoner of war.*

*Later, while a tour-expired 'screened gunner' at an OTU, I taught a rapid exit technique from the turret. There was a knack to it; some people were awkward and never got the hang of it.*

*On successfully abandoning the aircraft it was 'every man for himself'. We had lectures on how to evade capture. One talk was given by a sergeant who had done the impossible. He had evaded after baling out over Germany. He made his way into France by keeping to the fields, avoiding roads and staying out of sight during the daylight hours. On one occasion, in a starved condition, he came across a crop of carrots and ate so many his skin turned orange for a while. Later, he continued to serve his country by acting as a model for those cultivating survival and evasion skills. He made a lecture tour of the bomber stations, having shown that a 'home run' from Germany was possible without fluent German. In fact, he didn't speak a word of German!*

Ditching in the sea might result if an aircraft was damaged and lacked the fuel or power to make it home. This was a serious subject as survival time in the sea during Winter was measured in minutes. It was vital to do everything right. The 'J-Type' dinghy was stowed in the starboard wing. It could be released and inflated manually from the inside by pulling a cord or, from the outside, by pulling a loop on the starboard side, to the rear of the tailplane leading edge. There was, however, an immersion switch for automatic deployment.

*Smiles of relief: Freddie Wilmot and crew receive mugs of tea laced with rum from a WAAF as they await debrief. Wilmot's aircraft failed to return on his eighth operation, to Düsseldorf in June 1943. Wilmot (right) has no known grave and is commemorated at Runnymede. Photo: Vincent Holyoak.*

There were eight procedures for a Lancaster ditching, including lowering thirty degrees of flap and warning the crew 'Brace for ditching!' A further eighteen steps were set out in the drill for evacuation after the aircraft had settled on the water[20]. Heavery's crew practiced dinghy drill until they were confident they could survive if the aircraft stayed afloat long enough to allow them to get out.

Baling out over enemy territory was an occupational hazard. The crews received detailed briefings on German interrogation techniques. Under the Geneva Convention prisoners of war were required to give only their name, rank and service number.

> *The relative benefits of Luftwaffe custody were stressed, as the Gestapo had a well-deserved reputation for brutality. The Luftwaffe usually showed respect for fellow flyers. Capture by the Gestapo, however, was not our main concern. Fire was always our greatest fear. If the Lanc took a direct hit and disintegrated we would know nothing about it. Fire was something else. We didn't dwell on it but we spent a lot of time practising firefighting in the fuselage. As for potential ignition sources, we were more concerned about fighters than flak.*

The German nightfighters were a force to be reckoned with. They did much to dictate Bomber Command's strategy[21]. Many accounts of the bomber war refer to a nightfighter ploy involving two aircraft – with one standing off from the intended victim and acting as a decoy. Sidney Knott has no recollection of crew discussions about 'double act' fighter tactics and his doubts are supported by the record of Major Schnaufer's June 1945 interrogation. He said his unit, NJG.4, never carried out coordinated attacks, adding that any involvement of two fighters was coincidental. Schnaufer also pointed to the practical difficulties of flying together at night (Appendix 3; 14).

According to Schnaufer and his comrades, 98 per cent of the aircraft shot down by NJG4 were 'flamers'. The nightfighter pilots had noticed that the Lancaster caught fire more readily than the Halifax. The favoured aiming point was between the two engines on either side, hitting the fuel tanks, or the rear turret if the gunner opened fire. Of the bombers shot down by NJG4, 10 per cent fired or took evasive action first, 40 per cent did not fire or manoeuvre and 50 per cent fired or manoeuvred after the fighter opened fire. There was competition among the nightfighter pilots, to see who could shoot down the most bombers with the lowest expenditure of ammunition (Appendix 3; 9, 15, 16).

> *Competitive spirit also played an important part in the life of Bomber Command aircrew. Cochrane, Air Officer Commanding 5 Group, increased the pressure by introducing a new scheme. Lancaster Captains bringing back aiming point photos were awarded certificates. The photos, identified by crew, were displayed outside the Briefing Room. The snag, of course, was that we had to fly straight and level for 20 seconds or more after releasing the bombs, waiting for the photoflash to detonate. A variation on this theme was an open competition. Crews won status – if they lived long enough – by accumulating points awarded for photos showing bombs on target. This practice was dropped eventually, as only those aircraft in the initial wave could hope for a worthwhile photo. Later arrivals would find the target obscured by smoke.*

Bomber Command continued to recognise the role of competitive spirit in building and maintaining morale. This lived on, post-war, in the 'Bombing Ladder' – essentially a bombing competition between squadrons[22].

Good night vision had survival value. Front line squadrons had special night vision training rooms for air gunners:

> *Everyone has a 'preferred eye' with vision superior to the other eye. The preferred eye will focus first on an object. There is also a small blind spot in the field of vision when looking straight ahead, but this is not noticeable in binocular vision. During the day these effects were too minor to notice, but they made a big difference at night. We were taught that it was better to glance than to stare. Vision tends to fade when staring at an object. It was also better to look slightly to one side than straight ahead. There are more of the 'rods' required for night vision at the periphery of the eye. It was pitch black inside our night vision hut and aircraft recognition tests under these*

*conditions were tougher than the reality. It took around 20 minutes for our eyes to settle down in the darkened room. This is known as 'dark adaptation'. Maximum night vision is achieved after 20 minutes.*

The tension increased as the hours slipped away before a raid. Many operations were cancelled (scrubbed) but the tension remained, a solid lump in the stomach. It was difficult to unwind and get to sleep and some men developed highly individual ways of letting off steam. When an operation was scrubbed the crews gathered in the Mess or headed for the 'local' if time allowed:

*Ted and I usually returned before the others. Later, the others trooped in, wide awake and boisterous. Nick would perform his gorilla act, swinging around, jumping on the beds, running over Ted and screeching at the top of his voice. Ted was more strait-laced than most and he was always Nick's preferred target for 'monkey business'.*

Heavery's crew flew 11 different Lancasters on operations during their tour with 467 Squadron, from January to May 1943. Only one of the 11 aircraft survived into 1944 and that failed to return in the January. Nine of the bombers became casualties during raids; another was destroyed in an accident at Scampton and the remaining aircraft crashed:

*Lancaster W4823, 467 Squadron and subsequently 50 Squadron, destroyed at Scampton when Lancaster W4834 (57 Squadron) blew up on the ground, March 15 1943[23][24]. A 4,000 lb Cookie fell from the 57 Squadron aircraft and exploded at 09.00. It also wrecked two other 57 Squadron aircraft (ED306 and ED594), together with W4823 and two other visiting 50 Squadron aircraft (W4112 and W4196) positioned nearby. Five other Lancasters suffered significant damage in one of the worst incidents of this type during the war[25][26].*

*Lancaster ED500 (Q-Queenie), January 29 1943, crashed just south of Audlem, Cheshire, August 3 1943, when three engines failed in flight; salvaged but struck off charge (213 hours)[27][28].*

*Lancaster ED523, January 23 1943, failed to return from Stuttgart, March 11/12 1943 (69 hours)[28].*

*Lancaster ED524 (T-Tommy), January 23 1943, failed to return from Essen, April 3/4 1943 (111 hours)[28].*

*Lancaster ED530 (O-Orange), January 26 1943, ditched in English Channel on returning from Munich, October 2/3 1943[27][28].*

*Lancaster ED547 (M-Mother), January 28 1943, failed to return from Berlin, December 29/30 1943 (511 hours)[28].*

*Lancaster ED621 (V-Victor), from 39 MU March 22 1943, failed to return from Munich, October 2/3 1943[28][29][30].*

*Lancaster ED695 (J-Jig), February 28 1943, failed to return from Düsseldorf, May 25/26 1943 (148 hours)[28][29].*

*Lancaster ED737 (PO-F, then PO-P from April 20/21 1943, then PO-G from*

*June 12/13 to loss), March 1943, failed to return from Cologne, June 16/17 1943 (194 hours)*[28 30 31].

*Lancaster ED764 (N-Nuts), March 1943, failed to return from Peenemünde, August 17/18 1943*[28].

*Lancaster ED772, March 1943, went to 463 Squadron, November 1943, failed to return from Berlin, January 30/31 1944*[28].

# CHAPTER TWELVE

## *Simple Pleasures*

Dᴜʀɪɴɢ the late morning of Wednesday April 21, having slept off the exertions of long hauls to La Spezia and Stettin, Heavery's crew savoured the prospect of a few days off. They decided to spend the first 48 hours resting up.

Life in the Sergeants' Mess, for the most part, was much quieter than in the Officers' Mess, where boisterous games were played on occasion. They included 'High Cockalorum' (piling up furniture and planting sooty footprints on the ceiling) and 'Are you there, Moriarty?' (blindfolding two individuals, tying them together and encouraging them to beat each other with rolled-up newspapers). Such antics were unthinkable in Bottesford's Sergeants' Mess, tightly controlled by disciplinarians headed by a 'Chairman of Messing' renowned for his lack of *joie de vivre*.

Heavery's crew sought their entertainment elsewhere. They were in luck on Friday morning. Heavery was told his crew could have 24-hour passes provided no 'maximum effort' for that night had been called by noon. They made for the Flight Office to pick up the passes. Only the flight engineer cried off the visit to Nottingham. His six comrades left the main gate and began a brisk three-mile hike to Bottesford railway station.

*Our Engineer had a good reason for going solo, having been captivated by the charms of a 'temporary war widow'. He paid for this later, when an army sergeant returned unexpectedly from the Middle East and converted his face into a good likeness of a panda. He took it in good part, claiming the pleasure was worth the pain.*

*There was some good-natured argument about how to spend the day. Nick, our bomb aimer, was a little older and well-educated. Before the war he had worked as a trainee estate agent and had made the most of his few extra years by cultivating more sophisticated tastes. He insisted that our first priority should be a slap-up meal.*

*We began to trawl Nottingham's shabby wartime streets and Nick eventually found a promising restaurant. Well, it certainly looked posh in relation to the rest. We were easy to please, being accustomed to a standard diet of 'chips and beans with everything'. Bugger the expense! We had money in our pockets, not enough time to spend it and no reason to save. In wartime Britain the maximum charge for a restaurant meal was restricted by law to five shillings. This was no handicap to an expensive restaurant, as the regulations rather stupidly allowed a service charge.*

*Sophisticated tastes: Nick Murray, who was commissioned on completion of his tour with 467 Squadron. Photo: Flo Murray.*

*This was huge when all the 'extras' were added.*

*The restaurant occupied a basement and Nick led the way down the steps. We were shown to a nice table and began studying the menu. This appeared to be in a foreign language. Frankly, we were just kids from very modest backgrounds and we hadn't a clue. Nick dealt with our embarrassment by ordering crab salads all round. That was it! We left the restaurant in a bemused state and still very hungry. We now began to search for real food.*

The boys regarded Murray's 'slap-up-meal' as a mere starter. Crab salad was all very well, but they wanted real food which, by definition, is fried. During the afternoon they spotted one of Nottingham's many greasy cafés. The place looked promising as people were queuing outside, waiting for the crowded, sticky tables to become vacant. Inside, the room was full of customers. The atmosphere was smelly and heavy with tobacco smoke. Soon, Heavery and his crew were downing eggs, fried bread and soggy chips, with bread and butter to mop up the grease and egg yolk. Contentment settled over the group. Satisfaction had arrived at the modest price of just over one shilling a plate. There was still plenty of time to take in a show. They bought tickets for a music hall matinee and sat through a succession of acts of very mixed quality.

*It was still quite early – around seven in the evening – when we left the theatre. Beer was our next priority. Nottingham's many pubs were heavily patronised by aircrew. Popular haunts included the Black Boy and Flying Horse but we had our own favourite. The skipper loved a pint. Frank never drank alone as Ken, the mid-upper gunner, always kept him company. Their enthusiasm sorted out the rest of the evening. We knew the perfect place, where they were not too fussy about the rules. Most pubs shut early in the interests of the war effort and the need to keep workers committed to their 12-hour shifts.*

*We pushed through the blackout curtain and stepped inside. There was no bar – just a crowded room full of people enjoying a drink and a sing-song. My eyes watered, under attack from thick whirlpools of cigarette smoke. I blinked and focused on the familiar sight of the big woman bashing away on an upright piano. Her bulk dwarfed the instrument and, together, they filled a small stage.*

*We had visited this pub several times before. I don't know how it started but, whenever we turned up, the large pianist would play the hit song 'Jealousy'. It became our signature tune. A small group of people got up and found us a table. The beer soon arrived and we thanked the man who had paid for the round. We soon gave up trying to pay. More drinks arrived like clockwork, each donor acknowledging the treat with a brisk wave of the hand. Our table filled with glasses and still the beer continued to flow. We never bought a round. Later, reluctantly, we left the free beer, the piano and our friends. The strains of Jealousy, our tango, died away as we stumbled into the Nottingham Blackout. Making the most of a faint glimmer of light I looked at my watch. It was only nine o'clock!*

So far the crew had spent nine of their precious 24 hours – about as much time as it took them to fly to Pilsen and back a few days before. After two meals they had downed a series of pints. Now they were hungry once more, stomachs responding to the smell of nearby fish and chips as they ambled away from the pub. They ate their fill in the small fish shop's upstairs dining room, then set off in search of their beds. The accommodation had been booked on their arrival in Nottingham. Fortunately, they were very tired and in no mood to be fussy:

*This B&B was rough and ready, more like a small dormitory. I collapsed across the mean little bed and went out like a light until breakfast. Ideally, we would be through Bottesford's main gate about an hour before our passes expired. Sure enough, we arrived on the station at around 11 am, with plenty of time to change and claim lunch. Our crew – with the possible exception of the engineer – were always more interested in food than girls. We were permanently hungry.*

*As we travelled back to Bottesford on the train my mind chewed over the statistics. We had completed 23 ops. Seven more to go. We could make it! And we were on the Battle Order again. Having indulged in Nottingham's simple pleasures we felt invigorated and took this news in our stride. By mid-afternoon we were aloft in J-Jig (ED695) for a night flying test. Later, however, the operation was scrubbed.*

There was no flying for Heavery the next day, Sunday April 25. On the Monday morning, however, the crew began preparations for their last op in April. They flew J-Jig on the third attack against Duisburg in 19 days. Fortunately they were to enjoy a real break on their return during the early hours of Tuesday. It was to be a fortnight before they flew on ops again.

Others serving at Bottesford had more glamorous plans for short passes and leave. Section Officer Marie Cooper recalls that one popular Squadron Officer was more worldly-wise than most. This became evident when she and four others from Bottesford met up with him in London.

The party went on to a nightclub – a first for Marie: 'A table had been booked and, when eyes adjusted to the gloom and ears to the noise, we attacked our first bottle of whisky and danced on our allotted two square feet of floor. As the night wore on, another bottle was bought but we drank from the one that had been brought with us, being informed that, after the first bottle, subsequent ones were lethal and get more so as the clients get increasingly drunk. Wicked world!'[1].

'In the 'Ladies', instructing me as to how a new kind of suspender worked, the Aussie lady whom I shall call Anne told me that our Flight Lieutenant wanted to marry her. She had just got a divorce but, much as she liked him, she didn't want to do so. She hoped, very firmly, that he would find someone else. This prepared us for the little drama when the taxi stopped to drop her off at her flat and she tried to persuade him to stay with these nice young things, instead of following her inside. He was not to be put off and the nice young things went off on their own[1].'

Marie had more serious interests. She had worked hard to maintain her professional contacts in the world of archaeology by making regular visits to the British Museum and attending lectures. It was an uphill struggle:'Archaeology seemed utterly irrelevant. None of us knew what life would be like after the war, except that it seemed quite impossible that it could ever go back to pre-war days and values that were beginning to assume the qualities of a dream[1].'

CHAPTER THIRTEEN

# Frank's Shock Decision

In early May the accelerating deliveries of new aircraft made it possible to increase the strength of each Lancaster squadron to 26 aircraft, plus two reserves[1]. A stand-down from ops made life a little easier for Heavery's crew during the month and six days of precious leave gave them a much-needed respite.

> *Fifteen days had passed since our last flight, the Duisburg raid on April 26. We climbed into N-Nuts (ED764) at just after 14.30 on Tuesday May 11 for a routine night flying test. Our last trip in this aircraft had been to La Spezia, carrying that unusual all-incendiary load. We took off for the air test at 15.05, wondering why we felt so relieved to be back in the air. As usual, on landing back we had a good look around the aircraft, checking for glycol leaks and other potential problems that could affect serviceability for operations.*

The crew were allocated N-Nuts for Bomber Command's main attack on Wednesday May 12. At the station bomb dump the heavy bombs were taken from storage and loaded onto trolleys. As the navigators' briefing began the armourers worked up a sweat at the dispersal. 'Olive Oyl' would continue her hate campaign against Hitler that night and N-Nuts' bomb-bay was filled with 10 1,000 lb bombs. This was an unusual war-load. The growing air assault on Germany had put pressure on bomb supply and there were times when aircraft were bombed up with whatever was available.

Speculation over the target ended in the briefing room. The Main Force intended to raid Duisburg again – the fourth visit to this city during the Battle of the Ruhr.

The earlier raids had produced disappointing results. The outcome of this attack was to be different. A total of 572 aircraft were dispatched: 238 Lancasters, 142 Halifaxes, 112 Wellingtons, 70 Stirlings and 10 Mosquitos. Casualties were heavy; the 34 missing aircraft amounted to 5.9 per cent of the raiding force[2]. A total of 38 aircraft were struck off charge. The Ruhr defences were strengthened at this time, with more nightfighters deployed to airfields in the Netherlands[3].

Despite the air defence successes the city was ravaged. The marking by Oboe Mosquitos was accurate and the bombing was concentrated. The city centre and port area suffered severely. Around 1,600 buildings were destroyed and over 270 people died. In the dull, smoky light of the

following morning the population emerged unsteadily from their
shelters. They found that much of what had remained of Duisburg had
been flattened[2].

> *We took off for Duisburg at around midnight. The late start was due to the*
> *state of the moon. This raid was timed to ensure the moon had set before we*
> *crossed the coast.*

During their run over the target the Oboe Mosquitos dropped red TIs
with great accuracy. These were backed-up by green TIs. Around 80 per
cent of the reds fell within the aiming point. A photo reconnaissance
flight on Thursday morning found a 10,000 ft smoke plume towering
over the docks. Just a few hours before, on their way back from the
target, some returning crews could still see the fires at a distance of 150
miles, while over the Zuider Zee[4].

Duisburg had claim to the title of most attacked city in Happy Valley.
It received over 5,000 tonnes of bombs during the Battle of the Ruhr[5].

Heavery's crew flew home through the small hours of Thursday and
landed back at Bottesford at just after 04.00. Later, they heard that
Thiele had not returned but he was known to be safe. Their Flight
Commander's aircraft had taken a flak hit during the bombing run. The
shell had removed half of the starboard outer Merlin and damaged the
starboard inner. The explosion also blew out much of the cockpit
perspex. Thiele was struck on the head by a splinter. The aircraft made
a successful crash-landing at Coltishall and Keith Thiele received an
immediate DSO, the squadron's first[6].

After a few snatched hours of rest Heavery left his hut and walked to
the Flight Office. He then informed the crew that they were on the Battle
Order. Once again, they would be flying N-Nuts and the heavy petrol
load indicated a long trip.

> *Our next target turned out to be Pilsen again. Hopefully, our bombs*
> *would fall on Skoda this time. The bomb-load for this second attempt, a*
> *Cookie and five 1,000 lb bombs, was heavier by 3,000 lbs. We could carry*
> *a heavier bomb-load as we needed less fuel due to a more direct route. In*
> *April, the first Pilsen op had taken nine hours 10 minutes. On this occasion*
> *the shorter route reduced our time in the air to seven hours 45 minutes. This*
> *Flight Plan was influenced by the shorter nights of May. Inevitably, this*
> *made life more difficult for the raid planners.*

A force of 156 Lancasters and 12 Halifaxes made this second attempt
to destroy the Skoda Works but success eluded the raiders. Once again
the target proved difficult to locate and mark accurately and most bombs
fell on farmland to the north of the Skoda Works[7].

> *Pilsen was far beyond Oboe range. Unfortunately, the terrain on the*
> *approach to Pilsen rendered H2S ineffectual for orientation and target-finding*
> *purposes. Our earlier Pilsen losses went unavenged.*

There were consequences resulting from this second failure. Geoff
Whitten, a 35 Squadron PFF navigator in a Halifax II (JB786),
recalled in *Pathfinders at War*: 'The day after the raid on Pilsen, all

pilots, navigators and set operators of the marking crews were summoned to Group HQ at Wyton, where Don Bennett conducted a most clinically-cold post mortem. He had already had all the navigation logs sent to him and had worked through them all to discover where each of us had gone wrong. It was not very pleasant to have our errors publicly exposed by someone whose knowledge of air navigation brooked no contradiction[8].'

*We had a day off after the second Pilsen raid and this was followed by a welcome surprise. The squadron stood down from operations. Daily orders from Group continued this state of affairs for nine days. This was very unusual. We discovered later that the stand-down was general throughout Bomber Command.*

*At the squadron level, 467 had taken losses and a number of new crews were posted in as replacements. We returned to full strength and the stand-down was seen as an opportunity to cram in as much training as possible. While we were veterans we didn't escape the training blitz. We flew on seven of the nine stand-down days, practising high-level bombing, formation flying and air-firing. On May 22 we flew a short but exhilarating low-level cross-country. Most flights, however, were for bombing practice and each visit to the range involved ED772. This aircraft's bombing system had been upgraded and Nick was expected to master the new gadgets. We dropped our practice bombs over Wainfleet Range, in a remote corner of the Wash just along the coast from Boston.*

The bombing exercises followed a routine. The Flight Office telephoned RAF Wainfleet to book Heavery a place on the range. Sidney Knott visited Wainfleet – on the ground – for the first time after the war:

*It is a truly desolate place facing out into the Wash, the shallow water covering miles of mudflats at high tide. I stood there and remembered flying over the range just a few years earlier. In my mind I could hear Frank reporting in, giving our call sign and number. The range followed a strict timetable. Any delay meant forfeiting your turn and stooging around, with all eyes open for other aircraft in the same predicament. Nick dropped his bombs from 18,000 ft to 20,000 ft, releasing one on each run. On the ground recording stations took bearings on each practice bomb dropped.*

*The most serious problem for the crew during May was Frank's shock decision to go teetotal. This had an unfortunate influence on the quality of his landings. They went from smooth to appalling virtually overnight. We pleaded with him to come to his senses and swallow a beer. Happily, he had managed to frighten himself as well as the rest of us. He ordered a beer and was soon back on form.*

There was one spectacular Bomber Command operation during the stand-down. The Dams Raid was flown on the night of May 16/17 1943. Had Heavery's crew decided to join the 'special duties' squadron, Sunday May 16 might well have been their last day on Earth. It was for many 617 Squadron aircrew, including Vernon Byers and his crew, formerly of 467 Squadron.

The last three trips of Sidney Knott's first tour were to Ruhr targets: Dortmund, Düsseldorf and, finally, the dreaded Essen. Twelve cans of 30lb phosphorus incendiaries joined a 4,000 lb Blockbuster in the bomb-bay of Lancaster ED772 on Sunday May 23, a week after the Dams Raid. The big Cookie was hoisted into the bomb-bay first, at a position close to the aircraft's centre of gravity[9]. There were 15 bomb stations in the Lancaster's bomb-bay, arranged in three rows of five. The Cookie was secured to No. 13, the middle station.

The target, Dortmund, was among the most heavily defended cities in Happy Valley. This attack was the largest in the Battle of the Ruhr series, with 826 aircraft dispatched. The force consisted of 343 Lancasters, 199 Halifaxes, 151 Wellingtons, 120 Stirlings and 13 Mosquitos. The losses amounted to 38 aircraft (4.6 per cent) and the casualties included eight Lancasters[10]. A total of 41 aircraft were struck off charge.

Dortmund was a maximum effort for 467, with the squadron dispatching a record 24 aircraft[11]. The ground crews had made the most of the stand-down, bringing more aircraft to operational status. Within a few months of its establishment 467 had developed a reputation for high utilisation of its squadron strength.

The Dortmund attack was successful. The weather was favourable and the marking accurate. Destruction enveloped a large area of the city; some 2,000 buildings were wrecked and around 600 people died. Bomber Command found it unnecessary to visit Dortmund again for another year[10].

ED772 touched down at Bottesford at 03.10 on Monday May 24, bringing the crew's twenty-seventh sortie to a successful conclusion. They slept late and had the rest of the day free. Bomber Command mounted no large-scale raid that night.

> *The next op was to Düsseldorf, on the Tuesday. During the late afternoon we took ED772 on the usual half-hour night flying test. On our return the armourers loaded a Cookie and 12 SBCs. We got the green at 23.05 and ED772 began to roll.*

Another 758 aircraft were also on their way. The navigators had been briefed to concentrate over the city for a devastating assault. The participating aircraft consisted of 323 Lancasters, 169 Halifaxes, 142 Wellingtons, 113 Stirlings and 12 Mosquitos. A total of 686 aircraft attacked. The night's losses totalled 27 aircraft, or 3.6 per cent of the force (29 aircraft were struck off charge). The casualties included nine Lancasters. The raid was a failure due to marking problems caused by cloud and the bombing was scattered[12].

> *Our twenty-ninth operation was to Essen, perhaps the most feared in a long list of hated Ruhr targets. On Thursday May 27 we took off on what was to be our last flight in ED772. We were airborne at 21.55 and landed back five hours 10 minutes later, having emptied our bomb-bay over the home of Krupps.*

*On the move: Intelligence Officer Marie Cooper left Bottesford. This photograph of Marie and a 'Hillman Minx' was taken at Metheringham in 1944. Photo: Vincent Holyoak.*

The crew's Lancaster was one of 518 aircraft dispatched: 274 Lancasters, 151 Halifaxes, 81 Wellingtons and 12 Mosquitos. A total of 493 aircraft attacked. The losses amounted to 23 aircraft (4.4 per cent), including six Lancasters. Cloud required the use of sky-markers and the bombing was scattered. The results were disappointing but some 490 buildings were destroyed and nearly 200 people died[13].

During May 467 Squadron had dispatched 142 aircraft to seven targets, losing four crews (Mahoney, Parsons, Giddey and Desmond)[14]. By May 467 Squadron was operating a higher proportion of squadron strength than any other unit in 5 Group. Furthermore, its bombing results showed continuous improvement[15].

The last raid of the Battle of the Ruhr series was flown during the next month (the June 14/15 attack against Oberhausen)[16]. A total of 203 aircraft were dispatched. Seventeen aircraft failed to return.

Intelligence Officer Marie Cooper left Bottesford. Before posting to Metheringham, she was sent on an Intelligence course at Harrow-on-the-Hill. Soon after her arrival, when presenting a simulated briefing, she won a standing ovation for telling her audience that they wouldn't be able to see much on the ground as the visibility over the Ruhr tended to be poor. This experience did her no lasting harm. On the subsequent posting to Metheringham she was allowed to brief crews. At that time she was the only WAAF officer in Bomber Command to do so.

Later, Marie was posted to 617 Squadron at Coningsby, at a time when Leonard Cheshire was Squadron Commander. Some of the original Dambusters were still with the squadron. Marie later married Flight Lieutenant John Claridge, a New Zealander and a pilot with 106 Squadron.

# CHAPTER FOURTEEN

# *The Magic Number*

ONLY one to go! This thought was unspoken yet shared as Heavery placed his Lancaster on Bottesford's main runway, completing another safe return from Essen. Later, the tired crew left the debriefing room and stumbled out into the early hours of a new day, Friday May 28. A tantalising prospect beckoned – staying alive into the Summer of 1943.

*We had survived 29 trips. Surely it wasn't asking too much to live through just one more? Our skipper had shown it could be done. Frank had completed 30. He had made an extra trip as second dicky with another crew, in preparation for his first operational flight commanding a Lanc.*

*We had breakfast and turned in. Later that day we were called to Gomm's office. We stood there, assembled as a crew, as the Squadron Commander looked us up and down. Then he broke into a smile and announced that we had done enough. Frank had reached the magic number. Gomm said he would not split the crew just to ensure everyone had 30 in the logbook.*

*We filed out of his office in a state of shock. It was hard to believe. It was over! We had finished the tour and we were alive! We were, in fact, the first among a group of the first three 467 crews to survive a full tour on the squadron. This called for a real binge, beginning with the biggest fry-up money could buy. The next 'target' was our favourite café at Long Bennington, a nearby village on the Great North Road. The chips were soggy and the helpings generous. The ground crews were invited to the bash. After the meal we would make for one of the village pubs, the Reindeer or the Wheatsheaf, where Frank and Ken would give a masterclass in beer-drinking.*

Heavery's crew were confirmed tour-expired on June 9. The crews of Sergeant Ball and Flying Officer Cairney were confirmed tour-expired three days later.

*Frank was not the type to brood. It was finished and that was that! He didn't give a second thought to the fact that his tour had opened with Essen (his second dicky trip) and had ended with a repeat performance over that most feared of German targets. His thoughts were fixed on the evening's celebrations, with no room for looking back.*

*Ken and Johnny made the arrangements for the 'Great Long Bennington Fry-up'. We were sure of a warm welcome as a wartime transport café expected little trade in the evenings. The owners were always glad to see us. This was a rough and ready place. The chairs were hard and there was no menu. Our plates were filled with whatever was available, with an egg or sausage for decoration. We could be sure of fried bread, beans and plenty of lovely, greasy chips.*

The evening approached as Heavery's crew prepared for their last 'operation' together. This would be different: no flak, no fighters and no deep freeze in the rear turret. There would be no danger – other than the risk of drinking too much and falling into a ditch during the dark, two-mile walk back to the airfield. They were soon ready to leave, with the exception of Sidney Knott. The gunner had a reputation for taking his time when preparing for a night out:

*I told them to get going and promised to catch up. Their excited voices died away and the room fell silent. I sat on the bed as my body relaxed for the first time in months. I had been a bit of a dreamer before the war but there was no place for daydreaming in a Lanc's rear turret. I eased my legs onto the bed and settled back. I needed a few quiet, private minutes. I closed my eyes and saw familiar faces. They belonged to men who had failed to return over the past few months.*

*There was Sergeant Vine. He had died in February on his eighth operation, the raid on Wilhelmshaven. When we climbed away in the dusk Vine's Lancaster flew close to us. His rear gunner acknowledged my salute as I dipped and raised the guns. This crew had been with us since OTU and we were friends. Vine's aircraft slowly disappeared from view as the night closed around us and he was gone forever. Our Lanc was one of five from 467 Squadron flying to Wilhelmshaven that night. Only three came back. Flight Lieutenant Michie also failed to return from this raid. It was his tenth trip.*

*Pilot Officer Mant's face came into my mind. The Heavery and Mant crews had once shared an exercise to Thornaby and back, for circuits and landings in a Manchester. Mant and his crew failed to return from their tenth trip, to Stuttgart on March 11/12.*

*Sergeant Aicken's operational career with 467 was much shorter. This crew completed just four trips. They failed to return on the fifth, to Berlin on January 17/18. Flight Sergeant Parsons, a C Flight Lancaster Captain, died on his tenth op – to Düsseldorf just three nights ago.*

*Some individuals had no faces. They were just names to me. There was Flying Officer Giddey, who had also failed to return from Düsseldorf just a couple of days ago. It was his first op with the squadron. I never got the chance to know this crew as they had spent just eight days with 467 Squadron. Only the skipper's unusual name had stuck in my mind. He survived as a prisoner of war. He had been lost in J-Jig (ED695) – a Lanc we had flown four times on ops.*

*Two of our Lancs failed to return from that first trip to Pilsen. This botched raid ended in the bombing of an asylum – an error not without irony. Sergeant Wilson went missing. He and two others survived as prisoners of war. It was this crew's seventh trip, one more than Sergeant Stuart and his crew, who also failed to return that night.*

*The squadron also suffered casualties on the second Pilsen raid. Sergeant*

*Mahoney failed to return. He was one of several pilots who had flown with us as second dicky. He had accompanied us to La Spezia exactly one month before he became a casualty. He and his crew failed to return from their sixth trip.*

*Our own survival seemed miraculous as this parade of the missing continued. These crews – all of them – were gone by their tenth operation. Then there was Byers, who had taken our place on 617 Squadron. He and his crew had been the first to die on the Dams Raid, barely two weeks before. I had voted to go to 'Squadron X'.*

*I stared at the ceiling and was surprised as other faces came into view even with my eyes open. Some crews became casualties despite their great experience. Flight Lieutenant Desmond had gone missing only last night – just a few hours ago. I had flown with Desmond on two occasions. We were practising circuits and bumps at Woodhall Spa and two crews were allocated to the one aircraft. He had flown the Lanc and both crews back to Bottesford. Earlier, at 1661 HCU, I was among the gunners he took up for air-firing exercises. Desmond's crew were on their twenty-second op when they failed to return from Essen.*

*As a new squadron 467 had benefited from the arrival of several very experienced crews. The idea was to give us a head start. The veterans posted in included an American, Pilot Officer Wark, DFC. He and his crew arrived at Bottesford to complete their tour. It was an unlucky move: they failed to return from their second operation with 467. Wark's crew became the squadron's first casualties.*

*Then there was Squadron Leader Paape, DFC and Bar, B Flight's Commander. He was on his second tour and went missing on his eighteenth trip with 467. The target had been Essen.*

Knott jumped as the hut door slammed. There were wild shouts as he fought off sleep and tried to focus on his watch. He was still staring at it, eyes wide in disbelief, when the inner door burst open. Boisterous with beer, Frank and the others rushed in shouting: 'Where the hell were you?'

*Getting no response beyond stunned silence they tipped me off the bed, placed it on top of me, sat on it and began to tell me about the wonderful evening I had missed. I was mortified. I couldn't believe it! To this day I don't know how it happened. Thank God we went on leave in the morning. I had wanted to thank the ground crews and armourers who had looked after us so well. Now I couldn't look them in the eye!*

The crew returned from their end-of-tour leave. There was no immediate recognition of their dogged performance during a difficult tour. Apparently, there were no instant decorations for the mere achievement of staying alive, despite their many trips to tough targets and the fact that they never turned back.

The onward postings arrived. The flight engineer stayed on; Jock Rodgers hadn't finished. Of the other six, Ted Foster was posted to 26 OTU. The rest, Sidney Knott included, were posted as 'screened' aircrew to 17 OTU at Silverstone, Northants. The crew's hard-won experience was to be shared with those getting ready to join squadrons and

*467 Squadron's last casualties at Bottesford: pictured (left to right) are Squadron Leader William James Lewis (A Flight Commander), Wing Commander JR 'Sam' Balmer (Squadron Commander) and Squadron Leader Keith Sinclair, B Flight Commander. The photograph was taken in September or October 1943. Lewis and two of his crew died during an attack on Düsseldorf on November 3/4 1943 and were 467 Squadron's last operational losses while at Bottesford. Photo: Vincent Holyoak.*

commence their first tours. In mixing with the new boys, or 'sprogs', the crew returned to the OTU cradle as changed men. Their experiences in combat stayed with them for the rest of their lives.

Arrangements were made to fly the five to their new home at Silverstone. Their distinguished 'cab driver' was Squadron Leader Thiele, DSO, DFC and Bar:

> *Thiele was one of several outstanding New Zealanders serving on the squadron at this time. Thursday June 10 was the day of our departure from Bottesford. Thiele dropped Ted off at RAF Wing, Buckinghamshire, the home of 26 OTU. He began to taxi back along the runway, ready for the next leg to Silverstone. Ted climbed out when the Lanc drew alongside the Control Caravan. I remember Ted throwing out his two kitbags. That was one sure way of identifying aircrew – one kitbag for flying clothing and the other for the rest of your worldly possessions. Ted clambered down. We said our goodbyes, pulled up the ladder and closed the door.*

> *Years later – long after the war – Ted confided in me. He said that watching Thiele's Lanc take off that day had been the saddest moment of his young life.*

Sidney Knott had accumulated 373 hours 25 minutes in his logbook (242 hours five minutes at night). His operational flying over 29 trips totalled 179 hours five minutes. He had fired 1,400 rounds on ops (all at ground defences).

Heavery's crew left Bottesford unscathed but 467 Squadron's losses continued. In the period April – July 1943 15 crews failed to return[1]. During the war, 346 aircrew died while flying from Bottesford; 118 have no known grave and are commemorated at the Runnymede memorial to the missing[2].

In November 1943 467 Squadron moved to Waddington. In 1945, 467 Squadron moved again, this time to Metheringham[3].

In all, 467 Squadron flew 3,833 Lancaster sorties (over 26,000 hours and more than 4.5 million miles) and dropped 17,528 tonnes of bombs. The losses totalled 104 aircraft (2.7 per cent) in 299 bombing and 15 minelaying raids. Fourteen additional Lancasters were involved in crashes[4]. Over 700 squadron aircrew were posted missing on operations, of whom 282 Australians were confirmed as killed in action. Sources differ on the exact numbers. 467/463 Squadrons researcher Jim George, for example, notes that the Roll of Honour compiled by Frank Slack and Raymond Glynne-Owen lists 591 aircrew of all nationalities killed in action, together with 166 listed as POWs, evaders or 'safe' (landed in territory occupied by Allied armies), so producing a total of 757.

The squadron's Lancaster war losses, at 2.7 per cent, exactly match the percentage loss for 5 Group's Lancasters overall. The Group's Lancasters flew 52,262 sorties and 1,389 aircraft were struck off charge[5]. The squadron disbanded at Metheringham on September 30, 1945[6]. The squadron's gunners had accounted for six enemy aircraft. In addition, they probably destroyed another 13 and damaged 21 others. The squadron aircrew had been awarded five DSOs, 146 DFCs, 36 DFMs and two Conspicuous Gallantry Medals.

Heavery's crew had completed 29 operations with some close calls but free of serious mishap – a rare achievement. During the tour they dropped five mines, 25 4,000 lb Cookies, 21 1,000 lb bombs and over 20,000 incendiaries. Twenty-two of the targets were German and a

*End of an eventful year: Marie Cooper kept these signatures when Bottesford's Mess closed in November 1943, immediately prior to the arrival of the Americans. Bottesford WAAFs had a sense of humour, with addresses including 'no fixed abode', 'The Nunnery' and 'The Workhouse'. Paula, always known as 'Paul', claimed to reside at 'The Gasworks'. Vincent Holyoak*

number of the raids formed part of the Battle of the Ruhr series. Duisburg was visited five times, Essen raided on four occasions and Berlin three times.

Heavery and his team had done well to survive. Nine operations were flown in March and another nine in April. Nine raids per month corresponds with the number of nights when weather conditions might be expected to favour Main Force raiding. In effect, Heavery's crew had contributed a personal maximum effort.

During 1943 2,225 Bomber Command aircraft went missing on night operations. German nightfighter claims totalled 1,816 aircraft. Bomber Command still under-estimated the killing efficiency of the German nightfighters, putting losses from this cause at 964 bombers amongst the 1,537 cases where cause could be estimated. The nightfighters were also responsible for a large proportion of the 5,177 Bomber Command aircraft damaged. Some 14,000 Bomber Command aircrew died during 1943[7].

CHAPTER FIFTEEN

# Life With the Sprogs

JMOWLEM & Co. Ltd won the main contract to build RAF Silverstone. Construction of this airfield, to the west of the A5 near Towcester, was completed in early 1943 and the station opened in March. Silverstone had a typical wartime layout with three concrete runways. It became home to 17 OTU, part of 92 Group and operators of a collection of tired Wellingtons[1]. Five members of the crew arrived on June 10:

*I felt bewildered. I was a 'screened gunner' but had no idea what was required of me. Frank, Nick, Ken and Johnny were also in the dark. Ken and I set off to find the Gunnery Section, while the others did the same in their trades. This was easier said than done as Silverstone was disorganised and had the air of a very raw set-up. We were pleased, however, to learn we were billeted together.*

This OTU had moved to Silverstone from Upwood in April 1943 following a decision to lay hard runways at the latter airfield. In early June the OTU was still settling into its new home[2]. Fifteen days passed before Sidney Knott's first flight from Silverstone on June 25. During the wait things were sorted out and he was briefed on his duties:

*I took charge of air-firing to drogue and cine camera gun exercises for a group of sprog gunners. I relished the return to Wellingtons. We took up four gunners at a time: one occupied the rear turret on take-off whilst the others sat on the rest-bed at mid-fuselage. When the first gunner had fired his rounds or cine film he left the turret and another moved back to take his place. I controlled everything from the astrodome, using an Aldis lamp to communicate with the target tug or fighter.*

The novices wasted too much time changing over in the rear turret. Knott organised some ground training and demonstrated how to get in and out with greater ease. The sprogs soon achieved a faster turnround in the air.

*It didn't take Frank and Ken long to discover that plentiful beer was the one advantage of a posting to Silverstone. The village was close by - an easy walk of around one and a half miles. Better still, our hut was on the side of the airfield nearest the village. In wartime Britain pubs often ran out of beer but this never happened at Silverstone as the village had its own brewery! Frank and Ken could not conceal their delight. At that point in the war many pubs had meagre beer supplies and could open only two or three days a week. Silverstone, however, never ran dry and provided full service every day of the week.*

Ironically, Heavery and Butterworth were soon posted away from this earthly paradise. Together with Knott, they moved to a satellite airfield – RAF Turweston, in Buckinghamshire – after just four weeks at Silverstone. It was time to say farewell to Nick Murray and Johnny Lloyd. They stayed put as the Bombing and Wireless Sections remained at Silverstone.

Turweston opened in November 1942 and became Silverstone's satellite the following summer[3]. Some of 17 OTU's Wellingtons soon arrived. A Martinet and a Lysander were also on strength, for use during gunnery training.

*It is difficult to find something good to say about Turweston. The airfield was very dispersed. The screened gunners' hut was a long way from headquarters, the Mess and the Flight Office. Bikes were essential.*

*I got to know my fellow screened gunners. There was little 'Nobby' Clarke, who came from Portsmouth. There was also a big chap, Danny Towse, from Driffield. I remember thinking that 'Towsey' might have trouble getting out of an aircraft in a hurry. There was also Bill Harrall from High Wycombe, the proud possessor of a wonderful set of teeth. His ivories gleamed whenever he smiled.*

*As in my case, these gunners had been posted for a 'rest' on completion of their first tours. There was a good atmosphere in the billet, with plenty of jokes doing the rounds – including the pathetic one about new-fangled ammunition that took you prisoner if it failed to kill you at first attempt! Our happy gunners' hut contrasted with the Sergeants' Mess at Turweston, a dingy place lacking the basic amenity of a piano for a sing-song.*

*The new crowd soon got to know each other. We all had a history of first tour adventures. Nobby told Bill that his aircraft had run into trouble while returning from a trip. He had been ordered to bale out as the returning bomber crossed the English coast. Happily, he had landed safely in a field, where he was picked up by a farmer and treated to a huge breakfast in a warm kitchen. He would have had a different experience had he abandoned the aircraft over Germany.*

*Bill Harrall had served in the RAF Regiment, following its formation in February 1942. Subsequently, he volunteered for aircrew. He crewed up at 1654 Heavy Conversion Unit at Wigsley, Nottinghamshire, having completed a gunnery course in Scotland. This crew were posted to 44 Squadron at Waddington, where John Nettleton – destined to win the Victoria Cross on the Augsburg Raid – was Commanding Officer. Harrall later moved with this squadron to Dunholm Lodge, also in Lincolnshire. He took part in the first shuttle raid, to Friedrichshafen. His aircraft landed at Maison Blanche, where he was rewarded with a disgusting meal consisting of a heaped plate of rice decorated with chipolatas and half a peach, together with a mug of iced tea to wash it down. The crew made the best of it, acquired pith helmets and shorts and visited the local market to buy lemons, grapes and other delicacies long absent from British High Streets.*

*Bill's adventures when flying with his first tour skipper, Pilot Officer John Pennington, included a potentially fatal incident during the April 13 1943 raid on La Spezia. The port inner engine burst into flames as they flew south across France. The trail of fire extended back beyond Bill's turret. The mid-upper gunner fully appreciated the seriousness of their position when he heard Pennington mutter a prayer over the intercom as he and the flight engineer took emergency action. The prop was feathered and the engine extinguisher activated. They decided to press on but fire broke out once again and they realised it was impossible to continue. Pennington turned back and ordered the crew to jettison everything they could lay their hands on. Eventually, the crippled aircraft made a successful emergency landing at Tangmere, on the South Coast.*

Things were sorted out at Turweston within the space of a fortnight. A large wall board appeared in the Gunnery Leader's office. This listed all duties for screened gunners, together with flying times scheduled for the day, pupils' names and ground activities.

*Squadron Leader 'W', our Flight Commander, struck me as a man who got things done. He appeared to be a bit of a sergeant-major and this turned out to be an accurate first assessment. In fact, the atmosphere all round was very different from that of Silverstone. Turweston was more organised from the first. The satellite wasn't so crowded and that helped a lot.*

*My flying began on Wellington IIIs. A second Martinet also arrived to participate in the gunnery exercises. Flying began on July 18 but problems soon developed. Many of the experienced screened gunners were unhappy about flying with novice pilots. They felt they were re-living their own OTU courses! There was a lot of grumbling on the quiet yet we had no choice but to accept the risk of flying with sprogs. It dawned on us that Turweston might not be much of a rest as we faced up to the unpleasant realities. There were just not enough experienced pilots to go round.*

The doubts remained as a busy programme of training began. The veteran gunners' jaundiced view of their new role was reinforced by the antics of one inexperienced pilot:

*He put his Wimpy down heavily on one main wheel. The aircraft bounced, came down on the other and bounced again. The sprog pilot had made a common mistake: he had pulled back on the control column, instead of pushing forward and sorting it out with a touch of throttle. The aircraft stalled, fell onto the runway and repeatedly hopped from side to side, impersonating a waddling duck. This may have been entertaining for the onlookers but it was very uncomfortable for those on board. I was in my usual position, standing in the astrodome. Fortunately I retained my firm grip on two conveniently-placed leather straps as we continued to bounce along the runway.*

The window in Squadron Leader W's office gave him a panoramic view of Turweston's main runway. The speedy arrival of his staff car at dispersal suggested that he had witnessed everything:

*By the time the first pair of flying boots appeared on the Wimpy's ladder W was ready for action. The young pilot looked sheepish as he walked from the aircraft. He went white when he saw W and heard the Squadron Leader shout: 'That was the worst landing I have ever seen! Get rid of your kit and come to my office!' The staff car roared away, its rapid departure emphasising the Flight Commander's anger. They say every landing you walk away from is a good one but it would have been insensitive to argue this point before the Squadron Leader.*

The Wellington's undercarriage required a major overhaul and the aircraft was unserviceable for some days. The Flight Commander exacted his price for the misdemeanour. The unfortunate crew were put on circuits and bumps with a staff pilot.

*I felt sorry for W's victim as there was nothing really wrong with his flying. He just needed a little more experience. This pilot was efficient in the air when sitting alongside an instructor but he tended to lose confidence on his own. This showed in his landings but, admittedly, not always in such spectacular style!*

*I recalled that Frank Heavery, who had trained as a Blenheim pilot, required some extra help to master the heavier Wellington. Later, he also needed a little more patience from his instructor before going on to become an excellent Lancaster Captain. All it took was a few hours' additional instruction and an understanding instructor.*

The psychological turbulence was apparent at Turweston as tour-expired aircrew rubbed shoulders with those still under training. Many screened aircrew felt that 'rested' should mean just that. Why should they put themselves out? Attitudes changed, however, when they got to know their pupils and related raw inexperience to their own vulnerable situations just a few months before:

*Early on it had been argued that there had been no screened gunners at OTU to help us. We found out the hard way. Why should we make it easier for this lot? Gradually, however, such selfish attitudes melted away. We found we benefited, along with the pupils, from a positive approach that made the job more interesting. I had my share of sympathy for the sprogs. Many experienced the fear I had known when rotating the turret fully to the beam. The noise of the slipstream and the vibration made a beginner feel vulnerable until he became used to it. I also knew what was coming later, when they joined operational squadrons.*

*Most of our work focused on the sprogs, but there were exceptions - including Wing Commander Hilton. He was a highly experienced pilot but with no operational flying in his logbook. He had been kept back as an instructor. At long last, however, he and other experienced men were released for operations by the growing number of tour-expired pilots posted to OTUs.*

*Hilton was a pleasant chap. On July 21 I was briefed to join his crew with a party of three pupil gunners for a cine camera gun exercise. This work involved an interesting division of responsibilities. Hilton, as skipper, was in command of the aircraft while I had charge of the exercise. While waiting at dispersal, as our aircraft was readied, the Wing Commander started to ask about operational flying and the strange lifestyle surrounding ops. He wasn't too proud to ask me some very direct questions. I felt pleased that our difference in rank soon disappeared in a private and very frank discussion about flying in combat.*

Life at 17 OTU was a real rest in one important respect. There was no night-flying for Sidney Knott and the other screened gunners. Flying was restricted to the daylight hours and their sleep patterns, for the first time in months, were normal and undisturbed.

*Food was the biggest problem at Turweston. The Mess was a very long way from our remote billet. So-called 'suppers' amounted to a mug of cocoa and anything left over from tea. In the evening the sheer distance to the Mess put everyone off bar the desperate. The handful who bothered were more interested in chatting up the two WAAFs on duty than the slim prospect of a square meal. Then a solution was found. We began to scrounge bread and margarine. I wasn't much good at scrounging but Bill had the gift of the gab and his knowing smile could charm any WAAF. He would stuff the trophies – a loaf and marg – inside his battledress and head back to the billet. A hand-made wire toasting fork and the billet stove would be waiting, along with some hungry gunners.*

These minor successes provided a measure of independence from the Mess but Danny Towse had wider ambitions:

*Towsey was a country boy through and through. Our billet was close to an area of perimeter bordering a country estate and this corner of the airfield had a large population of rabbits. Towsey had a scheme to supplement the meagre meat ration at home. This involved the unauthorised use of billet coal bunkers. Every hut had a coal bunker and some huts nearby were unoccupied. We soon had several bunkers fitted under beds and camouflaged with biscuit mattresses and neat piles of blankets. We now had our meat lockers and Towsey showed us how to set the snares. He gave firm instructions. No smoker could handle the snares – the rabbits would avoid any noose tainted with nicotine.*

*The rest was merely a matter of organisation. Snares were laid and a rota organised. We rose early in the morning and checked the snares before the estate gamekeeper made his morning rounds. A second check was made every evening just before dark. Rabbits were plentiful. They were slipped into hessian bags and placed in the coal bunkers pending onward dispatch. One or two young rabbits survived capture in the snares. We adopted them and took them back to our billet as pets, only to discover that wild rabbits refuse to eat in captivity.*

*Leave was granted every 13 weeks on a non-operational station. Anyone going on leave from our hut took several rabbits from the store. Bill's mother was delighted, proclaiming: 'It's Christmas again!' Rabbit stew was a real boon for households struggling to make the most of wartime Britain's pitiful weekly meat ration.*

*We became bolder and distributed rabbits by post. This was simplicity itself. Each carcass was wrapped up in brown paper and addressed to the fortunate family. We would have been in serious trouble had the contents of the coal bunkers and parcels been discovered.*

*Our secret was well defended. We devised a second rota. Every morning two occupants of the billet slaved to keep our quarters abnormally tidy. Anyone inspecting our billet would take one look, be suitably impressed and disappear without bothering to look under the beds. The empty billets were always left alone. Our thriving rabbit industry was never discovered.*

OTU life ran on a seven-day week basis and weekends had no meaning. Fortunately, Turweston's understanding Gunnery Leader made life bearable:

*We had an arrangement. Half the billet had liberty on the Saturday evening and Sunday morning provided the work was covered by those remaining. No passes were issued. This system worked by word of mouth. When our turn came we cycled into Buckingham, a modest town in those days.*

*Our first priority was to find digs for the night. Bed and breakfast cost around five shillings. On one occasion we got off to a bad start as our usual place was fully booked and it proved difficult to find an alternative. By the time we gave up it was too late for the pictures. We went straight to a pub then on to a dance. We left the pub at around nine, to be sure of getting into the dance-hall. There would be no chance after 10, especially with a drink or two inside us.*

*It was a busy Saturday night and the dance-halls were packed. Eventually, we found a place to squeeze in. It was jammed wall to wall. We couldn't see the dance floor for feet. Moving to the music, couples were pushed close together like it or not. Dense blue spirals of cigarette smoke merged into the haze above their heads. Above all, there was absolutely no sign of the war.*

This interlude was brief as all Saturday dances ended at 11.30. The hall had to be cleared by midnight; no dance music was permitted on Sundays.

*The band finished the evening with the National Anthem. With no digs arranged we took the main road out of town, with the rather desperate idea of finding a comfortable haystack for the night. This was easier said than done. The only haystack around was a 2-star affair with unyielding, smelly straw. We settled in and pulled straw over ourselves to keep out the chill night air. We slept well enough but were wide awake just before dawn. We began to get our limbs moving but poor Nobby had seized up. We got him to his feet and held him up by the elbows, with his toes barely touching the ground. We marched him around until signs of life returned to his legs.*

*During that early August morning no-one witnessed our hilarious attempts to balance Nobby on his bike. It was still well before 6 am when we decided to head back to town in search of a hot drink. An early-rising local advised that the only hope of tea was a visit to the Fire Station. The fireman answering the door turned out to be the model of courtesy. Within minutes we were huddled round a fire, drinking steaming mugs of tea. Everything seemed right with the world and we stayed put for some time, lost in our thoughts. Eventually we claimed our bikes and headed back to camp, to find we had missed breakfast.*

Flying Officer 'P' had flying experience but was relatively new to twin-engined aircraft. On October 18 1943 he was briefed for a cine camera gun exercise. Sidney Knott arrived at the dispersal with his sprog gunners in tow. Now four months into the job, he knew exactly what was expected of him:

*With three gunners on the Wimpy's rest-bed and another in the rear turret, I returned to the astrodome and gripped the straps for take-off. I heard a loud bang just as we left the runway. The port wing dropped and the aircraft veered in that direction, but we were safely in the air within a fraction of a second. I ducked down and glanced forward. Things looked OK. I turned and looked towards the rest-bed, to meet the blank gaze of my band of innocents. They hadn't a clue!*

*We were now in the climb and, fortunately, the engines sounded sweet. Why not proceed with the exercise and use up some fuel? I knew we had lost a tyre on take-off but said nothing to the skipper. I merely asked him to let me know when we were at the briefed height and location for the simulated fighter attacks. The Wellington maintained its gentle climb and was soon approaching the required altitude. Flying Officer P's casual remarks confirmed he was unaware of the problem. The pupil gunner was ready in the rear turret and I saw no reason not to use the Aldis. I instructed the 'fighter' – in reality a Lysander – to commence its approach.*

Controlling the attacker from the Wellington's astrodome was straightforward. A steady green on the Aldis told the other aircraft to stand-by. Watching from the astrodome, Knott held the 'playmate' on green while the first of the novice gunners vacated his seat, having consumed some of the film held in two cine camera gun magazines. With the second gunner securely in place, Knott gave a flashing green - clearing the Lysander to begin a fresh series of attacks. This process was repeated until all four gunners had finished. Knott then gave the Lysander a red to signal an end to the proceedings. Feeling mildly surprised that, for once, the exercise had been completed in good time, his mind returned to the earlier problem:

*I told the pilot we had finished and then broached the subject of our unusual take-off. As I suspected, he was completely unaware of the problem. I suggested we reduce speed and lower the undercarriage. With the wheels down our problem was all too visible – the port tyre was shredded. It was time to take the necessary crash precautions, without unduly alarming my gunners.*

*Having taken in the bad news the pilot passed it on to Flying Control and this put them in a flap. They gave a typical response: 'Stand by' – a favourite when no-one is quite sure what to do next. The Duty Flying Control Officer informed the Flight Commander and W's unmistakeable voice came over the*

*R/T. He told us to make a low pass with the wheels down. I wasn't sure what good that would do, as there was nothing left of the tyre. It had disintegrated.*

Turweston, in common with most satellites, had hard runways:

*I expected the Flight Commander to order us to make a belly landing on the grass, to avoid obstructing the runway. I couldn't have been more wrong! He instructed Flying Officer P to put the Wimpy down on the main runway, with the wheels down. I told myself that our skipper had been on a training station for a long time and should be totally familiar with the drill. He needed to hold the port leg off the ground for as long as possible, with the help of a little extra port throttle. The Flight Commander then came on the R/T again, instructing our pilot to do an overshoot.*

Knott ministered to his sprogs and briefed them on crash drill. The last gunner was still in the rear turret. He was told to stay put and rotate the turret fully to port. Knott expected the aircraft to slew in that direction as soon as the port leg touched the runway and collapsed. With the rear turret doors to starboard the young gunner had the best possible chance of a quick exit. He was told to unlock the doors but keep them closed, with the additional instruction to leave by the usual means – the front hatch – if all went well on landing. Knott then turned to the three ashen-faced gunners on the rest-bed:

*I got them into their crash positions and told them to be ready to leave by the astrodome. There was a bit of a problem at this juncture, as there was just one intercom point by the rest-bed. I made a quick selection and told the brightest of the three to sit in the middle. I gave him the intercom point and told him to keep the others informed.*

*Was there anything in 400 hours of flying that might be useful in this situation? I asked the pilot if I could help with the landing. I recalled that instructors, during dual practice, always called out the airspeed during the approach. Our pilot might be more confident with a comforting voice in his ear. It would also give him one thing less to worry about. He liked the idea and asked me to come forward. I settled into the second pilot's seat while the bomb aimer went back to the navigator's station and sat with him. We did the overshoot and things were looking good.*

*I tried to be as lighthearted as possible in my exchanges with the pilot. As we passed Flying Control once again I had a good view of the crash tender and blood wagon, lined up and ready to follow us down the runway. I smiled when I saw the familiar shape of Squadron Leader W's staff car, positioned at the end of the runway and ready to pounce on the wreckage.*

*We went round again and began the approach. I called out the airspeed as we descended. When close to the stall and committed to a landing the aircraft floated for several long seconds before I felt the first contact with terra firma. Unfortunately, Flying Officer P had few hours on Wellingtons and this showed when he over-corrected, using too much throttle. I had expected a vicious ground-loop to port but the very opposite happened. The starboard undercarriage leg collapsed under the load, throwing us violently in that direction. Somehow we remained the right way up as we slithered to a standstill in a large cloud of dust. This began to clear as we registered our survival. I called: 'All switches off'. The pilot gave a terse reply – 'Check' – and began undoing his straps. I told everyone to leave the aircraft in a quiet, orderly manner, reminding them to take their parachutes. There was no panic. While confident there would be no fire, I didn't hang around. I left by the pilot's escape hatch - positioned above me - moved back along the top of the fuselage to the astrodome and helped the others out.*

*My sprogs were incredibly slow in leaving the aircraft. Thank God there was no fire! They stood in a circle, somewhat stunned and finding it difficult to take in what had happened. I rounded them up. Moving to the front of the aircraft I told the pilot we were all OK. He gave a gruff 'Same here' and thanked me, his gratitude heavy with relief. A familiar, strident voice then cut across this brief exchange. It was our Flight Commander. Glaring at the pilot, he snapped: 'Well, you grossly over-corrected. Now this aircraft is U/S'.*

*To be absolutely fair, I must add that this bollocking came after he had confirmed we were all in one piece. I walked over and said: 'Everyone's OK, Sir'. He was unimpressed and followed through with a pointed observation: 'Your lot took a long time to get out'. That was true but the comment could have waited! I thought we'd done well. I had expected a word or two of praise for the crew but W held true to character. He drove away smartly in his staff car, leaving me standing beside the battered Wellington, with a flea still bouncing around in my ear.*

Bill Harrall also had a nasty experience during a gunnery exercise:

*Shortly after take-off dense black smoke poured from an engine. Bill reported the problem to his pilot, together with a strong recommendation that he land as soon as possible. Harrall organised his sprog gunners at their crash stations and opened the escape hatch, just in case. He then went to collect his parachute, only to discover that he had left it in the crew room. He lost no time, went forward and reinforced his earlier advice: 'You'd better get this bloody thing down!' His skipper didn't argue the point. He saw a runway ahead and went straight in, presenting the neighbouring station's crash team with an opportunity to put their training into practice. Life with the sprogs turned out to be livelier than expected.*

Frank Heavery was recommended for a commission on completion of his tour with 467 Squadron. He became a Pilot Officer in August 1943. Sidney Knott was more than happy to join his former skipper for air-firing exercises, whenever possible. Flights involving air-firing, as opposed to the cine camera gun, were almost always given to experienced staff or screened pilots, due to the additional risks involved.

*It was like old times – Frank and I sharing a Wellington. Just before his commission came through Frank announced that he and Ted had been awarded the Distinguished Flying Medal (DFM). I was over the moon. The citation for Ted's DFM stated: 'His cooperation, coolness and devotion to duty have contributed in a large measure to the completion of his operational tour without a single unsuccessful sortie.' The Heavery crew's efforts had been recognised. I felt pride in my association with a crew who had served with distinction.*

Later, Knott partnered Heavery in the Martinet during a fighter affiliation exercise. This gave the rear gunner a completely fresh view of the challenges of fighter attack and gunnery. Knott served as lookout, an essential role during extreme manoeuvres. By early December Heavery's qualities received further recognition and he was made up to Flying Officer.

*More screened pilots and instructors arrived at Turweston at this time. We soon reached the point where all gunnery exercises, cine camera gun as well as air-firing, were flown by experienced pilots. Yet the occasional shortage of a key man could always disrupt the training schedule. In one case, an armourer – who happened to be our only trained drogue operator – was posted away. We were told to solve this problem and, after a little instruction on the electric winch, I became a part-time drogue operator. No record of these flights appears in my logbook as they were strictly unofficial. It resolved our difficulty, however, and gunnery training continued without pause.*

On completion of a gunnery exercise, it was normal practice for a tug aircraft to jettison the drogue and cable over a quiet part of the airfield. While an everyday ritual at OTU satellites, it was not without hazard. It was also difficult and time-consuming to retrieve the tackle and refit the cable to the tug's winch. Turweston's establishment became fed-up with this four-hour job and it was decided to speed things up by retrieving the drogue during flight.

In readiness for the launch, the drogue was folded neatly and rolled, rather like a flag ready to be unfurled. The launch was simplicity itself. All the winch operator had to do was throw it out of the hatch in the Martinet's floor. The cable ran out rapidly as the drogue opened in the slipstream. The operator had to react quickly, control the speed and avoid a cable break. The cable itself was colour-coded. This allowed the operator to gauge roughly how much remained on the winch drum.

*At the end of the next exercise I prepared for my first in-flight retrieve. This required careful handling. I took in the cable very slowly, controlling the drum speed with great care. The bobbin continued to feed the cable onto the drum in a neat, trouble-free manner. This was essential as a kink could cause a cable break. A steel cable released under load in a confined space could chop a man into pieces.*

*The Martinet's winch faced forward but I concentrated on the view through the hatch as the drogue slowly came into my line of vision, just below the tail. I brought it in to a point directly beneath the hatch and selected 'stop' on the winch. Extending my arm through the hole in the floor, I grabbed the thing and began hauling it in as quickly as possible. The experience was rather alarming at first as the drogue had a mind of its own. It made one hell of a racket as it slapped viciously against the aircraft's underside. I needed every ounce of strength at first but it became easier as more of the drogue was pulled inside. Pilots were always greatly relieved to hear that my struggles were over and the drogue was safely stowed. The Martinet was not a large aircraft and the drogue, even when gathered together, seemed to fill my entire cockpit space.*

Sidney Knott's operational experience with 467 Squadron was a treasure house for sprog gunners. They needed his help and support:

*I gave them frequent reminders that correct procedures must be followed at all times. My tasks in the air ranged from an intercom check with the rear gunner (primarily to ensure his safety catch was on) to helping clear a stoppage in the cine camera gun magazine. I made a point of showing them faster and easier ways of coping with problems.*

*We always had an end-of-course drink-up and the sprogs were generous with their thanks. I had a sharp lesson, however, at the end of the first course. Although I did my best I found it impossible to sink every drink put before me. These drinks were mixed with a vengeance; I became legless and had to be carried back to my billet. The next morning found no improvement in my condition. I couldn't get to my feet and it was three days before I managed to put my nose into the Mess. I was lucky to get away with this. Rendering oneself unfit to fly is an Air Force crime. My drinks were spiked but that was no defence! Happily, the other screened gunners covered for me, helped by the fact that our billet was in a remote and rarely visited part of the airfield. The sight of a normally serious gunnery instructor in a completely helpless state was regarded as a great joke! Fortunately, I have no memory of that night – my mind wiped clean by the long succession of beer and spirit cocktails. To this day, however, I never mix my drinks (or allow anyone to mix them for me).*

Knott was sympathetic towards sprogs who summoned up the nerve to voice the cliché: 'What's it like on operations?'

*I tried very hard to explain operational flying. I made it clear that it was completely different due to the fear factor. No-one knew, with certainty, how they would react until they faced that fear. I told them that survival required teamwork on a level far beyond the OTU experience. An operational crew had to work, think and live as a team. I did not say that a first tour posting to a heavy bomber squadron was, in effect, a death sentence for many.*

On one occasion Turweston's screened gunners were at a loose end and looking for something to break the monotony. Towse had an idea. He proposed a walk over the fields and promised something unusual to enliven this excursion:

*We reached a field boundary at the top of a steep slope. Towsey demanded silence as he divided us into two groups. One group waited silently at the top while the others walked slowly downslope, following the hedge. Arriving at the bottom, our country boy told us to spread out and stand still with our arms outstretched. It appeared that our friend had lost his marbles!*

*We waited patiently as he walked back to the other group. Then the fun began. The gunners at the top of the hill suddenly opened their arms and charged towards us, yelling like banshees. Immediately, dozens of hares hidden in the long grass leapt into the air and raced downslope towards us, dodging from side to side as they came. Their bodies twisted and turned, in frantic gyrations, as they sought to outmanoeuvre us at the bottom of the field. They shot past in an instant, large eyes bulging with fright. The stampede was over in a few seconds and we rolled around in the grass, convulsed with laughter. Having let off steam we walked back, still laughing, for a pint in the Mess. To this day I have no idea how Towsey knew the hares were in that field.*

Sidney Knott, in common with most, found that service life meant having too much to do or too little. The happy medium was a rare experience. Occasionally an aircraft went unserviceable and the gunners were left with time on their hands. This was an opportunity to catch up with outstanding ground jobs, including instruction on how to harmonise the guns:

*Fire from harmonised guns converged at a fixed point, with the rounds striking the enemy (hopefully) at a range of, say, 400 yards. When harmonising the Brownings we placed a board out beyond the aircraft. Sights mounted on the guns were used to range on the board, providing a concentration at the desired range. Harmonisation was really a job for armourers but sprog gunners were expected to understand such things.*

Late Summer slipped gently into Autumn and most screened gunners – Knott included – were made up to Flight Sergeant. The OTU Gunnery Leader then recommended Knott for a commission:

*I wasn't the type - I didn't want to be tied to a desk. I was quite content with*

*Recruitment drive: Flight Lieutenant Clive Walker (far right) had completed a first tour on Bostons, followed by a lengthy spell instructing. He wanted Knott as his rear gunner. Photo: Lucy Walker.*

*the practical side of OTU life. Eventually I found myself before the Flight Commander. He was surprisingly patient and listened as I explained my position. I didn't want to become his new Gunnery Leader or occupy the desk that went with the job. The proposal was dropped and there was no more talk of a commission during my RAF service.*

Attitudes towards training changed as the war progressed. Initially, pilots showing particular aptitude in the training role were held back from the operational squadrons, in recognition of their qualities as instructors. By late 1943, however, large numbers of screened pilots became Instructors on completion of their tours. Consequently, those who had been held back became free for posting to operational squadrons.

Sidney Knott's 'rest' neared its end:

*I was still at Turweston in the first half of January 1944. My first tour had ended over seven months earlier and I expected to be posted to an operational squadron in the very near future. One of our instructor pilots, Flight Lieutenant Clive Walker, approached me. He had been an OTU instructor for many moons, following a first tour of operations on Boston medium bombers with 107 Squadron, 2 Group. He had no operational experience on four-engined heavy bombers. Walker didn't beat about the bush. He was putting together a crew for operational flying and he wanted me as rear gunner. Walker had a friend called Crump, another instructor pilot busy recruiting. Obviously, they had talked things over. They had reached the conclusion that it was better to pick a crew of individuals with known qualities rather than go through the entire process blind, with no prior knowledge. I told Clive I would think about his offer - it wouldn't do to appear too keen. This decision was important as a bad move could have a serious impact on life expectancy!*

*When back in the billet I gathered my thoughts about Walker. I had flown with him on several occasions and he had rapidly gained my respect. I mentioned Walker's proposition to Bill Harrall, only to discover that Clive had already asked him to fill the mid-upper turret. We had a good laugh and told each other that this Flight Lieutenant displayed good taste. We decided to join Walker's crew but strictly on condition that he took both of us.*

The members of the new crew left for squadron duties during the second half of January. Knott walked through Turweston's main gate for the last time with 115 hours 40 minutes logged as a screened gunner. His final flight from the airfield was on January 15 1944.

*I said my goodbyes to Frank and Ken. Frank already knew what was going on. Walker must have said something to him. I rang Nick at Silverstone and received a typical Murray response: 'You bloody fool!' Sixty years on, examining a facsimile of Nick's logbook, I found that he went on to become a Bombing Leader that February, following the successful completion of a short course at the Air Armaments School, Manby. It appears that he didn't do a second tour.*

*I tried to contact Johnny Lloyd but had no luck. I had heard that he had found a WAAF he liked and was busy courting her. This was my last news of Johnny, the Heavery crew's wireless op.*

*Nick's reaction to my news was echoed by a senior officer at Turweston. He asked Bill and I why we were so keen to return to operational flying. He spoke to us almost as a father might talk to a son. He meant well but he had missed the point. Our return to operations was inevitable and imminent, whether we took the initiative or not. So, I made my rounds of Turweston's sections, sorting things out and getting clearance. I now had a new crew and looked forward to the flying training required to regain operational status.*

# CHAPTER SIXTEEN

# Apprentice Pathfinders

CLIVE Walker's crew were posted to a new Pathfinder squadron. The Pathfinder Force (PFF) was established in August 1942, despite stout resistance within the upper echelons of Bomber Command. The opponents included Air Vice-Marshal Cochrane, Air Officer Commanding 5 Group. Cochrane shared the view that the Pathfinders would 'skim the cream' from Bomber Command. It was argued that, in taking the best crews, PFF would reduce the Command's overall effectiveness as a fighting force.

The PFF concept appeared sound as it recognised that target finding and marking were tasks for specialists. The obvious weakness was demonstrated immediately, during the August 18/19 1942 raid on Flensburg. The Pathfinders fell foul of inaccurate forecast winds during their first operation. The bombers drifted to the north. Flensburg escaped but a number of Danish towns were hit[1]. Later, however, a combination of well-organised training, new technology, sophisticated pyrotechnics and fresh tactics brought the PFF to a pitch of high efficiency. In the early days oboe-equipped Mosquitos showed the promise of things to come[2]. By April 1945 PFF had 19 squadrons of Lancasters and Mosquitos. By the end of the European war PFF had flown over 50,000 sorties. The casualties totalled 675 aircraft and 3,700 aircrew[3].

On January 8 1943 the Pathfinder Force won its independence, becoming 8 (PFF) Group. It was commanded by the renowned Australian airman and navigator D.C.T. 'Don' Bennett, later Air Vice-Marshal Bennett, CB, CBE, DSO. He was just 31 when appointed AOC 8 Group. Bennett admired Harris. On the latter's appointment, Bennett wrote: '...my hopes for the bomber offensive and its ultimate destruction of Germany were revitalised[4].'

Bennett's vitriol was reserved for opponents to his own appointment and any critic of PFF and its performance. His blunt, aggressive style is conveyed in *Pathfinder*. He wrote: 'And to those charming and generous Air Force officers who so bitterly criticised my subsequent rapid promotion when the Pathfinder Force was formed, I would like to suggest that it was no fault of mine that the Royal Air Force, due to peacetime economies and restrictions, should, at the critical moment,

*PFF opponent: Air Vice-Marshal the Hon. RA Cochrane, AOC 5 Group. There were worries that the Pathfinders would 'skim the cream' from Bomber Command. Photo: Trustees of the Imperial War Museum.*

have been unable to produce a more senior Regular officer with the necessary combination of flying, navigation, radio, engineering and scientific knowledge suitable for the creation of such a force[5].'

PFF's establishment as 8 Group opened a year of rapid development in target finding and marking techniques. More effective target indicators (TIs) reached the squadrons in early 1943. The new pyrotechnics presented the German specialists responsible for ground decoys with increasingly difficult challenges. The TIs ranged from 250 lbs to 2,300 lbs. The latter was the 'Pink Pansy', an early TI utilising a 4,000 lb bomb casing and containing a red pyrotechnic, benzole, rubber and phosphorus[6].

The air war continued to grow in technological sophistication. The significance of this trend was recognised in late 1943, when 100 (Bomber Support) Group became operational[7]. This new Group concentrated on the rapidly expanding 'radio countermeasures' battle.

Relationships between 8 Group and 5 Group (and their respective commanders), however, remained difficult. Marie Cooper, the former Intelligence Officer at Bottesford, had arrived at PFF Headquarters having demolished what had been an all-male preserve. PFF Headquarters' pool of talent was exotic and included a direct descendant of 'Bloody Judge Jeffreys'. On one occasion, Marie was told to work through the night and list '50 best targets' for an orchestrated series of attacks on oil installations and marshalling yards in France: '...the haste was to prevent 5 Group from getting the best ones.' In the event, however, 5 Group had already 'got' most of the Top 20 on the list[8].

She recalls that Bennett, while a relentless worker, still found time to indulge personal whims. For example, a young member of the PFF Headquarters team with artistic talents was told to design a uniform for the International Peacekeeping Force Bennett was certain would be set up as soon as the Allies won the war[8].

The increasing complexity of the bombing war was reflected in PFF training. Sidney Knott and Walker's other veterans went back to school. They arrived at RAF Binbrook, near Grimsby, on January 26 1944, joining 1481 Bombing and Gunnery Flight for eight days of refresher training. They divided into their various trades and set to work:

> *The good news was a return to my old favourite, the Wellington. After my break from flying it felt great to be back in the turret. Flying from Binbrook began on January 28 with a cine camera gun practice and an air-firing exercise. I fired 500 rounds at a drogue.*

The next stop was RAF Lindholme, near Doncaster. Walker received his introduction to four-engined aircraft during this attachment to 1656 Heavy Conversion Unit. Knott also got to know the Halifax:

> *During four weeks at Lindholme I logged 30 hours 25 minutes on Halifaxes. We began to take shape as a crew. The most important factor – at least at this stage – was the working partnership between pilot and flight engineer. Clive began with the usual round of circuits and bumps. We progressed through increasingly complex exercises, including fighter affiliations (with Spitfires as 'playmates'), a Bullseye simulated raid and day and night cross-countries. The navigator and bomb aimer familiarised themselves with new and more advanced equipment while I polished my turret manipulation*

*skills. During our stay at Lindholme we switched to Lancasters – a Lancaster 'Finishing School' was also based at this station. We logged 10 hours 55 minutes on the Lancs. The switch made no difference to me as the Halifax and Lancaster rear turrets were very similar.*

Their next posting was to RAF Warboys, the Pathfinder training base near Huntingdon and home to the PFF Navigation Training Unit. The station, originally a satellite of Wyton, had close to 100 aircraft: Lancasters, Halifaxes and Mosquitos, the latter dedicated to Oboe training[9]. The crew

*Royal visitor: 8 Group AOC Don Bennett escorts H.R.H. Queen Elizabeth during a visit to Wyton on May 26 1943. Photo: Trustees of the Imperial War Museum.*

spent just a few days at Warboys and flew three Bullseye mock raids in this busy station's Lancasters. This completed the refresher and initial PFF training. Knott added 54 hours 45 minutes to his logbook while at Binbrook, Lindholme and Warboys. On April 1 1944 the crew were posted to a newly-formed operational unit, 582 Squadron, 8 (PFF) Group. The squadron badge carried the motto Praecolamus designantes (We fly before marking).

Little Staughton is situated between Bedford and Huntingdon, around four miles west of St. Neots. This station became an American base in January 1943. It had three hard runways (the main runway having a length of 1,920 yards). Little Staughton was transferred to Bomber Command on March 1 1944. The new squadron, 582, formed at the station just four weeks after the handover, its aircraft bearing the code 6O[10]. This Lancaster unit was formed by bringing together the C Flights from two 'founder' PFF squadrons, 7 Squadron (Oakington) and 156 Squadron (Upwood)[11]. Its first Lancaster was taken on charge on April 2 1944[12]. It stayed at Little Staughton until September 1945, sharing the station with 109 Squadron, flying the Mosquito XVI[13]. This Mosquito squadron played a crucial role in the success of the PFF. It had interesting origins, rooted in 1940 and the desperate struggle to counter the German beam bombing systems. A dedicated unit, 80 Wing, was formed to work with the Telecommunications Research Establishment (responsible for GEE and much else). One element of 80 Wing was the Wireless Investigation and Development Unit at Boscombe Down. This unit became 109 Squadron in late 1940 and was tasked with helping to develop British blind-bombing systems[14]. It flew a pressurised variant of the Wellington before converting to Mosquitos.

The Station Commander at Little Staughton was Group Captain RWP Collings. Walker's crew arrived on the day of the new squadron's assembly. Trying hard to ignore the date (April Fools' Day) they settled into their billets:

*Little Staughton had a dispersed layout but no bikes were available. Why were bikes so plentiful on training stations but like gold dust on operational stations? Amusing company compensated for the inconvenience of having to walk everywhere. Our mid-upper gunner, Bill Harrall, was good value as ever. The navigator was Flight Lieutenant L.D. Francis, a married man who had joined the RAF before the war. A sociable chap with a sharp sense of humour, he was Clive's age – around five or six years older than the rest of us. Bill spent part of a leave with him, visiting his home in Leighton Buzzard and meeting his wife.*

*The bomb aimer was Pilot Officer RGS 'Reg' Francks. He was from East London but was no Eastender. Reg had completed a full first tour. Bill Harrall recalls that he was 'a bit of a card'. He certainly had a sharp mind. I remember his poker-faced claim to be of the Greek Orthodox faith. Immediately before church parade began the order would be given: 'Other denominations, leave the parade ground!' Being of the Greek Orthodox faith, Reg hoped he would be in a congregation of one at Little Staughton. He was correct in this assumption.*

*Our wireless op, Flying Officer B.R. Rodgers, had not finished a full first tour. The Air Force refused to be short-changed and dealt with the outstanding balance later. When we finished our PFF tour he was told to stay on and continue to fly as a 'spare bod'. He accepted this without fuss and simply remarked: 'Apparently, I have a few more to do.'*

*Our flight engineer, Sergeant George Gledhill, also had operational experience. Gledhill was a dour Yorkshireman who came from Huddersfield. He was quiet by nature and troubles with a girlfriend kept him quieter still.*

*Everyone had flown operations on heavies with the exception of the skipper, but 582 soon put that right. We already knew that our pilot, Clive Walker, was a man of considerable depth. He came from the Bolton area, where his family had owned a tannery for over 100 years.*

Clive Walker was a member of a family prominent in the leather business[15]. He was just over 30 years of age. The impression of maturity was helped by his moustache – nothing too outlandish but in true RAF style. The crew called him 'Gus', after Gus Walker, a rugby player for Yorkshire, Barbarians and England who went on to make a name for himself in Bomber Command and the post-war RAF[16]. To their childish delight Clive hated this nickname.

Ronald Clive Walker was the youngest of four sons and the fourth generation of his family to join William Walker & Sons Ltd. The mere

*'Gus': Clive Walker – a man of considerable depth. Photo: Lucy Walker.*

fact of being a Walker cut no ice with the firm. He was expected to prove himself. He joined the company in 1932 as an apprentice, at the age of 18, on leaving Radley School. He broadened his education in the leather trades by working in France, Czechoslovakia and Germany during the 1930s. He became fluent in the three languages and made many friends on the Continent. This did not make his participation in the European bombing campaign any the easier.

He returned to England in 1938 and was commissioned in the Duke of Lancaster's Own Yeomanry. His Regiment went to France as part of

*The 'Three Musketeers': Clive Walker with Pat Crump and Tom Rushton. Photo: Lucy Walker.*

the British Expeditionary Force and eventually suffered the trauma of evacuation from the Dunkirk beaches. This debacle (particularly the ceaseless German air attacks) appears to have coloured the attitude of Captain Walker and his two closest friends, Pat Crump and Tom Rushton. All three left the Army and transferred to the RAFVR the following year. The 'Three Musketeers', as they were known, emerged from training as Pilot Officers[17].

Great Massingham, Norfolk, was home to 107 Squadron. The 'Three Musketeers' were posted to 107 in February 1942. Strings must have been pulled, with considerable efficacy, to ensure they stayed together. The squadron's Boston III aircraft began to operate on March 8 1942 with a medium level 'Circus' raid on Abbeville's rail yards. Walker's sortie was made in AL296. The squadron became medium and low level specialists, with strikes against rail targets, airfields and ports. This squadron, with the motto Nous y serons (We shall be there), suffered one of the highest loss rates in 2 Group (11 Blenheims and 26 Bostons).

A press visit to Great Massingham was organised on April 9 1942. Stories duly appeared in the following day's papers, including the *News Chronicle* and *Daily Herald*. The latter made a reference to the Three Musketeers. '...now taking their revenge. They vowed when the German bombers blasted them at Dunkirk that they would get their own back. Together they came back to England and transferred from the Army to the RAF. They were separated while they trained. Eight weeks ago they met again – on their first day with the Boston squadron. Since then, they have seen plenty of France, have withstood, on one raid, six successive attacks by the new Focke Wulf fighter, after which they shot one down, and came back with only one bullet hole...'[18].

The story was incorrect in some respects. The Three Musketeers occasionally flew together during training. Clive Walker's flying instruction began on June 2 1941, at No. 17 Elementary Flying Training School, North Luffenham, with a 35-minute air experience flight in a DH82A. He flew solo for 15 minutes just 11 days later, following 7 hours 30 minutes of dual instruction. He flew two or three times a day and he had 25 hours' dual and 25 hours' solo, together with 6 hours 25 minutes' dual instrument flying, by July 6 – at the conclusion of the EFTS course. Walker was rated 'above average' as a pilot.

On July 21 Walker had his first flight in the twin-engined Oxford, having been posted to No. 12 Service Flying Training School at Grantham. He flew solo on type six days later. He logged his first cross-country (Grantham/Upper Heyford/Grantham) on August 16. Walker was awarded his flying badge on October 1 1941, retaining an 'above average' assessment and with 132 hours 5 minutes in his logbook.

Clive Walker's next posting was to D Flight, No. 42 Operational Training Unit, based at Andover. Arriving in mid-October, he flew the Blenheim I for the first time on October 25. By December his training was assuming a warlike character, with 'medium dive and low level' bombing exercises. The move to Andover must have been a cause for celebration, as the Three Musketeers were reunited, with Walker occasionally flying with fellow pilots Rushton and Crump. Operational exercises and night-flying practice continued in January 1942. On February 7, Walker and his crew, Sergeant Perkins and Sergeant Lea, joined 107 Squadron's B Flight. Following Abbeville, Walker flew three more daylight Circus sorties in March, six in April and two in May – with targets ranging from rail yards to the docks at Calais and Cherbourg and power stations at Lille and Caen.

Walker must have felt some satisfaction on June 4, when he participated in a Circus attack on an oil tanker at Dunkirk docks, just two years after he and his two closest friends escaped from the area's heavily bombed beaches.

Walker's eight sorties in June included his first night operation, an intruder patrol to Leewarden on June 25 in Boston W8373. The month's sorties also included two North Sea search patrols for downed aircrew, both flown on June 30. On the second sortie Walker's crew located a dinghy. Walker had flown 20 sorties by the end of June. There was only one operation flown in July, a night intruder sortie to Borkum. Walker's logbook entry suggests that this was aborted due to compass failure and petrol leakage.

Walker's tour was over. He was posted to Upwood and B Flight of No. 17 OTU on July 29 1942, flying Ansons. Later, in August, he arrived at Castle Combe (Hullavington) to join a flying instructors' course. No. 3 Flying Instructors' School was equipped with Oxfords. Walker's assessment, at the end of August, was 'average' for both pilot and flying instructor. A logbook note adds: 'Instructional manner is good, but his flying could be improved'. He then returned to Upwood as an A Flight instructor on Blenheims.

During September he completed a 'BAT' (Beam Approach Training) course, on Oxfords. On September 29 he found an excuse to fly with Tom Rushton three times, taking a Blenheim I for air tests and a night-flying exercise. During October and November he flew with Pat Crump on four occasions. The last flight recorded in Clive Walker's first logbook was on November 21 1942, one hour and 10 minutes spent practising night circuits and landings. This brought Walker's total flying time to 519 hours 35 minutes. Walker was to continue instructing for just over a year.

*So, Clive had been an instructor for many moons, drawing on his experience on Blenheims and Bostons. He took charge with great efficiency and encouraged us to talk about our earlier operational experiences in four-engined aircraft engaged in night raids. He always showed that same pleasing lack of self-importance which led to my heart-to-heart about operational flying with Wing Commander Hilton some months back, while at OTU.*

*The Spring weather was warm and we sat in the sun, talking tactics. We came to a familiar conclusion: rigorous attention to detail and constant drills meant a greater chance of surviving the tour. We practised hard on the ground: abandon aircraft, crash drill, dinghy drill and so on. Our first tour lessons, including disciplined use of the intercom, were adopted immediately. We also placed much emphasis on the ability to cope if one or more crew members were injured.*

A notebook maintained by Walker during the war years contains a pencilled note headed 'Crew Interchangeability'. Each crew member had the ability to perform at least two and, in some cases, three other possible roles in an emergency. The engineer, Gledhill, was listed as pilot/bomb-aimer/gunner. Francks, the bomb-aimer, was also a potential navigator/wireless op/gunner, while Francis, the navigator, had the notations bomb-aimer/pilot/engineer against his name. Wireless op Rodgers could double up as gunner or navigator, while Harrall could move from mid-upper to rear turret if necessary, or take over as wireless op. Knott could operate from the mid-upper turret or, if necessary, take over Gledhill's duties as engineer. Each crew member practiced these alternative roles repeatedly during ground drills. Walker's organisational powers and strong sense of discipline produced a crew with a highly conscientious attitude.

*Clive was a good listener. He accepted advice and took sound decisions on matters new to him. We forgot all that 'skipper to rear gunner' nonsense. Our communications style in the air was straight to the point. When someone spoke we listened ...and they spoke only when necessary.*

*Clive never disappointed. He was an excellent skipper, mixing a warm personality with a command style requiring - and receiving - respect. As personalities, Clive Walker and Frank Heavery were poles apart, although both were expert Lancaster Captains. Frank had less command presence but always enjoyed the total loyalty of his crew. Clive had plenty of presence and there was a certain snap of authority in his voice. We liked that – nothing wrong with a strong character in the driving seat!*

Sixty years on, Knott and Harrall retain clear memories of Walker's military bearing and sharp, staccato voice:

*Things came together and we developed into a serious, hard-working crew. Our style was based on mutual support. We kept a close eye on each other and safe procedures always had priority. We wanted results but we intended to live, to continue to get results.*

*While no eccentric Clive did have a strange taste in pets. He kept a dog at Little Staughton. It was known as 'Thirsty', a name that speaks for itself. There was nothing unusual in keeping a dog on a wartime RAF base, but Thirsty was a Corgi, the first of its kind I had encountered. It was pretty enough but I didn't think much of it. Thirsty had an unpleasant temperament – a snappy little thing – yet Clive adored it and his feelings were reciprocated. Later, however, Thirsty took a shine to Bill Harrall. Clive was jealous and moaned at Bill, accusing him of illicitly feeding his four-legged friend in the Sergeants' Mess. Bill denied this but the dog's behaviour lent weight to Clive's allegations. The Corgi was quite content in Clive's company until Bill turned up. Thirsty would then desert his master and run to the gunner.*

Walker found his place in Little Staughton's folklore when Pathfinder AOC Don Bennett visited the station. The 8 Group Commander dined in the Officers' Mess, his staff car having been parked outside. During the evening all four tyres went flat. Bennett had a short fuse and declined to accept this as an Act of God:

*The big party was still under way when Bennett took his leave. The AOC's face was a picture when he spotted his flat tyres. Crimson with fury he strode back into the Mess and grabbed the first bod to hand. Sadly, it was Clive who received both barrels. Before an audience stunned to silence, Bennett snapped: 'Find a pump and pump up my tyres ...now!' Our navigator, bomb aimer and wireless op witnessed the whole thing and later described the scene, with great relish, for the benefit of the NCO crew members. Clive was innocent. He had nothing to do with the flat tyres and had no idea what Bennett was going on about. Our skipper had no choice but to swallow his pride and get on with it, the intensity of his own anger running a very close second to that of Bennett himself. Our navigator told us the story the following morning. I clearly recall his parting words: 'For God's sake don't let on to Clive that I told you. He's very cheesed off about it!'*

Walker's crew joined A Flight, commanded by Squadron Leader Walbourne. The facts of life and death on a Pathfinder squadron began to sink in. The RAF had fixed an operational tour at 200 hours at the beginning of the war, but this was changed to 30 operations for bomber crews. Bomber aircrew were also subject to a second tour, usually of 20 sorties. A Pathfinder tour, however, could amount to as many as 45 or even 60 operations. Mid-upper gunner Cliff Cooper's operational career paralleled that of Sidney Knott. He was a member of a 467 Squadron crew, skippered by Flight Lieutenant Leo Patkin, then did a second tour with 582 Squadron. Cooper completed 56 operations without the recognition of a 'gong'.

The Walker crew's flying from Little Staughton commenced on Wednesday April 5 with a three-hour flight in Lancaster L-Love (JA673). They took off at 11.00 for a Y-Run cross-country exercise using H2S radar. A new concept in bombing had developed within 8 Group. The method was based around a closely integrated 'bombing team' (involving pilot, navigator and bomb aimer), to achieve more effective marking and bombing. The bombing system itself was a considerable advance on earlier equipment and offered greater accuracy. Unfortunately, these improvements were not matched by more reliable weather forecasting. This remained Bomber Command's Achilles heel throughout the war.

Everyone was eager to get on with things and bring the new squadron to operational status. Later that Wednesday, at 20.00, Walker and crew were back in the air for another Y-Run and cross-country, landing away at Nuneaton after a flight of nearly two hours. They took the Lanc on the short hop back to base during the afternoon of April 7. The work-up continued the next day, with Walker taking S-Sugar (ND817) on a three hours 45 minutes Group navigation exercise. They landed back at 18.25, unaware that they would make their operational debut with PFF the following day.

# CHAPTER SEVENTEEN

## 'Two-Thirds Counts as One'

WALKER and his flight engineer took Lancaster ND818 along Little Staughton's main runway at noon on Sunday April 9. This flight combined a night flying test with an air-to-sea gunnery exercise and Sidney Knott fired 200 rounds at a sea target. They arrived back at 13.25.

During the morning Walker's name had appeared on 582 Squadron's first Battle Order. Main briefing was just a few hours away. The skipper progressed through his first day as an operational pilot on heavies as the aircraft were readied for the night's raid. Bombing-up commenced at the dispersal pans. Walker's aircraft was O-Orange (ND816) and its bomb doors gaped open. The long, dark cavern between the doors slowly filled with twelve 1,000 lb and two 500 lb bombs.

The afternoon slipped by. During the early evening Walker rather self-consciously led his crew into the briefing room. The large wall map of western Europe revealed the 'target for tonight', Lille's marshalling yards.

D-Day, the invasion of France, was just eight weeks away. A significant proportion of Bomber Command's effort was to be directed at French rail targets, a priority under the pre-invasion element of the 'Transportation Plan'. Bomber Command dropped 41,000 tonnes of bombs on the 37 rail targets allocated to it under this plan[1]. The aim was to create a 'railway desert' within 150 miles of Caen, to impede the reinforcement of the region by German armour and other forces[2].

The ruling that each sortie against a French target should count as only one-third of an operation caused great discontent on the squadrons. Some 582 Squadron cynics suggested that if trips to France were worth so little, perhaps they should take the place of night flying tests. Later, this controversial and deeply unpopular policy was reversed. It soon became apparent that French targets could be just as dangerous as their German counterparts.

This point moved beyond dispute in early May, when the Main Force suffered savage losses during a raid on German Army concentrations at Mailly-Le-Camp[3]. The attack during the night of May 3/4 involved 346 Lancasters and 16 Mosquitos. A total of 42 aircraft failed to return - an appalling casualty rate of 11.6 per cent[4]. Forty-five aircraft were struck off charge.

While such catastrophic losses occasionally occurred, the switch in emphasis from the area bombing of German cities to pre-invasion targets in France undoubtedly saved many aircrew lives. The night defences covering Germany had evolved into a finely tuned killing machine. Following the devastating Hamburg raids of mid-1943 and the use of 'Window' radar jamming, the German air defences were reconstituted. Window was the major stimulus, encouraging the Germans to develop highly effective new tactics including Zahme Sau (Tame Boar).

Wilde Sau (Wild Boar) pre-dated the Hamburg firestorm and accelerated the rapid evolution of German tactics by encouraging radical thinking. Wilde Sau can mean 'crazy' or 'bull at a gate'. Ironically, the expression was used originally in a negative sense, to undermine Major Hajo Herrmann's proposal to use single-seat day fighters in a freelance nightfighting role over the target. These tactics were used for the first time during a raid against Cologne on July 3 1943[5].

The Zahme Sau concept was altogether different and more deadly. It involved the infiltration of nightfighters into the bomber stream at the earliest opportunity. In one sense this made early identification of the target irrelevant to nightfighter controllers. Once the fighters entered the stream they flew with the bombers wherever they went. The deeper the penetration into German airspace the more time available to the accompanying nightfighters to find targets and make their kills. There was no effective counter to Zahme Sau.

Within a few weeks of the catastrophic Hamburg attacks Zahme Sau tactics were used for the first time. Zahme Sau was employed to counter an attack on Berlin on of August 23/24 1943. Bomber Command now had the ability to concentrate large forces in space and time. The aim was to swamp the defences by passing hundreds of aircraft over the target in an extremely short period. Yet this compressed bomber stream also presented Zahme Sau nightfighters with a concentrated target. All the Germans had to do was ensure their nightfighters congregate within the stream and remain with it for as long as possible. Large-scale Zahme Sau operations began on the night of August 23/24. Bomber Command dispatched 727 aircraft to Berlin and 56 (7.9 per cent) failed to return, making it one of Bomber Command's worst nights of the war. A total of 63 aircraft were struck off charge.

In encouraging the adoption of new and highly effective Zahme Sau tactics Window was a double-edged sword. The consequences were far worse than the original fear of reciprocal use of Window by German raiders[6]. In any event, by this stage in the war the German bombing force in the West was much reduced. From the German perspective, the Zahme Sau tactics gave all crews the chance to amass kills, in contrast to the earlier, more rigid box system of nightfighting monopolised by experten[7].

By April 1944 Bomber Command had an average daily availability of around 1,000 heavy bombers[8]. They were opposed by hundreds of nightfighters. Yet German nightfighting capabilities were tested severely by Bomber Command at this time. Harris often divided his force and attacked – with good results – two or more targets on the same night. The bomber streams were smaller than those encountered six months earlier and this made life more difficult for the Zahme Sau pilots[9].

Sidney Knott became aware of a change in his status at the start of the second tour:

> *First tour experience appeared almost irrelevant to the PFF. We were regarded as complete novices. In the first weeks of April we were allocated the apprentice role of 'Supporter'. Marking for the Main Force was no job for novices! Supporters bombed the markers just before the Main Force bombed. The idea was to give the Master Bomber a chance to assess how the bombs were falling on the target.*

Walker's crew logged four sorties in April, all against rail marshalling yards. In each case they bombed the markers in the Supporter role. On Sunday April 9 the first operation began as O-Orange moved off the perimeter track and responded to the green at 23.10, with Walker ready to counter the Lancaster's swing to port on the take-off run. They were back after just two hours 50 minutes in the air.

The Lancaster had bombed the red TIs over Lille at 0052.45 from an altitude of 16,000 ft, on a heading of 356 deg. Magnetic and an indicated airspeed of 155 kts. A large red glow illuminated the target area three seconds before the bombs dropped. There was a slight ground haze but visibility, overall, was good.

A total of 239 aircraft raided Lille. One Lancaster failed to return. The target area was pear-shaped, 2,500 yards by an average of 600 yards and with housing situated to the north, east and west[10]. Délivrance goods depot was struck by 49 bombs. Severe damage resulted and more than 2,000 rail wagons were destroyed. Sadly, many bombs fell wide and struck suburban housing in the city's Lomme district. Over 450 people died and more than 5,000 homes were destroyed or damaged[11]. In return, the destruction of this rail hub contributed to delays to the German reinforcement of Normandy, including the deployment of 1st SS Panzer[10].

The sortie left Walker's crew with just one-third of an operation to their credit. The widespread disgust at Bomber Command's accounting practices at least provided a common talking point. It served to break the ice and made it easier for Walker's men to get to know the other crews on the squadron.

Sidney Knott soon discovered that the policy for allocating Lancasters on 582 Squadron was as promiscuous as that of 467 Squadron. During the following afternoon, Monday April 10, the crew took O-Orange on a 35-minute night flying test but Walker was given ND438 for Tuesday's raid against Aachen's rail yards. During the night of April 11/12 Francks released a stick of 13 1,000 lb bombs across this target. The crew landed back at Little Staughton after a flight of three hours 35 minutes.

This successful raid by 341 Lancasters and 11 Mosquitos was Aachen's most damaging attack of the war. The casualties on the ground were heavy: 1,525 people died, including 212 children[12].

When the crew woke during the late Wednesday morning they were told they were not required for operations that day. Indeed, flying was confined to exercises for nearly a week; the training never stopped. This was an expression, at the squadron level, of PFF Commander Bennett's relentless search for perfection. Knott fired 400 rounds during an air-to-air gunnery exercise on the Thursday. Bombing exercises and night flying tests followed. The flying included Standard Beam Approach practice, a technique for landing in difficult weather conditions.

Walker's bomb aimer, Reg Francks, kept a car on the station. It trailed dense smoke, always a sign that the fuel was a concoction heavily reliant on aviation grade:

> *The station's motor transport was subject to the attentions of enterprising vehicle owners. Occasionally, Bill helped Reg pilfer petrol from a lorry whenever we required transport to St. Neots. After our SBA flight on Friday April 14 we were given 48-hour passes and a more ambitious excursion was in prospect. Reg acquired fuel and announced his plans to make for London. Space in his car was soon filled. Bill and I got a lift and we were dropped near a Tube station on the North Circular.*

> *We made our way to a 'Nuffield Centre' in the West End. Lord Nuffield, the car magnate, was exceptionally generous to service personnel. Nuffield Centres provided for all basic needs at very modest prices. Thanks to Reg and his car we arrived in good time to book bed and breakfast. The accommodation was clean yet spartan – a plain dormitory with bunk beds.*

> *London was showing signs of recovery from the Blitz. Bomb sites and other ugly scars of war were visible yet the capital was rediscovering its exciting, vibrant personality. There were plenty of good shows on offer. Bill and I liked the reviews with the long lines of statuesque girls skilled in the art of the high-kick. There were also some fine comedians. Most of the jokes were 'morale-boosting' but they were still very funny. The war had taken the starch out of society and an element of satire was beginning to appear.*

> *The best shows were at the Palladium, Victoria Palace and Prince of Wales. Food followed the entertainment. A good meal was always available at one of the many clubs open to the services. A drink was more challenging as the London pubs were so crowded. It took most of the evening to get served. London was full of service personnel. Americans, Canadians and Australians always made for the West End, despite the fact that the 'Bright Lights' had disappeared years ago with the imposition of the Blackout. London in April 1944 was still very much a city at war and, for the most part, it closed down quite early.*

Walker's two gunners had a good night's sleep then demolished substantial breakfast plates of sausages, beans and fried bread. They picked up their gas masks and went for a stroll:

> *I remember my sense of freedom on that Spring morning. The pavements were crowded, full of uniforms of all kinds. Hungry as ever we made short work of pie and chips at midday, leaving us with the entire afternoon ahead. Bill and I continued to walk and the hours passed quickly. Then a café caught our eye as it offered tea and music. We climbed the stairs and found seats. Tea was served on small tables laden with toast, jam and cakes. Three elderly ladies, positioned on a small stage at the end of the room, provided the entertainment. The piano, violin and cello produced pleasant music in the Palm Court style. While not to my taste it was enjoyable enough.*

*The London experience was another world and a sharp, almost bittersweet contrast to our strange life with an operational bomber squadron. In London, people seemed so friendly and the atmosphere itself was relaxing. The music in the café began to weave a protective spell around the afternoon. It stopped the clock and pushed aside unspoken fears shared by all aircrew. Another two hours slipped away.*

On leaving this refuge the gunners found the late afternoon had become quite foggy. They began to make their way back to the rendezvous agreed with Reg Francks:

*Reg was a reliable bloke but the fog had thickened by the time we reached Tottenham. It soon developed into a real pea-souper and I began to have doubts about our lift back to Little Staughton. Yet Reg turned up on time and was surprised to hear we had been worried.*

*Getting back, however, was far from easy. Our first problem was to find the Great North Road in thick fog and with the wartime absence of road signs. We made progress but the going was slow and Reg wondered whether we would have enough petrol to reach the station, given all the low gear work. The drive was difficult but Reg eventually entered familiar territory. Within minutes we recognised St. Neots and had just enough juice to drive through Little Staughton's main gate.*

A night flying test was combined with bombing and SBA exercises on Tuesday April 18. This was followed by an early evening briefing for an attack on the Noisy-le-Sec rail yards near Paris. Earlier, Wing Commander CM Dunnifliffe, DFC, had settled into his new office, having taken command of 582 Squadron.

Walker's crew made the acquaintance of yet another Lancaster on the squadron strength, N-Nuts (ND502). The bomb-load followed the Aachen pattern: 13 1,000 lb bombs rather than the mix of bigger blast bombs and incendiaries required for large-scale German city attacks. The raid involved 181 aircraft and four (all Halifaxes) failed to return. The attack wrecked the marshalling yards and some of the 200 delayed action bombs dropped were still exploding a week later. Repairs were not completed until 1951. The French casualties in this raid included 464 dead[13].

This sortie (the crew's third trip) was followed on Thursday April 20 by a flight of two hours 40 minutes practising Y-Run radar bombing procedures. On the Saturday a night flying test in ND818 was followed by briefing for an attack on Düsseldorf. This city's huge rail yards were the main objective. Walker was allocated N-Nuts, laden with six 2,000 lb bombs.

This raid on the night of April 22/23 marked a resumption of area bombing. It involved 596 aircraft and 29 failed to return (4.9 per cent of the raiding force). Thirty-one aircraft were struck off charge. The attackers dropped 2,150 tonnes of bombs on the city, hitting 56 large factories and destroying or heavily damaging over 2,000 homes. More than 1,000 people died[14].

The crew's Lancaster touched down at Little Staughton at 03.15 after four hours five minutes in the air. The airfield recognition letters were LX. Walker was heartened to see the red morse flashes in the darkness ahead from Little Staughton's mobile 'Pundit' beacon.

*This was our final op in April. Short trips flown in Spring weather were very different from Winter flying to long distance targets. They didn't seem as exhausting as my first tour trips with 467 Squadron. Our crew continued to develop as a team and grew more confident. Yet we were still put out by the fact that the two German trips counted as one op each, while the two French trips, added together, made just two-thirds. We were not greatly mollified by the concession that two-thirds should count as one. It still amounted to two for the price of one!*

Walker's crew were fortunate that their tour started at a time when Bomber Command switched the main emphasis from the costly, faltering area offensive against Germany to the bombing of French targets in preparation for the invasion. In contrast, the Heavery tour coincided with the costly Battle of the Ruhr. Bomber Command was close to exhaustion in the early Spring of 1944, after the exertions of the Berlin campaign. This had cost the lives of thousands of aircrew. The Battle of Berlin was Bomber Command's Calvary. During this campaign 1,303 aircraft became casualties (625 when attacking Berlin rather than other targets)[15].

The German night defences were formidable following their transformation after the Hamburg firestorm catastrophe of July 1943. In 1940 German nightfighters shot down 42 British bombers, rising to 421 the following year and 687 in 1942 (including 435 in the June-September period alone)[16]. Bomber Command's casualties continued to escalate during 1943. As a result of the following year's pre-invasion switch to French targets, however, casualties were lower than during the Battle of Berlin period. Yet these losses remained severe.

Bomber Command was under Eisenhower's control until late September. By that time Walker's crew had finished their tour. Bomber Command then began its final approach to the pinnacle of its striking power. In parallel, the German capacity for day and night defence commenced its terminal decline. The full destructive power of Harris' long-promised 'whirlwind' would be felt during the final nine months of war in Europe. By late August 1944, the ability to raid Germany in daylight underlined the new Allied long-range fighters' success in reducing the German fighter force. In the final quarter of 1944 Bomber Command dropped more bombs than in the whole of 1943 - and with greater accuracy[17].

Sidney Knott logged 33 hours 55 minutes with 582 Squadron during April, including 14 hours 25 minutes' operational flying:

*Squadron Leader Walbourne, A Flight's Commander, signed my logbook for the month. We had made a good start although we did get a little concerned about Clive after Noisy-le-Sec. We didn't want our skipper developing any false impressions based on his past experience over France – although that had been dangerous enough. We explained that the first three ops of our tour had been easy. Deep penetrations into heavily-defended German airspace were different.*

*If Clive harboured any lingering hopes that we were exaggerating they were dispelled during our fourth trip, to Düsseldorf. A Ruhr target always guaranteed a hot reception from seasoned flak crews. One taste of Happy Valley was quite enough to put Clive in the picture. On our return a pensive Gus climbed out of the Lanc, turned to me and said quietly: 'I see what you mean.'*

The Pathfinders' war grew in complexity. Important steps on the long, difficult road to effective target finding and marking were taken in late 1941. The idea of a dedicated target-finding force had a strong advocate in Air Commodore Sydney Bufton, Director of Bomber Operations at the Air Ministry. Bufton had pioneered target-marking with flares when in command of 10 and 76 squadrons[18]. Harris rejected the PFF concept when he took his seat at Bomber Command in February 1942 but he was ordered to proceed some months later.

The Pathfinder Force was established on August 11 1942, with Bennett in command and 1, 3, 4 and 5 Groups contributing 156, 7, 35 and 83 squadrons respectively. The PFF airfields were in Huntingdonshire and Cambridgeshire. The founder PFF squadrons operated a mix of aircraft (Halifaxes, Lancasters, Stirlings and Wellingtons).

The new force was established during a difficult period for Bomber Command. The German defences continued to develop and the growing efficiency of the nightfighters placed a premium on moonless nights. High casualties amongst the Halifax squadrons had required a stand-down. Furthermore, the Germans were starting to jam GEE. Yet there were positive developments, including the rapidly expanding production of four-engined bombers. In addition, American B17s began to operate on August 17 1942, opening with a modest attack on a French target. 'Round-the-clock bombing' was now in prospect[19].

The advantage began to swing towards Bomber Command during the final quarter of 1942. Oboe, the precision blind-bombing aid, arrived. While ground stations could control only a handful of Oboe-equipped Mosquitos at a time, this was just enough to deliver primary marking over targets within Oboe range. These markers were 'backed up' (replenished) by PFF heavy aircraft. The entire Ruhr was within Oboe range and this highly accurate blind-bombing/marking system was never jammed effectively by the Germans[20].

H2S ground-scanning radar entered service in early 1943. This could pick out rivers, lakes, coastlines and other ground features under favourable conditions. H2S had no range restriction as it was carried in the aircraft. The first H2S sets went to 7 and 35 PFF squadrons in January 1943. Every PFF heavy aircraft was equipped with H2S over the following months. Every Main Force squadron had H2S by early 1944. Oboe and, to some extent, H2S greatly enhanced Bomber Command's operational capabilities[20].

Mandrel and Tinsel were introduced during the final quarter of 1942. Mandrel was an airborne system for jamming German radars directing nightfighters. Tinsel was an airborne system broadcasting engine noise on German nightfighter frequencies. Tinsel, very unpleasant to the German ear, was given the name Seelenbohrer, or 'Soul-borer'[21]. Many more radio countermeasures followed.

The new target indicators had reached the PFF squadrons by January 1943. The bomb casings were filled with pyrotechnics of various colours – typically red, green, yellow and combinations. The pyrotechnic candles were released at various heights and fell slowly to the ground[22]. Constant innovation was important, to stay ahead of German expertise in the use of ground decoys. One marking device was the 'red spot fire'; usually set to burst at 3,000 ft, it had a distinct and vivid crimson glow[23].

Over a period of some eight weeks Bomber Command received Oboe, H2S, target indicators and new radio countermeasures. The Main Force, meanwhile, continued to expand. The new all-Canadian 6 Group became operational on January 1 1943. The PFF became 8 Group on January 8. By the end of 1943 Bennett's Group included four Mosquito squadrons: 105 and 109 for Oboe operations and 139 and 627 for general support. He named these squadrons the 'Light Night Striking Force'[24].

Bomber Command's striking power had been transformed. The all-Lancaster 5 Group could drop a greater weight of bombs in a single night than the whole of Bomber Command's Main Force a year earlier[22].

PFF tactics developed rapidly during the March-July 1943 Ruhr campaign. Oboe Mosquitos provided the primary marking with PFF 'Backers Up' dropping more markers on the primaries. Oboe-equipped Mosquitos of 109 Squadron, later to share Little Staughton with 582 Squadron, played a prominent role in PFF's evolution[25]. Target-finding and accurate marking remained a major challenge, however, when the Main Force operated beyond Oboe range.

Bomber Command spread consternation among the German defences on the night of July 24/25 1943, when Hamburg was attacked (followed very shortly by the raid that resulted in the catastrophic firestorm). Window - clouds of aluminium strips dropped to swamp enemy radars - was used for the first time. It paralysed the defences. Eventually, however, the Germans responded with new and extremely successful nightfighter tactics[26].

Window continued in use during the area bombing campaign. Stragglers were more vulnerable, however, if they strayed from the bomber stream and continued to drop Window. Many aircraft fell to nightfighters when they lost 'safety in numbers' and made matters worse by continuing to drop Window, so achieving exactly the opposite of the desired effect. In short, they were advertising their presence to German radar operators[21].

The pace of technological innovation accelerated during the final months of 1943. Mosquitos trialled the new 'GH' blind-bombing aid in October (with large-scale production and entry into service during 1944). In addition, two new radio countermeasures were introduced in October 1943. Corona broadcast false orders to enemy nightfighters, using German-speaking RAF personnel. There was also ABC (Airborne Cigar). This system, carried by specially-equipped heavy aircraft, disrupted German voice transmissions. Its warble attracted the epithet Dudelsack, or 'Bagpipes'[21].

Tactics reached new levels of sophistication. High-flying Mosquitos had been used as diversions, dropping flares and TIs to entice nightfighters away from the real target. The results were disappointing, however, as there were insufficient Mosquitos to achieve a convincing result. Bomber Command's solution was to dispatch small groups of heavy bombers on diversionary raids[27].

New 8 Group tactics were paying off. The flare-droppers ('Illuminators') went in first, before the 'Primary Markers'. With the target well lit, the first markers would be laid, followed by fresh markers of another colour dropped by the 'Backers Up'. If things went wrong markers of a different type and/or colour were used to cancel earlier markers[28].

Visual ground-marking was codenamed 'Newhaven'. If the target was obscured by cloud or smoke, to a degree ruling out Newhaven, blind ground-marking by radar (H2S) was used. This was known as 'Parramatta'. Oboe blind-marking was known as 'Musical Parramatta'. If the target was totally obscured a third technique - 'Wanganui' - was employed. This was blind-marking using parachute-equipped 'sky-markers'[28].

Bennett described how the marking methods found their names: 'I asked one of my Air Staff Officers, Squadron Leader Ashworth, '...Pedro, where do you come from?' And he replied, 'From Wanganui.' I then said, 'Just to keep the balance with New Zealand, we will call the blind ground marking by the name of Parramatta.' Then, looking for a third name, for visual ground marking, I pressed the bell on my desk and summoned Corporal Ralph, my confidential WAAF clerk. When she came in, I said, '...Sunshine, where do you live?' And she replied, 'Newhaven.' Thus it was that these famous codenames were born[29].'

Crews at Little Staughton were briefed on Wednesday May 3 for an attack on the Luftwaffe airfield and facilities at Montdidier. Clive Walker's aircraft was S-Sugar (ND817). The crew knew this Lancaster, having taken it on the Group navigation exercise flown on April 8. The bomber left the runway at 22.55 for a trip lasting three hours 15 minutes. The crew dropped a 4,000 lb Cookie and 13 500 lb bombs, two fitted with long-delay fuses. *The Bomber Command War Diaries* record that this attack was delivered by 84 Lancasters and eight Mosquitos. Four Lancasters failed to return, in exchange for severe damage to the target.

Walker's crew were fortunate to be tasked for the minor raid of the night. They might otherwise have participated in the main business of May 3/4 – the savagely-mauled attack on Mailly-le-Camp, when 42 aircraft failed to return.

Following a short break the crew were airborne again on Saturday May 6. They took S-Sugar for a night flying test that afternoon. On visiting the Flight Office after breakfast Walker had found his name on the night's Battle Order. The modest fuel load indicated another short trip to a French target. Some hours later one glance at the briefing room wall map revealed all. The rail yards at Gassicourt, Mantes-la-Jolie, were to be destroyed.

S-Sugar's bomb-bay held 12 1,000 lb bombs when Walker took off from Little Staughton at 00.45. The sortie took three hours 20 minutes. This raid inflicted heavy damage on the yard's sheds and depots, but some bombs fell wide and killed 54 civilians. The raid involved 149 aircraft and two Lancasters and a Halifax failed to return[30].

Pathfinder expertise was essential to the success of the French interdiction plan and, in particular, the dislocation of the rail transportation network. Great accuracy was vital when bombing key targets (some of a small, pinpoint nature), if French casualties were to be minimised[31]. Inevitably, however, many civilians died. Having completed six PFF trips Walker's crew 'graduated' and became Illuminators.

Walker's notebook contains the entry 'RCM Offensive'. He lists nine forms of radio countermeasures:

*Radar jamming: Window (Würzburg/AI), Mandrel (Freya) and Ground Grocer (AI jamming).*

*RT jamming: Airborne Cigar (VHF), Ground Cigar (VHF), Special Tinsel (HF), Corona (HF fighter control reportage transmissions) and Dartboard (MF jamming broadcasts).*

*W/T jamming: W/T Corona.*

The bombing offensive was now an electronic war rapidly extending the boundaries of 1940s technology:

*This second tour was a different type of war. Our aircraft were packed with new gadgets and we now had 'navigating teams'. Only the turrets and guns were unchanged. We flew as Illuminators on our seventh operation, a raid on Louvain during the night of May 11/12. This was yet another attack in the long series against major rail targets in the run-up to D-Day. Our aircraft for the night, J-Jig (ND899), was new to us although we had performed a brief night flying test in this Lanc earlier in the day. Before entering the aircraft, Clive had the usual walk round, examining the tyres and checking that all cowling and inspection panels were secure. We then climbed in and took our stations.*

*The Illuminators dropped parachute flares over the target, following the Master Bomber's instructions. We carried six flares and eight 1,000 lb bombs. The sortie went well and we dropped the flares in one stick squarely over the rail yards. This three-hour trip was our shortest to date, with the exception of the April 9/10 attack on Lille.*

The Louvain rail complex was struck by a hail of bombs from 105 Lancasters and workshops and storage areas suffered heavy damage. Four Lancasters failed to return. This important target was revisited the following night but Walker's crew did not participate. The second raid involved 120 aircraft, was more accurate and caused even greater destruction[32].

Bomber Command's agenda for May 11/12 provides an insight into Allied targeting priorities during the final countdown to D-Day. There were six targets that night. Beyond the Louvain attack, raids were flown against a large military camp at Bourg-Léopold and rail yards at Boulogne, Hasselt and Trouville, together with gun positions at Colline Beaumont[32].

*As the tour progressed we became skilled in the various PFF techniques. Flying as Illuminators, our flares offered the Master Bomber an overview of the target area. He then called in the Backers Up to reinforce the primary marking. During some attacks adjustments were made to the initial concentration of markers. It was not unknown for markers to fall short. This was 'creep-back', the product of a natural – and entirely understandable – tendency to drop a little too early. The Master Bomber made the necessary corrections to bring more bombs on target.*

On some occasions 'offset marking' was employed in an attempt to deal with Main Force creep-back. This involved dropping markers at a certain distance beyond the target, in the knowledge that creep-back would bring most of the bombs within the desired target zone. Offset-marking was also used to avoid problems caused by markers being obscured by smoke or overwhelmed by fire in the immediate target area[33].

*During my second tour PFF Commander Don Bennett issued instructions forbidding pilots to weave. He was concerned that this resulted in too many aircraft being late over the target. We had found that minimal time was lost by weaving (or the milder form of defensive flying known as 'jinking'). A good pilot and navigator always made up a few minutes of lost time with ease. Bennett's edict, however, had to be considered. Bill and I had a chat and then went to Clive with a proposition. Our navigator joined the discussion and we agreed we would continue to weave or jink whenever it seemed necessary to do so. The gunners maintained that it was better – even for a marking crew – to arrive two minutes late than not at all. The others were receptive to this line of argument.*

*The ridiculous idea of one-third of an op for a French target was abandoned at this time. This was a retrospective ruling – every sortie counted as one op. There was a rumour that the decision was taken following a special operation involving a small force of six aircraft attacking a French target. According to the buzz in the Mess not one bomber escaped. It was said that a nightfighter had been in the right place, at the right time, and had got the lot!*

Putting such rumours aside, many French targets were very dangerous. The slaughter of Mailly-le-Camp and the lesser known but costly minor raid on Salbris a few days later (May 7/8) made the point. The Salbris attack, on an ammunition dump, was successful but seven of the 58 participating Lancasters failed to return[34].

Following the Louvain attack, Walker's week was filled with training flights. On Saturday May 13 he took J-Jig for an exercise involving Y-Runs and a 15-minute fighter affiliation with a Hurricane. On Sunday he called in at A Flight's office and found he was booked for a night exercise. The crew took off at 23.00 in O-Orange (ND812) for bombing practice and a fighter affiliation, a rare event at night:

> *There was no moon but fighter and bomber soon found each other and the Hurricane set about trying to shoot us down. The training continued on the Monday and we readied ND909 for an afternoon radar bombing exercise. No practice bombs were dropped during these exercises. The purpose was to develop the navigating team's ability to work together smoothly during the final stages of the approach to the target.*

> *Our break from ops ended on the night of May 19/20 when we took O-Orange to Boulogne, along with 18 500 lb bombs. We were briefed as a Supporter.*

Boulogne's rail yards suffered heavily and there were no casualties among the 143 attacking aircraft. The main target was the northerly of two rail facilities – the marshalling yards. The crew of one 582 Squadron Lancaster, captained by Squadron Leader McMillan, had dropped flares but had not released the bombs when the signal to cease bombing ('cartwheel') was given. McMillan eventually ordered the bombs to be jettisoned over the sea. This aircraft suffered a final indignity at Little Staughton when the brakes failed and it ran out of runway[35].

On the night of May 21/22 Walker took O-Orange to Duisburg with a Cookie and incendiaries. The Lancaster was one of 510 heavy aircraft mounting the first large-scale strike against Duisburg for a year. The city was obscured by cloud but Oboe sky-marking produced good results. The bombers inflicted serious damage and 124 people died[36].

> *Briefed as Supporters, we took off for Duisburg at 22.50. The Lanc completed the climb to operational height as we headed out to sea. We dropped our load on the city, turned away and landed back at Little Staughton at 03.10. Our ninth PFF sortie was over.*

> *After a few hours' sleep and a meal Clive delivered the unwelcome news. We were going again that night. The skipper gave us the glad tidings on returning from his routine morning visit to the A Flight Office. Ground crews were already busy on the Lancs and bomb trolleys began the long crawl out to the dispersals. Clive said we had been given O-Orange once again. At 22.30 on that Monday the throttles were opened and we took off for Dortmund with six 2,000 lb bombs on board.*

This raid by 361 Lancasters and 14 Mosquitos, during the night of May 22/23, was the first major assault on Dortmund for a year. As a member of Heavery's crew Sidney Knott had participated in the last major attack on this target exactly 12 months before. Eighteen Lancasters (4.8 per cent of the force) failed to return from this fresh raid. The weight of the attack fell on the south eastern residential districts; over 360 people died and around 1,700 were injured[37].

Germany's nightfighter elite retained an ability to inflict losses out of all proportion to their numbers. On the night of May 24/25, for example, Bomber Command raided the rail yards at Aachen and 18 Halifaxes and seven Lancasters failed to return. Twenty-seven aircraft were struck off charge. Schnauffer, operating from the Belgian airfield of St. Trond, showed his prowess once again. He claimed five victims in the space of

14 minutes[38].

> *A few days later, on the night of May 27/28, we were flying over Rennes in O-Orange. We had been briefed as Illuminators and carried six flares and eight 1,000 lb bombs. Our stores were deposited on an airfield popular with the Luftwaffe.*

Walker's aircraft was part of a force of 78 Lancasters and five Mosquitos attacking this target in good visibility. The bombing was accurate and extensive damage resulted. Some crews reported a very large explosion - possibly a direct hit on the airfield's bomb dump[39].

Preparations for the invasion of occupied Europe now entered the final phase. Security was tight. French targets were allocated on the basis of two elsewhere for every one in Normandy, to keep the Germans guessing. Stern warnings were issued at the squadron level. A tough security message was delivered at a meeting of all aircrew at Little Staughton. Group Captain R.W.P. Collings looked serious as he scanned the attentive faces. The Station Commander favoured the blunt approach: 'You all know D-Day is imminent. You may see some unusual things when flying. You must keep your mouths shut when you get down.'

> *Collings' words stayed with us, on the ground and in the air. When we flew over the maze of creeks around Ipswich and Colchester we could see hundreds of empty barges. All manner of heavy equipment was stockpiled nearby, ready to load.*
>
> *As always, the Air Force kept us busy when we were not required for ops. There was more training, including Y-Runs, air-to-air firing and fighter affiliation with Hurricanes. We also completed a 'Fishpond' drill. Fishpond was a device that provided a warning of an approaching fighter. It used H2S radar to search for aircraft below. Any blip closing rapidly was likely to be a nightfighter. The crews didn't know, at that time, that the Germans had kept pace. They had developed a device, Naxos, that detected H2S transmissions. No wonder Fishpond worked so well!*

Naxos could not home onto an individual bomber using Fishpond but the device did reveal concentrations of H2S transmissions and, therefore, helped Zahme Sau nightfighters enter the bomber stream[40].

> *Over the next few days we saw the barges being loaded with equipment. Soon, presumably, troops would begin to board. The barges were packed together so tightly that the water in the creeks could no longer be seen. The view below looked like a floating honeycomb of arms and supplies.*

Four days of exercises ended on Wednesday May 31, when Walker's crew boarded Lancaster J-Jig (NE169):

> *After a 30-minute night flying test in this Lanc during the afternoon we were briefed as Illuminators for an attack on the rail yards at Tergnier. Our stores were identical to those carried on the Rennes operation: eight 1,000 lb bombs and six flares.*

The Tergnier attack was delivered by 111 Lancasters and four Mosquitos; two Lancasters failed to return[41]. The bombing results were good. With this raid over Walker's crew had completed 12 PFF sorties. They were given five days' rest from ops but were back in the air on Friday June 2. At 14.15 that afternoon Walker took J-Jig along the main runway and climbed away to the briefed height for a fighter affiliation, followed by more bombing practice and air-to-air firing. Their next op was flown during the first few hours of D-Day, Tuesday June 6 1944:

> *We took off at 02.50, having been briefed to bomb the powerful coastal batteries at Longues. J-Jig's contribution to D-Day consisted of 11 1,000 lb and four 500 lb bombs. No flares for this job! We had a briefed bombing height of just 8,000 ft - far lower than usual. The weather was cloudy and offered no opportunity to bomb visually. The entire force bombed blind through cloud, making good use of the new electronic bombing aids.*

> *As we left the target, at around 04.30, dawn was breaking on the momentous day leading to the liberation of Europe. It was unusually quiet over the target and Clive put the nose down as we headed for home. We broke cloud just off the Normandy beaches, to stare in amazement at a breathtaking sight. There it was - the invasion! Thousands of vessels were spread before us, some standing off and others approaching the shore. Our intercom discipline went to pot immediately. Everyone started talking at once as we tried to take it in. Bill Harrall remembers watching a monitor – a small vessel fitted with a single, battleship–sized gun for shore bombardment. The tiny warship heeled over violently every time the gun fired.*

> *Commonsense soon prevailed. Navy gunners had itchy trigger fingers and it was unhealthy to hang around. We turned out to sea, hugged the cloud base and made good speed back to Little Staughton. Before long I felt the aircraft take a slightly nose down trim as the undercarriage came down. We landed at 06.05, having completed our thirteenth op.*

Bomber Command flew a record 1,211 sorties that night. Eight aircraft failed to return, including one of the Lancasters attacking Longues. Most of the sorties (over 1,000) were directed against German batteries at 10 locations along the Normandy coast. Around 5,000 tonnes of bombs fell on these targets - yet another record for a single night[42].

> *Our brief yet inspiring glimpse of the invasion fleet made a deep impression on the crew. On the other hand, the station security warning had the desired effect. We said nothing to ground personnel after our debriefing. A public announcement had yet to be made but the BBC soon broke the story.*

> *I felt humbled by the sheer scale of the Normandy enterprise and the terrible risks faced by those storming the beach defences. Before turning in I found a quiet corner and prayed for their safety. I hoped our attack last night and the bombing over recent weeks had softened up the defences and wrecked the German supply lines.*

Bomber Command's war had become a battle of wits between the scientists. Research teams continued to produce a stream of new devices for more accurate navigation, blind-bombing and marking, together with defensive systems for early warning of nightfighter attack and the

*Pilotless plane: The V1 Flying Bomb opened the Germans' 'revenge campaign' against Britain. Trustees of the Imperial war Museum.*

jamming of German radar and communications. German scientists, in turn, showed great ingenuity in developing countermeasures and adding innovations to challenge their British counterparts.

Sidney Knott came face-to-face with German technological prowess during a sortie in July. A strange aircraft – some distance away and on an opposing course – swept past his turret at incredible speed. The Walker crew had seen their first jet, the Me 262:

*This came as a real shock. Aircraft without propellers! We had never heard of jets and were first introduced to the term by our Intelligence Officer at debriefing.*

The heavy bombers made an important contribution to the launch of Eisenhower's 'Great Crusade'. Following the attack on Longues Walker's crew were given leave. They were fortunate. All leave was cancelled for most service personnel, to reduce the pressure on the country's overworked rail system at this crucial point in a long war.

*I took Bill Harrall with me and introduced him to the delights of Leigh-on-Sea. He met my parents and we strolled around my old haunts. I had hoped for a chance to unwind but Flying Bombs heading for London roared overhead and rather took the edge off things.*

*Back at Little Staughton the training continued, including the usual Y-Runs and bombing practice. There was also something new: formation flying! This was not particularly pleasant or easy for Clive as the Lanc was relatively heavy on the controls. This training sequence ended on Thursday June 22 with a two-hour morning flight including a bombing exercise and air-to-sea firing. Later that day we were briefed for a night attack on Coubronne.*

*My log entry for this sortie, flown in B-Baker (PB136), carries the cryptic note 'P-Plane base'. P-Plane stood for pilotless plane or Flying Bomb, the latest unwelcome demonstration of German genius in weapons production. The VI 'Doodlebug' opened Hitler's so-called revenge campaign against Britain. Bill and I had been on the ground, looking up at the VIs, during our leave. It was with great pleasure, therefore, that we unloaded 11 1,000 lb bombs and three 500 lb bombs on that small yet very worthy target at Coubronne. We left Little Staughton at five minutes past midnight and arrived back just two hours later.*

In mid-December 1943 an Air Ministry appraisal of the V-weapons threat identified 69 P-Plane launch sites in northern France and warned that this number would probably increase to around 100. An all-out V-weapons assault on Britain was possible by February, but the report cautioned that some V1 sites would be ready to launch in early January. It was decided to commit the heavy bombers[43].

Bomber Command's first attack on the Flying Bomb sites occurred on the night of December 16/17 1943. The target was near Abbeville and was marked by Oboe Mosquitos[44]. American bombers were deployed in force for many of these early attacks. A total of 52 sites were bombed in the period to January 1 1944; German records suggest only seven were destroyed[45]. The bombing continued - with British night raids generally held to be ineffective[46]. After attacks on the night of January 25/26, Bomber Command's heavy aircraft were not directed at the VI sites again until after the D-Day landings in early June. The task was left, in the main, to American heavy bombers and 2nd Tactical Air Force[47]. Bomber Command was needed for strikes against the transportation targets prior to invasion.

By mid-May nearly 23,000 tonnes of bombs had been dropped on 96 VI launch sites. An optimistic view of the impact of these raids began to form, as the weapon had yet to be launched in anger[48]. The Germans, however, had been busy modifying the design of the large and relatively easy to spot 'ski' launch sites[49]. They even regarded the

*Tragedy in London: 121 people died when a V1 struck the Guards' Chapel, Wellington Barracks. Photo: Trustees of The Imperial War Museum.*

air attacks as useful, as they confirmed the need for less conspicuous launch sites for a sustained VI offensive before that offensive began[50].

The first of the VIs exploded at Gravesend, Kent, on Tuesday June 13[51]. The Flying Bomb campaign opened in earnest on June 15. By midnight on June 16 144 VIs, each with a 1,870 lb high explosive warhead, had crossed the coast; 73 reached Greater London[52]. By the end of the first week 723 people had been killed and 2,610 seriously injured in this new assault from the sky[53].

Bomber Command returned to bomb the VI sites on June 16[54]. The objective was to slow the rate of fire by disrupting the Flying Bomb supply organisation. The decision to give priority to attacking the so-called 'modified' launch sites, as well as the VI storage depots, was taken on Monday June 19[55]. It was the day after a Flying Bomb struck the Guards' Chapel at London's Wellington Barracks, killing 121 people. This tragedy ensured the VI sites retained their status as priority targets (with that priority exceeded only by the direct requirements of the invasion force ashore in Normandy)[56].

There were four VI-related Bomber Command strikes on June 23, involving a Flying Bomb supply depot (Oisemont) and three launch sites including Coubronne. These were the first of the modified sites to be attacked by Bomber Command. Walker's Lancaster was one of 81 heavy bombers dispatched to Coubronne[57].

The crews understood the significance of their sorties against VI sites, codenamed 'No-ball' targets. Success would mean fewer civilian deaths at home. Another P-Plane target was attacked on Sunday June 25. Walker was on the Battle Order for this night raid on Middel Straete:

> *We were determined to wipe out the VI sites. The crews saw this as an extremely worthwhile job. While heading out on night sorties we saw the bright exhaust flames of Flying Bombs travelling in the opposite direction, towards London. They gave me the creeps. The Doodlebugs had an eerie quality of menace. They were strange and unnatural at a time when people still expected flying machines to have pilots. P-Plane sites were small and extremely hard to hit. It was difficult, early on, to see how they could be beaten.*

On the night of June 24/25 739 bombers were dispatched to destroy seven launch sites in the Pas de Calais. A force of 80 Lancasters (including Walker's B-Baker) and five Mosquitos struck Middel Straete. Zero hour was 01.25, with Oboe Mosquitos responsible for ground marking. The force bombed on the red TIs[58]. The sky was free of cloud and there was a new moon setting at 00.45[59]. German nightfighters made the most of these clear conditions. Twenty two Lancasters failed to return from this series of attacks.

Despite the best efforts of Allied bombers in a growing air campaign against the V-weapons, the Germans maintained a launch rate of around 150 VIs every 24 hours throughout the second half of June[60].

Walker's crew had now completed 15 operations, all at night. The squadron's Gunnery Leader took the subject of night vision very seriously:

> *Little Staughton had an excellent Night Vision Room, a hut with no*

*windows and just the one door. All PFF gunners were expected to pass a series of night vision tests before being awarded the Pathfinder badge. We were human enough to want to feel special and the small, gilt Pathfinder badge was highly coveted. The badge was introduced by 8 Group and was worn under the brevet by crews who had qualified to full PFF status.*

*Unfortunately I never seemed to be around when the night vision 'examiner' arrived on our station. I'd be asleep, on a sortie or preparing for the next op whenever he put in an appearance. This may be why I never received my Pathfinder badge despite the completion of 35 PFF trips with 582. Bill Harrall received his badge, but two months after the tour ended. My badge must have got lost in the system and I never pursued the matter.*

Tactics on outbound flights during Sidney Knott's second tour differed greatly from the practice on 467 Squadron the previous year:

*My first tour operational flying took place in the January–May period. Many trips were long flights making good use of the long Winter and early Spring nights. We began a slow climb to operational height when far out to sea. This made it more difficult for the Germans to detect us early on. It also gave any diversionary raid the opportunity to work. During the climb we often entered thick cloud and Frank would worry about icing. When conditions were bad it was very difficult – and sometimes impossible – to reach the briefed height due to ice on the wings.*

*Quite different procedures were followed on the outward leg during my second tour. We set off at the allotted time and began an immediate climb. This tour ran from April to August. The nights were shorter and we climbed to bombing height over the airfield before setting course at the briefed time. The idea was to achieve a very dense bomber stream. There were other advantages, including the ability to find the wind strength at operational altitude from the very first.*

*The climb to operational height could take an hour and I have a sharp recollection of one unusual departure. There was a magnificent sunset as we stood around our Lancaster, waiting to go. The sun slipped down as we climbed aboard. Some minutes later, as we climbed, I watched enthralled as the ruby-gold sun put in a second appearance, seeming to rise in the west. It was a beautiful sight as it began to behave normally and commence its final journey below the horizon.*

During the late afternoon of Wednesday June 28 armourers and other ground personnel surrounded B-Baker, preparing the bomber for the night's raid. Within the past week, Walker's crew had taken this aircraft to the Coubronne and Middel Straete No-ball targets. They made their third successive sortie in B-Baker that night. The target was the rail complex at Blainville. As Illuminators they were briefed to drop six flares together with seven 1,000 lb bombs over the marshalling yards. Take-off was logged at 22.35:

*We were a confident bunch. The experience of 15 second tour trips had been added to our first tour operational flying. Only Clive was relatively new to heavy bomber ops but he had his first tour experience behind him and had already emerged as an excellent Lancaster Captain. At the same time we were not complacent. In fact Blainville was to make one point painfully clear: a premature end did not necessarily require the intervention of flak or nightfighters.*

Walker's aircraft was one of 28 Pathfinder Lancasters marking for 202 Halifaxes attacking rail targets at Blainville and Metz. Losses were high. Twenty aircraft failed to return - including one of the Lancasters marking Blainville[61].

*Blainville's rail yards received our bombs soon after the flares were dropped. We turned away and the navigator gave Clive his course for the first leg of the return. As we flew on Bill suddenly interrupted our thoughts with disturbing news. From his mid-upper vantage point he had just seen our starboard outer engine burst into flames.*

*A golden rule was drummed into every pilot and flight engineer: don't activate the engine fire extinguisher before feathering the propeller. Feathering was vital as it turned the prop blades edge on, reduced drag and prevented 'windmilling'.*

*The correct response sequence was all too easy to forget when faced with the unpleasant realities of an engine fire, but Clive and George did everything by the book. Their hands were on automatic as they worked the controls and switches – cutting the engine, diverting fuel elsewhere, reaching for the feathering button on the right of the panel and activating the extinguisher.*

*The pilot and flight engineer had just one chance with the Graviner extinguisher and it was tempting to 'press the tit' too quickly, ignoring the correct drill. As they worked fast in the cockpit I had no doubt about the seriousness of our situation. The fire had developed rapidly in the slipstream, producing a bright orange/yellow trail of flame long enough to be seen from the rear turret. It seemed like hours before Clive came on the intercom and said he was activating the extinguisher. Luckily it did the job. The skipper said the fire was out and this was confirmed by Bill.*

The crew took stock of their situation. A Lancaster flew well on three engines but B-Baker had some way to go and the fuel situation would need watching:

*The flight engineer finished his calculations. George told Clive we had lost a lot of fuel but there was still enough to reach Little Staughton. Our relief was tempered by more outbreaks of fire in the starboard outer. These involved small pockets of unburnt fuel. They were soon consumed but we were forced to reduce speed until there were no further flare-ups.*

*These inconveniences put us behind. The bomber stream forged ahead and left us in its wake as a straggler. We would make a tasty morsel for any nightfighter pilot worth his salt. Corkscrewing a three-engined, fire-damaged Lanc with no fuel reserve to speak of was an unhappy prospect. Bill and I kept vigil as B-Baker continued to make slow progress. Eventually we made a safe but somewhat overdue landing. We climbed out, walked forward and inspected the starboard outer. What a mess!*

*The engine was so badly damaged that it was impossible to draw any useful conclusions about the cause of the fire. Besides, there was no time to waste investigating what was, after all, hardly a rare occurrence. I told*

*Clive I didn't think we'd been hit by a nightfighter. It could have been flak but we had bombed from a height of around 12,000 ft. This put us above the light flak zone and a hit from heavier flak should have been self-evident. In all probability our adventure had resulted from a straightforward engine problem - perhaps a fractured fuel line.*

The damage looked worse than it was. The ground crews and engine fitters worked round the clock to restore B-Baker to operational condition. Within 48 hours, the Lancaster had completed an engine change and was ready to return to the war. Walker's crew boarded the aircraft at 11.00 on Friday June 30 and went through their checks prior to take-off for a night flying test.

*With the exception of the engine fire June had been surprisingly quiet for us, given the great events unfolding in Normandy. We made just four trips. We would have appreciated June even more had we known we would fly 14 ops in July - and all but four in daylight!*

During their Spring and Summer weeks at Little Staughton Sidney Knott and Bill Harrall had warmed to St. Neots, then a modest market town:

*We found a nice pub. Other members of the crew occasionally joined us for a day out. Cattle market day was best as the town's pubs always stayed open longer. Lunchtime drinking was extended to 4pm. We had a lot of laughs in that pub's back room, with its skittle table and other games. The landlord took a shine to us and eventually produced some bottles of Bass, carefully treasured and held in store for special occasions. This beer was far superior to the usual wartime brew. It was also much stronger. I learnt how to tip the Bass bottle carefully, to avoid its rich layer of sediment.*

*We joked, played the fool and forgot about the war. Occasionally we got into a bit of a state, our systems unaccustomed to such excellent beer. The swinging chuck used to knock down the skittles went everywhere but on target. Only Bill seemed immune to the glass in his hand. In fact, our mid-upper gunner excelled at all pub games and the consumption of beer had no influence whatsoever on his performance.*

*Bill's special game was shove-halfpenny. His father was a wood-carver and inlayer and he had made the Rolls-Royce of all shove-halfpenny boards. Bill was a natural and approached the game like a professional. He kept his own highly polished halfpennies. Bill's good nature was exploited ruthlessly and we were soon playing the game his way. This then spread to Little Staughton. Eventually, each Mess had its own shove-halfpenny board. They were highly polished to Bill's instructions, using linseed oil and nothing else! We organised competitions and shove-halfpenny gripped the entire station. With polished halfpennies and polished boards, friction was reduced to a minimum and the slightest touch was enough to send the coin shooting across the board.*

*I strongly recommend shove-halfpenny to anyone suffering from the stress of modern living. Forget yoga, counselling, anti-depressants and special diets. Try shove-halfpenny!*

# CHAPTER EIGHTEEN

# The War Against the Robots

AFTER a relatively quiet June the ops flown in July filled a page in Sidney Knott's logbook. The crew completed 14 sorties but only three involved German targets.

*Most of my July ops – 10 of the 14 – were flown in daylight. With one exception all the daylights were attacks on VI sites. On Sunday July 2 we took B-Baker (PB136) on a No-ball strike. Bomber Command's planners had decided to flatten the P-Plane base at Oisemont. We dropped nine 1,000 lb and four 500 lb bombs. Two of the latter were fitted with long delay fuses to make life more difficult for German repair teams and further disrupt the Flying Bomb launch schedules.*

*We continued to spot doodlebugs making for the English coast as we headed in the opposite direction to bomb their launch sites. The VI assault on London was now in full swing. Our job was to do enough damage to buy time for the fighter and gun defences to re-organise and meet this new threat. The Allied armies would eventually overrun the launch sites but no-one knew how long that would take.*

*For some weeks we carried the burden of reducing the scale of death and destruction raining down on London and its southern and eastern approaches. Oisemont was our seventeenth PFF op. It was very different - our first daylight sortie. We were given no opportunity to prepare ourselves and it felt strange to take off in a bombed-up condition at 'dinner time'. This was a short trip, just two hours 25 minutes. In fact the bombing up, briefing and debriefing took twice as long as the flight itself.*

Oisemont had been attacked without loss a few days before, on June 30, by 102 Lancasters and five Mosquitos. The crews encountered ten/tenths cloud over the target and results were uncertain[1]. It was attacked again on July 1. Bomber Command went back a third time the next day, to make sure. A total of 374 Lancasters and 10 Mosquitos attacked Oisemont and two other Flying Bomb launch sites. Damage resulted despite cloud obscuring the targets and all bombers returned safely[2]. German records at this time indicate that the blind attacks through cloud and large-scale night attacks were accurate in many cases[3].

*We were told to watch out for fighter escort on the Oisemont raid. If friendly fighters were around we never saw them. Anyway, there was little opposition over the target and we turned for home, hoping our bombing pattern had been tight enough to destroy the small No-ball site.*

Intelligence assessment and No-ball target allocation procedures had been streamlined, to respond immediately to reports from agents on the ground in France and feedback from air photo interpretation specialists:

*Over the following few weeks we became accustomed to mounting these attacks at ultra short notice. Our intelligence officers explained that some sites were mobile and, in these cases, we might get no second chance. If a prefabricated launch site survived an attack it could be dismantled and re-erected deep inside another wood. It might then escape the attentions of photo reconnaissance and the Resistance. In some instances we were in the air and on our way within two hours of receipt of orders at Little Staughton. This was Bomber Command's equivalent of a Fighter Command scramble!*

*No effort was made to prepare us for daylight ops. While our next sortie was a night attack this was followed by a long succession of daylights. Bill Harrall and I made use of the two days following Oisement to plan new gunnery tactics for daylight sorties. An entirely different search pattern was required. Enemy fighters would be likely to attack from out of the sun, rather than approach slowly from astern or below, as at night. There would be limited scope for evasive action when flying in formation. Bill and I were responsible for the defence of the aircraft. We worked out new tactics and presented our views to Clive and the others. A crew meeting was called and our ideas met with approval.*

*It was time to dig out my flying goggles, with the all-important sun visor. I hadn't seen them for weeks. I rummaged through my flying kit and eventually struck lucky. After some spit and polish they were put on a war footing and transferred to my locker in the crew room.*

*The night attack was mounted on Wednesday July 5. We took off at 23.20 in L-Leather (NE130), after a briefing to attack the P-Plane complex at Wizernes. Our stores were unusual: 11 1,000 lb American-made semi armour-piercing bombs, together with four 500 lb bombs. Two of the latter, once again, were of the long delay type to hamper repair work. Wizernes was a tough proposition as a night target; marking was a challenge as this No-ball site was positioned on the fringes of a wood. Our bombing height was an uncomfortable 8,000 ft - still within easy reach of some light flak.*

Four VI sites (two launch facilities and two storage complexes) were attacked on the night of July 5/6. These were large-scale assaults involving several hundred aircraft. Conditions were clear, with a bright moon. Four Lancasters failed to return[4]. The Wizernes attack was made by 81 Lancasters and five Mosquitos. Marking was accurate and the bombing concentrated, causing much damage[5]. The Walker crew's trip was very short, lasting just two hours. Another 582 Squadron Lancaster, however, was overdue. This aircraft was captained by Pilot Officer Manson, RCAF, and the word 'MISSING' was chalked against his name. There were no survivors[6]. Indeed, the aircraft was lost without trace.

During the Saturday morning, July 8, Walker's crew took their positions in B-Baker for a one hour fighter affiliation and bombing exercise. The fighter practice involved a Spitfire and Hurricane. This was Sidney Knott's first experience of mock attacks by a pair of fighters.

During the following day this Lancaster was prepared for an attack on the No-ball site at L'Hey. A total of 347 aircraft struck L'Hey and five other 'modified' launch sites. The results were mixed due to cloud cover over some targets. Two bombers failed to return[7]. The 52 Lancasters and five Mosquitos attacking L'Hey found their target obscured by cloud yet the launch platform and buildings suffered significant damage[8].

*Our Lanc had a typical bomb-load for this type of op: 11 1,000 lb and four 500 lb bombs, two with delayed action fuses. We were using American bombs again following an incident involving a Liberator. On taking off from a nearby airfield the American bomber got into trouble and attempted a landing at Little Staughton. It crashed next to our bomb dump. Thank god it didn't set the whole thing off! It would have blown us all to kingdom come. Anyway, it did enough damage to put the bomb dump out of commission for several days and our Station Commander solved this problem by asking the Americans for some of their bombs. After all, they created the problem and our need was greater - each Lancaster lifted around three times the bomb-load of a B24 Liberator or B17 Flying Fortress.*

The Americans remained committed to daylight bombing despite their frequent heavy losses, especially over Germany. Only the arrival of the Mustang long-range fighter eventually turned the tables.

*The Fortress had .5 machine guns all over the place while our lighter .303s were grouped in three turrets. There were two guns in the Lanc's nose turret but they were unmanned while over the target. The bomb aimer was at his bombsight – leaving us with little defence against head-on fighter attack.*

*Bill and I talked this over. One solution was for the wireless op to enter the astrodome and search ahead, but we couldn't afford to miss a wireless transmission. It was important to maintain a careful listening watch as the failure to receive a message could have catastrophic consequences, given our own troops' close proximity to many of the targets. A missed recall could lead to heavy loss of life from what is now known as 'friendly fire'. In the end we decided to leave the front guns unmanned during the bombing run and take a chance. After all, flak was a bigger threat than fighters.*

Monday July 10 began at an uncivilised hour for Walker's team and other 582 Squadron crews. Orders came through in the small hours. At the dispersal pans ground crews and armourers sweated despite the cool night air, struggling to meet the tight deadline set for bombing up and completion of all other preparations.

In the briefing room the bleary-eyed crews made the effort to look attentive as they were introduced to Nucourt, a large Flying Bomb storage facility. Air attacks had damaged the VI storage complex at St. Leu d'Esserent and this had prompted the Germans to transfer the weapons to the Nucourt caves. Nucourt had been attacked twice previously by American bombers. On July 10 it was to be attacked for the third time[9].

B-Baker left Little Staughton's main runway at 0445, heading in a southerly direction as the dawn sky brightened:

> *This P-Plane depot was some way inland. We found the target without much difficulty, thanks to GEE, and dropped the usual load – 11 1,000 lb bombs and four smaller bombs, two with long delays. We heard the Master Bomber urge the crews to maintain bombing height.*

This attack was pressed home by 213 Lancasters and 10 Mosquitos and there were no losses. Cloud over the target, however, resulted in scattered bombing.

A solution was tested under operational conditions the next day, when a small force of 26 PFF Lancasters and six Mosquitos delivered assaults on the VI complex at Gapennes, one of the modified launch sites[10]. Walker's crew, in B-Baker, had the honour of leading the Lancasters in

*Pulverised: the severely cratered entrances to the St. Leu d'Esserent Flying Bomb storage complex, pictured after the July 7/8 raid. The Germans transferred the weapons to the Nucourt caves, the entrances to which were attacked on July 10. Photo: Trustees of The Imperial War Museum.*

the first wave. Their Lancaster dropped 18 500 lb bombs (including two delayed action weapons). They bombed through total cloud cover[11].

The Gapennes raid introduced 'Heavy Oboe' tactics. Walker's Lancaster carried an eighth crew member that evening. He was blind-bombing expert Wing Commander George Grant, DFC, a Mosquito pilot with 109 Squadron – the Oboe specialists sharing Little Staughton with 582 Squadron. All Lancasters in the small formation released their bombs when Walker's Oboe-equipped aircraft dropped. This effective daylight blind-bombing technique – with the formation leader known as 'Ramrod' – brought more bombs onto the target. The chances of hitting small No-ball sites in cloudy conditions were suddenly much improved[10].

*We took off for Gapennes at 19.30 and landed back at 22.15. Clive's smooth touchdown marked the safe completion of my fiftieth op (29 with 467 and 21 with 582). This sortie was successful as our blind-bombing system was extremely accurate at such short range. In effect, we were adopting American bombing tactics: everyone dropped when the formation leader dropped. In our case everyone released under radio instruction from the leader. The 582 Squadron aircraft flew in three groups of three. Formation flying in combat put a terrific strain on the pilot as the Lancaster was not the easiest of aircraft to fly in such conditions.*

*Looking back, this switch to daylight operations was handled in a surprisingly casual way. We received no guidance on new gunnery tactics. Our pilots received no special instruction in combat formation flying. We were left to get on with it and there was no time to practice. Bill Harrall didn't think much of daylight formation flying over defended targets. He was not alone in concluding that it shifted the odds too far in favour of the 88 mm flak crews.*

*We did develop a safe technique for forming up. The lead aircraft flew at a low cruising speed to give the others a chance to catch up. We took off at one minute intervals and climbed gently onto a specified heading for a short period. The lead aircraft then entered a very wide turn to port. This offered the best possible visual cue for the following aircraft. It gave everyone a chance to 'cut the corner' of the turn and assume the correct position in the formation, with the more experienced pilots to the front.*

Heavy Oboe tactics were employed again during the following afternoon to destroy the modified launch site at Rollez. Walker flew as Ramrod leader and took off at 14.00 that Wednesday, commencing the crew's fourth No-ball strike in as many days. The first three were completed without a hitch in B-Baker but Rollez proved to be different:

*Our Lanc carried 16 500 lb bombs. Unfortunately, one grew very attached to us and stubbornly refused to drop when ordered. The English Channel was very busy at this time. It was full of Allied shipping and there was no convenient safe drop zone for jettisoning bombs in our area. We began our approach to Little Staughton with that 500 lb rogue still in the bomb-bay. On touch-down Reg went back and checked it was still secure before we began the taxi to dispersal. This bomb was returned to the armourers with the firm suggestion that they give it to someone else next time!*

A small PFF force of 18 Lancasters and five Mosquitos bombed the modified Flying Bomb launch site at Rollez. There were no losses and accurate marking contributed to a satisfactory bombing concentration[11]. Walker's crew had a break the next day, July 13, but operated on the two following days. On Friday July 14, flying Ramrod, they dropped 18 500 lb bombs (two fused for long delay) on the No-ball site at St. Philibert-Ferme. The nineteen Lancasters, controlled by Walker, dropped their bombs through thick cloud and there were no losses[12].

During the Saturday afternoon they returned to the VI storage depot at Nucourt. The 582 Squadron crews dropped their sticks of 1,000 lb bombs, once again using the new attack technique – with Walker's aircraft designated Ramrod and leading the formation. The attacking force consisted of 47 Lancasters, together with six Mosquitos from 105 and 109 squadrons. All aircraft returned safely[13]. As on July 10 this target was largely obscured by cloud[9].

> *There was an earlier start and a change of target on Tuesday July 18. Our Lanc, B-Baker again, was loaded with 11 1,000 lb and four 500 lb bombs. This time we were not going after a P-Plane site. We took off at 04.40 that morning on a close support mission for Second Army.*
>
> *Setting out on our twenty-fifth op with 582 Squadron we headed for Gagny, near Caen, to assist Second Army by softening up the German defences as a prelude to 'Operation Goodwood'. This was Montgomery's latest attempt at an armoured breakout (or, at the very least, continue the erosion of the German defence posture in Normandy). We were briefed to bring our bombs back if we had any doubts about our position relative to our own troops. Our bombing turned out to be too successful. It created a sea of rubble and helped the Germans dig in and further stiffen their defences. At the same time it impeded the progress of our own armoured vehicles.*

At this time reminders of the hard fighting in Normandy were to be found close to home. The tree-lined road from Little Staughton to Buckingham, for example, was used as an ammunition dump. The road's grass verges were dotted with small shelters packed with thousands of freshly produced artillery shells awaiting shipment to France.

In support of Goodwood a huge force of 942 aircraft attacked a chain of five fortified villages, including Gagny. American bombers also attacked these strongpoints. A torrent of 6,800 tonnes of bombs descended on the targets – with over 5,000 tonnes contributed by Bomber Command – and two German divisions were on the receiving end. Six British aircraft failed to return[14]. Goodwood, unfortunately, proved to be another false dawn. There was no 'breakout' and Goodwood petered out by July 20, producing only minor gains[15].

On the Wednesday morning, July 19, heavily laden bomb trolleys made their way towards Little Staughton's dispersals following orders for an immediate attack on a No-ball site discovered at Mont Candon. Eleven 1,000 lb and four 500 lb bombs were hoisted into the bomb-bay of D-Dog (PB149). Flying as 582 Squadron Ramrod once again, Walker took this Lancaster into the air at 14.30. Two Flying Bomb launch sites and a storage depot were attacked that afternoon by 132 Lancasters and 12 Mosquitos. There were no losses[16]. Thirteen Lancasters and two Mosquitos made the attack on the Mont Candon launch site[17]. The leading edge of Walker's bombs fell on crossroads to the west, undershooting the aiming point by around 500 yards.

A brief respite for the crew ended on Sunday July 23, when the last of Walker's Ramrod ops was flown. The target was the modified launch complex at Forêt-de-Croc and the crew, flying B-Baker, contributed a stick of 18 500 lb bombs. Half of this force of 48 Lancasters and 12 Mosquitos made a fresh attack on the Mont Candon installation[18]. Forêt-de-Croc and Mont Candon suffered heavy damage despite total cloud cover[19].

> *With one exception this was the last of our daylight ops. We had made the first of our attacks against the Flying Bomb sites four weeks earlier. It had taken around a month to achieve our main objective in the war against the robots. We had slowed the rate of fire. Meanwhile, our troops would soon begin to approach some of the forward launch sites.*

> *Our briefings for daylights always began with a promise of fighter cover. After a while the words 'fighter escort' triggered sceptical laughter in Little Staughton's briefing room. We never saw a single escort fighter or, come to that, a German opponent. I have no idea how we would have managed against determined fighter attack. In any event, most P-Plane sites were near the coast and the plentiful flak batteries in the coastal strip remained our biggest worry.*

> *Apparently, friendly fighters were around but they remained out of sight. The July weather was good and we felt naked, with no cloud around to provide cover from fighter attack. On most days the air was clear and the visibility excellent. We could see over enormous distances. Fortunately the German fighters failed to turn up. Most GAF day fighter units had been recalled by that time to protect the homeland. Yet we could never be sure and there was always the chance of surprise attack. The lack of opposition made many old hands develop a suspicious, uneasy attitude towards daylight ops.*

Bomber Command's attacks, especially strikes against supply depots such as Nucourt, succeeded in reducing the VI launch rate[20]. From the commencement of the VI offensive to the end of July, 5,853 Flying Bombs were fired and 734 crashed after launch. Those not dealt with by the defences killed 4,640 people, seriously injured 13,571 and slightly injured 17,083[21]. The death toll eventually rose to 6,184[22].

The Walker crew's final sorties in July were very different in character. They switched to German city targets, carrying the traditional PFF area bombing mix of a large blast bomb, incendiaries and flares.

They had a rude shock on returning from Forêt-de-Croc. Landing back at 10.15, after three hours in the air, they attended the debrief and were informed they were on again that night. B-Baker's engines were still warm when the ground crew and armourers began their lengthy preparations for a night raid.

> *We were not sorry to leave the daylight sorties alone. Combat flying in formation must be an acquired taste and certainly one I failed to acquire! It was*

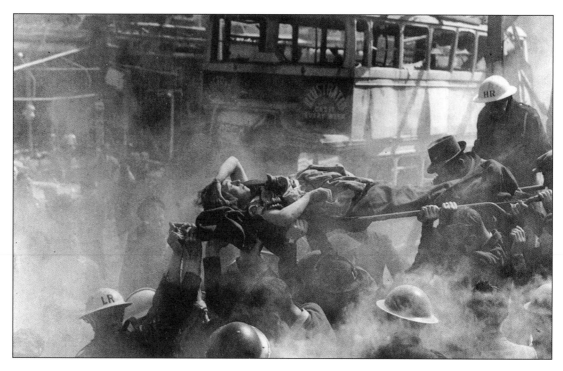

*a real headache for the gunners. We had to ensure the formation allowed us sufficient arcs of fire to defend our aircraft without the embarrassment of hitting other Lancs. The rear turret offered the best view for station-keeping. Clive called up repeatedly with the question: 'How are they doing?' He led small formations as Ramrod on six occasions. While he could see his wing partners to port and starboard, the rest were beyond his field of vision. On hearing from me he would instruct everyone to close up, to achieve a tighter bombing pattern over the target.*

*The two wingmen flew just below the leader to stay out of his propwash. The next vic of three flew a little lower still for the same reason. This also gave the gunners enough room to fire without hitting friendly aircraft. As rear gunner of the lead aircraft, I could fire down as far as the horizon without hitting a Lanc.*

During the early evening of Sunday July 23, still thinking about Forêt-de-Croc, Walker's crew filed into the briefing room for the second time that day. The tapes on the wall map gave them another unpleasant surprise. The 'target for tonight' was Kiel.

This highly skilled PFF crew were about to fly their twenty-eighth Pathfinder sortie. For the first time they were briefed as Secondary Blind Markers. The ground crew and armourers had finished with B-Baker. The Lancaster's bomb-bay now held a 4,000 lb Blockbuster, six 1,000 lb bombs, two Target Indicators and a further two TIs of the long-burning Wanganui type. B-Baker's take-off was logged at 22.40 and the Lancaster made good time as it headed out towards the hostile skies of north Germany.

The Kiel attack was Bomber Command's first major raid on a German city for eight weeks. A total of 629 aircraft participated and four failed to return – the low casualty rate reflecting the unexpected return to a German target, together with a sophisticated deception plan and extensive radio countermeasures. On the ground this raid claimed 315 lives. It took the authorities three weeks to restore gas supplies for cooking[18].

When B-Baker landed back at Little Staughton in the early hours of Monday July 24 the crew climbed out in an exhausted state. It was their longest day. It began at around 04.00 the previous day and had stretched to over 26 hours by the time they were debriefed. They downed the flying breakfast mechanically and stumbled into their beds. While they were left alone for the rest of Monday, they were listed on 582's Battle Order for the Tuesday - the day Wing Commander P.H. Cribb (later Group Captain, DSO, DFC) succeeded Wing Commander Dunnifliffe, DFC, as Squadron Commander. Walker, meanwhile, received some good news. He had been promoted to Squadron Leader.

Bomber Command planners hoped to maintain the element of surprise enjoyed by the force that attacked Kiel, by switching their attentions from north to south Germany the next night. Stuttgart was selected as the target for July 24/25. Perhaps surprise could be stretched by immediately returning to this target the following night?

Walker's crew were briefed as Secondary Blind Markers for the July 25/26 Stuttgart attack. On this occasion, however, their flares were not required by the Master Bomber and were returned to Little Staughton. Nevertheless, B-Baker parted company with the bombs - a Cookie and 10 500 lb bombs. The Lancaster touched down safely after a flight of seven hours 40 minutes - the longest trip during Sidney Knott's second tour.

A force of 461 Lancasters and 153 Halifaxes attacked Stuttgart on July 24/25 and 21 aircraft failed to return. This was the first of three major attacks on the city over a five-night period[23]. The second raid, on July 25/26, caused devastation on the ground. Twelve bombers failed to return[24].

*Our last sortie in July, in O-Orange (ND812), was flown on Friday July 28. This was the third attack on Stuttgart - a carbon copy of the raid three days before. We dropped a Cookie, four 1,000 lb bombs and incendiaries. We were Secondary Blind Markers but, once again, our flares were not required and stayed in the bomb-bay. We took off at 22.30 and landed back at 05.10, so completing our series of 14 ops in July.*

In the three raids on Stuttgart 1,171 people lost their lives and 1,600 were injured[23]. The third raid on Stuttgart was delivered by 494 Lancasters and two Mosquitos. British losses were heavy as nightfighters infiltrated the bomber stream early on, in conditions of bright moonlight. Thirty-nine Lancasters (7.9 per cent of the force) failed to return[25].

Bomber Command had a chance to inspect the latest German nightfighting technology on July 13, when a Ju88 G-1 landed at Woodbridge, Suffolk. The crew had got lost[26]. Their aircraft was equipped with the highly effective SN-2 AI radar and the Naxos Z device that homed onto H2S transmissions. Naxos Z had first entered service over six months before. The nightfighter also carried the Flensburg system that homed onto the British bombers' tail-warning equipment (Monica)[27]. Flensburg also homed onto Fishpond, the radar device searching the danger area below the bomber[28].

> *Most sorties in July were short flights but this period was very busy. We had no time for skittles and good beer at our favourite watering hole in St. Neots. Most of the P-Plane attacks had been flown in good weather. Overall, the defences were weak although there were many hostile pockets of light flak. In daylight, of course, we could see more and the flak certainly looked nasty - especially during the run-in over the coast. We were grateful to go on leave for six days.*

Harris, meanwhile, felt Bomber Command had not received due recognition for its contribution to the D-Day landings and the subsequent fighting in Normandy. At the beginning of July, he wrote to the Chief of the Air Staff, pointing out: 'There are over 10,500 aircrew in my operational squadrons. In three months, we have lost half that number[29].'

# CHAPTER NINETEEN

# *'Flak Happy'*

Fresh from their Summer leave Walker's crew returned to Little Staughton during the second week of August. Wednesday August 9 found them aloft in D-Dog (PB182), on a cross-country involving Y-Run bombing practice. The three-hour flight was followed the next day by a similar but shorter cross-country. They were to operate that Thursday and in the late afternoon the crew entered the briefing room. Dijon's rail yards were to be attacked and they were briefed as Illuminators. The armourers had already hoisted seven 1,000 lb bombs of US manufacture, together with six flares, into D-Dog.

The crew landed back with an empty bomb-bay at 03.05. Following the rituals of debrief they claimed their flying breakfasts and returned to the billets. Twenty Lancasters and 104 Halifaxes had attacked Dijon's marshalling yards; the bombing was accurate and heavy damage resulted[1].

*On Saturday August 12 we were briefed for a German target – the Opel motor works at Rüsselsheim, just south west of Frankfurt-am-Main. For the first time we were among the Primary Blind Markers/Illuminators. D-Dog carried a Cookie, four 500 lb bombs, six flares and four of the long-burning TIs to this target. Clive got the green at 22.05 and we were soon on course for Germany. We were in the air for four hours 30 minutes and brought back the flares and TIs, as they were not required. We left the bombs behind; they fell on the Opel complex.*

A force of 297 aircraft attacked Opel. Twenty bombers failed to return, in exchange for modest damage to the target. Most of the bombs fell in the surrounding countryside[2]. The majority of the attackers' 866 tonnes of bombs missed the Opel Works (believed to be contributing to VI production), but a second raid later in August resulted in severe damage[3].

*Now a veteran Lancaster Captain, Clive used his influence to secure the aircraft of his choice. We flew the same Lancaster, D-Dog, throughout August. Clive really liked this aircraft but it had an unfortunate turret problem. The rear turret's hydraulics were 'reliable', but only in the sense that I could rely on total failure after around four hours!*

*Fitters crawled all over D-Dog but couldn't find the hydraulic leak. The rear turret's oil pressure line ran from the port outer engine hydraulic pump, through the wing interior, into the fuselage and back to a master cylinder near my turret. I always checked the cylinder spindle before entering the turret. This spindle sat about six inches proud of the cylinder top and could be depressed only if there was air in the system. It was always as solid as a rock before take-off. Before landing, however, I would have trouble with the turret. Back on the ground I could depress the spindle – the sure sign of an oil leak. But where? On our return from Dijon, for example, the normally smooth traverse ended in a judder as the turret rotated out to the beam. This grew steadily worse and the turret failed completely just before we landed.*

*I talked it over with the ground crew. Before leaving for Rüsselsheim I called in at the Armoury to check that the problem had been fixed. The system had been bled and topped up and I was assured that everything was fine. We went out to the dispersal pan and climbed into D-Dog; I pushed down hard on the spindle and it was solid. I even checked again just before take-off. Yet, sure enough, my problem turret began to judder again after four hours in the air. I became seriously fed up at this point. We were close to home when the malfunction developed but we could bump into a German intruder at any time. The ground crew did what they could but the leak eluded them and air continued to enter the system whenever the turret was operated.*

Three days later, on Tuesday August 15, Walker's team were among the 582 Squadron crews briefed for a morning attack on Volkel, one of nine nightfighter airfields targeted in a coordinated assault by a massive force of 1,004 Bomber Command aircraft. Harris wanted to clear the way for a major revival of his night offensive against German targets. Clear visibility contributed to good results[4]. A force of 110 Lancasters and four Mosquitos heavily cratered Volkel and made both runways unserviceable[5].

*We were briefed as Visual Backers-Up and carried eight TIs, including four long-burners. This was our first daylight op as a marker. Our job was to renew the marking if asked to do so. We were asked and dropped all eight TIs, together with six 1,000 lb bombs.*

*Bill and I were expecting more daylights. Before the morning raid on Volkel we flew a brisk fighter affiliation with a Hurricane – a sharp reminder of what we might soon be facing.*

*After 14 ops in July Bill and I were probably getting flak-happy but I don't think we noticed at the time. Bill was shielded by his natural optimism. He never worried overmuch and, like me, he always felt different once the engines were started and we were on our way. Dijon was my sixtieth operational flight. While we were approaching the end of the tour I had no idea how many more we were expected to do. I still had my rabbit's foot and wishbone, but Bill had no good luck token. A girlfriend had given him a small doll and it became an honorary crew member during his first tour. He was upset when it was stolen during his short shuttle stay at Maison Blanche.*

While casualty rates declined, as a percentage of total sorties flown, in the final phase of Bomber Command's war, there were constant losses among 582 Squadron's aircrew. 582 Squadron Researcher Neil Cockburn observes that over one-third of all Bomber Command casualties were suffered during 1944. In the first two weeks of April 1944, 35 Lancaster Captains (including Walker) joined 582 Squadron. By the end of August,

15 of these crews had been lost and 92 men had died.

*On the quiet I had always envied the navigator, at his station behind the curtain and oblivious to the fireworks outside. In contrast, the rear and mid-upper gunners had a grandstand view of the flak. It chipped away at our nerves. This happened gradually and I didn't realise what was going on. Yet, strangely enough, I could always spot it in others. Some developed a tic around one eye, a twitch of the shoulder or shaky hands. I didn't notice anything about myself but, after the tour, my future wife noticed that my shoulder tended to jerk when faced with even the most trivial of problems. To some degree this stayed with me for the next 60 years.*

*I had flown 62 operations on returning from Volkel, 33 with 582. I was tired and I knew it. I began to feel fear. It is difficult to explain but I felt trapped in a permanent 'lull before the storm' state of mind. Would my luck hold? I asked myself that question time and again as we edged closer to the end of the tour.*

*The mood among the crews was quite different from that on 467 Squadron a year earlier. Pathfinder squadrons had a relatively high proportion of officers and this made for a less intimate atmosphere. Yet we grew very close as a crew. We remained confident in our abilities but a corrosive fatigue had set in. We found ourselves fighting the temptation to cut corners. This was a matter of life or death.*

*Bill remained an optimist but even he did not escape the strain of ops. He had an unpleasant, nerve-wracking flight with another crew. He was required to do the extra op early on, as a 'spare bod'. This involved a trip of two hours 20 minutes to Lens, back in June. Bill heartily disliked flying with people he didn't know.*

Harrall recalled that flight when he met Sidney Knott in July 2002 – their first encounter in 58 years:

*Bill described his flight with the other skipper as an uneasy affair; they lacked the crew discipline he was accustomed to. He added that he had never felt that way when flying with Clive Walker.*

On Wednesday August 16 the crew were on the Battle Order once again. They were briefed as Primary Blind Markers/Illuminators for an attack on Stettin. This raid marked Bomber Command's return to major German city targets. As the Allied armies advanced towards the German frontier Harris intended to deliver his long-promised 'whirlwind'. Two raids were organised for the night of August 16/17: 348 aircraft were dispatched against Kiel and 461 against the Baltic port of Stettin[6].

The entire character of the air offensive had changed by this time. Very early on in the war Bomber Command experienced a painful lesson. Its bomber aircraft had to operate at night if they were to stand any chance of survival. Five hard years had passed. The P-51D Mustang long range, high performance fighter eroded and eventually overwhelmed the German day fighter force in 1944. The point was fast approaching where night operations suited the German nightfighters more than British bombers, for the daylight air superiority battle was being fought and won over German soil[7].

*We got ready for a long night as the heavy petrol load indicated a deep penetration into Germany. This was confirmed at the briefing. The wall map tapes led to the Baltic coast and Stettin – a very long way east! D-Dog was loaded with a 4,000 lb Cookie, flares and TIs. We took off at 21.10 and landed back seven hours 35 minutes later.*

*I still fussed over my rogue turret. As usual the hydraulic system had been bled and topped up. Checks revealed no problems but that was nothing new. I said as much to the Chiefy, who responded sharply with the facts of life about this Lanc. He had orders to keep D-Dog flying until its due date for a major overhaul (and that was still some time away). He added, rather slyly I thought, that we could always turn back if the turret failed. That wasn't much help. By the time that turret died on me the target was bombed and we were heading for home. In any event, we had completed 33 sorties without turning back and we were certainly in no mood to start now!*

*I talked it over with Bill and we took a commonsense decision. My problem turret sucked in air only when operated. The obvious answer was to avoid using the turret until we entered enemy airspace. The Stettin sortie would require around eight hours in the air and I had a turret good for four hours. There was no choice but to conserve the turret. A detailed look at the Stettin flight plan suggested that I could begin to use the rear turret as soon as we crossed the Danish coast. When my turret was not in use Bill would modify his search pattern to cover my area as far as possible. In any event, I was still able to search astern and below.*

*As expected, my turret failed completely as we cleared the Danish coast on our return. I had a miserable trip home, sitting behind four useless guns. This Lancaster was a powerful late edition aircraft. Clive may have fallen in love with D-Dog but I hated its hydraulic guts! I had always maintained that a gunner's eyes were more important than his guns during night ops. Yet I found it very unpleasant to sit behind a battery of Brownings in a 'dead' turret. There is no doubt that this persistent problem with the turret added to the strain I felt at this late stage in the tour.*

The Stettin raid did heavy damage to the city's industrial areas and the port. Over 1,500 houses and 29 factories were destroyed and many others badly damaged. Around 1,150 bodies were recovered from the ruins and over 1,600 people were injured[6].

Two days later, during the afternoon of Friday August 18, the crew prepared for their thirty-fifth op together. They had been thrilled to learn that it would be their last. Sidney Knott continued his difficult discussions with the armourers. As far as they were concerned his jinxed turret was fully operational. Knott put their claim to the test. During a short test flight he put the turret through its paces by applying frequent, violent rotation. The results were predictable. Arriving back at Little Staughton he squeezed through the turret doors:

*I made my way back to the master cylinder. Sure enough, the spindle could be pushed down – a sign that my turret would fail. That hydraulic circuit still had a leak, somewhere! Tonight's petrol load indicated a German target and the prospect of flying across Germany with a duff turret, yet again, was not attractive. What a bloody awful worry on our last trip! Trying hard to keep the anger out of my voice I asked the armourers to bleed the system and top it up.*

The Walker crew's tour would end with Friday's night attack on Bremen. They were Primary Blind Markers/Illuminators, with stores identical to those carried to Stettin:

*I conserved the turret on the way out, then began the usual search routine as we crossed into Germany and turned onto the heading leading to the target. We dropped TIs, flares and a Cookie on Bremen. On the return my turret failed during the North Sea crossing.*

The August 18/19 Bremen attack, delivered by 288 aircraft, took place in good visibility and the marking was accurate. Around 1,100 tonnes of bombs cascaded across the city. This was Bremen's worst attack of the war and the results were catastrophic. Huge conflagrations developed – described in German reports as a 'firestorm'. Over 1,000 people died. One Lancaster failed to return[8]. A Halifax was also struck off charge:

*There were no fanfares for D-Dog on our return. The last of my operational sorties was over. Somehow I had survived both tours and 64 ops. I wasted no tears on D-Dog. That Lanc's rear turret was no longer my problem.*

*My war ended when we touched down at 02.30. Clive taxied in. We reached the dispersal pan and the engines fell silent. I sat quietly for a moment. Bremen was not only my last op, it was also to be my last flight in the RAF. It was finished. I sat behind the guns for a few seconds, paralysed by the thought that I had a future, after all.*

Sidney Knott may have finished but Bomber Command's war continued and the ferocity of its attacks intensified. During the final quarter of 1944 Bomber Command unleashed 163,000 tonnes of bombs[9]. In the first four months of 1945 Harris' whirlwind continued to devastate Germany: over 181,000 tonnes of bombs were dropped by Bomber Command aircraft – around one-fifth of the aggregate for the entire war[10]. This is the equivalent – in high explosive terms – of nine Hiroshima atomic weapons.

Sidney Knott's first tour operations spanned four months, from January 27 to May 27 1943. The second tour operations were flown from April 9 to August 19 1944. One obvious difference between the tours is the time of year. The first tour ran from Winter into late Spring while the second ran from Spring into high Summer. To some extent this is reflected in the operational hours flown, with far fewer long haul flights to distant targets during the second tour. Yet this is more an expression of new operational priorities than shorter nights. French targets in the run-up to D-Day and the campaign against the VI sites dominated the second tour.

Knott's 29 sorties with 467 Squadron amounted to 179 hours five minutes' operational flying. This was followed by 35 sorties, totalling 129 hours 45 minutes, with 582 Squadron. He accumulated 736 hours 40 minutes flying with the RAF, including 362 hours 20 minutes at night. The operational flying, totalling 308 hours 50 minutes, represented just over 40 per cent of Sidney Knott's total time in the air.

The first tour consisted of a mining sortie, followed by 22 operations to Germany and two each to France, Italy and Czechoslovakia. The second tour involved 25 ops to occupied Europe and 10 to Germany. Over the two tours Knott flew six operations against Duisburg, four against Essen and three against Berlin. He also operated twice against Nuremberg, Kiel, Stettin, Dortmund, Düsseldorf, Stuttgart and Pilsen.

A total of 2,157 Lancaster sorties were flown by 582 Squadron as a contribution to 165 raids. The first was to Lille on April 9/10 1944. The last was on April 25 1945, to Berchtesgaden. Twenty eight aircraft failed to return – a loss rate of 1.3 per cent. An additional eight Lancasters were struck off charge as a result of crashes[11].

The end of the war caught up with Little Staughton in late September 1945. The station was placed on the 'care and maintenance' list and much of the site returned to the plough. There was a brief revival in the 1950s, with the main runway lengthened to 3,000 yards to accommodate USAF jets. As in the case of so many wartime airfields, part of this former bomber base is now occupied by light industrial units[12].

During the tour with 582 Squadron Sidney Knott flew his operations in 11 Lancasters (by coincidence, the same number flown operationally during his first tour with 467 Squadron). The Walker crew dropped eight 4,000 lb Cookies, 12 2,000 lb bombs, 199 1,000 lb bombs, 164 500 lb bombs (including 16 with long delay fuses) and incendiaries. There was one 'hang-up' – a 500 lb bomb. They also dropped Target Indicators (including long-burners) and a large number of flares. A number of TIs and flares were brought back as they were not required by the Master Bomber.

These sorties contributed to the 608,612 tonnes of high explosive bombs dropped on primary targets by Lancasters. These bombs (around two-thirds of the total weight dropped by Bomber Command in the March 1942-May 1945 period) could have filled a freight train 345 miles long. The Lancasters also dropped 51.5 million incendiary bombs[13].

By October 1944 the effectiveness of the German nightfighter force was much reduced. During that month 54 Bomber Command aircraft failed to return from night operations. In January 1944 the nightfighters alone had claimed over 300 kills[14].

The fate of Walker's Lancasters contrasts sharply with the slaughter of the aircraft flown by Heavery a year earlier (virtually all were lost to enemy action over a six-month period). The 582 Squadron Lancasters, as listed below, fared better as a group. Five were lost in action but the others survived, to be lost in crashes or scrapped after the war:

*ND438, 156 Squadron (January 1944) and 582 Squadron (June 1944), then to 1667 HCU (December 1944), then to 35 Squadron and 156 Squadron, struck off charge May 22 1947[15].*

*ND502 (N-Nuts), 156 Squadron (January 1944) and 582 Squadron (April 1944), failed to return from Lens, June 15/16 1944 (274 hours)[15,16].*

*ND812 (O-Orange), 582 and 635 squadrons, overshot at Downham Market, October 23 1944 (250 hours)[16].*

*Devastation: Bomb damage around the entrance to the largest gallery at Wizernes. Photo: Trustees of The Imperial War Museum.*

*ND816 (O-Orange), 32 MU, 582 Squadron (April 1944), failed to return from Aachen May 24-25 1944 (121 hours)*[15,16].

*ND817 (S-Sugar), 32 MU, 582 Squadron (April 1944), failed to return from Mare de Magne August 7/8 1944 (246 hours)*[15,16].

*ND899 (J-Jig), 7, 582 and 156 squadrons, struck off charge March 25 1948*[15].

*NE130 (L-Leather), abandoned during return from Zeitz raid, January 16/17 1945*[15,16].

*NE169 (J-Jig), 582 Squadron (May 27 1944), failed to return from Wizernes, July 5/6 1944 (75 hours)*[15,16].

*PB136 (B-Baker), went to the Empire Air Armaments School in January 1945, then to 10 School of Technical Training*[15,16].

*PB149 (D-Dog), operated by 35, 582 and 156 squadrons, then to various conversion units; crashed October 31 1945*[15,16].

*PB182 (D-Dog), 32 MU, 44, 63 and 582 squadrons (July 1944), crashed January 20 1945 while landing at Oakington*[15,16].

The aircraft with ND/NE serials were among the 600 Merlin 38-engined Lancasters ordered from AV Roe (Chadderton) and delivered from December 1943 to May 1944. The three PB serials were among 800 Lancasters ordered from AV Roe (Chadderton) in April 1943 and delivered between May 1944 and March 1945[16].

Two Victoria Crosses are associated with 582 Squadron. Captain Edwin Swales, DFC, a South African, was awarded the Victoria Cross posthumously. He died on the night of February 23/24 1945 while acting as Master Bomber during a raid on Pforzheim. A fighter twice attacked his Lancaster, PB538, but Swales continued to broadcast instructions to the Main Force. Two engines were put out of action and the rear turret knocked out, but Swales still functioned as Master Bomber. Later, homeward bound, he lost control of the aircraft and ordered his crew to jump. Swales never got out. This was Bomber Command's last VC of the war[17].

Swales' citation described this attack as '...one of the most concentrated and successful of the war[18]'. The citation appeared in *The London Gazette* of April 24 1945. It added: 'Intrepid in the attack, courageous in the face of danger, he did his duty to the last, giving his life that his comrades might live.'

The second VC associated with 582 Squadron was awarded posthumously to a 24-year-old pilot from 109 Squadron. Squadron Leader Robert Palmer, DFC, was flying a 582 Squadron Oboe-equipped Lancaster, PB371, on December 23 1944, during a small-scale attack on the Gremberg rail yards, Cologne. It was Palmer's 110th operation. The plan for a radar-directed attack was scrapped when cloud cleared and visual bombing became possible. Sadly, Palmer failed to receive the order to switch to visual bombing. During the long Oboe run his Lancaster was hit repeatedly by flak and then attacked by fighters. Palmer's aircraft bombed the target but subsequently crashed. The rear gunner was the sole survivor[19].

# CHAPTER TWENTY

# *Absent Friends*

O N completion of his last trip with 467 Squadron sheer exhaustion overwhelmed Sidney Knott's planned participation in the crew's end-of-tour celebrations. Thirty-five trips later, the end of the second tour proved to be an even greater anti-climax.

*The crew went on extended leave after that last op to Bremen. Around three weeks later, during the second half of September, I received orders to report to Bourn, a holding centre in Cambridgeshire. At that time Bourn was home to 105 Squadron and its Mosquitos.*

*On my arrival I was surprised at the lack of activity. This was an operational base but nothing much seemed to happen, at least in my part of the station. There were very few people around. I decided to keep out of harm's way but the absence of Clive and the rest of the crew made me uncomfortable. When we said our goodbyes we had assumed we would be together again within a couple of weeks. Now I sat alone in the Mess anteroom, listening to the wireless and having a quiet drink. Perhaps 'rested' meant just that at the end of a second tour?*

*All this peace and quiet got me down after a while. I didn't know what to do with myself. Early one evening I settled down in Bourn's virtually deserted Mess anteroom and landed a pint on the table. Suddenly the phone rang. The call was for me and a girlish voice said: 'Ah! Found you at last! We didn't know where you were.' I was expecting fresh orders but this 582 Squadron WAAF gave me a shock: 'I have a message for you. You have been awarded the DFC and the CO sends his congratulations.' I didn't say a word. It didn't sink in. She chatted on: 'Well, let me add my congratulations. Would you like a copy of the message?' I muttered yes, put down the telephone and returned to my pint.*

*I sat in silence and studied the glass. What did she say? The Distinguished Flying Cross? It was the DFC, as opposed to the Distinguished Flying Medal, as I had been made up to Warrant Officer earlier that Summer. Normally, such things are an excuse for a boozy celebration but I had no crew and now lived a solitary existence on one of the RAF's quieter stations.*

Warrant Officer Knott relaxed in his chair, downed the first pint and felt rash enough to order another. While nursing the rare second beer his mind drifted back over the war years. He was a different person from that under-confident young man sitting with his father on a grassy cliff-top in 1940, watching German aircraft fly along the Thames to bomb London.

*I remembered women and children squeezing into makeshift bunks on the Underground platforms during the Blitz. That made a big impression on me. The young, old and sick huddled together, hoping for a decent night's sleep. I could still see their drawn, white faces. London took a terrible beating and the Germans went on to hammer Coventry. Other cities were laid waste by the Germans: Plymouth, Liverpool, Hull, Exeter, Canterbury and many more, in Britain and on the Continent. I played a part in Bomber Command's assault on Germany and had finished up with no regrets. I was fortunate to have had the chance to fight. What a contrast to the situation of the many thousands of merchant seamen who paid with their lives to keep Britain in the fight. They had no means to hit back yet the convoys continued to sail. I lifted my glass to their courage.*

*Hitler's regime had a unique character of distilled evil. It had conquered, exploited and tortured Europe without mercy. Bomber Command, together with the Americans, had helped reduce German military potential to the point where victory became possible in May 1945. Harris' squadrons, however, would have failed to bring the 'whirlwind' to Germany without the Canadians, Australians, New Zealanders and airmen of other Allied nations. Most of these men had no home leave during their entire service. I raised my glass again.*

It was a struggle to the death. Sidney Knott – and millions like him – often felt that the war would never end. During the second half of 1944, however, the Germans were forced back towards their eastern and western borders. Bomber Command and the American day bombers had degraded German fighting capacity. Much had been achieved by Bomber Command's thousands of young volunteers, the majority in their early twenties. While the casualty rate was appalling, there was no shortage of volunteers:

*I thought of names but I couldn't match them to faces. I could also picture many faces that were now nameless to me. I sat alone in Bourn's Mess. In other Messes I had been surrounded by the warmth of their company - excited voices, cigarette smoke and the comfort of well-worn jokes. One by one, their faces fell away from the crowd. An invisible presence had plucked them from view. Replacements arrived fresh from the Conversion Units, course photos still in their battledress pockets; they soon developed the haunted look of operational aircrew.*

*Painful mood swings were a symptom of this procession of triumph and tragedy. It affected everyone, not just the aircrew. I recalled our Chiefy on 467. One evening I spotted him sitting in a corner of Bottesford's Mess, drinking alone. Perhaps foolishly, I walked up to him and asked: 'What's up?' His brief, dull reply explained everything: 'Not much really - just a bad week'. A number of his aircraft had failed to return, along with the crews.*

*For all that heartache I had been part of an incredible, overwhelming enterprise. That thought, rather than the DFC, was a source of deep satisfaction. I raised my pint and whispered the right words: 'To absent friends!'*

The Distinguished Flying Cross is awarded for courage while flying on active service against the enemy. The ribbon is white with diagonal purple stripes. Sidney Knott did not receive his DFC at Buckingham Palace. The Palace found it impossible to keep pace with the number of awards. No doubt His Majesty took comfort in the knowledge that Britain, at that defining moment in its history, was a land rich in heroes.

*I remember my disappointment at the time. I had been excited and had sought advice on how investitures were organised at the Palace. Sadly, it wasn't to be.*

Knott had to wait three years, until August 25 1948, for his DFC. It arrived in the post, forwarded by RAF Records, Gloucester. It was accompanied by a letter from King George VI. It read: 'I greatly regret that I am unable to give you personally the award which you have so well earned. I now send it to you with my congratulations and my best wishes for your future happiness.'

Ted Foster, Heavery's navigator on 467 Squadron, had received a DFM 12 months earlier. He had attended the Palace, accompanied by his wife, Mary, and his mother. Frank Heavery also went to the Palace for his DFM, accompanied by his mother and brother.

As for Knott's 582 Squadron crew, Clive Walker, the skipper, received the DFC. The citation stated that the award was made '...in recognition of numerous operations against the enemy in which he has displayed the utmost fortitude, courage and devotion to duty.'

Bill Harrall was awarded the DFM, rather than the DFC, as his Warrant came through when the tour had finished. His parents accompanied him to the Palace. Little Staughton's Station Commander added a personal note to Bill's citation: 'Flight Sergeant Harrall has proved, in his operational career, to have outstanding courage and coolness. His high sense of duty makes him very worthy of the award of the DFM'.

In September 1990 the Post Office issued stamps featuring Royal Air Force decorations. By that time Sidney Knott had six grandchildren. He walked into Canterbury's main Post Office and purchased a First Day Cover for each grandchild. He attached a note, describing the decoration and what it represented.

Knott's citation, as published in *The London Gazette* of October 17 1944, reads as follows:

'This NCO is the rear gunner of a very determined and accurate marking crew. He has taken part in forty-nine attacks on heavily defended German, Italian and French targets, including fifteen as marker. His aircraft has on many occasions been attacked by enemy fighters which have been warded off by his accurate firing. He handles his guns skilfully, with a cool determination to protect his aircraft and crew. His crew have absolute confidence in Warrant Officer Knott as a rear gunner.'

In a minor reflection of the pressures of war, Knott's citation is inaccurate in its reference to the number of attacks flown (stating 49, rather than 64). It is easy to appreciate how this mistake may have arisen. Harder to understand are the references to fighter combats:

> *When I read the citation I was surprised, given that we had worked so hard to stay out of trouble. In these circumstances, however, you do not write to the King seeking a correction.*

# CHAPTER TWENTY-ONE

## 'Your Flying Days Are Over'

SIDNEY KNOTT'S flying career was over. He was one among thousands of aircrew awaiting 'reclassification' as the European war inched towards its close. The numbers of aircrew available far outstripped demand:

> Gunners were now surplus to requirements. My next posting was to the Scottish coastal town of Nairn and a remote airfield some three miles to the west, with views across the Moray Firth. This base was thinly occupied and my feelings of anticlimax deepened. I had been a gunner for three years. Gunnery was the sum of my adult life. What next?
>
> The station gradually came to life as a reclassification depot. I arrived during October - earlier than most. The station slowly filled with surplus aircrew of all ranks, kicking their heels and awaiting reclassification interviews. The Air Force intended to match former aircrew with available ground jobs. My main aim, as always, was to avoid a desk.
>
> Nairn's style was relaxed in the extreme. Orders were issued but there was little to do. With time on my hands I took to walking the surrounding countryside, often making for Nairn. The landscape was very different from that of the southern coastal towns, where most beaches were still disfigured by wire and pill-boxes. Nairn was a peaceful, sleepy backwater and I spent many soothing hours walking the deserted foreshore. Heading towards town, I developed the habit of buying a ticket for the pictures or calling at my favourite teashop. The natives were friendly and it wasn't long before I was invited into the teashop's parlour – a great honour in those days.
>
> Frank Heavery would have hated Nairn. The few pubs closed at 9 pm and strict licensing laws prohibited Sunday opening. This system was riddled with eccentricities. I could get a drink on Sunday but only if I qualified as a 'traveller', defined as an individual arriving on foot. I had to sign the 'Travellers' Book' and explain exactly how I had arrived at the pub. I could then have one drink ...and one only!

While walking the lonely beaches on bright, clear days Knott watched the distant Sunderland flying boats alighting on the Cromarty Firth. He missed flying and became determined to find a new Air Force job involving close contact with aircraft.

*I spent several months doing little or nothing and became increasingly bored. When it was my turn for interview I took a long shot. I told the officer I would be happy to go to the Far East with 'Tiger Force' if I could continue to fly. This was dismissed out of hand: 'No. That really isn't an option. Your flying days are over.' The Reclassification Officer had just two jobs on offer: driver or airfield controller. I expressed a preference for the latter as it meant daily contact with aircraft. My future decided, I went on leave to await my next posting.*

Three months had passed since Knott left 582 Squadron and Little Staughton. From Nairn the next posting returned him to the heart of 'bomber country' - to Elsham Wolds, Lincolnshire. He became an airfield controller U/T:

*Elsham Wolds, a 1 Group station, was home to the Lancasters of 103 Squadron. My squadron life, however, was finished. I belonged to the station rather than the squadron, one of a number of trainee airfield controllers.*

*It didn't take me long to get the hang of things. I assisted the flying control officer responsible for all aircraft movements. One of the qualified airfield controllers was friendly and suggested an outing to the nearest pub. He found me a bike and I soon discovered that the 'nearest pub' was a considerable distance away. We set off during a bitterly cold late afternoon in the second half of December. Fresh, thick snow lay across the lanes. Our progress was erratic but we battled on for several miles, only to find the pub closed. Refusing to accept defeat, we knocked smartly on the door - only to be told to 'get lost'. The pub had run out of beer and would stay shut until next week's delivery. We pedalled back in silence through the ice and slush, arriving at our billets sober in every sense of the word.*

*The Arctic freeze continued and more snow followed. Happy Christmas! Happy New Year 1945! The Station Commander celebrated by ordering everyone (no exceptions) to report to the main runway with shovels, but his attempt to keep the runway open was a losing battle. The long cold snap continued into early January and power cables came down, overwhelmed by the weight of ice encasing them. I woke one morning to find powdery snow blowing through an ill-fitting billet window and settling on my bed.*

*The Mess was a long way from our hut and the wind was sharp with ice crystals. On one occasion I took a short cut, following the hedgerow leading in the general direction of the Mess. The wind had banked up the snow and I soon found myself walking on a honeycombed crust of ice. Inevitably, this gave way and I sank up to my waist. It took a long time to struggle out and plod into the Mess - only to find I was too late for dinner. Lincolnshire, in the grip of a harsh Winter, can be a bloody miserable place!*

Knott was relieved when his next posting arrived. He made his way to Watchfield, near Swindon:

*The second phase of my training as an airfield controller began at Watchfield. The days were filled with lectures and practical work. Our instructors spent a lot of time explaining Flying Rules and procedures for laying a flarepath – setting out lights, gooseneck flares and other devices. This was an RAF course but we had all sorts in our group, including Fleet Air Arm and USAAF personnel. The Americans found it difficult to get to grips with our disciplined, very British approach to flying procedures.*

*There wasn't much to do during the evenings, but one member of our group saved the day. A gifted magician, he kept his hand in by putting on a daily show. He would demonstrate, very slowly, how each trick was done, then repeat it faster than the eye could follow.*

In February 1945 Warrant Officer Knott, sometime air gunner and now a qualified airfield controller, was posted to West Raynham in Norfolk. The airfield was two miles west of the village of the same name. At that time West Raynham was home to 141 and 239 Mosquito squadrons (100 Group). This station had two overworked airfield controllers responsible for providing 24-hour service. Not surprisingly, they were pleased to see the new arrival:

*West Raynham was different due to the presence of the Meteors. I had my first close look at a jet fighter. The early jet engines made a horrible racket – everyone hated the noise.*

The airfield controller acted as the flying control officer's extra pair of eyes. Flying Control had no clear view of the far reaches of the main runway. Many pre-war stations – originally all-grass airfields – had this problem. When the longer hard runways were constructed during the war the original hangars and other buildings often obstructed the view. The airfield controller, stationed in a caravan at one end of the runway, was linked by telephone to Flying Control. Landings were controlled by R/T and take-offs by Aldis lamp. The airfield controller's responsibilities, beyond logging aircraft movements and talking to Flying Control, included checking whether the undercarriage had been lowered as each aircraft began its approach.

'Darky Watch' was another important responsibility. If a pilot lost his bearings or had to get down quickly, he could call up 'Darky' and receive immediate assistance. This service utilised low power transmitters and receivers at most operational stations and some beacons. A 24-hour Darky Watch was maintained from Flying Control and the airfield controller's caravan. The duty controller listened out at all times, although the plaintive 'Hello Darky' call was a rare event:

*I remember only one and that was at extreme range. The maximum range was only around 10 miles, but that was adequate due to the sheer number of airfields in the region. West Raynham responded but the pilot was interested in a nearer airfield. Such excitement was unusual and airfield controlling proved to be a placid activity. The duties were organised around meal-times: breakfast to dinner, dinner to tea and tea to breakfast (the long shift). The rota was spread over a three-day cycle – dinner to tea on the first day and two shifts on the second day (breakfast-dinner and tea-breakfast), with every third day off. If one of the three airfield controllers went on leave or reported sick, the others were expected to cover for him.*

This sedentary existence was to continue for over a year; Sidney

Knott's nomadic Air Force life had ground to a halt. West Raynham was his longest posting by far:

> *West Raynham reminded me of Scampton, with its pre-war layout and buildings. The station's formal atmosphere was offset by a level of comfort superior to all earlier postings (with the possible exception of Scampton).*

Sidney Knott had two reasons to celebrate May 8 1945 - Victory in Europe (VE) Day. The end of the long European war coincided with his twenty-fourth birthday:

> *Better still, May 8 was the first day of my leave. I didn't go home directly but, instead, enjoyed a day out at Newmarket. During the war Newmarket was one of a handful of venues where racing continued. I put everything I had on dubious horses, lost the lot and still felt good! I had been robbed but I didn't give a damn. I hitched to Leigh-on-Sea, where I still had a few pounds tucked away in my room.*

By 1945 Bomber Command had 56 Lancaster squadrons on strength. Lancasters dropped 608,612 tonnes of bombs, the lion's share of Bomber Command's total of 955,044 tonnes. A total of 156,192 operational sorties were flown by Lancasters and 3,836 aircraft were struck off charge[1]. With the war in Europe over Bomber Command's gigantic infrastructure was dismantled. Twenty-six squadrons were disbanded in the first six months of peace[2].

In occupied, devastated Germany, the experts moved in to assess the damage caused by the Allies' bombing campaign. The US Strategic Bombing Survey was established in 1944. Headquartered in London, it was staffed by 1,200 officers and men. The British survey effort was set at a much lower level following intervention by Churchill – perhaps an indicator of political sensitivities.

The US Survey concluded: 'Allied air power ...made possible the success of the invasion. It brought the economy which sustained the enemy's armed forces to virtual collapse, although the full effects of this collapse had not reached the enemy's front lines when they were overrun by Allied forces. It brought home to the German people the full impact of modern war, with all its horror and suffering. Its imprint on the German nation will be lasting [3].'

Things changed after VE Day. Knott soon noticed the difference when he returned from leave:

> *While we were still at war with Japan the atmosphere was more relaxed. Flying continued but there were fewer aircraft movements. The most obvious change was the revival of sport. There was time, once more, for cricket, football, hockey and badminton. West Raynham had an excellent cricket pitch. I wondered whether I could still hit a cricket ball or kick a football. Matches were arranged between the Officers', Sergeants' and Airmens' Messes. I found myself in the Sergeants' Mess cricket team, playing against the officers. Our station had some outstanding sportsmen. The many well-known footballers and cricketers included Keith Miller, the Australian test player – then a Flight Lieutenant. He had done his initial training at Victor Harbour, South Australia, back in early 1942. We*

*had plenty of fielding to do whenever Keith batted.*

It was at this time that Knott made the acquaintance of Joan Jeary, a WAAF Corporal PT Instructor at West Raynham. They spent several enjoyable days out together, usually taking the train into Norwich. Joan recalls that his main topics of conversation were football and the 'stars' – passing on the knowledge shared by Ted Foster while at Bottesford.

In June Knott was sent to Castle Bromwich, near Birmingham. This three-week posting was to the grass airfield used by pilots (including the renowned Alex Henshaw) testing Spitfires, produced at the adjacent Vickers factory, prior to release to the squadrons:

> *This was cushy work. There was no flying control officer and I had nothing to do other than log occasional aircraft movements. This proved difficult, however, as communication with the factory left much to be desired. My first warning of a flight was usually the opening of the hangar doors. With the Spitfire rolled out the pilot would climb into the cockpit for a test flight of five to 20 minutes. A short flight usually meant there were problems with the aircraft. No-one bothered to visit my caravan (dubbed the 'coffee pot', due to its shape). I had to be content with a brief telephone call during the morning, outlining the day's programme.*

*Time for sport: with Victory in Europe, football and other sports were revived. Sidney Knott is pictured standing, to the far right. Photo: Sidney Knott.*

*I lived out, having found digs. I knew no-one and felt rather isolated. I used some of my free time to write to Joan – mainly complaining about lost opportunities to play football. I had no idea, at that time, that I would be back at West Raynham within a few weeks.*

The Vickers test pilots, meanwhile, retained their habit of taking off in virtually any direction across the grass. The problems of identification and logging were compounded by the fact that the aircraft had yet to

*A new friend: Sidney Knott met his future wife, Joan Jeary, at West Raynham. Photo: Sidney Knott.*

receive squadron letters. It was virtually impossible to read the much smaller aircraft numbers, even with binoculars. During the afternoon, as always, the phone would ring with instructions to close up for the day.

*From time to time this sedate lifestyle was interrupted by the arrival of a communications aircraft, usually an Anson, with a group of ferry pilots. They had the job of flying the latest batch of Spitfires to the squadrons.*

*Some days were entirely free of flying and I had time on my hands. Occasionally I ambled along the main road and caught the tram into Birmingham. This went into the Bull Ring, passing Aston Villa's ground on the way. I always sat on the top deck, enjoying the view. It was a comforting thing. Football somehow confirmed that the world was slowly coming to its senses. Perhaps we could now concentrate on sport, rather than blowing each other to bits.*

Knott returned to West Raynham in July, following the arrival of a permanent airfield controller at Castle Bromwich. A few weeks later, on Monday August 6, the city of Hiroshima was erased by an atomic bomb. This weapon had an explosive power 2,000 times greater than Barnes Wallis' Grand Slam 'earthquake bomb', carried by specially modified Lancasters and the largest conventional, air-dropped weapon used during the war. On Tuesday August 14 it was announced that the Japanese had accepted unconditional surrender after the dropping of a second atomic weapon, on Nagasaki:

*Terrible though the atomic bomb was, it brought the war to an immediate end. We had expected the bloody conflict to continue for years given the fanatical temperament of the Japanese. The Hiroshima and Nagasaki attacks finished a world war but the grotesque power of atomic weapons remained beyond understanding. Clearly, the world would never be the same again.*

The sudden advent of peace was seen as a serious threat to service discipline. West Raynham's Station Commander took the direct approach:

*He appealed to our better nature and warned against fancy stunts in aircraft. Instead, official entertainments were organised. In fact we were all well-behaved and celebrated VJ Day, August 15, with no displays of outrageous behaviour and no damage to the aircraft.*

*There was a big party in the Sergeants' Mess. The WAAFs were invited, including Joan. The Mess had a good pianist – a former member of Henry Hall's dance band. Then came the biggest challenge of my service career. Every member of the Mess had to sing a song on stage. Most took the safe option, singing well-known and extremely crude RAF songs. For some reason I decided to sing the Andrews Sisters' number Apple Blossom Time. Happily, the pianist gave a fine accompaniment and everyone took up the chorus. Apparently, it was a success - but I must have had more than a few beers before starting! I was told later that I had sung the only clean song all night. In future years, at house parties with some of my Air Gunners' Association friends, they often tried to persuade me to repeat this 'turn'. It was the only song I knew the words to, apart from Jealousy... and there isn't enough beer in the world to make me sing that!*

A few days later Knott took a telephone call in the Mess:

*It was Ted Foster, my 467 Squadron navigator. He was calling from Great Massingham, Clive Walker's operational base in 1942 and West Raynham's satellite until mid-1944, when it obtained independence as a full station. Ted had seen my name on Station Orders. Commissioned and reclassified, he was now Great Massingham's Equipment Officer. A desk job suited Ted but he found his new life boring. He spent most of his time issuing chits for coal! I was about to visit Great Massingham – a darts match had been arranged between our Mess and a pub in the village. We arranged to meet and it was great to see Ted again. We had a good laugh when I told him I preferred my situation to his. A Pilot Officer in the Officers' Mess was the lowest of the low and a Flying Officer wasn't much higher! In contrast, a Warrant Officer stood at the top of the ladder in the Sergeants' Mess.*

All the anxieties and pressures of war dissipated. RAF stations across the country began to normalise relations with their local communities. During the war tight security led to a ban on civilian visitors. In that first Autumn of peace the wartime restrictions were lifted and 'friends and neighbours' were welcome once again:

*There were some memorable sporting fixtures, including cricket at Holkham Hall, a Palladian mansion. I was always sure of getting a very good tea at these events. There was an exception, however, when we played a fixture against the staff of an asylum in Norwich. A sumptuous spread was prepared but all the cakes had disappeared by teatime. They were stolen and scoffed by the inmates.*

*My consolation that day was the presence of Joan. She was mad keen on sport. This was not surprising, given that she was a PT Instructor! I got to know her better by playing more than my fair share of badminton. Some hard-fought matches took place in West Raynham's lavishly-equipped gym.*

*I also taught myself to drive at West Raynham. It began on a very blustery day. The wind suddenly changed and this required a quick switch of runways. I couldn't drive but this minor detail was of no interest to the flying control officer. He ordered me to move the motorised control caravan. I explained the position and asked for a driver but no-one was available. I was told to get on with it. I managed it, with some violent abuse of the gears. My first driving lesson was a solo outing in a heavy vehicle.*

# CHAPTER TWENTY-TWO

# Civvy Street

THE demobilisation of millions of wartime service personnel was a huge undertaking. The release dates were announced on the wireless. Sidney Knott's 'demob' approached in the early Spring of 1946:

> I started thinking seriously about the future only when the war ended. While on operations no-one worried about what to do with the rest of their lives. This problem could best be described as theoretical given the high casualty rate. I considered staying on but soon decided against life in the peacetime Air Force. Back in 'Civvy Street', the fruit and veg trade seemed the obvious choice – but there would be no return to the family shop. My uncles, Tom and Jim Owen, offered a compromise. They had a shop and wholesale round in the Southend area and promised me a job after the war. Above all else I wanted to avoid shop work; I needed my Saturday afternoons to play football. I had some catching up to do!
>
> The demob interviews were an interesting experience, with some vigorous recruiting going on for the Police and Church. Many former aircrew drifted into the Church. Others favoured a Police career. Two friends of mine, both members of the Kent Branch of the Air Gunners' Association, each spent 30 years in the Police as a result of these interviews.

As for the Church, Flight Lieutenant John Williams, DFC, MA, was a notable example of a Bomber Command pilot with a religious calling. Williams had made up his mind, prior to the outbreak of war, to enter the Church. Williams served with 61 and 617 Squadrons and subsequently became vicar of St. Mary the Virgin, Rye. Knott heard this story from his navigator, Alan Talbot, who also entered the Church and subsequently became a vicar in Whitechapel. On February 17 1980 Canon Williams led the prayers at a service in St. Paul's Cathedral, giving thanks for the life of Barnes Wallis. The inventor of the 'bouncing bomb', used against the German Dams, died on October 30 1979[1].

> I stuck to my plans to join Tom and Jim. I outlined this idea to the officer. I must have convinced him as my demob papers carried the notation: 'It is considered that Warrant Officer Knott would be very suitable for employment as a salesman.' This proved to be correct. I retired from the fruit and veg business in 1983, at the age of 62 and after 37 years as a salesman.
>
> My demob date was Sunday April 7 1946. This was no simple matter and involved much more than reporting to an officer and signing a form. I had to visit

*every section of the station and obtain 'clearance' – including a check on any money owed and missing kit. My past caught up with me at this point. In my flying days I had been issued with underwear of unusually good quality. I never took to the vests and long johns – they were much too warm – but I thought my father might appreciate a couple of pairs. My rather predictable, weak alibi (that they had been lost in one of my many moves from station to station) cut no ice. I received the bill in due course. On the other hand I had more success with my uniform. The Warrant Officer's uniform, an officer's dress-type outfit, was quite expensive. A chap in the Mess was to be made up to Warrant Officer and he was about my height and build. When I told him my demob was imminent we struck a deal, all legal and above board as the uniform was my property.*

During the following day Sidney Knott joined a vast crowd of impatient Air Force personnel at Wembley Dispersal Centre. They were picking their 'civvies' from a strictly limited, standardised range of demob suits and other items of utility clothing:

*This was an odd experience. Before joining up I left clothes and similar matters to my mother. During my service years clothes came with the job. Now, for the first time in my life, I had to make up my own mind. I chose badly. Virtually everything turned out to be the wrong size. I then went on leave. Former aircrew were given 56 days' paid leave to sort out their futures. As I had already done this, beyond a final talk with my uncles, I was free to enjoy my first ever paid holiday.*

Sidney Knott's RAF career began on January 9 1941 and ended over five years later, on April 8 1946, when he was put on the Reserve List. He left the Air Force officially on June 3 1946, the day his demob leave expired. There was no new posting, only a stark warning printed on the last page of his demob papers:

*FOR ALL AIRMEN*

*Warning: you are reminded that the unauthorised communication by you to any person at any time of any information you have acquired while in H.M. Services which might be useful to an enemy renders you liable to prosecution under Official Secrets Acts 1911 and 1920.*

Sidney Knott used his last leave to take stock of his life:

*I had been changed and moulded by the Air Force. When I joined up I was an innocent. At demob I was a wiser man, with a much wider knowledge of the world. I had hardly ever left Leigh-on-Sea before joining the RAF. I went about as far as a bike ride would take me. A school trip to the Tower of London was a rare treat. During my service career, however, I mixed with men from every part of the country and, of course, from many other countries. While my entire service was in Britain I was fortunate to develop an appreciation of people from all backgrounds and walks of life. This was the big advantage of service in the Air Force. My old school friend, Johnny Martin, had joined the Territorials before the war. He was called up immediately, went straight to North Africa and stayed there for the rest of the war. He had no home leave for five years and spent all that time with men recruited largely from his own county.*

*Air Force life gave me a fresh perspective on my earlier years. I now realised my family were a strange lot. The shop was my mother's entire life. My father was easy to get on with when sober, but he was very different with a few drinks inside him. I had a comfortable home by the standards of the time but we were by no means a 'loving family'. I had been well looked after and well fed, but feelings were not expressed openly under our roof.*

*It was a claustrophobic start to life. Joining up freed me. It also gave me an insight into how other people lived their lives. When I returned home on leave I was always made welcome but, in fact, it was more the obvious place to go than anything deeper. During my first tour I began to talk to my father about my experiences. I didn't tell him much and he wasn't very forthcoming in his replies.*

*The Air Force helped me establish a new life and I had no regrets. I enjoyed squadron life, especially the warmth of close comradeship – perhaps because it was such a contrast to my earlier life at home.*

Sidney Knott's first 12 months in Civvy Street were spent working with his uncles. Tom and Jim Owen were getting on in years and the young man's arrival gave them the chance to take things easier:

*I moved back with my parents. This was a time of great upheaval. Mother's shop was sold – she became ill and couldn't cope with the business. In a remarkable coincidence the buyer turned out to be a chap I'd known at West Raynham. He was a Sergeant in the Armoury. While talking to mother he spotted my photo on the mantelpiece and recognised the face. The proceeds of the sale allowed my parents to buy a house. Father returned to carpentry and joinery. His skill in making doors, windows and stairs was in great demand as the rebuilding of bomb-damaged homes got under way.*

*I took on part of the wholesale round for the two old boys. Johnny Martin joined us following his demob. I took one lorry and he took the other. Fate took a hand after less than nine months, when Tom had a bad road accident. This set him back and he and Jim decided to close the wholesale business. This was serious. I was courting Joan and thinking of settling down.*

Joan Jeary is one of three sisters. All became WAAFs. The youngest of the three, Nicky, married a Warrant Officer wireless op/air gunner in 1944. The older sister was the last to join up. She married a former sailor after the war. The youngest of the family, a brother, did his National Service in the RAF.

Sidney Knott and Joan Jeary married on June 29 1947:

*Joan's family came from Norfolk while my people were from Essex. Joan delivered an ultimatum, as she was determined to be a June bride. One Sunday morning we sat round the table at my parents' house and talked things over. June had three weeks to run and if things were not sorted out very quickly our wedding would be in June 1948! We solved this problem by hopping on a bus, which happened to be going to Stanford-Le-Hope. We found a suitable church in the town but ran into problems with the vicar. He pointed out that we had to be resident in the Parish, but then offered a solution. There was a guesthouse nearby. Joan booked in and soon qualified as resident. The guesthouse also*

*A beautiful Sunday: Sidney and Joan on June 29 1947. Johnny Martin was Best Man. Joan's large bouquet was very much the fashion of the time, as were Sidney's gloves, bought for the occasion. There were no paid holidays and their honeymoon lasted 48 hours, at "The Pilot" on the Isle of Grain. Photo: Sidney Knott.*

*provided a venue for the reception – for close family only. We were married at midday on a beautiful Sunday.*

With the wedding approaching Knott looked hard for a new job. He soon decided to offer the problem to fate. He went to London, took a bus to Victoria Station and studied the departure boards. His eyes alighted on 'Brighton' and he boarded the next train for this South Coast resort:

*Brighton had a small wholesale fruit and veg market. I strolled around, chatting to the salesmen. One firm had a vacancy at its Eastbourne branch. Why not? I called on the manager of this small depot, which was about the same size as my uncles' defunct wholesale operation. I got the job and they promised to sort out some accommodation. By the time I arrived the following Sunday, however, the accommodation had been forgotten. I was told to find a place for the night at one of the many nearby B&Bs. One friendly landlady couldn't take me but directed me to a relative who had a room to rent.*

*Conditions immediately after the war were very austere. Joan and I lived in one room and spent a lot of time looking for better accommodation. Eventually we found a two-roomed basement flat. Fortunately, I liked the job at Eastbourne ...and my Saturday afternoons off! I joined Eastbourne Football Club and played in a league. I became serious about football and attended practice on Tuesday and Thursday evenings. My new employers were amenable. Very few houses had bathrooms at that time and, with this in mind, the firm allowed me to leave at*

*11.30 on Saturdays. This gave me the chance to collect my towel and soap and visit the public baths before the rush when work finished at noon. By late 1947 Joan was expecting Jean, our first daughter. We were to have three daughters – Jean, Judy and Melanie. In later years, each gave us two grandchildren.*

*One day during 1948 I spotted an advertisement in the Fruit Trades Journal. There was an opening for a salesman and accommodation went with the job. I applied and a few days later found myself at a manor house near Swindon – the company's base. This modest business supplied produce to local shops and operated a small fleet of three lorries. The accommodation looked promising. The ground floor of the building was used as offices while the first floor was divided into two flats. The manager had one half and we were to occupy the other. The flat proved to be better than the job. The business was badly run and I was out of work again within six months, shortly after the birth of our first child. I had no choice but to turn to my parents. We lived with them while we sorted ourselves out.*

Johnny Martin solved the problem. He repaid his old friend's earlier favour and found him an opening at his place of work, a market gardening/wholesale business at Thundersley, near Rayleigh. Johnny managed to buy a terraced house. He had married an Irish girl (Sidney Knott had given her away as she had no family in England). There were spare rooms and the Knotts needed no second bidding. They took the top floor.

*Something had to be done, however, to solve our accommodation problem once and for all. We wanted to buy a house but this was far from easy in the early post-war period. House-building had resumed but the emphasis was on repairs and the completion of houses started before the war and left unfinished for the duration. Eventually, we managed to buy a new bungalow in Rayleigh. We moved into our first real home during the Autumn of 1950 and our second*

*Helping hand from a friend: Johnny Martin managed to 'engineer' a job for Sidney Knott (far right) at Blake's, a market gardening/wholesale business at Thundersley, Essex. Photo: Sidney Knott.*

*daughter, Judy, arrived as a Christmas present. We were to stay in our bungalow for 17 years.*

Knott's job at Thundersley was demanding. During the Summer months he worked extremely long hours. Eventually, in 1956, the excessive hours persuaded him to explore opportunities at Spitalfields. There was a chance to earn more in a market ranking close to Covent Garden as the top London fruit and veg wholesale centre. The money was important as the Knotts now had a third daughter, Melanie.

The London market's curious name relates to the hospital (Spittle or Spittal) founded outside the City's Bishop's Gate in 1197[2]. Spitalfields (including the London Fruit Exchange and the flower market) was regarded as the world's largest covered market for fruit, vegetables and flowers. Knott found an opening with A. May, one of the major Spitalfields wholesalers:

*A. May specialised in potatoes and other veg and fruit. My job was to sell celery, carrots, onions, peas and cauliflowers. The cauliflowers came into the market all year round, with English caulis followed, in succession, by Jersey, French and Italian produce.*

*The fundamental purpose of a market like Spitalfields is to set prices. The aim, of course, is to sell for the highest possible price but, at the same time, ensure the produce is moved rather than held until it passes its prime. Market life was a wonderful experience but very up and down. Bad days were forgotten when the market bubbled and nothing I touched could go wrong. I got to know all the buyers and life was one big round of bid and barter. I thrived in this atmosphere and soon developed my own market personality. I became 'Sid of May's.'*

*The firm was very strict on cost control and every phone call was monitored. If the boss felt a call was unjustified, he'd soon appear and argue the toss. If we were having a good run on, say, Devonshire Swedes – the best in the country – he'd moan about the cost of calls for restocks. Telegrams were much cheaper than the telephone in those days but I liked instant results and worked better on the phone.*

*After some years I wanted a change and joined Dan Wuille & Co, later taken over by Francis Nicholls. These companies had a history stretching back a century or more but post-war Geest eventually acquired them.*

*Joan and I decided to move. We went to Romford in 1967 and stayed there until my retirement in 1983. We then moved to Kent and a chalet-bungalow in the village of Ash, near Sandwich.*

During his years at Spitalfields Sidney Knott made the acquaintance of former 617 Squadron navigator Alan Talbot, who had become vicar of a poor parish in Whitechapel. He had flown with John Williams on 61 and 617 squadrons. Williams' crew had moved to 617 when that squadron took heavy losses on operations after the Dams Raid. As in Williams' case, Talbot had always intended to enter the church.

*Our friendly clergyman, formerly a Flight Lieutenant, took to visiting us in the late morning – the end of the market day – when he knew he could buy a couple of bags of cheap vegetables. The market tended to attract its share of dodgy characters and, at first, Talbot was under suspicion as a possible 'bogus padre'. Yet we were soon convinced that he was genuine. Indeed, he was the vicar of a local church, St. Augustine with St. Phillip. The market's salesmen were pleased to help. The vegetables went to a woman who gave shelter to single, homeless women.*

*Talbot was a fascinating character. He became a missionary in East Africa. During his time in Africa he organised a cottage industry making Palm Sunday crosses, which were shipped to London. This allowed poor African communities to generate income. Later, in Whitechapel, he continued the business – importing the palm crosses from Africa and setting up a distribution facility in the Church Hall. This was an all-year-round activity, rather like the production of British Legion poppies. His Whitechapel parishioners also benefited, as they had the opportunity to 'earn a few bob' in the Church Hall. His enterprise became well known and he even gave a radio talk on the Palm Sunday crosses.*

*Alan Talbot kept in touch with his market friends when he 'moved up in the world,' taking a parish in Twickenham in the late 1970s. The Palm Sunday crosses continue to thrive, with over two million distributed every year in the United States alone.*

People in post-war Britain had to wait many years for any real improvement in their standard of living. This didn't come about until the 1960s. Rationing continued for many years after the war and shop queues were long and slow-moving. Housewives frequently had no idea what they were queuing for. They saw the long line of hopefuls and simply tagged on.

*Pay rates for everyday jobs were very low. While at Thundersley I earned £356 a year, with £55 deducted for tax. As a married couple with a young family we had nothing to spare. Joan worked on the land to supplement my wage, picking potatoes, peas and fruit. Joan also picked wild blackberries and I sold them to greengrocers for a shilling a pound. The extra money provided Winter outfits for the children.*

*Many wartime restrictions remained in place. My father, for example, wanted to buy a car but he had to put his name on a waiting list. We lived a mile or so from Rayleigh and always walked to the next bus stop to save fares. Things didn't improve for our generation until the late 1960s. We were then able to buy our first new car – a successor to several 'old bangers'. Our mortgage was nearly paid off by this time.*

*Things became easier when we moved to Romford in 1967. Joan went to work full-time, looking after the accounts of small firms in the area. Then she got the job she had always wanted. It was too late for her to train as a physiotherapist but she started work at two local hospitals, Oldchurch and Rush Green, as a physiotherapy assistant. She loved the work and continued until 1980. Joan only stopped when she had no choice due to the onset of painful arthritis.*

Sidney Knott retained his practical, no-nonsense approach to life and this attitude suited Joan. The couple never dwelt on the past:

*I had no trouble adjusting to Civvy Street. There were times when the war had seemed never-ending yet, afterwards, I had no nightmares or flashbacks. I just switched off. In later years holidays abroad meant flying but that didn't bother me. It was a novelty to fly straight and level above the weather! Frank and the rest of us thought the Lanc was big but it is a minnow alongside a 747.*

Knott was fortunate to escape physical disability. Many former aircrew suffered hearing loss in middle or late middle age:

*I had no health problems, just a big appetite for family life. Money was tight but our three kids were lots of fun. We made ends meet by doing things that, today, would seem odd – even eccentric. For example, if the GPO (as the Post Office was known at the time) decided to replace the telegraph poles in a road, one of the old poles could be bought for a few shillings. My father-in-law was a 'poleman' and he tipped me off about this. Coal was rationed and telegraph poles were a useful source of extra fuel. The polemen would saw a pole in half and put it in the front garden. It was soon sawn into sections, split with an axe and turned into logs.*

After the war Sidney Knott kept in touch with only one of his former crew members – Ted Foster, the Heavery crew's navigator. In 1961 Foster took his two children, David and Wendy, to London. They had arranged to meet Wendy's penfriend (from Germany, of all places). They left the car at Rayleigh and met up with Knott when he finished work. Such contacts were rare at that time:

*Ted and I continued to exchange occasional Christmas cards but that was about all. In the Air Force people became very close but, at the same time, they understood the realities of service life – one minute surrounded by friends and the next minute posted. This coloured the post-war attitude towards wartime*

*'Real food', by definition, is fried: Ted Foster cooks breakfast on the beach at Sandwich Bay, Kent, on the last morning of a holiday with the Knotts. Photo: Sidney Knott.*

*friendships. Besides, people were sick of everything about the war: the horror, waste of life, long working hours, short rations and general gloom. They wanted to forget and build a new and brighter future. After the lean years of austerity they focused on the new – a new home, a permanent relationship, family life and a fresh start, perhaps in a different career. It was time to let go of the wartime era.*

Attitudes changed again, however, as the years rolled by. Ted Foster, always a prolific letter-writer, set about tracing his 467 Squadron crew in the early 1980s:

*We met occasionally in our later years. I was surprised when I saw that he had lost that wonderful shock of blond, wavy hair! Ted also had three children, two boys and a girl. His Wendy was just a little older than our Jean. The two families had some good times together, including a number of memorable holidays. A few weeks after our return a long letter always arrived from Ted. He kept a diary of every shared holiday. Later in life, when Ted lost Mary, he often re-read the holiday diaries and savoured memories of happier times.*

One letter concerns a holiday divided between Kent and the Isle of Wight. It includes this comment:

*'The evening was spent in chin-wagging and the men were warned that the war was now over and a little less of the 'nothing on the clock, upside down and still climbing' would be appreciated for the next fortnight[3].'*

The Air Force was never far away, however, when Sidney Knott and Ted Foster were together. On that particular holiday, at the end of a long evening walk, they took a seat on the promenade. They were soon joined by an old man of 90, struggling along with the aid of two sticks. They struck up a conversation and it turned out that their elderly companion was once a top civil servant in the pre-war Air Ministry. In 1940 he had worked alongside Lord Beaverbrook and, later, had been instrumental in introducing the cine camera gun and the GEE navigational aid to Bomber Command. The three sat together, looking out to sea and sharing memories of a darker time.

*Ted took up his old trade of wool-sorting after the war. He found himself on a three-day week in 1951 and decided it was time for a change. He bought a newsagents in the Bradford area and led a seven-day week existence until 1966, when he obtained a good price for the shop. He took a job as an insurance collector but soon returned to the wool trade and the firm he had worked for before the war. He was a stock controller when he retired in 1983. He then had the time to track down his old crew. He had no need to go looking for the mid-upper gunner; Ken Butterworth came to him. One day, a new rep called at the Bradford shop, selling toilet rolls and paper towels. It was Ken, who still lived in Bolton.*

Sadly, Ted Foster died in 2002. Mary's death, some years previously, had toppled his world. They were married for 52 years. Nevertheless, Ted did his best to get on with things and remained extremely proud of 467 Squadron and his wartime service. During an April evening Wendy accompanied him to an Aircrew Association dinner and father and daughter had a wonderful time. Wendy drove him home and said goodnight. A neighbour became concerned when Ted's curtains remained drawn the following morning. He was found on the bedroom floor. Heavery's navigator had been putting his clothes away but he never got to bed that night. The family donated Ted Foster's DFM, other medals and logbook to The Yorkshire Air Museum at Elvington, near York.

*Ted's death came as a terrible shock. Joan and I went to the funeral. It was there that I met Clive 'Tubby' Watson, Ted's rear gunner during his second tour. This had opened with a raid on Bergen, Norway, on October 28 1944. We chatted quietly for a few minutes. He said Ted had saved the crew during the Bergen raid. Their pilot was very green and couldn't pull out of a steep dive. Ted came forward, took charge and used the trimmer. Ted flew 11 sorties during the tour, ending with an attack on Dortmund on March 12 1945. Over 1,100 bombers participated in this raid.*

Ted Foster had his chance meeting with Ken Butterworth, but Sidney Knott never met him again after the parting at Turweston in late January 1944:

*I have since, however, had the privilege of meeting his son, Kelvin. We got together in August 2002 and he talked about post-war life with his Dad. Ken had married in September 1946. He and Olive had three children. The first, Sandra, died as a baby. Kelvin grew up with another sister, Karen. Ken died in 1990 at the age of 68. Kelvin said his father had a spectacular end to his war, as part of a seven-man team 'liberating' Trondheim, Norway. Ken was a member of the crew of a Lancaster that dropped leaflets ordering the German garrison to surrender. The aircraft then landed. It was the evening of Wednesday May 9 1945 and they were the first Allied Forces in Trondheim.*

Their arrival caused a sensation and provoked some purple prose in the local newspaper: 'British lads, young, cool-headed, not to be upset by trifles, not even when the airfield suddenly became full of hundreds of Germans anxious to surrender. 'Take it easy! Take it easy! We can't take the whole garrison.' A moment or two later, all seven were taken in hand by Trondheim's young womanhood, who evidently found in all this their finest prize for years[4].'

*Lucky Ken! I have since tried to imagine him in this situation. He would have loved it. Ken would have been fluent in Norwegian (well, nearly fluent) by early the next morning!*

*Ken's family originally came from Rochdale. His father went to Bolton in search of work. After the tour with 467 Ken became friendly with a Canadian flyer and they stayed in touch after the war. Much later, in the 1990s, his friend visited Britain after the death of his wife. He stayed with the Butterworth family and eventually married Ken's sister.*

*Ken liked a drink and a smoke. At one point he was a 60-a-day man and blamed the war for this excessive attachment to tobacco. He put on weight in later life but remained his old gregarious self. Kelvin had little knowledge of his father's wartime experiences. Ken always refused to be drawn on his flying days. His son, however, often found an 'Airfix' Lancaster model among his Christmas presents.*

Sidney Knott never met Nick Murray after the war but he did knock on his door on one occasion. In 1963 the Knott family set out in their Morris 1000 and caught the ferry from Stranraer to Larne, to begin a 10-day touring holiday. Finding himself near Belfast, Knott decided to surprise his former bomb aimer:

*Nick's house was on the outskirts of the city. I knocked but got no reply. A neighbour said Nick and his family were on holiday in Scotland. We had missed each other. What rotten luck. I put a note through the door, together with a present. As a tribute to his skill in combing those wisps of hair in the 1940s I had found him an 18-inch giant comb!*

*Nick responded with a delightful letter. He wrote of his distress at having missed us: 'Dear me. When I think it is 20 years since you and I shared a Nissen hut and a Lancaster at Bottesford.' He added: 'Thanks a million for the miniature comb – just what I need for my lustrous, flowing curls.' He signed off: 'All the best, my dear, intrepid gunner.'*

*I never answered Nick's letter. I still don't know why. I retain my schoolboy loathing of putting pen to paper. I put it off again and again and, at some point, too much time had elapsed. I deeply regret this failure. I still have Nick's letter and regard it as a treasured possession. Nick died in 1995, aged 79, having enjoyed life to the full after the war.*

Ted Foster kept in touch with Nick Murray. They met when Murray came over for a short holiday. Later, Foster told Knott about this get-together. He said Murray was as irrepressible as ever – a little fellow with a spring in his step, bounding towards his former navigator with a warm smile.

*Nick Murray's first wife died suddenly. Later he met Flo and married again. They were together for 45 years and had two children, David and Helen. Nick's career prospered when he returned to the world of estate agency. He studied hard, did well in examinations and eventually became a Fellow of the Royal Institution of Chartered Surveyors. Subsequently he worked for the Government as a valuer. He lived in Belfast and, following promotion to District Valuer, moved to Coleraine.*

*A lifetime of service: RAF Strike Command made a presentation to Frank Heavery in 1984, marking his retirement from the Civil Service and his long association with the Air Force. Photo: Jennifer Walsh.*

Flo Murray adds: 'Nick enjoyed his work and he continued until he reached 65. We had a good social life. While Nick said little about his life in the RAF he occasionally talked about the crew. Nick was fun-loving, full of wit and a prolific reader. He would read the Bible, an educational book and some light reading every day. He remained keen on reading, walking and gardening in his retirement[5].'

Ted Foster's death occurred a few months after that of Frank Heavery, Knott's 467 Squadron skipper. Heavery passed away on January 4 2002 on his 79th birthday. Foster heard the news from Heavery's daughter, Jennifer, who lives in Ireland. A few days later Foster called Knott, broke the news and told him a strange story relayed by Jennifer. Heavery's wife died just 11 weeks before he passed away. The couple lived in sheltered accommodation. The night before he died the former Lancaster Captain surprised everyone by announcing his intention to go to the local pub and have a drink. Perhaps Heavery wanted to celebrate a life-long love of good beer. Perhaps, in those last few hours, he finally experienced a premonition.

As so often happened in the Air Force, Foster once bumped into Heavery in a Mess bar. This happened during the final weeks of the war in Europe. Foster noticed that the ribbon of the Air Force Cross had joined that of the DFM on Heavery's uniform. The war ended before Heavery could start a second tour. His great skills as a pilot were always in demand and he spent a lengthy period as an OTU instructor on Wellingtons:

> *Frank stayed in the Air Force after the war. He knew nothing else after Cirencester Grammar. Subsequently, he converted to jets. The Daily Mail of November 9 1955 carried a short news item headed: 'Motorist helps crash pilot.' It read: 'An unknown motorist helped a pilot, Pilot Officer Frank Heavery, from the wreckage of a Venom jet at St. Albans yesterday. The motorist drove Heavery, suffering only from cuts, to hospital.'*

During the 1990s, Foster passed Heavery's telephone number to Knott, who called his former pilot. He opened the conversation with: '1942-1943, 467 Squadron, Sidney Knott speaking.' 'Oh my God!' came the reply. When Heavery had collected himself, the two had a long conversation. Knott mentioned the Daily Mail story and Heavery replied: 'That was the day I broke my nose.' Heavery lived in South Wales and, subsequently, Sidney and Joan Knott were on holiday in the area. They agreed to meet but Heavery's wife fell ill and she went on to develop pleurisy. Sadly, the planned meeting between skipper and rear gunner never took place.

*Air Force wedding: Frank and May Heavery on their wedding day in August 1947. Photo: Jennifer Walsh.*

> *Even when his service career ended, Frank bounced back and began working*

*for the Air Force as a civilian. His enthusiasm for the RAF was as strong as ever. He continued as he started, when keenness led an honest man to add a year or so to his age.*

In a study of 1,590 aircrew buried at the war cemeteries of Rheinberg and Durnbach, the average age of the pilots was found to be 24.3 years. One per cent were in the 18-19 age range, seven per cent were 20, 10 per cent were 21 and 27 per cent were 22-24[6].

*Frank went solo on Lancasters in early December 1942, at the age of 19 years and 11 months. At that time I was 21 years and seven months but the skipper always claimed to be just six months younger than me. Certainly, Frank was among the younger Lancaster Captains. His true age was confirmed in the Spring of 2002 by Molly, his sister-in-law. He became 79 on the day he died. I had sent him a Christmas card a couple of weeks before and was not surprised at the lack of response. Frank also hated the chore of correspondence.*

Foster received a rare letter from Heavery in February 1993. It mentioned several operations and recalled the aftermath of a sortie to Nuremberg:

'It had been a moonlit night. Our Flight had lost three out of a strength of nine. I was in the office when Squadron Leader Thiele walked in. He looked at the Crew State Board on the wall and said: 'Wipe out those three crew names and move the rest up to fill the gaps.' And that was that[7].'

Following Heavery's death in 2002 Knott corresponded with his daughter, Jennifer, and obtained a deeper insight into his former skipper's background. Heavery's father had been an Army man, in the 'Ox and Bucks.' He served in India and fought in the Great War. Unfortunately, he contracted malaria in India and the disease eventually resulted in an early death when Frank was still a boy.

*Still flying: Frank Heavery (third from left) with squadron personnel in Malta. Photo: Jennifer Walsh.*

*Malaya: Frank Heavery
pictured during 1960.
Photo: Jennifer Walsh.*

Frank did well at school but there was no money for a university education. His mother wanted him to go into business and Frank reluctantly became a trainee manager with Sainsbury's. He lasted just three weeks, then joined the RAF. The false declaration of his age was discovered just after the outbreak of war and he was sent home to face his mother's displeasure. He had just over a year to wait until his eighteenth birthday and he occupied himself with casual work and the Home Guard.

This young man's life changed forever on August 18 1941, on the grass field of an Elementary Flying Training School at Burnaston. He was taken up for 'air experience.' He flew solo in a Magister just 12 days later. By the end of the following month he had flown his first cross-country solo and had 42 hours 35 minutes in his logbook.

Five years later, after active service with Bomber Command and long spells of instructing, Frank Heavery continued to serve in the peacetime RAF. In the late Summer of 1946 he was with 51 Squadron at Waterbeach, Cambridgeshire, flying regularly to the Far East to deliver aircraft, personnel and cargo. He met his future wife at Waterbeach. May served as a WAAF during the war and had spent much of this period in Fighter Command ops rooms. The couple married in 1947.

Heavery's expertise as a pilot exceeded his skills as a romantic. Jennifer recounts her mother's recollection of her first meeting with Frank, outside the Mess bar at Waterbeach: 'He asked her if she wanted a pint! Talk about love at first sight[8]!'

Jennifer, an only child, was born in 1949. She grew up on a series of RAF bases: 'I never thought much about it and it was only when I was older that I realised that not everyone lived like that! Nevertheless, I wouldn't have swapped my childhood. We lived in some funny places and sometimes it was hard to keep up at school, but RAF families often put their children into boarding school and I didn't like that idea[8].'

Jennifer enjoyed the family's time at Singapore, a three-year posting

*Before the world went to war: Clive Walker, 23, pictured with his mother, Beatrice, when attending a wedding. Photo: Janine Hillary.*

ending in 1962. Flying meant everything to her father and he remained an active pilot until his retirement in 1966. He was content to sacrifice promotion in his efforts to remain flying. Heavery flew at least 21 types during a flying career spanning some 26 years: Anson, Auster, Beaver, Blenheim, Canberra, Dakota, Devon, Dominie, Lancaster, Lancastrian, Magister, Manchester, Martinet, Meteor, Mosquito, Oxford, Pembroke, Varsity, Venom, Wellington and York. Interestingly, only the Venom – the type in which Frank crashed in 1955 – fails to appear in his list of Certificates of Qualification as Pilot.

On retiring from the Air Force Frank Heavery returned in a civilian capacity as a photographic interpreter at RAF Brampton. Later, Frank and his wife retired to Pembrokeshire.

Clive Walker was a very different character to Heavery. He came from a prominent family in the Bolton area. His ancestor, William Walker, was born in Darlington in 1800 and arrived in Bolton at the age of 23. He opened a small shop selling leather items required for the boom in steam-driven machinery. He specialised in the production of leather drive-belts and later opened a tannery at Rose Hill[9].

William Walker retired in 1872 and his two sons then controlled the business of William Walker and Sons. The firm prospered during the First World War and emerged as a major leather producer of national and international significance[9].

On completion of his second tour with 582 Squadron, in early September 1944, Clive Walker was posted to Pathfinder Headquarters at Huntingdon. Later, he returned to flying duties. During his service career he flew 20 types, including Wellingtons, Halifaxes and

Lancasters, together with the Mosquito and Hurricane. Sadly, the whereabouts of Walker's second logbook is unknown. The back of the first logbook, however, has an impressive list of 112 aerodromes at which he personally landed aircraft in the period 1941-45. Walker met his future wife at Huntingdon. Penny Foxwell was a WAAF Cypher Officer specialising in bomb damage interpretation. She was the daughter of the cartoonist Herbert Foxwell, who had found fame with his 'Tiger Tim' annuals.

Walker married Penny in September 1948. The couple returned from their honeymoon, an extended European tour, and established their first home in Heaton, Bolton. It became a family home with the arrival of two daughters, Victoria and Janine. They moved to The White House, Parbold, in 1952 and a third daughter, Lucy, was born in 1954. The three girls recall their father's reluctance to discuss the war years. Janine says: 'He was a very private person and never wanted to talk about his life in the RAF.' She also remembers a childhood incident when the family cat had kittens in a large box lined with her father's old flying jacket: 'When I asked him about his time as a pilot he shut up like a clam. During the next day the kittens were placed in another box, with an old blanket replacing the flying jacket.'

Brian, Clive Walker's elder brother, was killed on active service in Africa during the war. This loss may have heightened Clive's sense of responsibility towards the family firm when he returned from the RAF. William Walker & Sons became a public company in 1946, with Clive as a Director. The change in the company's status was accompanied by a drive to modernise and expand.

One strategy, the production of high quality coloured leathers for

*Wedding day: Clive and Penny married in September 1948. They met at Pathfinder Headquarters, Huntingdon. Photo: Janine Hillary.*

*VIP: Clive Walker hosts a visit to the Bolton tannery by Viscount Montgomery of Alamein. Photo: Janine Hillary.*

shoes and fashion accessories, was facilitated by Clive Walker's involvement in the pre-war recruitment of a German chemist. The latter's research paved the way for a successful and long-running business development programme and an office was opened in Bond Street, London, to promote fashion leathers[10].

Clive Walker travelled extensively on business, pursuing new markets and attending the major trade fairs in centres such as Frankfurt, Florence and Moscow. He had an easy, likeable manner and his languages and well-developed social skills paid dividends. This successful couple also enjoyed a busy social round. They were great party-goers and popular hosts. Lucy says: 'I remember him making cocktails for a big drinks party at home, showing us how to put salt or sugar on the rims of the glasses. He took extreme care to get the mix exactly right[10].'

A vast network of friends and acquaintances embraced the Walker family clan, business colleagues, sporting companions and friends across Europe. Clive Walker's sports were tennis, riding and skiing. He was a motoring enthusiast. Each vehicle received a name and personality (Tarquin, a dark green Jaguar, achieved prominence). He was also fond of gadgets of all kinds and the cine camera was a particular love. He would edit the reels for weekend viewing[10].

His family remained central to his life. Business consumed much of his time and energies but he did his best to keep the weekends free for the family. Favourite holiday destinations included Holy Island, where Clive had spent many happy days as a boy. The Walkers were also pioneering package holiday enthusiasts, enjoying the unspoilt delights of 1950s ski resorts and the Costa del Sol[10].

Yet there was another and heavier dimension to Clive Walker's character. He had few intimate friends – a reflection of his essentially private nature. He had left the RAF with many advantages: a good-looking, debonair man with a proud war record and a reputation for a strong sense of fun. He had a zest for life but his acute sensitivity left him no peace of mind. The great contrast between his happy pre-war experiences in Europe and the horrors of operational life as a bomber pilot undermined his resilience and left him with an unspoken inner sorrow[10].

This fundamental disquiet left him vulnerable to the stress of running businesses under increasing attack from cheap imports and the rise of plastics. No corner of the diverse leather market was untouched. Walker's responsibilities were considerable, including a series of directorships and senior roles within the British Leather Federation and The Leather Institute – now amalgamated into the British Leather Confederation. In 1962 these pressures overwhelmed him and he suffered a nervous breakdown, soon followed by a heart attack whilst on a business trip to Norwich[10].

Clive recovered and the family moved south to Buckinghamshire, to take him away from work pressures and closer to the side of the business he still enjoyed. He relinquished the Managing Directorship of Walker & Martin, became Chairman of Walker & Martin Leathers and concentrated on shoe and fashion leathers. Buyers included Rayne, shoemakers to the Royal Family. Penny was delighted when Sir Edward Rayne, the Chairman, sent a crate of shoes for her to choose from[10].

At the personal level a new social life developed, centred on tennis parties and Clive's passion for encouraging the young riders in his family. The former Pathfinder pilot appeared to move out of the darkness but in December 1965 he suffered a second heart attack. Once again, he had been on a business trip. He was found dead in his car, parked in a Northampton street. He was just 51. The shock of this loss

*Family life: holidays with Penny and the children offered respite from business pressures. Photo: Janine Hillary.*

was profound and remains with the family to this day.

Research associated with this book reunited Sidney Knott with his second tour mid-upper gunner, now living in Nelson. Bill Harrall married Irene in 1955. They have two daughters and one granddaughter and three grandsons. Sidney Knott and Bill Harrall talked together on the telephone in August 2002. They met up a few days later, coming face to face for the first time in 58 years:

*Reunited: Sidney Knott and Bill Harrall (right) pictured at the rear turret of Lancaster 'Just Jane' at East Kirkby, August 9, 2003. Photo: Philippa Redding.*

*It was wonderful to see Bill again. He is amazing – larger than life and still the proud possessor of his own teeth! He had no news of other members of the Walker crew, but quickly sketched out what had happened to him after our 582 Squadron tour had ended. It sounded familiar. He also wanted to continue flying but his request was refused. Having served with the crack 44 Squadron and then the Pathfinders, he was offered a job in an Orderly Room. Bill, in his typical blunt way, told them to 'bugger off'. His insolence earned him a posting to Nairn. He finished up at a Maintenance Unit in North Wales. He became a driver and went from manipulating a turret to wrestling with the steering wheel of one of the RAF's 'Queen Mary' heavy road transporters. He enjoyed service life and did not object to the wait for his demob date, which came up in February 1946.*

*On leaving the service Bill returned to the upholstery trade and High Wycombe – the 'home of furniture-making'. He became a foreman at E. Gomme, the makers of G-Plan furniture. The firm prospered and Bill was promoted to head of cutting and sewing. The family lived at Naphill, only a few miles away from Bomber Command's headquarters at High Wycombe. The company continued to expand and Bill was given the opportunity to establish a new factory in the north of England in 1960. He enjoyed the challenge.*

*Fifty-eight years is a long time. Encounters like that shake you up. When I met Bill again it took me half an hour to adjust. Then we were talking together as though we were young men again, fit and as sharp as you should be in your early twenties!*

# CHAPTER TWENTY-THREE

# *Back in the Turret*

G UNNERS became redundant when the jet bomber arrived in the 1950s. The aircrew category Air Gunner finally disappeared on January 1 1955.

Forty years on, in 1994, a party from the Kent Branch of the Air Gunners' Association visited the old Vickers site at Brooklands, Weybridge. The Weybridge plant, together with other plants at Chester and Blackpool, built 11,460 Wellingtons[1].

The gunners' outing had its origins in events at RAF Lossiemouth during the afternoon of New Year's Eve 1940. A Wellington, R-Robert (N2980) of 20 OTU, was in trouble within 20 minutes of take-off. The starboard engine failed and the pilot struggled to make it back to the airfield in rapidly deteriorating weather. The skipper, Squadron Leader

*A remarkable achievement: Wellington R-Robert at Brooklands Museum. Photo: Mike Talbert.*

Nigel Marwood-Elton, ordered his crew to bale out. Subsequently, he spotted a long expanse of water through a break in the thick cloud. Marwood-Elton decided to ditch.

The ditching went well. Pilot and second pilot had plenty of time to get out and enter the dinghy. They paddled ashore and watched R-Robert settle quietly into the depths of Loch Ness. The sole casualty was Sergeant Fensome, the rear gunner, who died when his parachute malfunctioned.

During 1976 American researchers using sonar located the remains of an aircraft in Loch Ness. Two years later this was confirmed as R-Robert. In 1984, 44 years after the ditching, the Loch Ness Wellington Association was formed with the aim of recovering the Wimpy.

John Rootes, then Chairman of the Kent Branch of the Air Gunners' Association, was at Lossiemouth in 1940 and remembered the ditching in Loch Ness. He arranged an outing for the Branch, to attend a preview before Brooklands Museum opened to the public. The Wimpy was in a sorry state and it was obvious that restoration would be a huge undertaking. Sidney Knott subsequently became Social Secretary of the Kent Branch. He organised a return visit to Brooklands three years later:

> *When the aircraft was raised from the bed of the loch it was found to be minus its rear turret. Subsequently, this was recovered and found to be in good condition. The restoration team had done a remarkable job on the Loch Ness Wimpy.*

*Fifty years on: Sidney Knott and Ted Foster prepare to board 'City of Lincoln'. Photo: Sidney Knott.*

*During this outing to Brooklands I discovered that the Frazer-Nash turret was secured to the airframe by just two bolts. Decades earlier, my young life had depended on the integrity of those slender steel pins.*

*On my first trip to Brooklands I had a chat with a member of the turret restoration team, a Vickers employee and son of a former air gunner. He and his colleagues had tried to obtain plans of the FN.20 turret but had been told that none of the drawings survive. How sad!*

A few years earlier Sidney Knott had enjoyed a closer reunion with the turret. Ted and Mary Foster were holidaying with the Knotts. The weather was fine and it was decided to attend the Biggin Hill air display. This was arranged by Melanie. The Knotts' youngest daughter lived nearby:

*Ted and I watched as City of Lincoln (PA474), the Battle of Britain Memorial Flight Lancaster, arrived at Biggin Hill. The familiar sound of four Merlins drifted across the airfield. We watched as City of Lincoln arrived at an enclosure, where the ground crew rigged safety ropes around her. Ted and I walked up, accompanied by the ladies. Joan – never particularly shy – called to one of the crew. He walked over and was told: 'I have two old codgers here who would love to look over your Lanc. They used to fly in them.'*

*The crew were as eager to speak to us as we were to them. If there was a 'generation gap' it vanished in moments. We were invited to board the aircraft. I made my way towards the front, stopping off at the navigator's station – Ted's territory. Later, we moved to the rear. As we approached the tail spar I noticed something was missing. 'Where's the Elsan?' I was told that the Elsan and much*

*It seems like yesterday: Ted Foster at the rear door of 'City of Lincoln'. Photo: Sidney Knott.*

*else had been removed to save weight.*

In order to prolong the life of this precious Lancaster's airframe the aircraft is kept as light as possible. The objective is to stay within a maximum all-up weight of 47,000 lbs².

*I showed the young crew member how I used to swing feet-first into the turret using straps hanging from the ceiling, but they had been removed long ago. I got carried away and gave my knee one hell of a bang on the superstructure. I went red in the face but never said a word; I don't think he noticed. I sat on the turret seat and chatted away.*

*All aircraft have a distinctive smell – a mixture of dust, rubber, hydraulic oil and a dozen other things. The Lancaster and Wellington had quite different smells and both were pleasant. The Blenheim, on the other hand, had a pungent odour dominated by hydraulic oil. The crews used to joke about this, calling it the 'smell of death'. Given the record of Blenheims on operations it took courage to see the funny side.*

*I looked around the rear turret once more, then clambered out and stiffly edged my way forward. City of Lincoln is a shell. The bare interior contrasted with my memory of a turret and fuselage packed with the equipment necessary to help us stay alive. The aircraft also seemed much smaller than my wartime Lancasters. In my day, the Lancaster was regarded as a huge aircraft. It sat low on the ground – much lower than a modern aircraft – and getting to the front was like walking up a steep hill within a confined space.*

*Ted and I climbed down the short ladder at the Lancaster's rear door. It was wonderful to visit City of Lincoln. We felt honoured to have had the chance.*

# CHAPTER TWENTY-FOUR

# Echoes of the Past

SIDNEY Knott was a founder member of both 467 and 582 squadrons. Sixty years on, his recollections of the first tour are much sharper than his memories of the second. This may reflect the sheer intensity of the first 29 operations. Knott's initial tour was completed at a time when casualties were extremely high:

*In many ways, my second tour – at least in retrospect – was easier. There was a 10-month gap between the tours and the character of Bomber Command's campaign (and the war in general) changed dramatically over that period. Bomber Command steadily gained strength and the casualty rate declined (although remaining at a high level). There was still plenty of stress but the atmosphere on 582 Squadron was different. The bonds between the first crew were closer as we were all sergeants. The second crew consisted of four officers and three NCOs who lived and messed apart. Many second tour trips were short and lower fatigue levels made a big difference, even during the hectic month of July 1944.*

Looking back across 60 years Knott's memories of operational flying

*The real meaning of survival: the families of many members of the Heavery and Walker crews, pictured with East Kirkby's Lancaster in August 2003, 60 years after the first tour of operations. Photo: Philippa Redding.*

remain fresh and his experiences live clearly in his mind:

> *It is strange, when over 80, to have such sharp memories of being so young.*
> *I wonder if today's worldly-wise young men would be prepared to accept such*
> *terrible risks? We were so different – an innocent, unquestioning generation.*
>
> *In the background, at all times, were the Germans. They were extremely fierce*
> *opponents. Today, however, I would be happy to sit down and have a beer with*
> *a former German nightfighter pilot. The RAF had great respect for the GAF*
> *and vice versa. There were many reports (some subsequently confirmed) of shot-*
> *down British aircrew being attacked and even lynched by civilians in heavily*
> *bombed German towns. I can understand the power of such bitter emotion. I felt*
> *it myself, perhaps to a lesser degree, when I sat on the cliff top with my father*
> *in 1940 and watched over 100 German bombers come in over the sea and fly*
> *along the Thames to London. I felt elation when one bomber was hit and went*
> *down over Thorpe Bay. I always thought it would be very bad news to bale out*
> *over Berlin or a Ruhr city. Perhaps it is time to push aside such dark thoughts,*
> *once and for all.*

Francis Mason, in *The Avro Lancaster*, observed: '... the tragedy of the
Allied bombing was that it was never possible at 20,000 ft on a dark night
to distinguish the guilty from the innocent[1].'

The human dimension of bombing came home to Knott in the
unlikely setting of Bridgnorth Castle. On a Sunday outing during
2001, Sidney and Joan were taking a stroll along the castle walls. The
visibility was good, with fine views down to the lower area of the town
and the Severn beyond:

> *Joan wanted a rest and she found a seat. I walked forward to the parapet*
> *and took in the view. A woman sat down next to Joan and struck up a*
> *conversation while her husband joined me, looking out over the wall. He told*
> *me he lived locally and began to point out how far the river could spread in*
> *flood conditions.*
>
> *His wife told Joan she was German and that she had met her husband*
> *during his National Service in the BAOR (British Army of the Rhine). Joan*
> *asked where she was from. The response – 'Essen' – produced an involuntary*
> *'Oh!' She saw something in Joan's face and a question followed: 'Do you know*
> *Essen?' Joan explained that I had been in the Air Force during the war.*
>
> *The German woman then told her story. As a young girl in Essen she had*
> *been bombed out no less than six times. These events belonged to a different life;*
> *she had lived in England for many years and now regarded the UK as her*
> *home. Driving away from Bridgnorth, Joan recounted the conversation. Rather*
> *facetiously, I said I had nothing to do with at least two of the six incidents, as I*
> *went to Essen on just the four occasions.*
>
> *Later, I turned things over in my mind. This is a reminder, if one is needed,*
> *that bombing cities means bombing people. Yet, 60 years on, my confidence in*
> *the justification for the mass bombing of Germany remains unshaken. Area*
> *bombing made an important contribution to the defeat of Nazi Germany, a state*
> *founded on the imposition of terror. It helped free Europe from enslavement by*

*For our children and grandchildren: Sidney and Joan Knott, pictured in 1992, on the occasion of Joan's seventieth birthday. The grandchildren (from left to right, standing) are: Sarah, Christopher, Tim and Hannah. Sitting are Karen (left) and Helen. Photo: Sidney Knott.*

*a regime of unbridled evil. It helped free the German people from this evil. As a result, Germany today is part of a Europe characterised by democracy, rather than the concentration camp.*

*The critics of area bombing tend to ignore the facts. The Germans pioneered area bombing. The people living in German cities produced the munitions required to defeat the free world and deliver victory for the 'Master Race'. Germany was so strong that its eventual defeat involved a long and costly battle of attrition. In the east the great tank battles fatally weakened the German army. In the west, round-the-clock bombing tied down the human and other resources which would otherwise have filled out both front lines defending Germany. In addition, the bombing made weapons production much more difficult. German morale, nevertheless, remained firm throughout. The woman we met in Bridgnorth had been bombed out six times but her family stayed in Essen! Yet the bombing continued and helped to grind down the German capacity to wage war. We attacked docks, rail yards, munitions plants and, of course, the towns and cities where the factories were located and the workers lived.*

Bomber Command had to operate at night for most of the war in order to survive. It lacked the ability to engage in precision bombing. The choice was between making the entire city the target (area bombing) or ending the bombing and, in effect, relinquishing Britain's only offensive capability in the war against Germany. As John Terraine points out, in the context of total war this 'meant no choice at all'[2].

Bomber Command suffered heavy casualties throughout the war. While the casualty rate fell (to just over one per cent) in the final six months of the war, 649 bombers failed to return in that period[3]. In total, around 15,000 young men died in Lancasters. They represent around one quarter of Bomber Command's war dead[4]. Naturally, there are conflicting views as to whether the damage done was worth the sacrifice of many thousands of young lives:

> *In my own mind I am quite sure their sacrifice shortened the war. At the individual level, however, every young man lost was some mother's son. They died for us, our children and grandchildren. I was very lucky to survive, to enjoy 60 years of tomorrows – a future denied to so many of my friends.*

> *At the same time it is impossible (at least, until very recently) to fight a war without incurring heavy losses. Despite the human cost we retained confidence in our leaders and Butch Harris in particular. He was respected. He faced many very difficult decisions, night after night, and carried an immense burden.*

Harris, as AOC Bomber Command, provided a convenient focus for post-war criticism of the bombing campaign. His critics are fond of discussing the 'immorality' of area bombing:

> *All acts of war are immoral. It is pointless to single out an element of war and describe it as 'more immoral' than any other. It is important to remember that Nazi Germany wanted war. Most critics of Harris and Bomber Command were not around at the time. It is important to understand that we were within a hair's breadth of losing the war in May 1940. Our leaders were poor and our military capability virtually non-existent. Britain was about to tumble into the abyss and only the width of the English Channel and Fighter Command kept us free. Rather than discuss immorality (within a free society bought by the lives of too many of my contemporaries), I would rather talk about the moral duty – clear to us at the time – to crush Nazi Germany. I never heard any doubts expressed over the bombing of Germany.*

James Hampton, in his fine book *Selected for Aircrew*, makes the point: 'During the war, the aims and execution of the strategic bomber offensive against Germany had seemed clear and uncomplicated. They had enjoyed the fullest support and approval of almost every member of the population from the Prime Minister downwards. However, in the post-war years, with the country safely delivered from the prospect of defeat and the imposition of an unspeakable tyranny, Bomber Command became a subject of much controversy. Operations of enormous significance and acts of great courage and high endeavour were trivialised and denigrated[5].'

The frontline crews had no illusions about area bombing; to suggest otherwise would insult their intelligence. WAAF Officer Marie Cooper recalled that one 467 Squadron officer caused a stir when he thumped the table and declared that, tonight, he wanted 30,000 less women and children in Berlin. 'You understand? Thirty thousand Germans less! So get out and do it!'

Those words were frozen in Marie's memory: 'There was, after an initial moment of silence, an audible gasp and murmuring, but the briefing continued. After it, however, a delegation protested against his ever being allowed to add his bit to briefings in the future!

'This is interesting because, of course, this was in fact what the aircrew were being asked to do – kill women and children. But, in order to do this, one half or, perhaps, all of their minds had to turn it into a successful operation with aiming point photographs, a cull of enemy fighters and a safe return to base. The object of the exercise was to defeat Germany, which did indeed include killing non-combatant civilians, as they were doing to us, but to make the killing of women and children the primary directive was very bad taste, to say the least[6].'

Area bombing was the only offensive option open to Britain. This was recognised as early as July 8, 1940, when newly-installed Prime Minister Winston Churchill wrote to Lord Beaverbrook, Minister for Aircraft Production: 'When I look round to see how we can win the war, I see that there is only one sure path. We have no continental army which can defeat German military power. The blockade is broken and Hitler has Asia and probably Africa to draw on. Should he be repulsed here or not try invasion, he will probably recoil eastwards and we will have nothing to stop him. But there is one sure way that will bring him back and bring him down, and that is an absolutely devastating, exterminating attack by very heavy bombers against the Nazi homeland[7].'

The mass bombing of Germany produced a major victory for the Allies. The point was acknowledged by Albert Speer, Hitler's Armaments Minister, who described the bombing offensive as Germany's greatest lost battle. As Overy points out (*Bomber Command 1939-45*): 'The critical question is not so much 'What did bombing do to Germany?' but 'What could Germany have achieved if there had been no bombing?'[8].'

The air defence of Germany absorbed around one million service personnel and 10,000 88mm flak guns – weapons which might otherwise have paralysed the great land offensives, had they been deployed in the anti-tank role[9]. In the critical year of 1944, defending the German home front from strategic bombing absorbed 30 per cent of all artillery produced, 20 per cent of heavy shells, 33 per cent of the optical industry's production of sights and 50 per cent of Germany's entire electro-technical output[10]. In contrast, the bombing offensive accounted for just seven per cent of Britain's war effort[11]. What other option could have done such damage to Germany for less than 10 per cent of the war effort?

Harris may have been a ruthless, relentless pursuer of area bombing strategy, but he was not its architect. In 1941 – before Harris became AOC Bomber Command – the Air Staff proposed an expansion of Bomber Command to a force of 4,000 heavy bombers. This ambition was beyond reach. Bomber Command achieved a maximum strength of 1,994 operational heavy aircraft in May 1945. The total stood at 654 when Sidney Knott joined 467 Squadron for his first tour[12].

In a memorandum from the Chiefs of Staff to Churchill it was argued early on that the bombing offensive should be on the heaviest possible scale. The only limits to its size should be those imposed by operational difficulties in the UK. The Chiefs of Staff declared: 'As our forces increase, we intend to pass to a planned attack on civilian morale with the intensity and continuity which are essential if a final breakdown is to be produced.' The memorandum continued: 'We have every reason to be confident that if we can expand our forces in accordance with our present programme, and if possible beyond it, that effect will be shattering[13].'

Sidney Knott has no illusions about the treatment of Harris after the war:

> *It was a matter of politics. The Russians pressed Churchill, demanding air attacks on the eastern cities. Bomber Command gave them Dresden. Harris was pressed to raid the city. Churchill then disowned Harris. He wasn't the first politician, or the last, to do a U-turn. I have always admired Churchill but, in the final analysis, he was a politician to the core. Surprisingly, Harris – despite his close relationship with Churchill – appears to have overlooked this fact. Perhaps his direct contact with Churchill blinded him to political realities? Perhaps the apparent depth of Churchill's support, including his comment after the 1942 '1,000 raid' against Cologne, clouded Harris' judgement?*

After Cologne, the Prime Minister told Harris: 'This proof of the growing power of the British bomber force is also the herald of what Germany will receive, city by city, from now on[14].'

In considering the human cost of area bombing, one must also consider the overriding moral duty to defeat the obscenity of Nazi Germany. In the words of a prominent politician of today, this defeat '...gave humanity a future. Almost everything we value about our life today – freedom, democracy, prosperity, let alone an existence without the constant fear of the firing squad, the death camp and the torture chamber – exists only because Hitler was crushed[15].'

The Victory Edition of *Royal Air Force Journal*, published in May 1945, featured a statement attributed to Walter Darre, one of Hitler's more minor ministers, responsible for agriculture and much more – including active participation in the establishment of the SS 'Race and Resettlement Office'. The comments were made in April 1942 and amount to a declaration of intent following the defeat of Britain: 'As soon as we beat England we shall make an end of you Englishmen once and for all. Able-bodied men and women will be exported as slaves to the Continent. The old and weak will be exterminated. All men remaining in Britain as slaves will be sterilised; a million or two of the young women of the Nordic type will be segregated in a number of stud farms where, with the assistance of picked German sires, during a period of 10 or 12 years, they will produce annually a series of Nordic infants to be brought up in every way as Germans. These infants will form the future population of Britain. They will be partially educated in Germany and only those who fully satisfy the Nazis' requirements will be allowed to return to Britain and take up permanent residence. The rest will be sterilised and sent to join slave

*The warmth of comradeship: members of the Kent Branch of the Air Gunners' Association beside 'City of Lincoln', during one of the Lancaster's visits to Manston. Standing (second from the left) is Ken Apps, who baled out from the rear door of his Lancaster and became a prisoner of war. Standing (third from left) is Ron Wilson, from Margate, who completed a tour on Stirlings. During a rough trip one of his crew was fatally wounded. Wilson got him to the rest-bed and comforted him. Standing (fifth from left) is the late Jasper Matthews, from the Dover area, who served with a Special Duties Squadron and then became a Pathfinder. Between Jasper and Sidney Knott (standing, far right) is George Bishop, from Canterbury, who completed a Lancaster tour and then became an airfield controller. Kneeling, far left, is Tom Lockett GM, now living in Hampshire, who spent 30 years in the Police after service in Bomber Command. Next to Tom is the late John Rootes DFM, from Margate, a long-standing Chairman of the Kent Branch. Photo: Sidney Knott.*

gangs in Germany. Thus, in a generation or two, the British will disappear.'

Many Bomber Command crews developed bonds stronger than those existing within their own families. These relationships were broken by death or at the end of the tour, when the crews dispersed. With the end of the war, however, attitudes changed:

*In the immediate post-war period there was a great sense of wanting to get on with life. Few were prepared to dwell on the past. There was a baby boom. Ex-servicemen were pre-occupied with their young families and the challenge of making a living. Things were hard for many years. Many found their lingering memories of war unsettling – a reminder of how close they came to losing the future. When those young families grew up and the standard of living improved, however, there was the time and inclination to look back.*

The expansion of the Air Gunners' Association was largely the result of the efforts of former gunner Freddie Gill, then a Sergeant in the Metropolitan Police:

*The London Association ticked along for years, but it wasn't until the early 1970s that attitudes changed and more former aircrew felt the need to revisit the past and make contact with wartime friends. The Association's branches began to multiply; membership was open to any gunner who had earned his brevet.*

*I enjoyed many years of warm comradeship as a member of the Kent Branch of the Air Gunners' Association. In our heyday the Kent Branch annual dinner in Canterbury was attended by around 150, including, of course, the ladies. At our last Christmas dinner we were down to 20. The Association's National Committee took the tough decision in 2002 to close in the Spring of 2003. With such an elderly membership closure was inevitable,*

*although some local branches soldier on, including the Kent Branch.*

Many organisations still provide a framework for Bomber Command veterans to come together and draw strength from each other. They include the Royal Air Force Association, the Aircrew Association, the Bomber Command Association, the Pathfinder Association and the many squadron associations.

In 2001 Sidney and Joan Knott moved from the Kent village of Ash to a small community near Stoke-on-Trent. They now live close to Jean, their eldest daughter. The nearest branch of the Air Gunners' Association was some distance away, in West Bromwich. For this reason, Sidney Knott joined his local Aircrew Association branch. In 2003 he attended his first 467/463 Squadrons Association gathering, held at Waddington on ANZAC Day.

Decades have slipped by since the end of the war and Sidney Knott and other veterans have seen the very fabric of British society change almost beyond recognition:

> *The greatest change is in the degree of personal wealth. People today have an extraordinary level of disposable income. When the war in Europe ended I owned nothing other than an ill-fitting demob suit. I think it is wrong, however, to go through life expecting people to express constant gratitude for wartime sacrifices. At the same time, Remembrance Sunday should continue*

*Guests of the station: members of the Kent Branch of the Air Gunners' Association in the Mess bar at RAF Manston, pictured with the Station Commander. Immediately behind the Station Commander is Len Whitehead, who flew to Berlin on his first operation, which was only his second flight at night. Whitehead was a 'spare bod'. His Captain on that operation was John Williams, who later flew with 617 Squadron and, subsequently, became vicar of St Mary the virgin, Rye. Pictured front, far left, is the late Mike Henry DFC, author of the book Air Gunner. Photo: Sidney Knott.*

*Runnymede: Sidney Knott in a reflective mood at the RAF Memorial to the missing – those with no known grave. Photo: Joan Whitehead.*

*to be observed. The young men who died should not be forgotten.*

*Occasionally, on an 'off day', I find myself thinking that too much freedom is a curse. Perhaps, after our experience of war, hardship and loss, we gave our children and grandchildren too much freedom. There is a tremendous gulf between today's 21-year-old and the Lancaster Captain in the Mess bar at Bottesford in 1943. What would today's young man and Sergeant Vine have in common? The biggest difference, surely, was the huge weight of responsibility on Vine's shoulders.*

*Those wartime experiences are ancient history to our grandchildren but just an eyeblink away to us. Sixty years sounds like a long time yet, in a very real sense, that wartime world still exists – hidden away in a corner of the mind. I returned to Bottesford long after the war. I had memories of a bustling community of over 2,000 people. In their absence, it is a deserted and forlorn place. One or two buildings still stand. I couldn't see the runways from the road but large sections of concrete perimeter track were visible. Only the thin, patchy grass marks the passing of the bombers and my absent friends.*

## RUNNYMEDE

*Yes, sorrow lives at Runnymede,*
*Its granite walls to hold*
*So many dreams that were not dreamed,*
*So many loves untold;*
*But love is there for each mother's son*
*Whose name doth hold his place*
*On these cold stones,*
*And that love you will find*
*Bestows serenity and peace*
*That's restful and most kind*
*To those who mourn*

# 467 Squadron Personalities

*Roll of Honour: 467 Squadron:*

A TOTAL of 1,814 aircrew operated with 467 Squadron. The youngest was 17 and the average age was around 24 years. The scale of human loss was enormous: one source (Slack/Glynne-Owen) states that 591 squadron aircrew (32.6%) were killed in action and 155 have no known grave.

The squadron had seven commanders (including a temporary CO killed in action within 48 hours of Cosme Gomm's death). In the period from establishment on November 7 1942 to disbandment in 1945 five of the squadron's seven COs were killed in action.

Sidney Knott's recollections of 467 Squadron Lancaster Captains include the following, who were killed in action:

Sergeant Kenneth R Aicken, 25, no known grave. (commemorated at Runnymede, Panel 199)

Pilot Officer Vernon Byers, 32, no known grave. (Runnymede, Panel 175)

Flight Lieutenant John M Desmond, 24, Reichwald Forest War Cemetery. (Grave 22-E-9/13)

Wing Commander Cosme L Gomm, DSO, DFC, 30, Calvados St. Desir War Cemetery. (Grave 7-G-C-6)

Squadron Leader Donald C MacKenzie, DFC, 21, Rheinberg War Cemetery. (Grave 3-A-3/7)

Sergeant Kevin E Mahoney, 21, Hanover War Cemetery. (Grave 8-J-8/14)

Pilot Officer Graeme S Mant, 26, Durnbach War Cemetery. (Grave 8-F-20)

Flight Lieutenant James B Michie, 31, no known grave. (Runnymede, Panel 120)

Squadron Leader Arthur M. Paape, DFC and Bar, 24, Reichwald Forest War Cemetery. (Grave 10-E-1)

Flight Sergeant John M Parsons, 29, Schoonselhof Cemetery, Wilrijk, Antwerp. (Grave ii-G-4)

Squadron Leader Alfred S Raphael, DFC, 27, no known grave. (Runnymede, Panel 119)

Flight Sergeant Maxwell P Stewart, 26, Durnbach War Cemetery. (Grave 11-G-25/28)

Sergeant Raymond C Stuart, 21, Poix-de-la-Somme Church, France. (Grave E-15)

Sergeant Henry B Vine, no known grave. (Runnymede, Panel 168)

Pilot Officer Albert M Wark, DFC, no known grave. (Runnymede, Panel 178)

Flight Sergeant Basil F Wilmot, 28, no known grave. (Runnymede, Panel 194)

*Survivors: 467 Squadron*

The surviving aircrew of 467 Squadron included 122 prisoners of war and 27 evaders[1]. Lancaster Captains surviving their tours with 467 and recalled by Sidney Knott include:

Sergeant A C Ball

Flight Sergeant John Binnie, DFM (prisoner of war)

Flying Officer J W Cairney, DFM

Squadron Leader John Good, DFC and Bar

Squadron Leader David Green, DSO, DFC

Flight Sergeant Brian Howie, DFM

Flight Lieutenant Bill Manifold, DFC and Bar

Pilot Officer J H Smith

Squadron Leader Keith Sinclair, DFC

Squadron Leader Keith Thiele, DSO, DFC and Bar

Pilot Officer George Tillotsen, DFC

Sergeant B.C. Wilson (prisoner of war)

Flying Officer W.L. Wilson, DFC

*Failed to Return:*

*Wing Commander Cosme Gomm, DSO, DFC*

A number of popular leaders of the highest quality were amongst those who died. They included Wing Commander Cosme Gomm, DSO, DFC, 467 Squadron's first Commanding Officer. He was killed in action on the night of August 15/16 1943. He was the skipper of Y-Yankee (ED998) and failed to return from an attack on Milan[2].

Cosme Gomm was born in 1913 in Curitiba, an industrial town in Parana State, Brazil. The Royal Air Force was his life. He was granted a Short Service Commission only a week before his twentieth birthday, on

November 7 1933. He was confirmed in the rank of Pilot Officer on New Year's Day 1935 and became a Flight Lieutenant in August 1938. Gomm's war began with a posting to 77 Squadron at Driffield. Flying Whitleys, his first tour of 33 sorties ended in April 1941 – the month his DFC was gazetted. During a raid on Bordeaux on December 27 1940 Gomm's Whitley was damaged over the target, resulting in a crash-landing at Abingdon. There were no crew casualties[3].

On completing the tour Gomm was posted to a nightfighter squadron equipped with Beaufighters and commanded by John Cunningham. Cosme Gomm flew 19 operational patrols and was credited with 2½ victories, involving a Ju88 and two He111s[3].

On November 7 1942, his 29th birthday, Gomm arrived at Scampton with orders to form 467 Squadron RAAF. The new squadron moved to Bottesford just over two weeks later. Gomm's second bomber tour opened on the night of January 16/17 1943 with a raid on Berlin. The crew completed their eighteenth operation with 467 Squadron on the night of May 23/24. This was an attack on Dortmund; they were coned by searchlights for six minutes[3].

On June 11 1943 Wing Commander Gomm's DSO was gazetted. The citation concluded:

> 'His enthusiasm, energy and keenness, tempered with a quiet, efficient and cheerful personality, have created an exceptional spirit of keenness and determination in the Squadron.
>
> On operations, he has always displayed exceptional courage and determination and has consistently brought back photographs of the target area.
>
> Wing Commander Gomm, through his personal example and high qualities of leadership, has proved himself to be an inspiration to his squadron and has not only won the respect and admiration of all his men, but through his magnificent efforts has built up a Lancaster Squadron which is probably second to none.'

Gomm's tour continued with a raid on Friedrichshafen (Operation Bellicose) in Y-Yankee, during the night of June 20/21. After bombing the target Gomm was among those who flew on to Algeria, where his Lancaster was turned round. The crew bombed La Spezia on the way home, in the first of the shuttle raids[3].

The Friedrichshafen attack was made by 60 aircraft. The raid was directed at the Zeppelin Works on the shores of Lake Constance. At that time it was a major production centre for the Würzburg radars used to control German nightfighters. The raid, while involving a relatively small force of Lancasters, called for the early use of the Master Bomber technique. Group Captain Leonard Slee, DSO, performed this role until his aircraft developed engine trouble. His deputy, Cosme Gomm, took over. The attack was delivered in bright moonlight and the intention was to bomb from heights of between 5,000 ft and 10,000 ft, but the flak was very heavy and Gomm instructed the force to add 5,000 ft to their heights. Stronger winds at the higher altitudes caused problems but around 10 per cent of the bombs hit the relatively small target. There were no losses on this raid and no casualties among the 52 Lancasters going on to North

Africa and, subsequently, bombing La Spezia on the return[4].

The return of Gomm's crew to England marked the completion of 20 operations. Second tours typically consisted of 20 trips and Gomm was on his third (including the second tour, on nightfighters). Yet the Squadron Commander continued his operational flying. There were two sorties to Hamburg in July, followed by a raid against Genoa on August 7/8. One week later, on Sunday August 15, the Lancaster Gomm had taken to North Africa and back (Y-Yankee) was bombed up for the Milan raid. This city was subjected to a series of three attacks within the space of a few days. A total of 199 Lancasters were readied for the latest raid. Highly concentrated bombing was achieved but Gomm's aircraft was among the seven casualties that night[5].

Some aircraft ran into accurate flak around Chartres but the nightfighters inflicted most of the losses. They fell among the bombers as they flew across occupied France. Y-Yankee probably fell victim to a nightfighter. The aircraft blew up in mid-air and wreckage landed over an area of two square miles. Much of the debris fell to earth near the village of Beaumont, Normandy. The youngest crew member, 20-year-old flight engineer Sergeant James Lee, survived and parachuted to safety. The chute had been damaged and he fell fast, but had the luck to land on a hayrick. He suffered burns and spent the rest of the war in captivity[6].

Gomm's death was a severe blow to the squadron and was catastrophic at the personal level for Section Officer Paula Fisher, a member of the Intelligence Section at Bottesford. Paula was well-known, often debriefing crews returning from sorties. She and Gomm had formed a relationship. Paula was devastated by his death but the Air Force was unmoved. She was told to pull herself together. Subsequently, she was posted from Bottesford[3].

After the war Gomm's mother presented a Book of Citations to 467 Squadron. This book, given in memory of her son, was presented to the Australian War Memorial, Canberra[3].

### Squadron Leader A M Paape, DFC and Bar

Paape was another very popular leader. He and his crew joined the squadron on its formation in November 1942. They went missing on April 3/4 1943 during a raid on Essen. It was the eighteenth operation of Paape's second tour. Sidney Knott recalls:

*This Squadron Leader commanded B Flight. He was known affectionately as 'First Back' Paape, as he always seemed to be the first to return from a raid. There were many jokes about how he did this, but I suspect the sheer efficiency and experience of this crew had much to do with it. Paape's positive influence spread throughout the squadron.*

The respect accorded to Paape acknowledged his selection of tough targets for his own operations. His sorties included four trips to Berlin, two to Nuremberg and three to Essen – including the last, when he failed to return. His Lancaster was among the 21 aircraft missing that night (24 were later struck off charge). Paape's crew died with him: Sergeant LT Fulcher,

RCAF (flight engineer), Flying Officer H North (navigator), Sergeant DJR Robinson (bomb aimer), Flying Officer T Dring, DFC (wireless operator) and gunners Sergeant GR Johnson and Flying Officer JM Stewart, AFM. They were in Lancaster ED524. Frank Heavery had taken this aircraft to St. Nazaire and Berlin in late February/early March 1943[3].

### Sergeant K R Aicken

Ken Aicken was a New Zealander. He and his comrades joined 467 Squadron on its formation and they became the second crew to fail to return. Their tour opened in early January 1943 with a mining operation, followed by two trips to Essen and one to Berlin on the night of January 16/17. They were on the squadron Battle Order for the following night. Once again Berlin was the target and their Lancaster (N-Nuts: W4378) failed to return on this, their fifth operation[3].

### Pilot Officer A V M Byers

Vernon Byers and his crew joined 467 Squadron on February 5 1943. They made only three sorties before being posted to 617 Squadron (in place of Heavery's crew) the following month. Byers failed to return from the Dams Raid[3].

### Flight Lieutenant J M Desmond

John Desmond was an Australian. He and his crew reported to 467 Squadron on its formation in November 1942. Many of the toughest German targets were added to their logbooks, including Duisburg (four trips) and Essen (three trips). A number of 467 Squadron Lancaster Captains flew as second dicky with Desmond, to gain an introduction to operations. They included Sergeant Stuart, who died with his crew on April 16/17 during the first of two attacks on Pilsen.

Flight Lieutenant Desmond's twenty-second operation was a return to Essen. It was one trip too many. Until the night of May 27/28 ED504 had been lucky for Desmond's crew; the last trip was their sixteenth in this Lancaster[3].

### Squadron Leader D C MacKenzie, DFC

Don 'Mac' MacKenzie joined 467 Squadron on its formation and became an extremely popular B Flight Commander. He died on the raid against Düsseldorf on the night of June 11/12 1943. There were no survivors. This loss was particularly tragic. The crew were killed very close to the completion of the tour, having survived sorties to many of the most heavily defended German targets. They had made four trips to Duisburg, three each to Essen and Berlin and two to Hamburg. They failed to return from their second sortie to Düsseldorf. An eighth crew member also died. He was Squadron Leader Ambrose, the newly-appointed Commander of C Flight, who flew as second dicky with MacKenzie that night. Their Lancaster was W4983 – the first B.III Lancaster built. It was manufactured at

Metropolitan Vickers in September 1942[3].

### Sergeant K E Mahoney

Kevin Mahoney was an Australian. He and his crew arrived at Bottesford on April 10 1943. They lasted barely one month. Sergeant Mahoney joined Heavery and crew for his first operational flight. He was second dicky when Heavery took Lancaster ED772 on the nine hours 50 minutes marathon to La Spezia on the night of April 13/14. He also flew as second dicky on the Stettin raid a few days later. Mahoney's crew failed to return from the May 13/14 Pilsen raid, their sixth operation[3].

### Pilot Officer G S Mant

Mant's crew were posted to 467 on the squadron's formation in early November 1942. Mant was commissioned shortly afterwards. They failed to return on the night of March 11/12 1943. They had taken Lancaster ED523 on their tenth sortie, with Stuttgart as the target. Heavery had taken this Lancaster on three operations during February, to Lorient, Nuremberg and Cologne. Mant's crew usually took O-Orange (ED530). Byers – lost on the Dams Raid – flew as second dicky with Mant on a trip to St. Nazaire two weeks before the Stuttgart raid[3].

### Flight Lieutenant J B Michie

The fate of Michie and his crew paralleled that of Mant. They joined 467 on its formation and failed to return from their tenth operation. Michie's crew flew extensively in January–February 1943, visiting Essen three times and Berlin twice. They went missing in Lancaster ED525 on the night of February 19/20, during a raid on Wilhelmshaven[3]. Two of the five aircraft dispatched by the squadron that night failed to return.

### Flight Sergeant J M Parsons

Parsons flew as second pilot with Heavery to Essen on April 3/4 1943. He and his crew failed to return from their tenth operation, a raid on Düsseldorf on the night of May 25/26. Three of the crew died that night in ED768. They were shot down by flak near Antwerp (Flak Regiment 295). The kill was disputed by a nightfighter pilot who claimed to have fired on ED768. He may well have after the Lancaster was struck by flak. The four survivors from this crew became prisoners of war: Sergeants J J Vaulkhard, JP Egan, FJ Selman and RA Hunt[3]. The three killed in action were Parsons, together with Flight Sergeant B Spencer and Sergeant T Chalmers.

### Squadron Leader A S Raphael, DFC

Raphael and crew arrived at Bottesford on April 19 1943. They were already operational and Raphael made no second dicky trip. The crew flew three sorties at the end of April, six in May and continued to operate successfully into August. They failed to return from the

Peenemünde attack on the night of August 17/18 (their nineteenth operation). The Peenemünde attack saw the first use by the Germans of the new Schräge Musik upward-firing cannons. Raphael may have been one of the first victims, as two Schräge Musik-equipped nightfighters shot down six of the 40 aircraft lost that night. When Raphael died in the Peenemünde raid he had been temporary Commanding Officer of 467 Squadron for barely 48 hours, following Cosme Gomm's death in the Milan attack[3]. Wing Commander J R Balmer, DFC, OBE, took command of 467 Squadron the following day, August 19 1943. John Balmer RAAF was killed in action on May 11/12 1944, in an attack on the military camp at Bourg-Léopold. His Lancaster, LL792, was shot down by a nightfighter and was one of five that failed to return from this raid. Balmer was 33 when he died[1].

### Flight Sergeant M P Stewart

Stewart was an Australian. He and his crew joined 467 Squadron on its formation. Sortie thirteen was unlucky for them. They took off in ED526 to raid Nuremberg on February 25 1943. The aircraft failed to return and they were all listed killed in action. In six weeks of operations their sorties included two trips each to Berlin, Essen, Düsseldorf and Wilhelmshaven[3].

### Sergeant R C Stuart

Raymond Stuart's crew were posted to 467 Squadron in February 1943. They joined C Flight on its formation at the end of March. All seven men died on the night of April 16/17, during the first of the Pilsen attacks. It was their sixth operation[3].

### Sergeant H B Vine

Sergeant Vine was posted to 467 Squadron in January 1943. He was not required to make a trip as second dicky and his crew's first operation was a Gardening mining sortie on the night of January 12/13. They made eight sorties in all, including four to Lorient. The eighth trip, to Wilhelmshaven in ED529, was flown on the night of February 19/20 and proved to be the last. Their aircraft failed to return and there were no survivors[3]. The Heavery and Vine crews were very close. ED529 was one of two 467 Squadron Lancasters missing that night (the other was captained by Michie).

### Pilot Officer A M Wark, DFC

It appears Wark and his crew were experienced when they joined 467 Squadron just after its formation, as there was no second dicky trip. This crew became the squadron's first casualties. They took ED367 on a mining sortie on January 2/3 1943. A few days later, on January 8/9, they took the same aircraft to Duisburg and failed to return. All seven were killed in action[3]. Their aircraft was lost without trace.

*Flight Sergeant B F Wilmot*

Freddie Wilmot was an Australian. He and his crew were posted to 467 Squadron in April 1943. Their sorties were flown against tough targets: Duisburg (twice), Düsseldorf, Pilsen, Dortmund, Essen and Wuppertal. Their last sortie was flown in D-Dog (ED304) on June 11/12 – the second trip to Düsseldorf. Their aircraft failed to return and there were no survivors[3].

## AMONG THE SURVIVORS

*Sergeant A C Ball*

Ball was a 467 Squadron founder member. His sorties included four trips to Duisburg, three each to Berlin and Lorient and two to Essen. This crew completed their tour and Ball was posted to 17 OTU on June 12 1943[3]. Sidney Knott had moved to Silverstone/Turweston only a few days earlier. Knott flew with Ball on several exercises in Wellingtons and as drogue operator in a Martinet.

*Flight Sergeant J E Binnie, DFM*

John Binnie and crew arrived at Bottesford on April 25 1943. He made an immediate start, flying as second pilot with Heavery to Duisburg on April 26/27. This crew's eighth operation was flown to Bochum in ED695 – an aircraft familiar to Heavery's crew, who had taken it to Berlin, Essen, Stettin and Duisburg in the March–April period. During the Bochum trip they were attacked twice by a nightfighter. The crew fought off the attacks but the rear turret was crippled and the fuselage and starboard wing damaged. Binnie elected to press on and bomb the target. The crew returned safely, landing back at Bottesford with a flat tyre. Binnie received the DFM in recognition of his determination to complete the sortie. The crew's luck then ran out. They took ED737 to Cologne on June 16/17. Once again, this aircraft had been flown on ops by Heavery's crew, on a sortie to Kiel in early April. The Lancaster failed to return from Cologne. Binnie survived, together with two others. The rest of his crew died that night, together with a second pilot, Flying Officer A Smith[3].

*Flying Officer J W Cairney, DFM*

Cairney and crew reported to Bottesford in December 1942. They flew 28 operations, including four trips to Duisburg and three each to Essen and Berlin. Cairney was posted to 17 OTU on June 12 1943 on completion of the tour[3]. The Cairney, Ball and Heavery crews were close. They were RAF, joined 467 Squadron in its formative weeks, survived their tours and were then posted to 17 OTU. Cairney's period with 467 Squadron was not without incident. During a practice bombing exercise he had been forced to ditch in shallow water, in the Wash.

*Squadron Leader J Good, DFC and Bar*

Johnny Good was an Australian. He and his crew were posted to 467 Squadron in February 1943. It appears that Good made no second dicky trip. Their tour began with a mining sortie on February 26/27. The tour included five trips to Essen, together with two each to Dortmund and Düsseldorf. This crew's last sortie, flown on July 12/13, was a close-run thing. An engine failed on the outward flight to Turin. They continued but only managed to make enough height to cross the Alps when all moveable items (apart from the bombs) had been jettisoned. They bombed and obtained an excellent photo of the target. On the return, while over the sea in daylight, Good spotted another Lancaster in distress. They moved alongside the damaged bomber, ignoring the danger of fighter attack, and escorted it back. Good's crew also took part in the shuttle mission to Friedrichshafen/North Africa/La Spezia. When tour-expired the crew were posted on July 28. Good went to 27 OTU. Subsequently he returned to operations and completed a second tour with 466 Squadron (September 1944–April 1945)[3]. Good's flight engineer, Flight Sergeant SA Heslop, occasionally operated with Heavery and Michie.

*Squadron Leader D A Green, DSO, DFC*

David Green's crew were posted to 467 Squadron to finish their tour. They completed 17 sorties from Bottesford. This crew attacked many heavily defended targets, visiting Berlin on six occasions and participating in four Essen raids. When tour-expired Green was posted to 5 Group headquarters on July 5. The crew's last operational flight together was to Essen on April 3/4[3].

*Flight Sergeant B M Howie, DFM*

Brian Howie and his crew were among the 467 Squadron founder members. They came to the squadron as an experienced team requiring 10 additional ops to complete their tour. Their trips included two sorties each to Essen and Berlin. Their final op was a long haul to Nuremberg in ED541, on March 8/9. Howie was posted to 1654 Conversion Unit two weeks later[3].

*Flight Lieutenant W G Manifold, DFC and Bar*

Bill Manifold and crew arrived on the squadron during December 1942. Manifold flew as second dicky with Pilot Officer Mant on the Wilhelmshaven attack of February 19/20 1943. A mining trip followed on February 27/28. This crew's tour included three trips to Duisburg and two each to Essen, Berlin, Dortmund and Düsseldorf, together with long hauls to targets such as Munich, Pilsen and La Spezia. The penultimate operation was to Cislago, northern Italy, on July 16/17. They attacked a facility supplying power to the region's rail network and industry. The bomb aimer was Sergeant AC Brown, DFM. He found the target obscured and asked Manifold to circle until he could bomb accurately (despite the attention of fighters). The tour finished with a trip to Leghorn on July 24/25. They were then posted, as a crew, to 156 Squadron in August[3].

### Pilot Officer J H Smith

Smith was a New Zealander. His posting to 467 Squadron reflected the policy of reinforcing new squadrons with experienced crews. Smith and crew arrived at Bottesford on December 19 1942. They completed their tour, making six trips with 467 – including three to Essen. The last sortie was in ED545 to Turin on February 4/5. Smith was posted to 1654 Conversion Unit as an instructor[3].

### Squadron Leader E K Sinclair, DFC

Keith Sinclair's crew were posted to 467 Squadron on November 7 1942. Their tour, however, did not open until March 22/23 1943, when they joined the attack on St. Nazaire. Tough targets followed, including three trips each to Essen and Duisburg and two to Dortmund. During his tour Sinclair took along no less than 10 pilots as second dicky (together with a sergeant as second bomb aimer). His tour was spread over seven months. The last operation was a sortie to Mannheim on September 5/6, in ED657. Earlier in the Summer, on June 20/21, Sinclair and his crew had boarded this aircraft for the shuttle raid on Friedrichshafen (Operation Bellicose). The Lancaster was hit by flak, resulting in an engine fire. The fire was extinguished and the aircraft continued to fly the shuttle route to Blida, North Africa. The flight over the Alps on three engines was a considerable achievement. The aircraft stayed in North Africa for repairs. Sinclair took advantage of the fact that another 467 Squadron crew had completed 30 ops on the way out. He decided to take Stu Hooper's aircraft, ED538, back to Bottesford, bombing La Spezia on the way[7]. Sinclair succeeded MacKenzie as B Flight Commander when the latter failed to return from Düsseldorf on June 11/12. Sinclair was 467's first Australian Flight Commander. When tour-expired he was posted to 1654 Conversion Unit on September 30[3]. Keith Sinclair had an unusual claim to fame. A journalist from Melbourne, he had interviewed Hitler on one occasion. Bill Manifold noted that he eventually returned home to edit the Melbourne Age[8].

### Squadron Leader K F Thiele, DSO, DFC and Bar

New Zealander Keith Thiele was another outstanding leader. Thiele commanded C Flight on its formation at the end of March 1943. This crew's tour included four trips each to Berlin and Essen and two each to Düsseldorf and Nuremberg. Thiele took Heavery with him as second pilot on his third sortie, the attack on Essen on January 12/13 1943. Desmond, Byers, Manifold, Sinclair and two other Captains also flew second dicky trips with Thiele.

Squadron Leader Thiele lost a crew member during his fourth sortie (the January 16/17 raid on Berlin), when a gunner (Flight Sergeant A J

Broemeling) died due to an oxygen supply problem.

On the May 12/13 raid against Duisburg Thiele's Lancaster (LM310) was hit by flak. This put two engines out of action yet the crew returned safely to Bottesford. This was their second return on two engines – the first occurred when V-Victor (ED621) was hit over the target on the April 14/15 raid against Stuttgart.

On his return from Duisburg Thiele was awarded an immediate DSO. When tour-expired he requested to revert to Flight Lieutenant and start a second tour immediately. This was refused. Subsequently he transferred to Fighter Command and was reported missing on March 2 1945. Later, he was classified 'safe'[3].

Sidney Knott has vivid memories of Thiele:

> *He was one of those rare men who didn't understand the meaning of the word fear. Thiele was captivated by operational flying. He didn't want to stop! At the same time who knows what really goes on inside a man's head? I remember the aftermath of a crew night out in Nottingham. When we got back to the railway station in the late evening we saw many familiar faces from the squadron. Then we noticed Thiele sheltering in a corner. He had enjoyed a very boozy evening. We went to the rescue, guided him gently into the guard's van and watched over him during the journey home. He was dead to the world most of the time. Somehow we got him back to camp, footslogging the final three miles. We pushed him, safe and sound, into the Officers' Mess. Happily, this brave man survived the war.*

### *Pilot Officer G F Tillotsen, DFC*

George Tillotsen and his crew reported to Bottesford on March 25 1943. Their first sortie was a mining operation. A few days previously, Tillotsen had flown as second dicky with Flight Lieutenant Desmond (Essen) and Squadron Leader Good (Kiel). This crew's 30-trip tour included three sorties to Cologne and two each to Düsseldorf, Gelsenkirchen, Dortmund and Hanover. The tour was completed on October 1/2 with a sortie to Hagen. This crew participated in the August 17/18 raid on Peenemünde. Their Lancaster, ED549, was attacked repeatedly by a nightfighter and they survived thanks to teamwork and sharp gunnery[3].

### *Sergeant B C Wilson*

An Australian, Wilson was posted to 467 Squadron on March 10 1943. He flew as second dicky twice, with Ball to Duisburg and with Cairney to Berlin. The first operation was to St. Nazaire on April 2/3, flying Y-Yankee (ED651). They were also flying this Lancaster when they failed to return from the Pilsen raid of April 16/17. Four of the crew died. Wilson, together with his navigator and bomb aimer, became prisoners of war[3].

### *Flying Officer W L Wilson, DFC*

'Pluto' Wilson, an Australian, also arrived at Bottesford on March 10

1943. The next day he joined Thiele's crew as second dicky for a sortie against Stuttgart. Future operations involved heavily defended targets such as Dortmund, Duisburg, Essen, Düsseldorf, Gelsenkirchen and Berlin. He and his crew also attacked La Spezia three times, the last on the return from the North Africa shuttle. This crew participated in the August 17/18 attack on Peenemünde, flying ED545. They were attacked by a fighter and the aircraft was damaged by cannon fire. The rear gunner was wounded and his turret set on fire. Nevertheless, he and the mid-upper gunner managed to shoot down the fighter. They then fought the fire and brought it under control. The crew continued on to bomb the target and make a safe return to Bottesford (although not without difficulty). The Lancaster was also damaged several times by flak during this sortie. The members of this skilled, courageous crew were heavily decorated. Those who flew with Wilson included the recipients of a CGM and five DFMs. With his tour completed Wilson was posted to 1660 Conversion Unit on September 25[3].

# *467 Squadron Statistics*

THE statistics below are presented on the 467 Squadron History Website (www.467463raafsquadrons.com). The first operational sorties flown by 467 Squadron crews were to Furze on the night of January 2/3 1943 (minelaying). The last operational sorties were flown on April 25/26 1945, an attack on Tønsberg oil refinery, Norway.

A total of 258 complete crews were posted to 467 Squadron for operations; 74 crews finished their tours and 115 crews failed to return. Other crews were posted during their tours or were still operating when hostilities ceased. A total of 230 sorties were completed in aircraft damaged by the enemy. There were 77 early returns (28 due to engine failure).

A total of 225 Lancasters were operated; each crew flew an average of 14.76 operations. Squadron aircraft dropped 17,578 tonnes of bombs.

# APPENDIX III

# *Interrogation: Major Schnaufer*

*Secret ADI (K) Report No. 551:*

THE following information has been obtained from P/W. As the statements made have not as yet been verified no mention of them should be made in intelligence summaries of commands or lower formations, nor should they be accepted as facts until commented on in air ministry intelligence summaries or special communications.

*The German Night Fighter and the RAF Night Bomber*

*RAF and GAF Aircrew compare notes.*

1. During the investigations of GAF night fighter organisation conducted at Schleswig on 21st May 1945 by a panel of DAT, Air Ministry, two RAF heavy bomber air gunners interviewed three experienced nightfighter officer pilots of NJG4 in order to ascertain the effectiveness and failings of RAF heavy bomber combat tactics against German nightfighters.

2. The nightfighter pilots were the well known Major Schnaufer, Kommodore of NJG4, and two of his Gruppenkommandoure and the result of their interrogation is set out in the present report exactly as received from the DAT panel. It was pointed out in preamble to that report that all three of the German officers knew little of the activities of other units beyond their own and that the information is therefore largely based on the opinions and experience of the pilots of NJG4.

3. It is perhaps worth adding that the present interrogations largely confirm and amplify the views of German nightfighter aircrew captured in operations since the middle of 1944 and reported notably in AID (K) 283, 508, 599, 620 and 700/1944 and 125/1945.

*Method of Search and Attack*

4. Major Schnaufer said that jamming and concentrated bomber streams rendered AI useless. He would fly to the position where jamming was greatest and then search visually. He was convinced

that the majority of the inexperienced pilots had little success and that most chances were made by the experienced pilots. He considered that after eight victories a pilot was good for a long life. The majority of those shot down were at their fourth to sixth victory stage.

5. On a dark night, once the stream was intercepted, the number of bombers seen by each fighter averaged one to three. This number increased with better visibility and on a bright moonlit night would be anything up to 25. The experienced pilot would attack an average of three on a dark night, the inexperienced one or none. Schnaufer claimed nine in 24 hours on 21 February 1945 (a 5 Group raid on Munster), two early in the morning and seven in the evening.

6. Pilots and crews always searched upwards and the type of attack favoured was to approach from below, fly a little ahead of the bomber, climb and drop back until guns came on, fire and break away down. Firing range on a dark night was 100 metres or less, sometimes as close as 30 metres, and on a light night 200 metres or less. The same approach was used for an attack with upward firing guns. The pilots of this NJG had not been briefed on Fishpond cover and no approaches were made from above or level dropping below the bomber inside Fishpond minimum range.

7. Schnaufer considered that in the later stages of the war 50% of all the attacks were carried out with upward firing guns. With the less experienced pilots the tendency was towards upward firing guns. One reason for this was the little difference in the speeds of the Ju88 and the Me110, compared with the Lancaster and Halifax. When approaching from astern and below for the attack with forward firing guns, if the bomber corkscrewed it was most difficult for the fighter to gather speed quickly enough to follow it down in the initial dive.

8. Schnaufer had attacked 20 to 30 bombers with his upward firing guns at about 80 yards range and of these only 10% saw him at a range of approximately 150 to 200 metres and corkscrewed before he could open fire. This pilot claimed to have shot three bombers down with his upward firing guns while they were actually corkscrewing, and Krause claimed six corkscrewing bombers with his upward firing guns, but all three pilots admitted that it was most difficult to shoot down corkscrewing bombers with this type of armament. They said it was possible for a fighter to remain under the bomber and corkscrew with it but only if the manoeuvre was not violent. The fighter would fire when the bomber changed direction, usually at the top.

9. Pilots would usually aim to hit the bomber between the two nacelles on either side, or if the rear turret became troublesome they would aim at that.

10. Pilots had the greatest respect for the mid-upper turret at the commencement of the corkscrew. They said that if they approached from below and the bomber commenced to corkscrew with a dive in their direction it gave the mid-upper gunner a perfect view and a good chance to fire. This would normally be at fairly close range.

11. On the approach if the bomber commenced corkscrewing, or opened fire at the fighter at a reasonable range, the fighter pilots would usually break away and either leave the bomber and look for another target, or sit off in a position where they could not be seen by the bomber and come in again in approximately five minutes even to the second and third time. If they were about to open fire when seen or fired at, they would press the attack. The less experienced pilots would usually press the attack anyway; Schnaufer thought the reason for this was probably lack of confidence in finding another target and their keenness to get a kill.

12. Schnaufer and the other experienced pilots usually carried flares to drop when they found the stream. These flares were of great assistance to the less experienced pilots, enabling them to find the stream and its direction.

13. In a brilliantly lit target area when single engined fighters would be carrying out target interception, Schnaufer said the twins would also go in and attack over the target. He could not be sure how many would do this and he thought that it was a matter of courage and keenness on the twin engined pilots' part. He personally would attack in the target area, rather than follow a bomber out into the darkness.

14. In NJG4 no co-ordinated night attacks were ever carried out and Schnaufer thought that if a bomber was attacked by two aircraft at the same time it was merely coincidence. He pointed out that it was most difficult to formate with another fighter at night.

15. Of the bombers shot down by NJG4 pilots, approximately 40% did not fire or manoeuvre, 50% fired or manoeuvred after the fighter had opened fire, and 10% fired or manoeuvred first. About 98% were flamers. Pilots always carried maximum ammunition load and used their maximum fire power; there was a certain amount of competition in the Staffel as to who could shoot down the most bombers with the least ammunition.

*The Corkscrew*

16. All pilots considered the corkscrew a most effective evasion manoeuvre but they were of the opinion that a corkscrewing Halifax was an easier target than the Lancaster, although the Lancaster caught fire, when hit, more easily. Their idea of the Halifax was a robust but slower aircraft than the Lancaster, less manoeuvrable and with a poorer search.

17. The pilots could not distinguish between different types of corkscrews and usually followed the target aircraft through one complete movement of the corkscrew, which enabled them to anticipate change of direction. They invariably attacked on the change of direction at the top. If the bomber was not shot down at this stage the experienced pilots would break away altogether, or sit off for a time as they thought that to attempt a second attack on the aircraft straight away would be suicidal. Pilots did not hold off from a corkscrewing bomber and fire on the changes of direction, as they considered it was too difficult to anticipate the position of these changes.

18. Schnaufer said the more violent corkscrew, started with a really steep dive and turn, was usually most successful as the nightfighters hadn't the speed to follow. He added that the general manoeuvrability of the Lancaster, and the most violent manoeuvres carried out by some Lancasters he had attacked, amazed him. On the other hand he said that he'd never lost a corkscrewing bomber, but he thought that less experienced pilots may do so.

19. The majority of bombers tended to corkscrew to port but all three pilots maintained that they could not base their attack on this. However, Schnaufer stated repeatedly that he preferred to attack on the starboard side and break away to starboard, as he thought there was less chance of collision with the bomber.

*Banking Search*

20. The banking search was considered most successful, as the pilots could not tell whether they had been seen or not; it definitely put them off.

*Bombers' Fire*

21. All three pilots considered that the bomber's tracer or gun flash did not give away the bomber's position and Schnaufer remembers only two or three cases when bombers have been shot down due to this. He said he rarely saw the bomber's tracer and, therefore, it did not worry him unduly while aiming. He was of the opinion that the bomber gunners did not fire nearly enough or soon enough. He was convinced that had the bombers fired more and used much brighter tracer, many of the pilots, the less experienced especially, would not have attacked. Asked if bright tracer fired from fighters interfered with his aiming, he said it did and appreciated that it would be the same for the bomber gunners.

22. Schnaufer said that in 1942 they were told that the heavies were carrying a .5 under gun. He was very worried about this until he found that very few bombers were in fact carrying it.

23. Schnaufer had been surprised twice by fire from a bomber which he

had not seen and, in each case, the fire was accurate; these bombers he did not attack. He said that, generally, the bomber fire was accurate but, once again, emphasised that we did not fire enough or open up soon enough.

24. He had been hit seriously twice and on numerous other occasions had arrived at his base to find his aircraft damaged. He thought that the most dangerous range for the fighter was from 300 to 100 metres and considered ranges of less than 100 metres were less dangerous due to the fact that he would have either surprised the bomber or be breaking away at this range. Most of the fire from bombers was at about 150 to 200 metres range. On one occasion Schnaufer was shot at at 800 to 1,000 metres range and he said that the fire was so accurate that he could not approach the bomber.

25. The bomber gunners invariably fired once they were in the corkscrew manoeuvre but rarely during the initial stages. It was thought that they were either afraid of disclosing their position or the G forces were too great. In some cases they continued firing accurately even when the bomber was in flames and going down.

*Identification*

26. Schnaufer said he could usually recognise each bomber he attacked as he invariably came in close enough to see the guns. The first indication would be the silhouette then, on the Halifax, the exhausts could be seen faintly at four to five hundred meters from below. With the Lancaster, the exhausts can only be seen when the fighter is flying directly astern and in line with it. On a dark night these would sometimes be visible at a range of 800 metres, but usually less. Night glasses were not worn.

27. Schnaufer said that he attacked a Fortress on a Frankfurt raid at night in 1943 and made three attacks before being seen, but on the fourth attack the bomber fired and shot him down. The Fortress also went down.

*Contrails*

28. The pilots always took advantage of contrails. They were able to estimate the approximate distance of the bombers ahead by the density of the contrails which they followed and, as the end of the contrail was approached, would weave from side to side in search of a bomber. Also contrails gave fighters the true direction of the bomber stream. Schnaufer added that he found it most difficult to see the bomber which was creating the contrail and he also realised that it was difficult for the gunner of the bomber to see the fighter.

*Searchlights*

29. Searchlight crews were instructed not to cone a bomber with more

than six searchlights when working with the fighters. Pilots were able to see their targets satisfactorily with this number. The searchlights blinded the pilots just as they did the bomber gunners; this was due to the ground crews all wishing to take part in the victory.

*Fighter Losses*

30. Losses in NJG4 during the last seven months of the war were 50. Of these, 30 were shot down by Mosquitos, five by heavy bombers and 15 due to reasons unknown. It was estimated that each pilot flew 30 to 40 sorties in that time and the number of aircraft available was at first 50 and latterly down to 15. In addition to these losses, a number of aircraft would crash on landing or be compelled to belly-land due to damage caused in combat. Schnaufer said that the maximum nightfighter effort put up against any one raid was 150 to 200 aircraft.

*General*

31. Pilots had not been told that some bombers were carrying .5 armament in the rear turret, but said this would not have worried them.

32. Pilots were told in July 1944 that AGLT existed but it did not worry them unduly as, with their type of attack, when they were at close range they were out of AGLT and rear turret cover until the last moment.

33. To Schnaufer's knowledge no Allied types of aircraft were employed at night at any time. He thought that if bomber crews had reported this it was probably due to friendly aircraft shooting at each other. On one occasion, when about to attack a Lancaster, another Lancaster shot at it and he sat off and watched both Lancasters shoot each other down (it was omitted to ask if he claimed these two as destroyed).

34. Pilots were familiar with the fields of fire of bombers and based their tactical approach on this.

35. The pilots had no knowledge of any rocket projectiles of the type reported by crews in late 44/early 45. They said that they would definitely have been briefed to this effect had such weapons been used. Schnaufer added that if something of the type was used it would be fired by flak personnel and probably in an area where fighters were not operating.

36. Schnaufer considered the lanes of flares used in the Berlin raids, to assist the fighters to intercept, was the best tactic developed by the German nightfighter force. He said it was being planned to use this method on all targets.

37. It was said that in 1942-43 some bombers, when attacked, fired off

a white flash which blinded the fighter pilots and caused them to lose their target. They thought the idea most effective and could not understand why it was not continued.

ADI (K)
US Air Interrogation
24th June 1945

S D Folkin,
Group Captain

# *Glossary*

*ABC:* Airborne Cigar – a system for disrupting German fighter controller voice transmissions.

*AC2:* Aircraftsman, Second Class.

*AGLT:* Automatic gun-laying turret (system known as 'Village Inn').

*AI:* Airborne Interception radar.

*Air Armaments School:* gunnery school.

*Air Experience:* A familiarisation flight for those with little or no flying experience.

*AFC:* Air Force Cross.

*Airborne Cigar:* Jamming system, with a receiver automatically scanning R/T frequency bands and transmitters for sending jamming signals.

*Aldis Lamp:* Signalling lamp.

*Anson:* Twin-engined general reconnaissance aircraft.

*AOC:* Air Officer Commanding.

*Backers-up:* Aircraft briefed to assist in marking.

*Beaufighter:* Twin-engined fighter bomber, employed as a nightfighter.

*Benzedrine:* An amphetamine.

*Big City:* Berlin.

*Biscuits:* small, square mattresses (three arranged together form a bed).

*Blackout:* Extinguishing/hiding artificial light, to help protect a city from air attack.

*Blenheim* Twin-engined aircraft.

*Blitz:* Bombing campaign by the Luftwaffe against London and other British cities in 1940-41.

*Blitzkrieg:* 'Lightning War'.

*Blockbuster* or *Cookie:* A 4,000 lb high capacity blast bomb.

*Bloodwagon:* Ambulance.

*Bull:* 'bullshit' – discipline.

*Bullseye:* Mock raid – a simulated attack exercise flown during advanced training.

*Can:* Small Bomb Container (SBC).

*CGM:* Conspicuous Gallantry Medal.

*Circuits and Bumps:* practice take-offs and landings.

*Cookie:* 4,000 lb high capacity blast bomb ('Blockbuster').

*Corkscrew:* Evasive action – a diving turn, followed by a climbing turn in the opposite direction.

*Corona:* The use of German-speaking RAF personnel to broadcast false orders to enemy nightfighters.

*DA:* Delayed action bomb.

*D-Day:* June 6, 1944 – the invasion of Normandy.

*Defiant:* Largely unsuccessful single-engined fighter equipped with a four-gun turret.

*DFC:* Distinguished Flying Cross.

*DFM:* Distinguished Flying Medal.

*Dispersal:* A system for distributing, over a wide area, aircraft, buildings and other facilities, to reduce losses in the event of air attack.

*Dogleg:* A change of course, often adopted to confuse the German defences.

*Doodlebug:* Popular name for the VI Flying Bomb.

*Drift:* Action of the wind on the direction of flight.

*Drogue:* A fabric target towed behind an aircraft and used for air-firing practice.

*DSO:* Distinguished Service Order.

*Dual:* Flying instruction – pupil pilot and Instructor.

*Elsan:* Chemical toilet.

*ENSA:* Entertainments National Service Association.

*ETA:* Estimated time of arrival.

*Evasion:* Avoiding capture on being shot down.

*Feathering:* Propeller blades turned edge on, to reduce drag and prevent windmilling.

*Fifth Columnists:* Hostile infiltrators.

*Fishpond:* Radar device warning of an approaching fighter.

*Flak:* Anti-aircraft fire/guns.

*Flarepath:* Runway illuminated for use at night or in bad weather.

*Flight:* A squadron sub-unit (typically of six or eight aircraft, in a heavy bomber squadron).

*Freya:* German ground radar system.

*Funnels:* Final approach for landing.

*GAF:* German Air Force.

*Gardening:* An operational sortie involving the dropping of mines.

*GEE:* Navigational aid utilising signals from ground transmitters (pulse-phasing position fixer).

*GH:* Blind-bombing system.

*Gooseneck Flares:* Paraffin-fuelled flares.

*Grand Slam:* 22,000 lb deep penetration ('earthquake') bomb.

*Ground Grocer:* Ground-based transmitters for jamming German nightfighter radars.

*Ground Speed:* The speed of an aircraft relative to the ground.

*H2S:* Navigation and target identification radar system (pulse reflector).

*Happy Valley:* The Ruhr Valley region of western Germany.

*Hard Runway:* Concrete/tarmac runway, as opposed to a grass field.

*HCU:* Heavy Conversion Unit.

*Home Guard:* A volunteer, part-time military force.

*Home Run:* Successful escape or evasion, ending in a return to the UK.

*Illuminators:* Flare-droppers, providing illumination over the target.

*ITW* Initial Training Wing.

*Ju88:* Twin-engined fast bomber, with variants developed for nightfighting.

*LDV:* Local Defence Volunteers, later known as the Home Guard.

*Lewis Gun:* Air-cooled, drum-fed, gas-operated machine gun.

*Lichtenstein:* German nightfighter radar.

*Magister:* Two-seater trainer.

*Main Force:* A large group of bombers attacking a target.

*Manchester:* Twin-engined heavy bomber.

*Mandrel:* System for jamming German radar stations.

*Manipulation:* Movement of the turret/guns.

*Martinet:* Single-engined target tug.

*Master Bomber:* Operationally experienced pilot using VHF to broadcast instructions to control the progress and accuracy of a raid.

*Maximum Effort:* an order for mobilisation of the maximum number of aircraft to attack a given target or targets.

*Munich Crisis:* Ended by a pact signed by Germany, Britain, France and Italy on September 29 1938. The crisis concerned Czechoslovakia and ended with the ceding of the Sudetenland to Germany.

*Musical Parramatta:* Oboe blind-marking.

*NAAFI:* Navy, Army and Air Force Institute.

*Newhaven:* Visual ground-marking of a target.

*Nickelling:* Dropping leaflets over enemy or enemy-occupied territory.

*Nissen Hut:* a building of semicircular section, constructed from corrugated steel sheet.

*Oboe:* Blind-bombing system.

*Op:* Operation – an operational flight.

*Orderly Room:* A room used for general administrative work.

*OTU:* Operational Training Unit.

*Overshoot:* To fly too far down the runway before touching down.

*Parramatta:* Blind ground marking by H2S.

*Perimeter Track:* Concrete/tarmac tracks allowing aircraft to taxi from the runway to other locations on the airfield.

*PFF:* Pathfinder Force.

*Pillbox:* Small concrete fortified emplacement.

*Pinpoint:* Visual acquisition of a feature giving a precise location.

*P-Plane:* Pilotless plane – VI Flying Bomb.

*QFE:* Air pressure at the airfield, allowing the altimeter to be adjusted for changes (the instrument reading zero on landing).

*RAAF:* Royal Australian Air Force.

*RCAF:* Royal Canadian Air Force.

*RAFVR:* Royal Air Force Volunteer Reserve.

*Reciprocal Course:* A course 180 deg. from the previous or assumed course.

*RPM:* Revolutions per minute.

*Reserved Occupation:* An occupation excluding the individual from military service.

*R/T:* Radio-telephone/telephony.

*Run-in:* Final approach to the target.

*Satellite:* Airfield associated with a main base.

*SBC:* Small Bomb Container.

*Scarecrow:* Anti-aircraft shell designed to simulate exploding aircraft (the existence of which was denied, postwar, by the Germans).

*Schräge Musik:* Twin 20 mm cannons, fuselage-mounted to fire upwards, just forward of the vertical.

*Second Dicky:* Second Pilot.

*Selection Board:* A group selecting candidates for commission as officers.

*Skipper:* Captain of the aircraft; pilot.

*Small Bomb Container:* SBC – container for incendiary bombs.

*Sortie:* An operational flight.

*Sprog:* A new recruit; an individual under training.

*Squarebashing:* Drill on the barrack square.

*Stirling:* The first of the RAF's four-engined heavy bombers to enter service.

*Target Indicators:* TIs – pyrotechnic flares used to mark targets.

*Target Tug:* aircraft towing a drogue target, used for gunnery training.

*TA:* Territorial Army.

*Tinsel:* Airborne system broadcasting engine noise on German nightfighter frequencies.

*Tour:* A Bomber Command first tour consisted of 30 operations, followed by a second tour of 20 operations. A Pathfinder tour, however, could involve 45 or more sorties.

*Tracer:* Incendiary ammunition that can be observed in flight.

*Trimmer:* Small control surface on the elevators, allowing the pilot to trim the aircraft.

*U/S:* Unserviceable.

*VI:* Flying Bomb.

*VE Day:* Victory in Europe Day – May 8 1945.

*Vegetables:* Sea mines dropped by aircraft.

*Vulture:* Rolls-Royce engine powering the Avro Manchester.

*WAAF:* Women's Auxiliary Air Force.

*Wanganui:* Radar-assisted blind-marking of an obscured target using parachute-equipped pyrotechnics – 'sky markers'.

*Wellington:* Twin-engined bomber.

*Watch Office:* Flying Control (control tower).

*Whitley:* Twin-engined heavy bomber.

*Wilde Sau:* 'Wild Boar' – nightfighting tactics employing single-seat day fighters using illumination over the target to find the bombers.

*Window:* Aluminium strips dropped to swamp enemy radars.

*Würzburg:* Radar used to control searchlights, flak and fighters.

*WVS:* Women's Voluntary Service.

*Y-Run:* Integrated bombing exercise using H2S radar.

*Zahme Sau:* 'Tame Boar' – an air defence strategy based on the infiltration of nightfighters into the bomber stream, allowing them to accompany the Main Force.

# APPENDIX V

# *Notes to Chapters/Appendices*

*Chapter One: The Choice*

1. Cooper, A W (1993), *The Men Who Breached the Dams*, 170.
2. Sweetman, J (1993), *The Dambusters Raid*, 60.
3. Middlebrook, M and Everitt, C (1990), *The Bomber Command War Diaries*, 386.
4. Sweetman, J (1982), *Operation Chastise*, 125-126.
5. Euler, H (2001), *The Dams Raid Through the Lens*, 92.
6. Holyoak, V (1995), *On the Wings of the Morning: RAF Bottesford, 1941-1945*, 60.

*Chapter Two: The Air Gunner's Brevet*

1. Falconer, J (1995), *RAF Bomber Airfields of World War 2*, 61.
2. Bowyer, C (1979), *Guns in the Sky*, 34-35.

*Chapter Three: Crewing Up*

1. Foster, E, unpublished manuscript.
2. Middlebrook, M and Everitt, C (1990), *The Bomber Command War Diaries*, 269.
3. Robertson, B (1964), *Lancaster – The Story of a Famous Bomber*, 122.
4. Middlebrook, M and Everitt, C (1990), *The Bomber Command War Diaries*, 258.
5. Ibid, 724.
6. Robertson, B (1964), *Lancaster – The Story of a Famous Bomber*, 10.
7. Mason, F K (1989), *The Avro Lancaster*, 39, 54, 55, 57.
8. Ibid, 281.
9. Postlethwaite, M (2002), *Lancaster Squadrons in Focus*, 91.
10. Holmes, H (2001), *Avro Lancaster: The Definitive Record*, 43.
11. Garbett, M and Goulding, B (1983), *Lancaster at War*, 14.
12. Holmes, H (2001), *Avro Lancaster: The Definitive Record*, 165.
13. Yates, H (2002), *Luck and a Lancaster*, 115.
14. Bennett, D C T (1983), *Pathfinder*, 175.
15. 467 Squadron History (www.467463raafsquadrons.com).
16. Mason, F K (1989), *The Avro Lancaster*, 309.

*Chapter Four: Operational At Last!*

1. Holyoak, V (1995), *On the Wings of the Morning: RAF Bottesford, 1941-1945*, 7.

2. Ibid, 8.
3. Ibid, 10.
4. Lake, J (2002), *Lancaster Squadrons 1942-43*, 30, 81.
5. Holyoak, V (1995), *On the Wings of the Morning: RAF Bottesford, 1941-1945*, 104.
6. Falconer, J (1995), *RAF Bomber Airfields of World War 2*, 20.
7. 467 Squadron History (www.467463raafsquadrons.com).
8. Holyoak, V (1995), *On the Wings of the Morning: RAF Bottesford, 1941-1945*, 60.
9. Robertson, B (1964), *Lancaster – The Story of a Famous Bomber*, 118.
10. Holyoak, V (1995), *On the Wings of the Morning: RAF Bottesford, 1941-1945*, 61.
11. Ibid, 20.
12. Ibid, 62.
13. Ibid, 71-72.
14. Lake, J (2002), *Lancaster Squadrons 1942-43*, 24.
15. Holyoak, V (1995), *On the Wings of the Morning: RAF Bottesford, 1941-1945*, 15.

*Chapter Five: Under Fire for the First Time*

1. Terraine, J (1988), *The Right of the Line*, 505.
2. Overy, R (1997), *Bomber Command 1939-45*, 111.
3. Ibid, 98.
4. Bowyer, C (1977), *Pathfinders at War*, 40.
5. Mason, F K (1989), *The Avro Lancaster*, 84.
6. Bennett, D C T (1983), *Pathfinder*, 182.
7. Ibid, 183.
8. Ibid, 185-186.
9. Hampton, J (1993), *Selected for Aircrew*, 42.
10. Longmate, N (1988), *The Bombers*, 232.
11. Mahaddie, T G (1990), *Hamish: The Story of a Pathfinder*, 54.
12. Hampton, J (1993), *Selected for Aircrew*, 35.
13. Bowyer, C (1979), *Guns in the Sky*, 48.
14. Mason, F K (1989), *The Avro Lancaster*, 76.
15. Middlebrook, M and Everitt, C (1990), *The Bomber Command War Diaries*, 349.
16. 467 Squadron History (www.467463raafsquadrons.com).
17. Holyoak, V (1995), *On the Wings of the Morning: RAF Bottesford, 1941-1945*, 60.
18. Mason, F K (1989), *The Avro Lancaster*, 80.
19. Middlebrook, M and Everitt, C (1990), *The Bomber Command War Diaries*, 355.
20. Rolfe, M (2001), *Flying into Hell*, 60.
21. Hinchliffe, P (2001), *The Other Battle*, 140.
22. Middlebrook, M and Everitt, C (1990), *The Bomber Command War Diaries*, 356-357.
23. Hampton, J (1993), *Selected for Aircrew*, 195-197.
24. Overy, R (1997), *Bomber Command 1939-45*, 130.
25. Hinchliffe, P (2001), *The Other Battle*, 108.
26. Ibid, 113.

*Chapter Six: 'It All Looked Very Unfriendly'*

1. Letter from Marie Claridge (née Cooper), former Intelligence Officer at Bottesford, to Vincent Holyoak, author of *On the Wings of the Morning*.
2. Tubbs, D B (1972), *Lancaster Bomber*, 104-106.
3. Hampton, J (1993), *Selected for Aircrew*, 36.
4. Ibid, 203.
5. Manifold, B (1986), *Never a Dull!*, 73.
6. Hinchliffe, P (2001), *The Other Battle*, 113.
7. Middlebrook, M and Everitt, C (1990), *The Bomber Command War Diaries*, 359.
8. Holyoak, V (1995), *On the Wings of the Morning: RAF Bottesford, 1941-1945*, 62-67.

*Chapter Seven: The Turret and the Guns*

1. Bowyer, C (1979), *Guns in the Sky*, 30-31.
2. Tubbs, D B (1972), *Lancaster Bomber*, 71.
3. Bowyer, C (1979), *Guns in the Sky*, 32-33.
4. Tubbs, D B (1972), *Lancaster Bomber*, 75.
5. Mason, F K (1989), *The Avro Lancaster*, 293.
6. Terraine, J (1988), *The Right of the Line*, 463.
7. Hampton, J (1993), *Selected for Aircrew*, 247.
8. Ibid, 248.
9. Hinchliffe, P (2001), *The Other Battle*, 174-175.
10. Holyoak, V (1995), *On the Wings of the Morning: RAF Bottesford, 1941-1945*, 64.
11. Ibid, 81.
12. Middlebrook, M (1990), *The Berlin Raids*, 377-378.
13. Hampton, J (1993), *Selected for Aircrew*, 181.
14. Hinchliffe, P (2001), *The Other Battle*, 82.
15. Ibid, 173.
16. Garbett, M and Goulding, B (1984), *Lancaster at War: 3*, 112.
17. Hinchliffe, P (2001), *The other battle*, 111.

*Chapter Eight: 'This Stuff is all Around Us!'*

1. Terraine, J (1988), *The Right of the Line*, 518-519.
2. Middlebrook, M and Everitt, C (1990), *The Bomber Command War Diaries*, 365–366.
3. Mason, F K (1989), *The Avro Lancaster*, 129.
4. Cooper, A (1992), *Air Battle of the Ruhr*, 39.
5. Middlebrook, M and Everitt, C (1990), *The Bomber Command War Diaries*, 366–367.
6. Holyoak, V (1995), *On the Wings of the Morning: RAF Bottesford, 1941-1945*, 60.
7. Manifold, B (1986), *Never a dull!*, 77.
8. Holyoak, V (1995), *On the Wings of the Morning: RAF Bottesford, 1941-1945*, 68.
9. Ibid, 76
10. Letter from Marie Claridge (née Cooper), former Intelligence Officer at Bottesford, to Vincent Holyoak, author of *On the Wings of the Morning*.
11. Middlebrook, M and Everitt, C (1990), *The Bomber Command War*

*Diaries*, 368.

12. Foster, E, unpublished manuscript.

13. Charlwood, D (1984), *No Moon Tonight*, 98.

14. Middlebrook, M and Everitt, C (1990), *The Bomber Command War Diaries*, 370-372.

15. 467 Squadron History (www.467463raafsquadrons.com).

16. Mason, F K (1989), *The Avro Lancaster*, 104.

*Chapter Nine: The Hardest Month*

1. Middlebrook, M and Everitt, C (1990), *The Bomber Command War Diaries*, 374.

2. Letter from Marie Claridge (née Cooper), former Intelligence Officer at Bottesford, to Vincent Holyoak, author of *On the Wings of the Morning*.

3. Holyoak, V (1995), *On the Wings of the Morning: RAF Bottesford, 1941-1945*, 11.

4. Ibid, 60.

5. Ibid, 73.

6. Manifold, B (1986), *Never a dull!*, 103.

7. Ibid, 104.

8. Ibid, 75.

9. Tubbs, D B (1972), *Lancaster Bomber*, introduction by Group Captain Leonard Cheshire, VC, DSO, DFC.

10. Mason, F K (1989), *The Avro Lancaster*, 92.

11. Middlebrook, M and Everitt, C (1990), *The Bomber Command War Diaries*, 375.

12. Ibid, 376.

13. Tubbs, D B (1972), *Lancaster Bomber*, 25.

14. Middlebrook, M and Everitt, C (1990), *The Bomber Command War Diaries*, 379.

15. Freeman, R A (2001), *Bases of Bomber Command, Then and Now, 11*.

16. Middlebrook, M and Everitt, C (1990), *The Bomber Command War Diaries*, 380.

17. Ibid, 381.

18. Rolfe, M (2001), *Flying into Hell*, 84.

19. Mason, F K (1989), *The Avro Lancaster*, 131.

20. 467 Squadron History (www.467463raafsquadrons.com).

*Chapter Ten: It's a Long Way to Pilsen*

1. Middlebrook, M and Everitt, C (1990), *The Bomber Command War Diaries*, 378-379.

*Chapter Eleven: Odds Against Survival*

1. Hampton J (1993), *Selected for Aircrew*, 112-113.

2. Middlebrook, M and Everitt, C (1990), *The Bomber Command War Diaries*, 708.

3. Hampton, J (1993), *Selected for Aircrew*, 269-270.

4. Bowyer, C (1979), *Guns in the Sky*, 45.

5. Longmate, N (1988), *The Bombers*, 182

6. Letter from Marie Claridge (née Cooper), former Intelligence Officer

at Bottesford, to Vincent Holyoak, author of *On the Wings of the Morning*.

7. Manifold, B (1986), *Never a Dull!*, 82.
8. Hampton, J (1993), *Selected for Aircrew*, 265.
9. Holyoak, V (1995), *On the Wings of the Morning: RAF Bottesford, 1941-1945*, 69-70.
10. Bird, T (2000), *A Bird over Berlin*, 79.
11. Holyoak, V (1995), *On the Wings of the Morning: RAF Bottesford, 1941-1945*, 91-92.
12. Ibid, 96.
13. Terraine, J (1988), *The Right of the Line*, 534-535.
14. Cooper, A W (1989), *Bombers over Berlin*, 223.
15. Hampton, J (1993), *Selected for Aircrew*, 146.
16. Ibid, 150.
17. Mason, F K (1989), *The Avro Lancaster*, 7.
18. Bowyer, C (1979), *Guns in the Sky*, 35-36.
19. Rolfe, M (1999), *Hell on Earth*, 79.
20. Bob Baxter's Bomber Command (www.bomber-command.info).
21. Mahaddie, T G (1990), *Hamish: The Story of a Pathfinder*, 51.
22. Mason, F K (1989), *The Avro Lancaster*, 81.
23. Robertson, B (1964), *Lancaster – The Story of a Famous Bomber*, 154.
24. Mason, F K (1989), *The Avro Lancaster*, 345.
25. Freeman, R A (2001), *Bases of Bomber Command, Then and Now*, 70.
26. Mason, F K (1989), *The Avro Lancaster*, 131.
27. Ibid, 357.
28. Robertson B (1964), *Lancaster – The Story of a Famous Bomber*, 159-160.
29. Mason, F K (1989), *The Avro Lancaster*, 359.
30. Holmes, H (2001), *Avro Lancaster, The Definitive Record*, 99.
31. Mason, F K (1989), *The Avro Lancaster*, 360.

*Chapter Twelve: Simple Pleasures*

1. Letter from Marie Claridge (née Cooper), former Intelligence Officer at Bottesford, to Vincent Holyoak, author of *On the Wings of the Morning*.

*Chapter Thirteen: Frank's Shock Decision*

1. Mason, F K (1989), *The Avro Lancaster*, 133.
2. Middlebrook, M and Everitt, C (1990), *The Bomber Command War Diaries*, 384.
3. Hinchliffe, P (2001), *The Other Battle*, 140.
4. Cooper, A (1992), *Air Battle of the Ruhr*, 65.
5. Longmate, N (1988), *The bombers*, 237.
6. Holyoak, V (1995), *On the Wings of the Morning: RAF Bottesford*, 1941-1945, 74-75.
7. Middlebrook, M and Everitt, C (1990), *The Bomber Command War Diaries*, 385.
8. Bowyer, C (1977), *Pathfinders at War*, 88.
9. Mason, F K (1989), *The Avro Lancaster*, 131.
10. Middlebrook, M and Everitt, C (1990), *The Bomber Command War Diaries*, 390-391.
11. Holyoak, V (1995), *On the Wings of the Morning: RAF Bottesford, 1941-1945*, 76.

12. Middlebrook, M and Everitt, C (1990), *The Bomber Command War Diaries*, 392.
13. Ibid, 393.
14. 467 Squadron History (www.467463raafsquadrons.com).
15. Mason, F K (1989), *The Avro Lancaster*, 104.
16. Ibid, 134-135.

*Chapter Fourteen: The Magic Number*

1. Holyoak, V (1995), *On the Wings of the Morning: RAF Bottesford, 1941-1945*, 71.
2. Ibid, preface.
3. Robertson, B (1964), *Lancaster – The Story of a Famous Bomber*, 118.
4. Middlebrook, M and Everitt, C (1990), *The Bomber Command War Diaries*, 774.
5. Ibid, 783.
6. Holmes, H (2001), *Avro Lancaster, The Definitive Record*, 79.
7. Hinchliffe, P (2001), *The Other Battle*, 232.

*Chapter Fifteen: Life With the Sprogs*

1. Falconer, J (1992), *RAF Bomber Airfields of World War 2*, 64.
2. Freeman, R (2001), *Bases of Bomber Command, Then and Now*, 339.
3. Falconer, J (1992), *RAF Bomber Airfields of World War 2*, 77-79.

*Chapter Sixteen: Apprentice Pathfinders*

1. Middlebrook, M and Everitt, C (1990), *The Bomber Command War Diaries*, 301.
2. Longmate, N (1988), *The Bombers*, 231-232.
3. Postlethwaite, M (2002), *Lancaster Squadrons in Focus*, 49.
4. Bennett, D C T (1983), *Pathfinder*, 141.
5. Ibid, 112-113.
6. Tubbs, D B (1972), *Lancaster Bomber*, 71.
7. Neillands, R (2001), *The Bomber War*, 272.
8. Letter from Marie Claridge (née Cooper), former Intelligence Officer at Bottesford, to Vincent Holyoak, author of *On the Wings of the Morning*.
9. Mahaddie, T G (1990), *Hamish: The Story of a Pathfinder*, 96.
10. Postlethwaite, M (2002), *Lancaster Squadrons in Focus*, 81.
11. Freeman, R A (2001), *Bases of Bomber Command, Then and Now*, 328.
12. Mason, F K (1989), *The Avro Lancaster*, 311.
13. Falconer, J (1992), *RAF Bomber Airfields of World War 2*, 51.
14. Hinchliffe, P (2001), *The Other Battle*, 60-61.
15. Kelvin Butterworth, newspaper cutting, *'Flying Cross Award'*.
16. Hampton, J (1993), *Selected for Aircrew*, 102-103. Gus Walker was Syerston's Station Commander when he lost his right arm in 1942. He had been watching the Lancasters depart when he saw burning incendiaries tumble from a bomb-bay. He pursued the Lancaster in his car, jumped out and ran towards the aircraft as the 4,000 lb Cookie exploded. The blast wave removed his arm. Guy Gibson was at the scene. Walker is said to have asked Gibson to find the arm as it had a new glove. He also urged Gibson to telephone the AOC and ask him if he would accept a one-armed Station Commander in two months'

time. He returned to duty as Syerston's Station Commander within eight weeks. In later years he became Inspector-General of the RAF (Sir Augustus Walker, GCB, CBE, DSO, DFC, AFC, MA).

17. Gunn, P B (1990), *RAF Great Massingham, A Norfolk Airfield at War, 1940–1945*, 54.
18. Daily Herald, *'The Boston Boys'*, April 10, 1942, 2.

*Chapter Seventeen: 'Two-thirds Counts as One'*

1. Lacey-Johnson, L (1991), *Point Blank and Beyond*, 5.
2. Ibid, 46.
3. Ibid, 206.
4. Middlebrook, M and Everitt, C (1990), *The Bomber Command War Diaries*, 505.
5. Hinchliffe, P (2001), *The Other Battle*, 131-133.
6. Ibid, 144.
7. Ibid, 233.
8. Ibid, 262.
9. Ibid, 278.
10. Lacey-Johnson, L (1991), *Point Blank and Beyond*, 69.
11. Middlebrook, M and Everitt, C (1990), *The Bomber Command War Diaries*, 492.
12. Ibid, 494.
13. Ibid, 495.
14. Ibid, 497.
15. Middlebrook, M (1990), *The Berlin Raids*, 306.
16. Hinchliffe, P (2001), *The Other Battle*, 107.
17. Hampton, J (1993), *Selected for Aircrew*, 68.
18. Lake, J (2002), *Lancaster Squadrons*, 1942-43, 52.
19. Middlebrook, M and Everitt, C (1990), *The Bomber Command War Diaries*, 297-301.
20. Ibid, 334-335.
21. Hinchliffe, P (2001), *The Other Battle*, 195-197.
22. Middlebrook, M and Everitt, C (1990), *The Bomber Command War Diaries*, 336.
23. Terraine, J (1988), *The Right of the Line*, 541.
24. Hinchliffe, P (2001), *The Other Battle*, 221.
25. Middlebrook, M and Everitt, C (1990), *The Bomber Command War Diaries*, 363.
26. Ibid, 411.
27. Ibid, 418.
28. Neillands, R (2002), *The Bomber War*, 130.
29. Bennett, D C T (1983), *Pathfinder*, 187.
30. Middlebrook, M and Everitt, C (1990), *The Bomber Command War Diaries*, 506.
31. Hampton, J (1993), *Selected for Aircrew*, 62-63.
32. Middlebrook, M and Everitt, C (1990), *The Bomber Command War Diaries*, 509-510.
33. Hampton, J (1993), *Selected for Aircrew*, 252.
34. Middlebrook, M and Everitt, C (1990), *The Bomber Command War Diaries*, 507.
35. Lacey-Johnson, L (1991), *Point Blank and Beyond*, 95-96.

36. Middlebrook, M and Everitt, C (1990), *The Bomber Command War Diaries*, 513.
37. Ibid, 513-514.
38. Hinchliffe, P (2001), *The Other Battle*, 280.
39. Middlebrook, M and Everitt, C (1990), *The Bomber Command War Diaries*, 516.
40. Hinchliffe, P (2001), *The Other Battle*, 199.
41. Middlebrook, M and Everitt, C (1990), *The Bomber Command War Diaries*, 517.
42. Ibid, 522-523.
43. Darlow, S (2002), *Sledgehammers for Tintacks*, 20.
44. Ibid, 21.
45. Ibid, 29-30.
46. Ibid, 31.
47. Ibid, 37.
48. Ibid, 44.
49. Ibid, 38-39.
50. Ibid, 45.
51. Ibid, 49.
52. Ibid, 50.
53. Ibid, 75.
54. Ibid, 52.
55. Ibid, 64.
56. Ibid, 63.
57. Ibid, 70.
58. Ibid, 79.
59. Ibid, 80.
60. Ibid, 100.
61. Middlebrook, M and Everitt, C (1990), *The Bomber Command War Diaries*, 535.

*Chapter Eighteen: The War Against the Robots*

1. Middlebrook, M and Everitt, C (1990), *The Bomber Command War Diaries*, 536.
2. Ibid, 537.
3. Darlow, S (2002), *Sledgehammers for Tintacks*, 100.
4. Middlebrook, M and Everitt, C (1990), *The Bomber Command War Diaries*, 538.
5. Darlow, S (2002), *Sledgehammers for Tintacks*, 115.
6. Ibid, 116.
7. Middlebrook, M and Everitt, C (1990), *The Bomber Command War Diaries*, 540.
8. Darlow, S (2002), *Sledgehammers for Tintacks*, 132.
9. Ibid, 135-136.
10. Middlebrook, M and Everitt, C (1990), *The Bomber Command War Diaries*, 541.
11. Darlow, S (2002), *Sledgehammers for Tintacks*, 139.
12. Middlebrook, M and Everitt, C (1990), *The Bomber Command War Diaries*, 542.
13. Ibid, 543.
14. Ibid, 544-545.
15. Terraine, J (1988), *The Right of the Line*, 655.

16. Middlebrook, M and Everitt, C (1990), *The Bomber Command War Diaries*, 546.
17. Darlow, S (2002), *Sledgehammers for Tintacks*, 147.
18. Middlebrook, M and Everitt, C (1990), *The Bomber Command War Diaries*, 548.
19. Darlow, S (2002), *Sledgehammers for Tintacks*, 152-153.
20. Ibid, 197.
21. Ibid, 163.
22. Ibid, 194.
23. Middlebrook, M and Everitt, C (1990), *The Bomber Command War Diaries*, 549.
24. Ibid, 550-551.
25. Ibid, 552.
26. Bowyer, M J F (1979), *Action Stations 1: Military Airfields of East Anglia*, 220.
27. Mason, F K (1989), *The Avro Lancaster*, 191-192.
28. Neillands, R (2001), *The Bomber War*, 333.
29. Hampton, J (1993), *Selected for Aircrew*, 66.

*Chapter Nineteen: 'Flak Happy'*

1. Middlebrook, M and Everitt, C (1990), *The Bomber Command War Diaries*, 559.
2. Ibid, 561.
3. Darlow, S (2002), *Sledgehammers for Tintacks*, 181-182.
4. Middlebrook, M and Everitt, C (1990), *The Bomber Command War Diaries*, 563.
5. Darlow, S (2002), *Sledgehammers for Tintacks*, 186.
6. Middlebrook, M and Everitt, C (1990), *The Bomber Command War Diaries*, 569.
7. Neillands, R (2001), *The Bomber War*, 329.
8. Middlebrook, M and Everitt, C (1990), *The Bomber Command War Diaries*, 570.
9. Terraine, J (1988), *The Right of the Line*, 674.
10. Ibid, 678-679.
11. Middlebrook, M and Everitt, C (1990), *The Bomber Command War Diaries*, 776.
12. Freeman, R A (2001), *Bases of Bomber Command, Then and Now*, 329.
13. Holmes, H (2001), *Avro Lancaster, the Definitive Record*, 165.
14. Hinchliffe, P (2001), *The Other Battle*, 307.
15. Mason, F K (1989), *The Avro Lancaster*, 327-415.
16. Robertson, B (1964), *Lancaster – The Story of a Famous Bomber*, 145-211.
17. Middlebrook, M and Everitt, C (1990), *The Bomber Command War Diaries*, 669.
18. Mason, F K (1989), *The Avro Lancaster*, 203.
19. Middlebrook, M and Everitt, C (1990), *The Bomber Command War Diaries*, 636.

*Chapter Twenty-One: 'Your Flying Days Are Over'*

1. Lake, J (2002), *Lancaster Squadrons 1942-43*, 7-8.
2. Postlethwaite, M (2002), *Lancaster Squadrons in Focus*, 94.
3. Neillands, R (2001), *The Bomber War*, 383-384.

*Chapter Twenty-Two: Civvy Street*

1. Chandler, C (2002), *Tail gunner*, 115-116.
2. *Fruit, Vegetable and Flower Markets of England: Spitalfields* (1954), 21.
3. Letter from Ted Foster to Sidney Knott, April 26 1990.
4. 'The English are here! Seven British Airmen – The First Invaders,' Trondheim, Friday May 11 1945.
5. Letter from Flo Murray to the author, March 2003.
6. Hampton, J (1993), *Selected for Aircrew*, 141.
7. Letter from Frank Heavery to Ted Foster, February 26 1993.
8. Letter from Frank Heavery's daughter, Jennifer, to Sidney Knott, December 11 2002.
9. Information from the Bolton & District History Society, provided by Kelvin Butterworth.
10. Letter from Clive Walker's daughter, Lucy, to the author, March 25 2003.

*Chapter Twenty-Three: Back in the Turret*

1. Overy, R (1997), *Bomber Command 1939-45*, 58.
2. Garbett, M and Goulding, B (1984), *Lancaster at War: 3*, 150.

*Chapter Twenty-Four: Echoes of the Past*

1. Mason, F K (1989), *The Avro Lancaster*, 7.
2. Terraine, J (1988), *The Right of the Line*, 502-503.
3. Mason, F K (1989), *The Avro Lancaster*, 201.
4. Garbett, M and Goulding, B (1984), *Lancaster at War: 3*, 22.
5. Hampton, J (1993), *Selected for Aircrew*, 7.
6. Letter from Marie Claridge (née Cooper), former Intelligence Officer at Bottesford, to Vincent Holyoak, author of *On the Wings of the Morning*.
7. Hampton, J (1993), *Selected for Aircrew*, 32-33.
8. Overy, R (1997), *Bomber Command 1939-45*, 199.
9. Hampton, J (1993), *Selected for Aircrew*, 315.
10. Neillands, R (2001), *The Bomber War*, 385.
11. Overy, R (1997), *Bomber Command 1939-45*, 202.
12. Ibid, 211.
13. Terraine, J (1988), *The Right of the Line*, 291.
14. Ibid, 487.
15. Neillands, R (2001), *The Bomber War*, 388, quoting the Rt Hon Michael Howard QC MP.

*Appendix I: 467 Squadron Personalities*

1. www.467463raafsquadrons.com.
2. Rolfe, M (1999), *Hell on Earth*, 81.
3. Research commissioned by the late Ted Foster, Frank Heavery's navigator.
4. Middlebrook, M and Everitt, C (1990), *The Bomber Command War Diaries*, 399-401.
5. Ibid, 422.
6. Holyoak, V (1995), *On the Wings of the Morning: RAF Bottesford, 1941-1945*, 90-91.
7. Manifold, B. (1986), *Never a Dull!*, 109.
8. Ibid, 97.

# APPENDIX VI

# *Selected Bibliography*

Bennett, D C T (1958), *Pathfinder,* Frederick Muller, 1983.

Bird, T (2000), *A Bird over Berlin*, Woodfield Publishing.

Bowyer, C (1977), *Pathfinders at war*, Ian Allan.

Bowyer, C (1979), *Guns in the sky*, J M Dent & Sons.

Bowyer, M J F (1979), *Action Stations 1: military airfields of East Anglia*, Patrick Stephens.

Chandler, C (1999), *Tail gunner*, Airlife Publishing, 2002.

Charlwood, D (1956), *No moon tonight*, Goodall Publications, 1990.

Cooper, A W (1982), *The men who breached the dams*, Airlife Publishing, 1993.

Cooper, A W (1985), *Bombers over Berlin*, Patrick Stephens, 1989.

Cooper, A W (1992), *Air battle of the Ruhr*, Airlife Publishing.

Darlow, S (2002), *Sledgehammers for tintacks*, Grub Street.

Euler, H (2001), *The Dams Raid through the lens*, After the Battle.

Falconer, J (1992), *RAF bomber airfields of World War 2*, Ian Allan, 1995.

Freeman, R A (2001), *Bases of Bomber Command, then and now*, After the Battle.

Garbett, M and Goulding, B (1971), *Lancaster at war*, Ian Allan, 1983.

Garbett, M and Goulding, B (1984), *Lancaster at war: 3*, Guild Publishing/Ian Allan.

Hampton, J (1993), *Selected for aircrew*, Air Research Publications.

Hinchliffe, P (1996), *The other battle*, Airlife Publishing, 2001.

Holmes, H (1997), *Avro Lancaster: the definitive record*, Airlife Publishing, 2001.

Holyoak, V (1995), *On the wings of the morning: RAF Bottesford 1941-1945*, Vincent Holyoak, Leicester.

Lacey-Johnson, L (1991), *Point Blank and beyond*, Airlife Publishing.

Lake, J (2002), *Lancaster squadrons 1942-43*, Osprey Publishing.

Longmate, N (1983), *The bombers*, Arrow Books, 1988.

Mahaddie, T G (1989), *Hamish: the story of a Pathfinder*, Ian Allan, 1990.

Manifold, B (1986), *Never a dull!*, Ausbooks.

Mason, F K (1989), *The Avro Lancaster*, Aston Publications.

Middlebrook, M and Everitt, C (1985), *The Bomber Command war diaries*, Penguin Books, 1990.

Middlebrook, M (1988), *The Berlin raids*, Penguin Books, 1990.

Neillands, R (2001), *The bomber war*, John Murray (Publishers), 2002.

Overy, R (1997), *Bomber Command 1939-45*, Harper Collins Publishers.

Postlethwaite, M (2002), *Lancaster squadrons in focus*, Red Kite.

Robertson, B (1964), *Lancaster – the story of a famous bomber*, Harleyford Publications.

Rolfe, M (1999), *Hell on earth*, Grub Street.

Rolfe, M (2001), *Flying into hell*, Grub Street.

Sweetman, J (1982), *Operation Chastise*, Jane's Publishing Company (1990); *The Dambusters raid*, Arms and Armour Press (1993).

Terraine, J (1985), *The right of the line*, Sceptre, 1988.

Tubbs, D B (1971), *Lancaster bomber*, Pan/Ballantine, 1972.

Yates, H (1999), *Luck and a Lancaster*, Airlife Publishing, 2001.

*Sidney Knott's Logbook Entries: First Tour, 1943, 467 Squadron*

**First page spread:**

| 1943 Date | Hour | Aircraft Type and No. | Pilot | Duty | Remarks (including results of bombing, gunnery, exercises, etc.) | Flying Times Day | Night |
|---|---|---|---|---|---|---|---|
| | | | | | Time carried forward :— 146.20 / 100.10 / 46.10 | | |
| JANUARY | | MK I LANCASTER | | REAR GUNNER | | | |
| 3 | 18.45 | 4378 | Sgt Heavery | " " | BULLSEYE | | 4.20 |
| 9 | 14.15 | 4823 | " | " | N. F. T. | .40 | |
| 9 | 17.40 | " | " | " | BULLSEYE | | 5.00 |
| 26 | 12.25 | 438A | " | " | N. F. T | 1.00 | |
| 26 | 18.25 | 4825 | " | " | BULLSEYE | | 4.00 |
| 27 | 17.40 | 4823 | " | " | GARDENING (5 VEGS) 34.15T 500 RDS. AT S/LIGHTS | | 4.5 |
| 30 | 15.10 | 363 | " | " | N. F. T | .30 | |
| | | TOTAL 6 BULLEYES | | | | | |
| | | TOTAL | | FOR | JAN. 27.   500 RDS FIRED) | | |
| | | " | | | MONTH      DAY    2.10 | | |
| | | [signature] S/Ldr %c B. FLIGHT | | | NIGHT   18.15 | | |
| | | | | | TOTAL   20.25 | | |
| | | | | | GRAND   TOTAL   DAY   102.20 | | |
| | | | | | NIGHT   64.25 | | |
| | | [signature] N/C. %c 467 R.A.A.F Sqdn. BOTTESFORD. | | | TOTAL   166.75 | | |
| | | | | | B/F   FILM FIRED   150FT / RDS   "   DROGUE 4850 | | |
| | | | | | "   A&S   2850 | | |
| | | | | | "   A&A   200 | | |
| | | | | | "   A&S   200 | | |
| | | | | | 7,600   TOTAL TIME ... | | |

**Second page spread:**

| 1943 Date | Hour | Aircraft Type and No. | Pilot | Duty | Remarks (including results of bombing, gunnery, exercises, etc.) | Flying Times Day | Night |
|---|---|---|---|---|---|---|---|
| | | | | | Time carried forward :— 166.45 / 102.20 / 64.25 | | |
| FEBUARY | | MK III LANCASTER | | | | | |
| 4 | 14.05 | 524 | SGT. HEAVERY | REAR GUNNER | 8NT. X Country . recall. 6.10HRS | 4.30 | 1.40 |
| 5 | 15.45 | " | " | " | N.F.T & L O/Bombing. | 1.45 | |
| 16 | 19.00 | 523 | " | " | LORIENT 1. 4,000 12 CANS 8×30 | | 6.10 |
| 19 | 17.55 | 530 | " | " | WILHELMSHAVEN 1. 4,000 12 CANS | | 4.45 |
| 25 | 11.30 | 523 | " | " | N. F. T | .35 | |
| 24 | 12.00 | " | SGT CODLIN | " | " " | .30 | |
| 25 | 19.50 | " | SGT HEAVERY | | NUREMBURG 1. 4,000 10 CANS 90×4 | | 7.25 |
| 26 | 19.00 | " | " | | COLOGNE 1. 4,000 12 CANS 90×4 | | 4.50 |
| 28 | 12.10 | 524 | " | | N. F. T | .25 | |
| 28 | 18.45 | " | " | | ST. NAZAIRE 1. 4,000 11 CANS 90×4 | | 5.45 |
| | | | | | TOTAL   FOR   MONTH   DAY   7.45 | | |
| | | | | | NIGHT   30.35 | | |
| | | | | | TOTAL   38.20 | | |
| | | [signature] S/Ldr %c B. FLIGHT | | | TOTAL   FLYING   HOURS | | |
| | | | | | DAY   110.05 | | |
| | | | | | NIGHT   95.00 | | |
| | | | | | TOTAL   205.05 | | |
| | | | | | OPERATIONAL   HOURS   TO   DATE   33.50 | | |
| | | | | | NUMBER   OF   TRIPS   6   TOTAL TIME ... | | |

Time carried forward :— 205·05 / 110·05 | 95·00

| Date | Hour | Aircraft Type and No. | Pilot | Duty | Remarks (including results of bombing, gunnery, exercises, etc.) | Day | Night |
|---|---|---|---|---|---|---|---|
| | | MK III LANCASTER | Sgt HEAVERY | | | | |
| MARCH | | | | | | | |
| 1 | 18·45 | 524 | | REAR GUNNER | BERLIN 1,4000 10 CANS 90×4 | | 7·10 |
| 3 | 12·10 | 547 | " | " | N.F.T. | ·25 | |
| 3 | 1900 | 544 | " | " | HAMBURG 1,4000 12 CANS 90×4 | | 5·30 |
| 5 | 14·00 | 544 | " | " | N.F.T | ·20 | |
| 5 | 19·05 | 544 | " | " | ESSEN 1,4000 12 CANS 90×4 | | 4·35 |
| 6 | 11·40 | 547 | " | " | N.F.T | ·20 | |
| 7 | 14·20 | 547 | " | " | N.F.T | ·20 | |
| 8 | 13·40 | 547 | " | " | N.F.T | ·20 | |
| 8 | 19·35 | 547 | " | " | NUREMBURG 1.4000 12 CANS 90×4 | | 7·50 |
| 9 | 20·45 | 544 | " | " | MUNICH 1.4000 10 CANS 90×4 | | 7·32 |
| 11 | 11·30 | 547 | " | " | N.F.T | ·20 | |
| 12 | 14·25 | 500 | " | " | N.F.T | ·30 | |
| 12 | 19·25 | 500· | " | " | ESSEN 1.4000 12 CANS 90×4 600 R/S FIRED AT GROUND DEFENCES | | 4·15 |
| 14 | 12·15 | 500 | " | " | N.F.T. | ·30 | |
| 26 | 19·00 | 530 | " | " | DUISBURG 1.4000 12 CANS 90×4 | | 4·45 |
| 27 | 2020 | 530 | " | " | BERLIN 1.4000 11 CANS 90×4 | | 6·50 |
| 29 | 12·20 | 695 | " | " | N.F.T. | ·20 | |
| 29 | 21·45 | 695 | " | " | BERLIN 1.4000 12 CANS 90×4 | | 7·30 |

TOTAL TIME ... 113·30 | 157·00

---

Time carried forward :— 264·30 / 113·30 | 151·00

| Date | Hour | Aircraft Type and No. | Pilot | Duty | Remarks (including results of bombing, gunnery, exercises, etc.) | Day | Night |
|---|---|---|---|---|---|---|---|
| APRIL | | LANCASTER MK III 'S | SGT HEAVERY | REAR GUNNER | | | |
| 2 | 12·30 | 310-L·M | SGT HEAVERY | REAR GUNNER | TO LINTON – OUSE RETURN ON AND | 1·10 | 89·50 |
| 3 | 19·35 | 695 | " | " | ESSEN 1.4000 12 CANS 90×4 | | 5·15 |
| 4 | 20·55 | 737 | " | " | KIEL 1.4000 12 CANS 90×4 | | 5·50 |
| 8 | 11·15 | 772 | " | " | FORMATION FLYING AIR TO SEA 300 R/S | 1·35 | |
| 8 | 20·50 | 621 | " | " | DUISBURG 1.4000 12 CANS 90×4 | | 6·05 |
| 9 | 20·35 | 621 | " | " | DUISBURG 1.4000 12 CANS 90×4 | | 4·35 |
| 11 | 11·30 | 772 | " | " | FISHTER AFFILIATION AND N.F.T. | 1·30 | |
| 13 | 20·40 | 772 | " | " | SPEZIA 4.1000 5 CANS 90×4 | | 9·50 |
| 16 | 21·20 | 772 | " | " | PILSEN 1.4000 2.4000 300 R/S AT GROUND DEFENCES | | 9·10 |
| 17 | 11·30 | 772 | " | " | BOSCOMBE DOWNS TO BASE | ·55 | |
| 18 | 21·10 | 764 | " | " | SPEZIA 14 CANS 90×4 | | 9·00 |
| 20 | 21·35 | 695 | " | " | STETTIN 1.4000 9 CANS 90×4 | | 8·05 |
| 24 | 14·45 | 695 | " | " | N.F.T. | ·25 | |
| 26 | 23·55 | 695 | " | " | DUISBURG 1.4000 12 CANS 90×4 | | 4·55 |

TOTAL FOR MONTH   DAY   5·35
" "   NIGHT   62·45
" "   TOTAL   68·20

TOTAL FLYING HOURS   DAY   119·05
" "   NIGHT   213·45
TOTAL   332·50

OPERATIONAL HOURS TO DATE   152·35
" TRIPS   24

*(signature)*   Sqd Ldr O/C FLIGHT

| Date | Hour | Aircraft Type and No. | Pilot | Duty | Remarks (including results of bombing, gunnery, exercises, etc.) | Day | Night |
|---|---|---|---|---|---|---|---|
| | | | | | Time carried forward :— | 332·50 | |
| | | | | | | 119·05 | 213·45 |
| 11·5·43 | 1505 | 764 | SGT HEAVERY | R/GUNNER | N. F. T. | ·40 | |
| 12·5·43 | 00·05 | 764 | " | " | DUISBURG 10 1,000 | | 4·00 |
| 13·5·43 | 21·35 | 764 | " | " | PILSEN 1 4,000 5 1,000 | | 7·45 |
| 15·5·43 | 11·55 | 764 | " | " | FORMATION & AIR FIRING | 1·20 | |
| 16·5·43 | 13·50 | 772 | " | " | H·L·B· | 2·00 | |
| 16·5·43 | 23·55 | 772 | " | " | H·L·B· | | 1·50 |
| 17 — | 16·20 | 949 | " | " | A & E TEST | 1·30 | |
| 18 — | 11·40 | 772 | " | " | H·L·B | 1·20 | |
| 19 — | 15·10 | " | " | " | H·L·B | 2·05 | |
| 20 — | 15·15 | " | " | " | H·L·B | 1·50 | |
| 22 — | 14·30 | " | " | " | LOW LEVEL X COUNTRY | 1·00 | |
| 23 — | 22·20 | " | " | " | DORTMUND 1·4,000 12 CANS 8x30 | | 4·50 |
| 25 — | 14·35 | " | " | " | N. F. T. | ·30 | |
| 25 — | 23·05 | " | " | " | DUSSELDORF 1·4,000 12 CANS 90x4 90x4lb | | 4·45 |
| 27 — | 21·55 | " | " | " | ESSEN 1·4,000 12 CANS | | 5·10 |
| | | | | TOTAL FOR | MONTH DAY 12·15 | | |
| | | | | " | NIGHT 28·20 | | |
| | | | | | TOTAL 40·35 | | |
| | | | | TOTAL | FLYING HOURS DAY 131·20 | | |
| | | | | | NIGHT 242·05 | | |
| | | | | | TOTAL 373·25 | | |

O/C C FLIGHT
Sqn/Ldr.
No 467 RAAF SQUADRON BOTTESFORD.
W/C

OPERATIONAL TRIPS TO DATE 29   OPERATIONAL HOURS TO DATE 179·05

### Second Tour, 1944, 582 Squadron

| Date 1944 APRIL | Hour | Aircraft Type and No. | Pilot | Duty | Remarks (including results of bombing, gunnery, exercises, etc.) | Day | Night |
|---|---|---|---|---|---|---|---|
| | | 582 SQUADRON | | LITTLE | STAUGHTON. Time carried forward :— | 543·50 | |
| | | | | | | 283·45 | 260·05 |
| | | LANCASTER | | | | | |
| 5 | 11·00 | JA 673 | F/LT WALKER | R/GUNNER | Y CROSS COUNTRY | 3·00 | |
| 5 | 20·00 | ND 503 | " | " | " " " LANDED NUNEATON | 1·50 | |
| 7 | 16·00 | ND 503 | " | " | NUNEATON TO BASE | ·30 | |
| 8 | 14·40 | ND 817 | " | " | GROUP NAV. EX. | 3·45 | |
| 9 | 12·00 | ND 818 | " | " | N.F.T & AIR TO SEA FIRING 200RDS 2 - 500lbs RAIL YARDS | 1·25 | |
| 9 | 23·10 | ND 816 | " | " | LILLE 12 - 1,000lbs SUPP ⅓ | | 2·50→ |
| 10 | 15·00 | ND 816 | " | " | N. F. T. | ·35 | |
| 11 | 20·50 | ND 438 | " | " | AACHEN 13 - 1000lbs SUPP RAIL YARDS | | 3·35→ |
| 13 | 14·00 | ND 816 | " | " | AIR TO AIR (DROGUE) 400RDS. | 2·05 | |
| 14 | 11·50 | JA 673 | " | " | BOMBING & N.F.T. & S.B.A. | 1·20 | |
| 18 | 11·10 | ND 812 | " | " | " " " " | 1·40 | |
| 18 | 21·45 | ND 502 | " | " | NOISY-LE-SEC (PARIS) 13-1,000 SUPP RAIL YARDS ⅓ | | 3·55→ |
| 20 | 10·50 | ND 502 | " | " | Y RUNS AND BOMBING | 2·40 | |
| 22 | 14·10 | ND 818 | " | " | N.F.T. & S.B.A. | ·40 | |
| 22 | 23·10 | ND 502 | " | " | DUSSELDORF 6 - 2,000 SUPP RAIL YARDS | | 4·05 |
| | | | | | 33 HRS - 55 MINS | | |
| | | | | | TOTAL FOR MONTH FLYING | 19·30 | 14·25 |
| | | | | | AIR TO DROGUE 400RDS FIRING | | |
| | | | | | " " SEA 200 | | |
| | | | | | OPS. 2⅔. OPS HRS 14·25 HRS. MINS. | | |
| | | | | | ⅔ to count as one. | | |
| | | | | | Total Time :— | 303·15 | 274·30 |

Sqn/Ldr O/C
A FLT. 582 SQDN. LITTLE STAUGHTON.

577.45

| | | | | | | Time carried forward :— | 303.15 | 274.30 |
|---|---|---|---|---|---|---|---|---|
| **Date** | **Hour** | **Aircraft Type and No.** | **Pilot** | **Duty** | **Remarks** (including results of bombing, gunnery, exercises, etc.) | | **Flying Times** | |
| | | | | | | | **Day** | **Night** |
| **1944** | | | | | | | | |
| **MAY** | | **LANCASTER** | | | | | | |
| 3 | 22.55 | ND 817 | F/LT WALKER | A/G | MONTDIDIER (DROME FRANCE) 1.4,000 11.500 2 L.P 500 PRACTIC BOMBER | | | 3.15 |
| 6 | 15.35 | ND 817 | " | " | N.F.T. | | 30 | |
| 6 | 00.45 | ND 817 | " | " | MANTES GASSICOURT (RAIL YARDS) 12.1,000 PRACTIC BOMBER | | | 3.20 |
| 8 | 15.25 | ND 860 | " | " | 'Y' EX. | | 2.10 | |
| 11 | 15.20 | ND 899 | " | " | N.F.T. | | .45 | |
| 11 | 22.30 | ND 899 | " | " | LOUVAIN 8 1,000 (RAIL YARDS) 6 FLARES X4X7" ILLUMINATOR | | | 3.00 |
| 13 | 11.30 | ND 899 | " | " | 'Y' RUNS F/A HURRICANE 15 MINS. | | 2.05 | |
| 14 | 23.00 | ND 812 | " | " | NIGHT F/A NO MOON & BOMBING | | | 1.50 |
| 15 | 15.00 | ND 909 | " | " | 'Y' EX. | | 1.40 | |
| 19 | 14.45 | ND 812 | " | " | N.F.T. F/A HURRICANE 15 MINS | | 1.15 | |
| 19 | 23.45 | ND 812 | " | " | BOULOGNE SUPP 18 X 500 | | | 2.45 |
| 21 | 22.50 | ND 812 | " | " | DUISBERG SUPP.16 S.B.C 8X30 1.4,000 | | | 4.20 |
| 22 | 22.30 | ND 812 | " | " | DORTMUND SUPP. 6 2,000 | | | 4.00 |
| 25 | 15.05 | ND 812 | " | " | N.F.T. | | .20 | |
| 27 | 23.25 | ND 812 | " | " | RENNES 8 1,000 (DROME RAIL YARD) 6 FLARES X4X7 ILLUMINATOR | | | 3.55 |
| 27 | 10.30 | ND 812 | " | " | FISH POND & BOMBING | | 2.20 | |
| 30 | 10.25 | ND 169 | " | " | F/A 15 MINS HURRICANE AIR TO DROGUE FIRING 400 RDS BOMBING | | 2.40 | |
| 31 | 10.45 | ND 899 | " | " | Y EX. & BOMBING | | 2.10 | |
| 31 | 15.55 | ND 169 | " | " | N.F.T. | | 30 | |
| 31 | 00.30 | ND 169 | " | " | TERGNIER 8 1,000 (RAIL YARDS) 6 FLARES X 4X7 ILLUMINATOR | | | 3.35 |
| | | | | | | | 16.25 | 30.00 |
| | | | | | | TOTAL TIME | 319.40 | 304.30 |

---

624.10

| | | | | | | Time carried forward :— | 319.40 | 304.30 |
|---|---|---|---|---|---|---|---|---|
| **Date** | **Hour** | **Aircraft Type and No.** | **Pilot** | **Duty** | **Remarks** (including results of bombing, gunnery, exercises, etc.) | | **Day** | **Night** |

HRS - MIN
TOTAL FOR MAY DAY 16 25
NIGHT 30 . 00
TOTAL 46 . 25

*Dh Walbou* W/CDR
'A' FLT 582 SQD LITTLE STAUGHTON.

ROUNDS FIRED TO DROGUE 400
F/A WITH HURRICANE DAY MIN 45
NIGHT MIN 15
OPS 8 HOURS 28.10

| | | | | | | | | |
|---|---|---|---|---|---|---|---|---|
| **1944** | | **NE 169** | | | | | | |
| JUNE 2 | 14.15 | LANCASTER | F/LT WALKER | A/G | F/A 15 MINS HURRICANE AIR/AIR 400 RDS FIRED & BOMBING | | 2.15 | |
| 5 | 02.50 | " | " | " | LONGUES D-DAY 11 1,000 BOMBER (FLAK BATTERY) | | 3.10 | 3.15 |
| 16 | 14.55 | NE 821 | " | " | N.F.T. | | .40 | |
| 17 | 15.05 | " | " | " | " | | .40 | |
| 18 | 10.35 | ND 889 | " | " | 'Y' RUNS & BOMBING | | 1.35 | |
| 20 | 10.50 | PB 136 | " | " | FORMATION & BOMBING | | 1.50 | |
| 20 | 16.30 | ND 899 | " | " | 'Y' RUNS & BOMBING | | 1.25 | |
| 21 | 15.30 | PB 136 | " | " | FORMATION | | 1.45 | |
| 22 | 11.00 | PB 136 | " | " | AIR TO SEA FIRING 400 RDS BOMBING | | 2.00 | |
| 23 | 00.05 | PB 136 | " | " | COUBRONNE (P.PLANE BASE) 11 1,000 BOMBER 3.500 | | | 2.00 |
| | | | | | | TOTAL TIME | 331.50 | 309.45 |

641·35

| | | | | | | Time carried forward :— | 331·50 | 309·45 |
|---|---|---|---|---|---|---|---|---|

**1944**

| Date | Hour | Aircraft Type and No. | Pilot | Duty | Remarks (including results of bombing, gunnery, exercises, etc.) | Flying Times Day | Night |
|---|---|---|---|---|---|---|---|
| JUNE | | LANCASTER | | | | | |
| 24 | 15·10 | PB 136 | F/LT WALKER | A/C | FORMATION (P.PLANE) BOMBER | 1·25 | |
| 25 | 00·25 | PB 136 | " | " | MIDDLE STRAETE 16·500 2·500Lg | | 2·00 |
| 25 | 15·20 | NE 140 | " | " | GROUP 'Y' CHECK | 2·05 | |
| 28 | 22·35 | PB 136 | " | " | BLAINVILLE 6 FLARES 4×7 STAR/OUTER 1,000 CAUGHT FIRE ON RETURN | | 6·05 |
| 30 | 11·25 | PB 136 | " | " | N. F. T. | ·35 | |
| | | | TOTAL FOR | | JUNE DAY 16·25 NIGHT 13·20 TOTAL 29·45 | 16·25 | 13·20 |

|  | AIR-SEA 400RDS | AIR-AIR 400RDS |
|---|---|---|
| ROUNDS FIRED | | |
| F/A WITH HURRICANE | 15 MINS | |
| OPS. 4 | HRS 13·20 | |

*DM Walbourn* W/CDR %c
'A' FLT 582 SQD LITTLE STAUGHTON

| | | | | | | Total Time …. | 335·55 | 317·50 |

---

| | | | | | | Time carried forward :— | 335·55 | 317·50 |
|---|---|---|---|---|---|---|---|---|

| Date | Hour | Aircraft Type and No. | Pilot | Duty | Remarks (including results of bombing, gunnery, exercises, etc.) | Flying Times Day | Night |
|---|---|---|---|---|---|---|---|
| 1944 | | LANCASTER MK III | | | | | |
| JULY 1 | 11·50 | PB 136 | F/LT WALKER | A/C | AIR TEST & BOMBING | ·35 | |
| 2 | 12·40 | " | " | " | OISEMENT 2·6,000 2·500LD P.PLANE SITE | 2·25 | |
| 5 | 23·20 | ND 130 | " | " | WIZERNES 4,000(O.S.A) 2·500LD P.PLANE SITE | | 2·00 |
| 8 | 11·25 | PB 136 | " | " | FORMATION HURRICANE F/A OP TWO & SPITFIRE 15 MINS & BOMBING | 1·00 | |
| 9 | 12·40 | " | " | " | L HEY 4·1,000 2·500LD P.PLANE SITE | 2·05 | |
| 10 | 04·45 | " | " | " | NUCOURT 4·1,000 2·500LD P.PLANE STORAGE | 2·50 | |
| 11 | 19·30 | " | " | " | GAPENNES 16·500 2·500L·D P.PLANE 'RAMROD' SITE | 2·45 | |
| 12 | 14·00 | " | " | " | ROLLEZ 16·500 P.PLANE 'RAMROD' 1 HANG UP SITE | 2·20 | |
| 12 | 11·15 | ND·817 | S/C COLLINGS | " | LOCAL | ·20 | |
| 14 | 14·45 | PB 136 | F/LT WALKER | " | ST AYIHIBERT FERNE 16·500 P.PLANE SITE 2·500LD 'RAMROD' | 2·45 | |
| 15 | 15·15 | " | " | " | NUCOURT 9·1,000 P.PLANE 'RAMROD' STORAGE | 3·05 | |
| 18 | 04·40 | " | " | " | GASNY 11·1,000 P.PLANE 4·500 SUPPORT | 3·05 | |
| 19 | 14·30 | PB 149 | " | " | MONT CANDON 11·1,000 P.PLANE 4·500 SITE RAMROD | 2·35 | |
| 23 | 07·15 | PB 136 | " | " | FORET DE CROC 18·500 P.PLANE SITE RAMROD | 3·00 | |
| 23 | 22·40 | PB 136 | " | " | KIEL 6·1,000 2×T.I L·B/WAN. FLARE 1·4,000 2×T.I S·-B-M | | 5·20 |
| 25 | 22·05 | " | S/LDR WALKER | " | STUTTGART 16·500 14·000 1 S·B C×X·X FLARES WAN 2·500 FLARES MAPPED S-B-M | | 7·40 |
| 27 | 11·15 | ND 182 | " | " | A/C CHECK & BOMBING | 1·05 | |
| 28 | 22·30 | " | " | " | STUTTGART 1·4,000 1 S·B·C× 4×WAN FLARE 4·1,000 FLARES MAPPED S·-B-M | | 6·40 |
| | | | | | | 29·20 | 21·40 |

| | | | | | | Total Time …. | | |

| Date | Hour | Aircraft Type and No. | Pilot | Duty | Remarks (including results of bombing, gunnery, exercises, etc.) | Day | Night |
|---|---|---|---|---|---|---|---|
| | | | | | Time carried forward:— | 704.45 | |
| | | | | | | 365.15 | 339.30 |
| 1944 | | LANCASTER | | | | | |
| Aug. 9 | 11.25 | PB.182 | S/LDR WALKER | A/G | 'Y' X COUNTRY 9 BOMBING | 2.55 | |
| 10 | 10.35 | " | " | " | " | 1.25 | |
| 10 | 21.25 | " | " | " | DIJON RAIL YARDS | | 5.40 |
| 12 | 22.05 | " | " | " | RUSSELSHIEM OPAL P.B.M.I | | 4.30 |
| 12 | — | " | " | " | GROUND BACK | | |
| — | 11.25 | " | " | " | F/A HURRICANE N.F.T. | 1.00 | |
| 15 | 10.25 | " | " | " | | 2.55 | |
| 16 | 21.10 | " | " | " | VOLKEL | | 7.35 |
| 16 | 14.45 | " | " | " | STETTIN P.B.M.I | .50 | |
| 18 | 21.25 | " | " | " | N.F.T. BREMEN P.B.M.I | | 5.05 |

# Summary: Air Operations, Bomber Command, 64 Raids

Air Gunner 1268143:
Warrant Officer Sidney James Knott, DFC

467 Squadron (5 Group), Bottesford (first tour)
582 Squadron (8 Group), Little Staughton (second tour)

| First tour totals: 29 sorties, 467 Squadron RAAF | | | | | | | | | | |
|---|---|---|---|---|---|---|---|---|---|---|
| Operational Sorties | Main Force | Minor Operations | Total Sorties | Struck Off Charge | % | Killed | Injured | POW | Evaded Capture | Interned |
| | 12296 | 684 | 12980 | 577 | 4.45 | 2834 | 69 | 561 | 51 | 14 |
| | Outcome (%) if shot down or crashed on return | | | | | 80.31 | 1.96 | 15.90 | 1.45 | 0.40 |

| Second tour totals: 35 sorties, 582 Squadron RAF | | | | | | | | | | |
|---|---|---|---|---|---|---|---|---|---|---|
| Operational Sorties | Main Force | Minor Operations | Total Sorties | Struck Off Charge | % | Killed | Injured | POW | Evaded Capture | Interned |
| | 20500 | 4907 | 25407 | 542 | 2.13 | 2639 | 48 | 556 | 246 | 7 |
| | Outcome (%) if shot down or crashed on return | | | | | 75.49 | 1.37 | 15.90 | 7.04 | 0.20 |

| Combined totals: 64 sorties | | | | | | | | | | |
|---|---|---|---|---|---|---|---|---|---|---|
| Operational Sorties | Main Force | Minor Operations | Total Sorties | Struck Off Charge | % | Killed | Injured | POW | Evaded Capture | Interned |
| | 32796 | 5591 | 38387 | 1119 | 2.92 | 5473 | 117 | 1117 | 297 | 21 |
| | Outcome (%) if shot down or crashed on return | | | | | 77.91 | 1.67 | 15.90 | 4.23 | 0.30 |

Source: Barry Hope

# APPENDIX IX

# *Index of Personalities*

NOTE: In most instances, ranks cited are those current at the time of first reference